The Margraten Boys

Also by Peter Schrijvers

BLOODY PACIFIC: AMERICAN SOLDIERS AT WAR WITH JAPAN

THE CRASH OF RUIN: AMERICAN COMBAT SOLDIERS IN EUROPE DURING WORLD WAR II

LIBERATORS: THE ALLIES AND BELGIAN SOCIETY, 1944–1945

THE UNKNOWN DEAD: CIVILIANS IN THE BATTLE OF THE BULGE

The Margraten Boys

How a European Village Kept America's Liberators Alive

Peter Schrijvers

*Senior Lecturer, School of History and Philosophy,
University of New South Wales, Australia*

© Peter Schrijvers 2012

All rights reserved. No reproduction, copy or transmission of this publication may be made without written permission.

No portion of this publication may be reproduced, copied or transmitted save with written permission or in accordance with the provisions of the Copyright, Designs and Patents Act 1988, or under the terms of any licence permitting limited copying issued by the Copyright Licensing Agency, Saffron House, 6-10 Kirby Street, London EC1N 8TS.

Any person who does any unauthorized act in relation to this publication may be liable to criminal prosecution and civil claims for damages.

The author has asserted his right to be identified as the author of this work in accordance with the Copyright, Designs and Patents Act 1988.

First published 2012 by
PALGRAVE MACMILLAN

Palgrave Macmillan in the UK is an imprint of Macmillan Publishers Limited, registered in England, company number 785998, of Houndmills, Basingstoke, Hampshire RG21 6XS.

Palgrave Macmillan in the US is a division of St Martin's Press LLC, 175 Fifth Avenue, New York, NY 10010.

Palgrave Macmillan is the global academic imprint of the above companies and has companies and representatives throughout the world.

Palgrave® and Macmillan® are registered trademarks in the United States, the United Kingdom, Europe and other countries

ISBN: 978-0-230-34663-5   hardback
ISBN: 978-0-230-34664-2   paperback

This book is printed on paper suitable for recycling and made from fully managed and sustained forest sources. Logging, pulping and manufacturing processes are expected to conform to the environmental regulations of the country of origin.

A catalogue record for this book is available from the British Library.

A catalog record for this book is available from the Library of Congress.

10 9 8 7 6 5 4 3 2 1
21 20 19 18 17 16 15 14 13 12

Printed and bound in Great Britain by
CPI Antony Rowe, Chippenham and Eastbourne

For my great-grandfather Victor Rigo –

Soldier in World War I
Resistance fighter in World War II

These American boys run the risk of dying twice. They have already been killed on the battlefield. They would die once again when we stop remembering them. We cannot let that happen.

A Margraten adopter

Contents

List of Illustrations viii
Preface xii
Acknowledgments xvii
Abbreviations xx
Note to the Reader xxii

1. A Debt of Honor 1
2. A Web of Intimate Relations 33
3. Saying Goodbye 60
4. The War Turns Cold 79
5. A Long and Dark Shadow 109
6. The End of History 134
7. A Global Village 157
8. The Return of History 186
9. Of Paramount Importance 218
10. The Audacity of Hope 243

Postscript 268

Notes 273
Bibliography 298
Margraten Boys Index 309
General Index 312

List of Illustrations

1. Overjoyed inhabitants pose with American soldiers who have liberated Maastricht, a town just west of Margraten. September 1944. (Courtesy Regionaal Historisch Centrum Limburg and photographer Jef Naseman, Maastricht, the Netherlands) xiv
2. An American bugler at Margraten cemetery blows taps in May 1945. (Courtesy US National Archives and Records Administration) 6
3. Margraten's Father Heuschen and three of adoption's administrative volunteers at the American cemetery's wooden chapel in 1946. The chapel, erected by German prisoners of war, was torn down when the permanent cemetery structure was built in the 1950s. (Courtesy Foundation Akkers van Margraten) 12
4. In one of their last moments together, Warren and Mabel Rose Feil rest on a bench in their garden in Alabama in April 1944. The touching story of the young widow and the private killed in Germany on his birthday played a key role in galvanizing the Margraten adoption community in 1945. (Courtesy Regionaal Historisch Centrum Limburg and photographer Johan Martens, Ghent, Belgium) 15
5. As the wife of the Maastricht mayor and baron, the well-connected Emilie Michiels van Kessenich after the war came to play an increasingly important role in the Margraten adoption committee. (Courtesy Regionaal Historisch Centrum Limburg and photographer Johan Martens) 19
6. The mayor of Montgomery, Alabama, welcomes Mrs. Michiels van Kessenich. Mrs. Michiels van Kessenich is accompanied by the grandfather of Lt Harte. 36

List of Illustrations **ix**

7. Frank Harte was the pilot of a B-17 Flying Fortress that was downed by German fighters and one of many airmen buried at Margraten. (Courtesy Regionaal Historisch Centrum Limburg and photographer Johan Martens) 36
8. The mother of a Margraten boy from North Carolina tries to get in touch with Mrs. Michiels van Kessenich following her talk on CBS's *We, the People* in 1946. Hers was just one of many attempts by grieving American parents and siblings to find out more about the faraway resting places of their loved ones. (Courtesy Regionaal Historisch Centrum Limburg and photographer Johan Martens) 38
9. A studio photo of the Evancho family in Pennsylvania around 1920. World War II would take the lives of brothers George and Peter, here seated left and right of their parents at ages three and five respectively. Both lie side by side in Margraten. Baby sister Helen (here on her mother's lap) made contact with her brothers' new adopter, a Belgian, shortly before her death in 2008. (Courtesy Mary Anne Fedor and Erik De Bruyne) 77
10. Women and girls jostle to have their picture taken with American liberators in Maastricht in 1944. Females of all ages would play a crucial role in Margraten's adoption program. (Courtesy Regionaal Historisch Centrum Limburg and photographer Jef Naseman) 83
11. One of the thousands of typed index cards in the 1946 wooden chest of drawers linking European adopters with fallen American soldiers and their families overseas. This is the card for Gussie Knierim, an infantryman who grew up on a small farm in Missouri, and his adopters from the Dutch town of Maastricht. Today adoption data are safely stored in computer files and constantly updated. (Courtesy Maria Duizings-Croonen, Reijmerstok, the Netherlands) 132
12. Felix Prevoo says a prayer for Sergeant Ralph Wheeler, a New Yorker who died when his bomber was downed in February 1944. Deeply involved in adoption since the end of the war, Felix at the start of the 1960s stepped forward to run the program's administration single-handedly for the next four decades. (Courtesy Felix Prevoo, Margraten) 140

13. Lieutenant and flight nurse Wilma 'Dolly' Vinsant from Texas. One of the four Margraten girls. (Courtesy John Gouverne, Maarheze, the Netherlands) 163
14. Shortly after liberation in 1944, children in the Limburg town of Valkenburg have their picture taken near an American piece of artillery. The boys have borrowed helmets from the GIs in the background. The war made an indelible impression on the very young and caused many to become committed adopters later in life. (Courtesy Miets Stevens) 193
15. Back of the bracelet of S/Sgt Albert Kielblock, killed in October 1944 aboard a B-24 Liberator from the 392nd Bomber Group. From this bomber group alone, the names of 80 men are engraved on Margraten's headstones and walls of the missing. (Courtesy US National Archives and Records Administration and Annette Tison) 222
16. George W. Bush and Queen Beatrix side by side at the Margraten cemetery during the American president's visit in May 2005. (Courtesy Stichting Margraten Memorial Center) 229
17. To signal that his remains have been recovered at last, a bronze rosette is placed before Shannon Estill's name on the Wall of the Missing in the presence of the fighter pilot's daughter in 2007. (Courtesy Sharon Estill Taylor) 237
18. Efforts to safeguard the memory of the Margraten boys continue unabated. Since 1945, four generations of the same family have watched over Albert Gackowksi, a private from Illinois in the 89th Infantry Division. It took his adopters until very recently to get in touch with relatives and obtain family pictures. One photo shows
19. Albert (left) with his brother Leo. Another shows Albert (crouched on the right) with his parents and brothers Leo and Norbert. Albert was the only son not to come home from the war. He rests in Plot A, Row 2, Grave 4. (Courtesy Laura Lange-Gackowski and Inge Burlet) 248
20. Many American families were made to pay a terrible price in World War II. In April 1944, Ben Allen proudly poses with his big brother Bill on the farm in Illinois. Less than a year later, the final offensive in Nazi Germany had

claimed not only the life of Bill but also that of sister Elizabeth's husband. Bill and his brother-in-law both rest in Margraten and are being watched over by a fourth generation of the same Dutch family. (Courtesy Benton Allen and Pauline Roukens-Göttgens, Landgraaf, the Netherlands) 252

21. Key members of the Adoption Foundation Margraten accept the prestigious Limburg Award in 2008. Most of the prize money would be donated to the American World War II Orphans Network. In the background is a photo projection of Sgt. Walter Pete of the 29th Infantry Division whose name is among more than 1,700 on the Wall of the Missing. (Courtesy Adoption Foundation Margraten and Jo Purnot) 255

22. African-American troops of the 3136th Quartermaster Service Company and Dutch civilians engaged in the backbreaking work of digging graves in Margraten's rich soil in 1945. (Courtesy Stichting Akkers van Margraten and Joseph Layne, Richmond, Virginia) 265

23. Gerda Roebroeks-Nelissen shows a photo of her sister Nettie at the grave of Henry Wolf of the 774th Field Artillery Battalion. Gerda was 13 when Henry spent several weeks on their farm before being sent to the Battle of the Bulge. The American asked Gerda's parents to stay in touch with his wife in Ohio. They kept their promise, only to learn at the end of the war that Henry had been killed and buried in nearby Margraten. At the start of a new century, ageing witnesses like Gerda find much comfort in the knowledge that a third and fourth generation are keeping adoption promises made many decades ago. (Courtesy G. Roebroeks-Nelissen, Sint Geertruid, the Netherlands. Photographer José Manuel Alorda, Barcelona, Spain) 271

Preface

She gently pressed his gloves against her chest. She had come, she told the young man in the small and unassuming office, to see her son Jack. Jack Taliaferro. A soldier in the 12th Regiment of the 4th Infantry Division. The man carefully wrote down the details and politely asked her to take a seat.

He returned much sooner than she had expected. They stepped out of the office and into a chill wind that brought back memories of the night when Jack was born in a modest house in southern Oklahoma. The early spring morning on the prairie had been cold with a dusting of snow.

But that was 1924 and Wilma Taliaferro's world had been turned upside down many times since. The Great Depression had come and hung around for much longer than she cared to remember. Then there had been the terrible shock of the devastating Japanese attack on Pearl Harbor. Next she had gone through the heartbreaking experience of watching her son depart for war in Europe. At the bus station in Duncan, he had asked her to hold his gloves as he went to buy his ticket. It was only when the bus had disappeared from sight and she lowered her hand that she noticed her fingers still clutching his gloves.

Jack never returned to wear his gloves again. The man from the office guided Mrs. Taliaferro past a tranquil rectangular pond covered with white lilies. Together they climbed a series of wide steps that took them to a broad platform. From it she could see a giant American flag at the far side of a sea of thousands upon thousands of white marble crosses and stars organized into neatly rippling waves.

They walked onto the soft grass in total silence and pensively wound their way between row on row of American names. Jack had been laid to rest in Plot G, Row 14, Grave 13. Besides his name, rank, unit, and state only a date was etched into the shiny marble:

29 November 1944. Mrs. Taliaferro had not been so near her son for several decades. She quietly wished she could return the gloves to his warm palm, whisper encouragements into his ear, and smell the familiar scent of his skin. But the sweeping wind made her feel very cold and empty, and all she could do was press her boy's gloves closer to her chest as she read his name over and over again.

When Mrs. Taliaferro at last turned to walk back in the direction of the cemetery's office, in the distance she caught a glimpse of an ancient windmill nestling in the gentle folds of the rich soil. In May 1940 the Nazi-German invasion had hit the neutral Netherlands like lightning out of a clear blue sky at a time when in America boys Jack's age had been more interested in hunting quail or poring over the latest baseball statistics. But fate slowly and insidiously had brought the Dutch and boys like Jack together. By May 1945 the war had caused some 230,000 of the small Dutch nation's 9 million inhabitants to lose their lives, including more than 100,000 people of Jewish ancestry. By that time too, more than 405,000 young American soldiers had sacrificed their lives in defense of the Dutch and of many victimized peoples like them worldwide.[1]

Jack Taliaferro and some 8,300 other soldiers rest in what is the only American military cemetery in the Netherlands. The names of another 1,700 American boys whose bodies have never been recovered are recorded on two Walls of the Missing at the entrance to the cemetery. The field of honor lies in the small village of Margraten. The village is tucked away among the softly curving fields and meadows of southern Limburg, a predominantly rural area of wheat farmers and fruit growers, and a Catholic region in what is otherwise a mostly Protestant country. It is located six miles east of the city of Maastricht, just a few miles north of the Belgian border, and barely 14 miles west of Aachen, the first German city captured by American troops in World War II.

Together with the British and Canadians, the Americans loom large in the Dutch collective memory of liberation from Nazi oppression. However, with the exception of the towns and villages in the Arnhem corridor of Operation Market Garden, nowhere has the relationship with the Americans been more special than in Margraten and southern Limburg. Wedged into the narrow salient between northern Belgium and Germany, the Dutch in southern Limburg, like the Belgians, experienced a lightning liberation in the still balmy days of September

1944. They embraced the Americans with ecstatic joy as they shared the expectation of Allied commanders and soldiers alike that the war might be over in weeks.

1. Overjoyed inhabitants pose with American soldiers who have liberated Maastricht, a town just west of Margraten. September 1944. (Courtesy Regionaal Historisch Centrum Limburg and photographer Jef Naseman, Maastricht, the Netherlands)

But then the Allied campaign suddenly ground to a halt. Logistical lines stretching all the way back to Normandy snapped. Operation Market Garden, the airborne attempt in the autumn of 1944 to cross the Rhine and deal a lethal blow to Germany's industrial heartland, failed. Mauled German troops fell back on the Siegfried Line and took up positions in what soon would be the deathtraps of Aachen and the Hürtgen Forest. If until 13 September 1944, the day on which Margraten was liberated, the Allied offensive had been "rapid and sweeping," a US Army report on the Dutch cemetery noted, soon after "the advances were measured by thousands of yards and by a heavy price in casualties and material for every yard gained." With the approach of winter came frost and snow that made the lives of American troops even more miserable.[2]

Unlike the population in the greater part of the Netherlands, who were condemned to a horrendous 'hunger winter' and would remain under the Nazi yoke until May 1945, the civilians in southern Limburg were extremely fortunate to be free. Their bonds with the Americans grew deeper still as they watched the boys transform from seemingly carefree liberators into exhausted frontline troops hammering the Siegfried Line and pushing back the Ardennes bulge. Their awe for the indomitable American spirit knew no bounds when, early in 1945, they saw tens of thousands of troops flood training camps and rest and recreation centers and unfold the might of the Ninth Army for the final spring offensive against a Nazi Germany teetering on the brink of collapse.[3]

Like so many of the parents, siblings, girlfriends, fiancées, wives, and children of the Margraten boys, Wilma Taliaferro never fully recovered from the numbing blow that World War II had dealt her. Yet, on the day of her visit to Margraten, she, like so many other Americans, may at least have taken some comfort from knowing that the Dutch refuse to forget why Jack and thousands of boys like him will rest in their soil forever.

Anyone visiting the Netherlands American Cemetery and Memorial today may be surprised to find that so many graves are adorned with a single rose, an impressive bouquet, a card with some kind words, pebbles on a marble star, orange candy on a gleaming cross. Some of the flowers and tokens have, of course, been left behind by American visitors. But most are being placed there throughout the year by people from Margraten and surroundings, from across Limburg province, and from all over the Netherlands.

They do this because they have joined a unique, locally organized program of grave adoption that has ensured continuity of gratitude and remembrance into a third and even fourth generation since liberation. In less than a year after the war, locals young and old had adopted all of the many thousands of graves with barely any prompting. Today, some 70 years later, at a time when few of those who lived through the war are still around, there is a waiting list of people keen to adopt a grave as soon as one becomes available. Indeed, so many Dutch people insist on continuing to pay tribute that a few years ago it was decided to also put up for adoption the names of the American soldiers on the Margraten Walls of the Missing.

This book recounts the moving and largely unknown story of how the lives and deaths of thousands of American boys have become indelibly bound up with the memory of a Dutch community. When the Dutch talk about the soldiers whose graves they have adopted, they rarely mention ranks or last names. Instead, they speak of Jack, Gustav, or Antonio or, just as naturally and caringly, of 'our boy.' For if the Margraten boys belong to America, the Dutch in whose soil they will rest forever, just as gratefully consider them theirs too.

The proud Dutch adopters were more than willing to talk when called upon to contribute to the making of this book. With the kind help of the Margraten Adoption Foundation, a questionnaire was included in the 2008 annual adoption newsletter. In the first week following its delivery in early spring, my inbox was overflowing with more than 100 responses. I have been inundated with reactions and follow-ups ever since, and in a recent tally identified more than 1,100 different respondents. Among them are surgeons and truck drivers, lawyers and construction workers, teenagers and octogenarians. They have written, sometimes very emotionally, about their motivation to adopt a grave and about what they remember of occupation and liberation and of the experiences passed on by parents and grandparents.

Many of the Dutch adopters one way or another have managed to learn much about American soldiers who, before they were killed in the war as infantrymen or flyboys, were fruit growers in California, farmers in Nebraska, autoworkers in Detroit, shopkeepers in Atlanta, or office clerks in New York. The adopters have shared often very touching letters as well as intimate photos of GIs and their families posing on front porches and in living rooms across America. They have scanned and mailed rare German documents reporting on American plane crashes. They have sent hard copies of thick US Army files documenting the cause and circumstances of a Margraten boy's death in painstaking detail.

It goes without saying that this unique trove of memories and documents forms the backbone of a story that is simultaneously harrowing and redeeming.

Acknowledgments

This is the kind of book that could not have been written without the help of literally hundreds of people from all over the Netherlands, Europe, and the United States. That is why it is impossible for me to express my gratitude to everyone in person. There are, nevertheless, a number of people who are deserving of special mention.

The unwavering support of the highly motivated volunteers who run the rejuvenated Adoption Foundation at Margraten has been absolutely crucial from the very moment I started research for this book in 2007. They helped locate witnesses, documents, and photographs, and over the years answered telephone, letter, and email queries too many to count. Special thanks go to the Foundation's president Fien Opreij, secretary Jacques Aussems, and local historian Jo Purnot. I am honored to have been lucky enough also to talk with some of the pioneers of the adoption program: Lies Köster, Felix Prevoo, Annie Prevoo-Frijnts, and Maria Prevoo-Ramakers.

By far the most important contribution of the Adoption Foundation has been to enable me to get in touch, through their annual newsletter, with the vast community of adopters spread out over the province of Limburg, the Netherlands, and other European countries. Amazingly, over the years close to 1,200 adopters of all ages have taken the time not only to reply to the specific questions of a questionnaire, but to make available for my book all kinds of moving stories, newspaper clippings, documents, and photographs relating to 'their' Margraten boys. Together they have succeeded in enriching this book with a uniquely personal dimension.

Whenever the information coming out of the adoption community threatened to overwhelm, Frans Roebroeks stood ready to provide advice and clarity in his capacity as archivist at the Regionaal Historisch Centrum Limburg. I have benefited immensely not only from his knowledge of the region and World War II, but also from his tips with regards to sources in Limburg, The Hague, and Washington, DC. From Maastricht he has replied, with admiring patience, to an endless barrage of emails being fired off from Sydney. And I have much enjoyed his perceptive comments and dry wit during the long talks we had whenever I was back in the Old World.

Lucie Beckers-van den Boorn was kind enough to allow me unfettered access to a personal archive that was a veritable treasure trove still carefully hidden away in cardboard boxes so many years after the end of the war. It is with much sadness that I learned she passed away at age 87 not long after her enthusiastic contribution to this book. A special word of thanks also to Jenneke Meyer Viol and her brother for granting permission to examine valuable papers and reproduce rare photographs that once belonged to their mother Emilie Michiels van Kessenich. To Maria Duizings-Croonen for providing me with information from and photos of the original index cards that sit in the 1940s chest of drawers in her home. To Paul Bronzwaer for sharing his extensive knowledge about the German occupation of Limburg and to John Gouverne for doing the same with regards to the liberation of the area by American troops. To Mieke Kirkels of the Foundation Akkers van Margraten for passing on various kinds of useful information with seemingly inexhaustible energy. And to filmmakers Albert Elings en Eugenie Jansen for their eye-opening television documentary on the construction of the American cemetery in Margraten in 1944–45 and for the inspiring talk I had with them in the shadow of the Sydney Opera House.

I would like to single out for special mention also L. J. P. M. Frissen, former Governor of the Dutch province of Limburg. The mayor of Margraten and his administrative staff, most particularly Leon Urlings en Ria van Wissen. Emile Ramakers at the City Library of Maastricht. And finally also Bert Kleijnen, Frank Lahaye, Luc Wolters, and the superintendent of the American military cemetery in Margraten, Keith Stadler.

I received warm encouragement and incalculable help also from countless people on the other side of the Atlantic Ocean. They are too many to list individually, but I cannot bring this research journey to a close without at least mentioning Benton Allen in Galesburg, Illinois; Mary Anne Fedor in Pennsylvania; Carl Hodges' son in Tennessee; Patricia Morrow in Houston, Texas; Gerarda (Grada)

Sumner-Dorscheidt in Cranston, Rhode Island; Charles Taylor in Iowa; Sharon Estill Taylor in Seattle, Washington; and Annette Tison in Virginia. Many thanks also to my dear colleague Professor Kurt Piehler, now the new director of the Institute on World War II at Florida State University.

My colleagues at the University of New South Wales in Sydney provided me with much intellectual and moral support, while the School of History, conscious of the expensive nature of conducting research from Down Under, made sure to offer vital financial support. Many thanks also to Professor Bruce Scates at Monash University in Melbourne.

The team at Palgrave Macmillan has, once again, been most instrumental in helping to mold one of my ideas into a book. Special thanks to Michael Strang for identifying the potential of what I had in mind early on and to Ruth Ireland and Jenny McCall for seeing the project through with a keen instinct and a firm hand. Thanks also to Tracey Dando for her editorial comments.

As always, my deepest gratitude goes to my extended family. I am afraid that, over the many years, my book projects have slowly but steadily taken on the form and shape of a family enterprise. Time and again my father has been willing to come out of retirement to perform various urgent research tasks. I have turned the Belgian homes of my sister Christel and brother Jan into research bases for extended periods of time. My linguist sister Karin read drafts of the English-language manuscript whilst highly pregnant and I think she finished the final chapter on the way to the hospital in London. Caroline Finch, Karin's mother-in-law in Norfolk, was kind enough to agree to submit the English text to yet another round of careful scrutiny.

Most of all, however, my mother and father, brother and sisters, nieces, and family-in-law have steadfastly refused to roll their eyes whenever I am expounding, even before one book has been completed, what the next one will be on. That alone must be seen as a sure sign of love. Somehow, however, I sense that my wife Elle may secretly roll her eyes upon reading this paragraph. If so, I have no problem forgiving her this. She has, after all, forgiven me so much more.

Abbreviations

ABMC	American Battle Monuments Commission
AFCENT	Allied Forces Central Command
AFNORTH	Allied Forces North Europe
AGRC	American Graves Registration Command
AVM	Foundation Akkers van Margraten
AWON	American WWII Orphans Network
BCM	Papers Burger-Comité Margraten, GAM
CKL	Papers Commissaris van de Koningin in Limburg, RHCL
DIB	Dienst Identificatie en Berging, Ministerie van Defensie, Nationaal Archief, The Hague
DL	*De Limburger*
DNL	*De Nieuwe Limburger*
GAM	Municipal Archives Margraten
GVL	*Gazet van Limburg*
HQ	Headquarters
IDPF	Individual Deceased Personnel File
JFC	Allied Joint Force Command
LD	*Limburgs Dagblad*
MACR	Missing Air Crew Report
MBZ/NA	Ministerie van Buitenlandse Zaken, Nationaal Archief, The Hague
MVK	Family Papers Michiels van Kessenich, RHCL
NARA	National Archives and Records Administration, Washington, DC
NIB	Netherlands Information Bureau
NWGC	Netherlands War Graves Committee
PJP	Papers Jo Purnot
PLB	Papers Lucy Beckers

PM	Parish Archives Margraten, RHCL
QAM	Questionnaire Adoption Community Margraten
QM	Quartermaster
QMG	Quartermaster General
RG	Record Group, NARA
RHCL	Regionaal Historisch Centrum Limburg, Maastricht
SAM	Foundation Adoption Margraten

Note to the Reader

"The past," the great American novelist William Faulkner famously observed, "is never dead. It's not even past." That is certainly true of the Margraten boys and the Dutch community in whose midst they rest. In the course of writing this book, stories of the unique relationship forged in and around the village of Margraten have continued to surface among Dutch adopters as well as American relatives of the World War II fallen. Those readers who find that their story, too, should be preserved as part of the expanding Margraten memory are warmly encouraged to contact the author at:

themargratenboys@yahoo.com

It goes without saying that readers are also warmly encouraged to visit the Netherlands American Cemetery and Memorial and to listen to what it is the Margraten boys are trying to tell them even today. To make it easier for readers to locate the final resting places of some of the individual American soldiers mentioned in this book, I have put the exact coordinates at the end of each relevant note (in bold type) as well as in a separate section of the index.

1 A Debt of Honor

The early evening of Wednesday, 24 January 1945, was pitch dark and biting cold. But that did not stop half a dozen prominent inhabitants from gathering in Margraten's town hall for an urgent initiative. Since their liberation in September 1944, men and women in the area had clung adoringly to American soldiers stationed in their homes and schools and in tents dotting fields and meadows. The Dutch in Limburg province had struck up friendships with GIs. They had cried whenever soldiers were ordered back to the front lines. They had been heartbroken when truck upon truck returned from the battlefield loaded with the corpses of boys who had brought so much hope and optimism to their war-worn lives. For some time now, people had been feeling a need to demonstrate their appreciation for the American troops in a more organized and relevant manner than the occasional offer of warm water for a morning shave or an evening meal in the family home.

It was beyond doubt for all involved that evening that any such initiative was to revolve around the vast, bloodstained field of honor in their midst. Since November 1944 thousands upon thousands of dead soldiers had been brought to the American cemetery in Margraten from vicious battles for the Siegfried Line, the German city of Aachen, and the Hürtgen Forest. In the wake of the ferocious Ardennes counteroffensive that had just been blunted, the giant field on the main road from Maastricht to Aachen continued to absorb casualties at a sickening rate. Despite one of the coldest winters on record, many saddened civilians had been finding their way to the cemetery to pay tribute. But what more could be done? The villagers at the town hall hurriedly dispensed with the formalities. In no time they decided to organize themselves into what would henceforth be officially known as the Civilian Committee United States Military

Cemetery Margraten. A quick succession of ballots determined who would be the committee's president, secretary, and treasurer. Then the newly minted committee members plunged into the chilling cold again. They headed for the nearby school, where Captain Joseph Shomon of the 611th Graves Registration Company had his office.[1]

In the mind of Captain Shomon, the 611th by now had become "part of the family in Margraten," and the officer from Connecticut was more than happy to receive the Dutch delegation. The villagers immediately explained to him that they had just created a committee whose goal it was "to do as much as is currently possible for the fallen allied soldiers." "We as Dutch citizens," they solemnly declared, "feel an obligation towards the American soldiers who died not just for their country, but also for our freedom, and we want to do something for them in return." They had already decided, they hurried to announce, that the committee would collect money to buy flowers and to pay for a Holy Mass in the fallen boys' honor on each third Sunday of the month. But surely, they asked, as unit commander at the American cemetery he could give them advice on still better ways to pay tribute?

The initiative caught the New Englander off guard. Captain Shomon made sure to express his heartfelt thanks to the delegation and instantly lauded the idea of flowers and church services. Beyond that, however, there was little else he could advise them to do, apart from trying to use their influence to help find new land for the local farmers who had been hurt by the sudden transformation of fertile fields into an American burial site. Moreover, he felt obliged to point out that, quite possibly, the cemetery was not there to stay. At some point in the future, the Margraten boys might be transferred to cemeteries in Belgium and France or even repatriated to America. The members of the committee nodded but left undeterred. They had finally found a way of channeling the community's gratitude into purposeful action with the approval of the appropriate American authority, and for now that was all that mattered. They returned to a freezing town hall to talk things over. A decision was made to have a new meeting after Mass that Sunday to which they would now also invite Father Ramakers as well as Mayor Ronckers whom they had just designated honorary president of the Civilian Committee. Then they went home and straight to bed. There was much work to be done in the months that lay ahead.[2]

1

As the war drew to a close in Europe in 1945, an early spring descended upon Margraten with an exceptional mildness that encouraged growing crowds from across the region to flock to the cemetery. Visitors were allowed onto the terrain only during strictly limited hours so that American troops could continue the processing of casualties and digging of graves with the least interruption. This was absolutely vital as an endless procession of two-and-a-half ton trucks and one-ton trailers was now rolling in from deep inside Germany with the bodies of GIs killed during Operation Grenade, the offensive to cross the Roer River, and Operation Plunder, the final push across the Rhine River. Indeed, by the end of March, the exhausted African-American diggers could no longer keep up the pace and Captain Shomon once again had to call on all able-bodied men in Margraten to report to the cemetery with shovels. Still, each time the gates briefly swung open for visitors, people from across southern Limburg patiently stood waiting at the main entrance to get in, their arms loaded with flowers.

When the war finally came to an end in Europe in early May 1945, Margraten, in the words of Captain Shomon, "went wild." The church bells rang and Mayor Ronckers proclaimed a holiday. There was singing, dancing, drinking, and parading in the streets. Children with beaming smiles, dressed in their finest clothes, went from door to door. People cried and rushed to church. Many headed for the American cemetery with flowers and flags to say thanks. For the first time since the cemetery's creation on 10 November 1944, Captain Shomon closed the gates early. He issued passes for his men and with some fellow officers hurried over to Ronckers' home. The officers opened a bottle of champagne and, before long, the mixed crowd was singing national anthems and any old song they could think of. Then Joseph Shomon raised his hand and proposed a toast. "Here's to victory in Europe – may the war end soon in the Pacific. God bless the Allies and our good friends here in Margraten and the world over."

The following day, work at the cemetery resumed early as more bodies had been trucked in from Germany during the night and previous day. With an eye to the first Memorial Day to be held at the end of May, Captain Shomon decided that the time had come to set in motion at least some rudimentary beautification of the cemetery. Norwegian spruces from the woods near Wittem were planted to serve not only as a windbreak, but also as a screen to shield the place from the view of American troops still rolling by on the road to Aachen. Trucks hauled loads of majestic blue and golden cedars from a German nursery in Münster to provide the burial ground with some serenity. Gravel from the banks of the Meuse River turned muddy tracks into neat paths and rubble from the pounded city of Aachen served as demarcations for the burial plots. The cemetery's first flower beds were created with pansies from local Dutch gardens and the Ninth Army allowed Captain Shomon to hire additional civilian labor from Margraten and villages as far away as Vaals near the German border to speed things up.

Within less than three weeks after the creation of the Civilian Committee, appeals during church services and in town hall posters had raised enough money in the impoverished parish of Margraten for Holy Masses in honor of the slain GIs to be scheduled for the next five years. The Civilian Committee had also hurried to organize a memorial service on 15 April 1945 for President Roosevelt, whose sudden death had caused an outpouring of grief and anguish throughout the community. But the first real opportunity for the committee to show its mettle came when the May Memorial Day approached much faster than Captain Shomon had wanted. The American company commander had hoped to have flowers on each of the 17,000 GI graves by the time of the commemoration. But in the final week of May, the American officer had to admit that he could gather neither enough flowers nor enough men to accomplish this. When they became aware of the snag, the Civilian Committee immediately offered to come to Shomon's aid. In January they had solemnly promised flowers for the cemetery. Now they set about to deliver on their promise.

On Memorial Day, barely three weeks after the defeat of Germany, the people of Margraten witnessed the first of many gatherings of high-ranking military and civilian officials to come. General William Simpson, commander of the Ninth Army, was the principal speaker. He was flanked by no less than 16 corps and division commanders. Their ranks were swelled by chaplains and clergymen of all faiths, Dutch government representatives, and ranking military leaders of other Allied nations. From as early as eight in the morning, the Dutch had begun pouring in from all over Limburg province. They arrived on foot, on bicycles, in carriages, on horses, and only very occasionally in cars. When the ceremony finally commenced at eleven, an estimated 30,000 civilians formed a packed cordon around the cemetery. They listened in awe to Simpson's solemn speech and the 21-gun salute, watched more than 30 war correspondents take notes, and observed aircraft overhead charged with making photos to be rushed to the London press corps. A deep hush fell as Simpson stepped down from the platform, was handed a wreath, and proceeded to carry it to the grave of an unknown soldier. The hush lingered while each of Simpson's lieutenants peeled off to place a wreath on the grave of a soldier from their own outfit.

Impressive though the official wreaths were that day, they barely stood out against the mass of garden flowers that had been spread across all of the 17,000 American graves. On the day preceding the commemoration, 20 trucks of Captain Shomon's unit had made the rounds of 60 villages in the area to pick up freshly cut flowers, put at the disposal of the Americans as a result of a massive effort coordinated by the Civilian Committee. Close to 200 men, women, and children had worked deep into the night to have all of the graves adorned with a touch of color.

Now, as the Memorial Day ceremony came to a close and the officials began heading back to their vehicles, thousands of locals refused to return home. They gathered around Father Heynen who so often in the past half year had spent time in these grounds to say prayers during burial ceremonies. Father Heynen quickly improvised a special service. The Americans brought out their chaplain's small wooden altar and Father Heynen concluded the afternoon by reciting the rosary with his loyal flock. Upon leaving the cemetery later that day, each Dutch family received one of 20,000 memorial cards, courtesy of the Civilian Committee, and paid for with money collected by office workers at a Limburg coalmine. On the card's back, a text in English and Dutch exhorted visitors never to forget the price paid for their freedom by thousands of "buddies and brothers." "We consider them," the text concluded, "as our proper heroes." Captain Shomon later recalled that at the end of that day he had "felt an even greater gratitude to the people of Holland for their magnificent tribute to our dead comrades."

6 The Margraten Boys

2. An American bugler at Margraten cemetery blows taps in May 1945. (Courtesy US National Archives and Records Administration)

Two days later, on 1 June 1945, the 611th Graves Registration Company received orders to prepare to leave Margraten. The proud unit turned over the military cemetery, records and all, to the men of the 603rd Graves Registration Company, who would continue to dig still more American graves for the next ten months. There was anxious talk of a new assignment for the 611th in the Pacific. "We were a sad outfit," Shomon wrote. "We hated the thought of leaving our beloved Margraten, our friends, and our cemetery."

On the morning the Americans left, the entire village turned out to say goodbye, crowding the streets. Father Heynen said a parting prayer and Mayor Ronckers made a farewell speech. The Americans stood in formation, facing the Dutch. Captain Shomon returned the honors. "We leave you in sadness," he addressed the crowd. "You have been good to us and we respect you above any people we have met in this war. This is how we feel this morning; we shall always feel this way. May God bless you and your good work. May He look after the dead which we leave in your care this bright but sorrowful June morning." Many a villager cried when the American vehicles lined up and headed for Maastricht.[3]

2

Margraten's Civilian Committee had played a key role in the Memorial Day tribute at the end of May 1945. But even before that, they had begun to be involved in another initiative that was to take on proportions no one could have foreseen at the time. As happened at American cemeteries all over liberated Europe, within months of its creation, civilians were visiting the Margraten cemetery not just out of gratitude to the US and its mighty military, but often also to safeguard the memory of a particular GI.

Some had learned that a soldier whom they had befriended, or fallen in love with, during the heady days of liberation had lost his life within weeks or even days of crossing the nearby border with Germany and been returned to southern Limburg to rest there forever. Captain Shomon in spring had seen a Dutch girl visit the grave of her American friend several times a week. She and her mother would bring flowers, kneel and pray at the grave, and then sit there for hours with tearstained eyes and nothing to eat. Shomon's men had taken pity on the women and made a habit of bringing them sandwiches.

Other civilians had begun to spend time at a soldier's grave not because they had known him personally, but because a close comrade had implored them do so. A family from Heerlen regularly undertook the six-mile trip to the grave of Preston Clark of the 30th Infantry Division because a GI who had stayed at their home had been devastated by the death of the lieutenant from North Carolina in November 1944. Before moving on to Germany, the GI had a picture taken of himself at Lieutenant Clark's grave and asked his Dutch hosts to make sure his comrade would not be forgotten.[4]

In January 1945, Captain Lane had approached Joseph van Laar with a similar request regarding another lieutenant of the 30th Infantry Division from the Carolinas. Because of his good command of English, van Laar, the town clerk from Margraten who had helped Captain Shomon locate the right spot for the American cemetery the previous fall, acted as a translator and liaison between the municipality and the 611th Graves Registration Company. In that capacity, he was one of the few civilians authorized to be at the cemetery outside visiting hours. Captain Lane had traveled to the cemetery to pay a visit to the freshly dug grave of his cousin John Land. A promising medical student from South Carolina, the 24-year-old officer had been killed in the vicinity of Aachen two days after Preston Clark. His parents and young wife were heartbroken, the American officer told van Laar, and he hoped that a letter about his visit would at least somewhat assuage their grief. Could he perhaps be bothered, the captain anxiously inquired, to take some flowers to his cousin's grave from time to time?

Joseph van Laar's response was instant. The haunting things he had experienced at the massive cemetery in the past months – the rows of mutilated dead, the ceaseless digging, the howling wind – had made a deep impression and left him with a strong sense of responsibility. "I will take care of your cousin's grave as if he were my own family," he solemnly promised. "Indeed," van Laar resolved, "I will adopt his grave." The American officer had needed a few seconds to allow this to sink in and had then thanked the Dutchman profusely and from the bottom of his heavy heart.

In March of that same year, Joseph van Laar had received a letter from Anderson, South Carolina. In it, John Land's parents expressed their deep gratitude to the Dutchman who they thought unusually kind for wanting to adopt their son's grave. By then, so many American soldiers visiting Margraten cemetery had asked van Laar to do the same that finally he felt the need to take the matter up with the mayor of Margraten. "I find myself," he explained to Mayor Ronckers, "saying 'yes' time after time, but I cannot possibly continue to do this for much longer." "Why," the town clerk suggested to the mayor, "do we not ask more people to step forward and accept such responsibility?"

Mayor Ronckers had instantly sensed that such an adoption program would present the perfect opportunity for the Civilian Committee to prove its real worth and for the broader community to give wholehearted expression to its deep feelings of sympathy for the Americans. Known for his determination, the mayor wasted no time in putting together a group under the auspices of the Civilian Committee tasked specifically with organizing an adoption program.

He had harbored little doubt about who would be the ideal person to head it: the man who, just the previous autumn, had arrived in Margraten as Father Ramakers' right-hand man. In neighboring parishes, Johannes Heuschen, a handsome and robust 33-year-old, had come to be known as a formidable footballer and, above all, as a priest with boundless energy.[5]

In Margraten the young Father Heuschen had immediately lived up to his solid reputation. It was he who had been the driving force behind the initiative that saw all of the 17,000 American graves bedecked with flowers on Memorial Day 1945. Yet, despite his involvement in this, he had also managed to have locals adopt several hundred graves even before the departure of Shomon's 611th Graves Registration Company in June 1945.

For the remainder of the year, the Civilian Committee undertook to offer assistance in countless other activities aimed at paying tribute to the American liberators. In the summer, they helped organize visits to the cemetery for more than 50 local organizations from across southern Limburg. On 4 July, to mark the anniversary of American independence, they accompanied Prime Minister Schermerhorn during the wreath-laying on behalf of the Dutch government. In November, to commemorate the departed on All Souls' Day, the committee paid for special masses in honor of the fallen heroes in all of the region's parishes liberated by American troops.[6]

Others too came up with initiatives that centered on the massive cemetery to express the population's gratitude to the United States. On 13 September 1945, the first anniversary of the liberation of Margraten, the Jonkheden, a social organization of unmarried men aged 16 and older, with its roots in medieval times, put together an impressive procession. Carrying wreaths and flags, mayor and aldermen, clergy, the local brass band and shooting club, schoolchildren, and almost all of Margraten's inhabitants assembled in front of the church and then snaked their way to the military cemetery. When the year drew to an end, blueprints were being examined in the office of Limburg's governor for what was described as a 'Memorial Hotel.' The impressive construction was to be built in Epen, on the Dutch side of the border with Belgium, exactly halfway between the American military cemeteries of Margraten and Henri-Chapelle. Its purpose was to serve as high-quality accommodation for visitors from the United States and elsewhere. The ambitious plans were later shelved, however, no doubt because of a dire lack of funds so soon after the devastation of war.[7]

Still, amidst all these manifestations of gratitude, the one thing that was mobilizing the Dutch more than anything else since Memorial Day, was the news that individual American graves were up for adoption under the auspices of the Civilian Committee and with permission of the American military authorities. The committee had become better known in the region through their repeated involvement with the cemetery. And they now resolutely added to their agenda as a core activity "the encouraging and administering of grave adoption by the civilian population." As a result, more and more people began to approach the committee with requests for adoption.[8]

These requests came as a godsend to the mayor of Margraten. By the summer of 1945, as postal services in Europe began to function normally again and more and more Americans learned of the locations of the various military cemeteries, relatives and friends of GIs who had been reported killed or missing had begun a desperate search to obtain more news. Many simply addressed a letter to the mayor of Margraten in the Netherlands.

The stories that reached Mayor Ronckers were heart-rending. For those whose next of kin had gone missing, the agony of not knowing what had happened was unbearable. At the end of the summer, the American Graves Registration Command (AGRC) had started a large-scale operation in the European theater aimed at locating unburied remains of American military personnel and the bodies of GIs interred in other than American military cemeteries. For this purpose, special detachments had been sent to the Netherlands as well, and they were racing against time from north to south in the hope of completing the task before the onset of winter and frozen soil. American authorities provided Dutch radio and press with notices encouraging the population to contact their burgomasters with any information they might have concerning such remains or graves.[9]

All this did not stop Captain Ellis Middleton's father from organizing his own search. A well-to-do lawyer in patent and trademark causes with offices in Washington, DC, and New York's Rockefeller Plaza, he had the Dutch embassy send pamphlets to the governors of several Dutch provinces. In mid-September 1945 a copy also reached the office of the Margraten mayor. It showed a photo of a handsome 24-year-old fighter pilot whose P-47 Thunderbolt had last been seen on 23 September 1944 in the midst of the fierce battle for Arnhem during Operation Market Garden. Now, almost a year later, the desperate father was appealing to the Dutch "to help me locate my son if living or his body if dead." He implored mayors as well as newspapers, schools, and churches to make an announcement asking for information. His son, the pamphlet suggested, might possibly be suffering from amnesia. In that case, it could be helpful to know that he smoked Camel cigarettes and loved reading poetry, and that his favorite magic trick was to make a thimble disappear from his finger. Or still, that he might respond to the name of his wife Anne, daughter Hart, or Danish dog Beowulf. Prepared for the worst, the grief-stricken father also provided the details of the fighter pilot's 1941 dental chart.[10]

Others knew for certain that their loved ones had been killed and now lay interred at the Margraten cemetery. But they, too, had a burning desire to know more. In August 1945, a Dutchman from The Hague wrote to Mayor Ronckers that he had received a letter from a friend in Bloomington, Indiana. The American had asked him to travel to Margraten and to send him a photo of his brother's grave. But the Dutchman had just recently been liberated from a German concentration camp and was still too weak to make the trip. Could the mayor be so kind as to provide him with a few photographs for which he would be more than willing to pay? He would be all too glad to take care of the American grave at a later stage.

Such requests told the burgomaster that what was needed were local people who could comfort American families without delay by putting flowers on the soldiers' graves, describing their visits in letters, and forwarding the much-sought-after photos of names of loved ones on wooden crosses and stars.

Meanwhile, as the letters from America continued to arrive and growing numbers of Dutch were stepping forward as adopters, Father Heuschen, with financial assistance from the Civilian Committee and the support of several young volunteers, found himself pouring more and more of his energy into the adoption program.[11]

3. Margraten's Father Heuschen and three of adoption's administrative volunteers at the American cemetery's wooden chapel in 1946. The chapel, erected by German prisoners of war, was torn down when the permanent cemetery structure was built in the 1950s. (Courtesy Foundation Akkers van Margraten)

3

The indomitable village priest would soon be scrambling for reinforcements for his adoption team. This had everything to do with unexpected developments taking place in the nearby city of Maastricht. Willem Michiels van Kessenich – aristocrat, lawyer, and son of a prominent political family – had been mayor of the capital of

Limburg province for almost three years when the Germans overran his country in May 1940. Like many mayors across the country, Baron Michiels van Kessenich had taken the decision to stay at his post and undertake the delicate balancing act of engaging in a constructive relationship with the Germans for the benefit of the people he represented. This frustrating effort had collapsed, however, when in the summer of 1941 the German occupier disbanded all municipal councils and instructed mayors to begin governing unambiguously according to Nazi principles. For the mayor of Maastricht this was the final straw and in the autumn he, like many other Dutch mayors, tendered his letter of resignation.

Soon after the liberation in September 1944, Baron Michiels van Kessenich had been reinstated as mayor of Maastricht and the 42-year-old now seemed to be set for a promising postwar political career. It soon turned out, however, that his brief stint as wartime mayor had sufficed to cause his reputation considerable damage. There were those in Maastricht, especially in resistance circles, who refused to forget the role he had played in the hostage affair during the very first days of the war. It was true that the German invaders in almost every Dutch city had demanded lists with the names of inhabitants to be held hostage and threatened with execution with an eye to ensuring the population's docility. But the fact that Michiels van Kessenich had been too compliant in providing the Germans with a list of names some saw as most inappropriate, indeed as odious, and they were keen to remind people of it at every turn.[12]

In such circumstances, Baron Michiels van Kessenich must have realized that there was much political benefit to be gained from cozying up to the Allied liberators and wrapping himself tightly in the American flag. The perfect person to help him achieve this goal was his wife Emilie. Charming and gracious, the slender mother of eleven children, Emilie had quickly succeeded in ingratiating herself with the highest-ranking officers of Maastricht's American garrison: General Hobbs, commanding officer of the 30th Infantry Division; General Corlett, commander of the XIX Corps; and even General Simpson who was in charge of the entire Ninth Army.

Emilie van Kessenich appeared untiring in devising schemes aimed at making relations between the GIs and the local population as agreeable as possible. In October 1944, she became one of the driving forces behind an organization that set out to organize dances where American troops taking short breaks from the front could relax and meet "politically and morally screened" Dutch girls under the strict control of a committee that included local clergy. In the next few months, some 2,500 girls signed up for this program. Mrs. van Kessenich was happy to find herself transformed from a housewife into someone being driven around in American staff cars, running meetings, and battling against some in the clergy and press opposed to what they saw as a grave loosening of morals. Morals had truly spun out of control when the war in Europe suddenly ended in May 1945 and a hurried demobilization of American troops in no time came to resemble an organized rout. Amidst collapsing discipline and escalating alcohol abuse, the once successful dance scheme quickly had to be abandoned.[13]

Emilie van Kessenich returned home from her previous duties just in time to lend her full support to a husband fighting for his political life. Just days after the victory in Europe, Queen Wilhelmina had ordered the formation of a new Dutch government, and Michiels van Kessenich had been suggested for the key post of Minister of the Interior. This, however, was now causing a political storm, as former members of the Maastricht resistance vehemently protested his candidature and gladly stoked publicity about his role in the hostage affair. In June the people charged with forming the new government withdrew their offer to the mayor of Maastricht. To make matters worse, in the second half of 1945 a commission set up to look into the conduct of mayors in wartime began a close examination also of the case made against Willem Michiels van Kessenich.[14]

Amidst these gathering clouds, the mayor apparently decided to attempt to replenish his political capital by further cultivating relations with the Americans. He may well have done so on the advice of his wife, who admitted in her journal to having been "deeply hurt" by the ministerial affair. In any case, in July Willem Michiels van Kessenich sat down to write a stirring tribute to the American people for their part in restoring peace to his city and country. He signed the letter as the mayor of Maastricht, sealed the envelope, and had a secretary mail it to America's hugely popular magazine *Life*.[15]

On 12 September 1945, a letter arrived from the US for Mayor Michiels van Kessenich. It had been written by a young woman from Demopolis, Alabama. She said that *Life* had published his letter in

4. In one of their last moments together, Warren and Mabel Rose Feil rest on a bench in their garden in Alabama in April 1944. The touching story of the young widow and the private killed in Germany on his birthday played a key role in galvanizing the Margraten adoption community in 1945. (Courtesy Regionaal Historisch Centrum Limburg and photographer Johan Martens, Ghent, Belgium)

the late August issue and that she had been very pleased to learn his full name so that now she was able to contact him at last. Her husband Warren Feil, a private in the 84th Infantry Division, had been killed in Germany on his birthday, 18 April 1945, and now lay buried in the American military cemetery of Margraten, which she knew was located not far from Maastricht. "Since you live so near it," she pleaded, "I will be grateful to you all the days of my life if you can get me a snapshot of his grave." Mabel Rose Feil said she would be glad to reimburse the mayor for any expenses incurred. "My husband and I were so young," she said in closing, "and he was my whole life to me."[16]

Two days later, this anguished sentence was quoted in an article in the *Gazet van Limburg*. Exactly one year after the liberation of the region, amidst all kinds of commemorations, the article called upon the people of Limburg to remember the terrible pain so many American families must be suffering and to consider caring for the grave of a Margraten boy as if it were the grave of a family member. The article signaled the start of a cooperative effort between Margraten and Maastricht aimed at massively expanding the adoption program. Although it was Emilie van Kessenich, the Maastricht mayor's wife, who had given the impulse for the article and provided the newspaper with Mrs. Feil's letter, people interested in caring for a grave where urged to contact Margraten's Civilian Committee to be registered as candidates. The response to the call was overwhelming. Within ten days, the committee received no fewer than 3,000 letters with the names and addresses of adoption candidates from across the province.[17]

In Margraten Father Heuschen hurriedly called for more volunteers to lend support in sifting through the piles of mail and keeping close track of which graves were being assigned to which Dutch families. Priority was given to the growing number of letters that were arriving from America with the express wish from relatives and friends to have someone take care of a particular grave. Heuschen had soon assembled a team of seven or eight villagers. These young people had just set out on their own careers and were putting in long hours during the day. Two of them were men who served as municipal clerks; the others were women who held various administrative jobs. Still, drawn by the pleasure of each other's company, and inspired by Heuschen's charismatic leadership and the lofty goal of doing right by the American liberators, none objected to working at the priest's home in the evenings and even on weekends.[18]

In Maastricht, meanwhile, Mrs. van Kessenich proved to be at least as hard driving. Motivated by an urge to serve the good cause as well as her husband's political career, at the end of September 1945 the beleaguered mayor's wife decided to write a long letter to none other than President Truman, begging him to forgive her this "dreadful impudence." She described the nature of the adoption program set up by the Margraten Civilian Committee and told the American president that she had joined forces with them and was now "propagating their splendid work," among others by calling upon the thousands of young women who had once attended the GI dances she had helped organize in the final months of the war.

Emilie van Kessenich clearly had ambitious plans for the adoption program that would involve all of the 17,000 American graves. So much so even, that she brazenly appealed to the American president with not one, but two requests for assistance. As the American cemetery authorities refused to provide the committee with the full details of the deceased and the exact locations of their graves, she was hoping that the president could refer her to higher authorities that would prove more cooperative. Simultaneously, Mrs. van Kessenich thought that perhaps, too, President Truman could appoint an officer in the US with the responsibility to coordinate the many requests from American families "according to the help we can offer them." She even suggested as a candidate Lieutenant Colonel Leo Senecal, former mayor of Chicopee, Massachusetts, and former commanding officer of the Civil Affairs detachment in Maastricht, with whom she and her husband had entertained most cordial relations after the city's liberation in September 1944.[19]

With the letter on its way to the White House, Emilie van Kessenich also contacted Dutch Foreign Minister van Roijen and American ambassador Stanley Hornbeck to gain support for the adoption program. At about the same time, the mayor's wife took two of her small daughters and some flowers to the Margraten cemetery. She snapped a photo of the girls posing at the wooden cross that had Warren Feil's name on it. Next she enclosed the photograph in a letter to the private's mourning wife in Demopolis, Alabama.[20]

In Washington, DC, Emilie van Kessenich's letter slowly made its way through the War Department's swollen bureaucracy. At the end of October 1945, the Director of the Civil Affairs Division was advised that some of the division's officers "have personal knowledge of the activities of the Mayor of Maastricht and his wife gained while they were stationed there and feel that they can commend the earnestness and sincerity of these people." A week later, however, such recommendations had done nothing to prevent the office of the Quartermaster General from sending Mrs. van Kessenich a brief letter politely thanking her for the "kind sentiments" she had expressed while regretting "that we are not in a position to supply the information you desire."[21]

But if the November letter from Washington, DC, did much to dampen Mrs. van Kessenich's hopes of playing a major role in Margraten's adoption program, the letter and photo to Alabama had set in motion an unlikely chain of events. Back in Demopolis, Warren Feil's widow was so struck by the kind gesture of the Dutch mayor's wife that she passed the snapshot on to *Life* together with a letter telling the story of how her husband's grave had come to be adopted. The mass-circulation magazine on 11 February 1946 not only published Mrs. Feil's letter and photo but, at the urgent request of the widow, some time later also agreed to print the details of Mrs. van Kessenich's address "for all to see who have soldiers buried at Margraten." *Life*'s stories on the adoption program now caused a deluge of mail from America to find its way to the offices of the Maastricht and Margraten mayors. Emilie could hardly believe her eyes when bags of American mail began arriving at her husband's office in Maastricht. By the third week of March, more than 1,200 letters had been received and more were pouring in each day.[22]

Father Heuschen and Emilie van Kessenich were aided in their response to the staggering American appeal by the fact that earlier in the year they had formalized their cooperation. Emilie had been made patroness of Margraten's Civilian Committee for which Heuschen now acted as indefatigable secretary. Moreover, both she and the priest had been made members of the Netherlands War Graves Committee (NWGC) in Amsterdam, a newly created national body that was to serve as an umbrella for all local organizations concerned with the care of Allied graves on Dutch soil. It had caused the members of Margraten's committee great pride to learn that the national committee had decided to use their pioneering adoption program as a model for other committees in the Netherlands to emulate where it concerned the fallen of Great Britain and Canada.[23]

Even within these structures, however, the demands on Margraten's committee remained overwhelming. Heuschen's young volunteers worked ceaselessly until deep into the night on workdays and sacrificed

5. As the wife of the Maastricht mayor and baron, the well-connected Emilie Michiels van Kessenich after the war came to play an increasingly important role in the Margraten adoption committee. (Courtesy Regionaal Historisch Centrum Limburg and photographer Johan Martens)

weekend after weekend. At one point, the committee began paying several of them some kind of salary for a number of months, especially when it became clear that with even harder work it might prove possible to accomplish a most ambitious plan: to have all of the by now nearly 18,000 graves adopted by Memorial Day of 1946. The war had caused everything to be in short supply. But in a sweeping gesture the director of the Royal Dutch Paper Mill in Maastricht gladly used his influence to solve the committee's paper pinch. And Mayor Michiels van Kessenich did his part, too, allowing at least two of his secretaries to take time out to lend his wife a hand in the adoption program. These young women were equally happy to extend their work as volunteers in the evening. Indeed, on several occasions they took the bus to Margraten after work, only to return to Maastricht the following morning.[24]

Meanwhile, a special network of close to 50 volunteers was set up in villages across southern Limburg. Their specific task was to help adopters who lacked sufficient knowledge of English to correspond with American families who were anxiously awaiting letters with more details on the resting places of their loved ones.²⁵

4

If the appeal for a word of comfort was massive among American families, it was easily matched by the outpouring of solidarity among Dutch families. By 30 March 1946, the date on which the last burial took place at the Margraten military cemetery, some 14,000 Dutch requests for adoption had been processed through Herculean effort. Meanwhile, the Civilian Committee relentlessly kept up calls for more adopters through churches, newspapers, schools, and the scouting movement. On 30 May 1945, the local population, under the auspices of the Civilian Committee, had enthusiastically succeeded in putting fresh flowers on the grave of each GI. By the time of Margraten's second Memorial Day in May 1946, the committee was exceedingly proud to announce that families from across the province and beyond had pledged to care for close to all of the nearly 18,000 American graves. These pledges were solemnly confirmed in certificates issued by the Civilian Committee, indelibly linking Dutch names and addresses with the names of American boys and grave locations. Volunteers in turn meticulously typed these data onto tens of thousands of index cards stored in the home office of Father Heuschen in Margraten.²⁶

The Memorial Day ceremony on 30 May 1946 was still more impressive than the very first one the year before. This time Prince Bernhard, representing the Dutch Royal Family, joined the large delegation of American generals and admirals, Dutch government officials, and ambassadors from across the world in paying tribute to the Americans who had sacrificed their lives. Civilian turnout was higher even than in 1945, with an estimated 40–50,000 people now descending on the cemetery early in the morning. American MPs and hundreds of Dutch police forces were kept busy until late in the evening with crowd and traffic control. The *New York Times* reported that such a mass turnout on Memorial Day was "believed to be without parallel in a foreign country."²⁷

Impressed as the Dutch were by the Memorial Day ceremony, they did not need visiting authorities and formal speeches to remind them of why they had agreed to adopt American graves. "We did so," summed up a woman whose family was caring for the graves of three soldiers, two from Illinois and one from North Carolina, "because of our tremendous and endless appreciation and gratitude." "Everyone," emphasized another woman whose parents had received a certificate with a paratrooper's name, "wanted to adopt a grave."[28]

Many in Limburg's newly liberated territories had painful and often traumatic memories of a long German occupation that had ceased only with the arrival of the Americans. In some places the memories were still more vivid than in others. In Kerkrade, a town of some 30,000 inhabitants on the German border just north of Aachen, the Nazi occupier had ordered the civilians out of their homes when the front line rapidly drew closer at the end of September 1944. The forced evacuation in a battle zone had been a horrendous and lethal experience. Only a few hundred people had managed to stay behind, stubbornly clinging to their homes in the fury of battle. One of them, a 16-year-old girl, remembered that when the GIs at last arrived in their battered street, they dressed even their dog in orange, the national color of Holland, from sheer mad joy. For her family then, adopting the grave of Leo Marceau from Massachusetts, an infantryman who had died across the border in March 1945, was no more than the natural thing to do.[29]

Families who returned home after Kerkrade's liberation had been no less happy. Immediately after the war, one such family was determined to set out on a pilgrimage to Margraten. Accompanied by neighbors and friends, they first took the steam train to Valkenburg, and then covered the remaining four miles on foot. Some time after that visit, they accepted responsibility for the grave of a paratrooper of the 101st Airborne Division slain during the fierce fighting in the Arnhem corridor in 1944.[30]

In other towns and villages near the German border and front line, many also had experienced sufficiently narrow escapes during the bombardments to remain eternally grateful for the liberation. A child who lived through the war in Heerlen recalled that she slept in a potato crate in the basement and that a hole had been made in the wall they shared with the neighbors so that they could crawl through it in case of a direct hit. During many nights on end, the murmurs of people reciting the rosary had drifted through the hole. The girl's parents later became the proud adopters of a Kansas infantryman from the equally proud Big Red One.[31]

For a child further north in Geleen, the war had been compressed into the memory of Allied air forces mistakenly bombarding her town. Her father had rushed her and her three sisters to the basement just in time. When the dust settled, they found their house badly damaged and the street unrecognizable. A priest could be seen crawling across the rubble on his knees, saying the last rites for neighbors trapped and dying. It was an awful price to pay for liberation. Still, when the long-awaited day finally arrived, her family gladly abandoned their bedrooms again, this time to make room for American soldiers. And when her mother in January 1945 gave birth to a boy in their battered home, GIs elbowed each other to spend time at his crib. The same girl from Geleen would never forget how, right after the war, she and her family had asked an uncle to drive them to Margraten to visit the adopted grave of James Stirling, an Ohioan and private from the 30th Infantry Division, the first division to have made its way from Belgium into the Netherlands.[32]

From the outset, however, the initiative for American adoptions was by no means limited to the inhabitants of Limburg. Many in the neighboring province of Brabant hurriedly responded to calls from local newspapers to accept special care of graves in the American cemeteries of Son and Molenhoek. These cemeteries were located in the infamous Arnhem corridor, the site of the courageous but ill-fated airborne operation of September 1944, which had been aimed at capturing the Lower Rhine bridge and sweeping into Germany to end the war before the year was out. When in the late 1940s these graves were transferred to Margraten, the adopters from Brabant refused to abandon their boys and insisted on continuing their obligations towards them in Limburg.

But even among the Dutch who had not been liberated by American troops, there were myriad reasons for adopting GI graves soon after the war ended. One woman recalled that as soon as her mother arrived in Maastricht after marrying her father, she joined the adoption program to take care of the grave of an air force lieutenant from Pennsylvania for the rest of her life. She had suffered unspeakable hardships during the hunger winter in Amsterdam in 1944–45, a famine that had caused some 16,000 Dutch to die and a quarter of a million to suffer from malnutrition. Both her parents, the daughter testified, "were mad with joy when the Americans came with freedom and bread."[33]

In Limburg and beyond, certain communities of shared suffering were especially keen on adopting Margraten graves. Those, for example, who had served in the Dutch armed forces and had been swept aside by Germany's blitzkrieg in just four days. Humiliating as this had been, it had not made the fear and suffering of Dutch soldiers less. For a Geleen family that adopted infantryman Robert Rowse from Massachusetts in 1946, the invasion of 1940 was a central theme. In 1939 nervous rumors of war had prevented the newlyweds from venturing further than Luxembourg for their honeymoon for fear of a German invasion. Barely a year later, many fearful weeks had gone by following the chaotic Dutch surrender before news at last arrived that the fresh husband had survived the ordeal unscathed. The husband's brother, however, had never returned from the punishing German bombardments in the front lines.[34]

Grateful for having survived the terror of the Nazi security services, many who had been in the resistance, too, could not think of a more potent gesture than the adoption of a liberator's grave. Among the earliest adopters, the whole panoply of resistance was represented: families who had hidden Jews and young Dutch men evading forced labor in Germany, men who had returned downed airmen to the Allied side, women who had gathered intelligence and relayed messages.[35]

In Maastricht, one such resistance member had played a key role in a pilot escape line, putting to good use an underground network of caverns and tunnels dug out in the region's characteristically soft marlstone. As if all that was not dangerous enough, he and his wife had also offered refuge to a Jewish couple. In August 1944, just weeks before the liberation, someone tipped off the Germans. The Jewish couple managed to escape, but the resistance man and his wife were arrested and dragged off to a Maastricht prison. One of the first things the Americans did when they liberated Maastricht was to throw open the Nazi prison gates. President Truman later directed General Eisenhower to express to the resistance man "the gratitude and appreciation of the American people for gallant service in assisting the escape of Allied soldiers from the enemy." The courageous couple from Maastricht in turn thanked the American people for their sacrifice in the common struggle by adopting the Margraten grave of a Montana corporal from the 99th Infantry Division.[36]

Young men who had been among the tens of thousands who had gone into hiding from as early as 1943 to escape forced labor in Germany formed another group keen on becoming Margraten adopters. In 1942 one such adopter had been a relatively carefree student. A year later, however, he had been on his way to the Dutch camp of Ommen, notorious for its brutal regime, and from there to Germany to join the pool of forced labor from across Europe. In May 1944, however, he had managed to escape and reach southern Limburg where he went underground. Four months and several close calls later, the 20-year-old had been liberated in Ulestraten. "It was Sunday, 17 September 1944," the man recalled, "in some sense the happiest day of my life." Back in America, for the family of Lieutenant Robert Strong, Friday, 2 March 1945, was without a doubt the saddest day of their lives. On that day, the fighter pilot from New York had failed to return from his mission. In 1946 the former Dutch forced laborer did not know the details of the American pilot's death beyond the scanty data on his Margraten cross. But as one young man to another, he did know that he owed him a lifelong debt of honor.[37]

Perhaps no one sensed this debt more intensely than the few Jews who had survived the near annihilation of their people in the Netherlands. For a Jewish woman from Maastricht, the adoption of Charles Miller from the 36th Tank Battalion served a double purpose. It was to remind her forever of what the war had taken away from her and what the liberation had allowed her to hold on to. In the summer of 1942 her Jewish husband had been arrested and deported to the east. The woman had desperately grabbed her son and daughter and, together with her sister and brother-in-law and their two daughters, tried to cross into Switzerland. When that failed, the family went into hiding in various places in Belgium. In Brussels the Nazis were tipped off and she and her sister's husband, who was also her husband's brother, were sent to the notorious Dossin Barracks in Mechelen, and from there in a cattle wagon to the camps. The woman's children, her sister, and both nieces escaped arrest and continued to hide in Belgian safe houses until the end of the war. The woman's husband and his brother perished at Auschwitz. She herself somehow managed to hang on to life in the factory of death and eventually became reunited again with her children. That the adopted Connecticut tanker's first name was the English for Karel and that, like her son, he was born in 1924, may well have been a quirk of fate. But the bereaved Jewish mother must have sensed that all this had to be more than just a coincidence.[38]

Total war had forced children to share its hardships, too, which gave them just as many reasons as adults for wanting to become involved in adoption. A girl who was 16 at the time of liberation remembered the German occupation in Limburg essentially as a time of "much fear." That painful memory explains why she helped take care of the resting place of Theodore Hemmingson, an Iowa sergeant from a tank battalion, from as soon as the adoption program took off. For another girl, barely twelve when the war came to an end in Munstergeleen, the Nazi regime had caused her to sense acutely the strain that her parents were under while helping downed Allied pilots to escape and hiding young Dutch men. The liberation came, she recalled, "as a gift from heaven." Helping her father commemorate the five Americans he had adopted by the summer of 1946 was the least she could do in return.[39]

That same year, a mother from the tormented town of Kerkrade agreed to have her son sign on to the adoption program in his own name. The 15-year-old attended the Memorial Day service in May and made a point of carrying flowers to the cemetery on his bicycle on at least one other occasion that same year. Sixty years later, he was still honoring the annual rituals.[40]

5

The groundswell of sympathy for the liberators had not just sprung from past suffering, but also from fond memories of the American troops stationed in the region. For people who had known many years of harsh rationing, the rich stocks of American food inevitably formed a central theme in their gratitude. The child of adopters in Valkenburg loved to think back to the two GIs at their dinner table sharing their ration of meat and beans as well as the deliciously soft white bread. The ritual of one American offering her his fork for this feast and the other his spoon was forever seared into her memory. An adopters' daughter in Meerssen, in whose home the Americans had happened to install a kitchen, would always carry with her the deep impression this made. "We shared food with them," she mused, "what a wonderful experience. I will never forget the taste of egg powder, something we had never seen before. And then there was the canned food they left behind. We carefully stashed the cans away. Just in case there would be another war."[41]

An eight-year-old adopters' son in Heerlen was convinced that there would be no more war now that the Americans had arrived. For him the German invasion of May 1940 had meant joining the stream of refugees and his father telling him to select no more than one toy for the trip. This had been followed by an occupation which in his mind was above all a time of stubborn lice due to a chronic lack of soap. With the GIs had come a giddy atmosphere of security, plenty, and optimism. His mother had kept a journal just to record the excitement of what she would forever refer to as "the American days."[42]

Those days had belonged to cocky young men who impressed the Dutch with their generosity and big smiles. Women happily offered to do their laundry, knowing full well that they would be recompensed with more soap than they could have dreamed of months earlier. Their husbands just as gladly accepted the much-needed business that American forces brought to Limburg. An adopter from Simpelveld had enjoyed the brisk business of repairing a constant stream of 'liberated' radios that the GIs carried back from Germany when taking a break from the front lines. Another adopter had been forced to call on his children to help out in his printing business as the demand for personalized letterheads and Christmas cards soon became too much for him to handle on his own.[43]

The presence of the Americans had been reassuring in many other ways. One adopters' couple would never forget that when their daughter broke a leg, an American medic came to the rescue, gently placed the girl on the kitchen table, and then swiftly put her in a solid cast. Adopters in Berg en Terblijt were eternally grateful for the Americans who in a jeep had rushed their son all the way to a hospital in the Belgian city of Liège after German shelling had ripped off one of the boy's fingers.[44]

But after four years of enemy occupation, the small gestures of friendly foreigners resonated just as much as the big ones. How could adopters forget, for example, that when their son was born on 24 November 1944, the four GIs billeted in their home had paid a visit to the local bank in Waubach, opened an account in the newborn's name, and deposited several guilders?[45]

In this era of good feelings, the color of the soldiers' skin had mattered little, although most in southern Limburg had never before seen a black person in the flesh. How could adopters in Mheer not think back with a warm glow to the days when more than half a dozen African-American soldiers in their home had sat around the stove in the evening regaling them with stories? These, after all, were the same black GIs who had made their four-year-old daughter squeal with joy by walking up and down the stairs to her bedroom on their hands. So fond were the mutual memories that when, later in the year, the Dutch family had another baby, several of the African-Americans had used their leave to drop by all the way from Germany.[46]

It had not been easy for impoverished people in a war-torn country to think of ways to thank liberators who seemed to have it all. But that had hardly stopped them from trying. In a Heerlen theater, schoolchildren had huddled together on stage and, wearing wooden shoes for the special occasion, had danced their hearts out to please a charmed American crowd. Still in Heerlen, an adopter's children had brought kettles of hot water to the Americans living in tents in the adjoining field so that they could shave. In the evening, their aunt and her girlfriends had brought over a gramophone player and some records, and invited the boys in for a dance. Before being sent to bed, the children had sung 'God Bless America' for the GI visitors and been plied with chocolate "and other candy we had never tasted before."[47]

For young women in particular, the era had been one of a romantic chemistry that could be explained only by the intensity of war and the joy of deliverance. "Some weeks after the liberation," a woman from Meerssen wrote, "I celebrated my 22nd birthday at home with some of the Americans stationed nearby. I will never ever forget that birthday!" In 1946 the same woman found herself dutifully tending the grave of a Georgian private from the 9th Infantry Division. She was just one of countless young women who played a crucial role in making the Margraten adoption program a resounding success.[48]

For women and men alike it had been heartbreaking to witness firsthand what changes life in the front lines could wreak in young men whom they had first gotten to know in the relative peace of the rear. This was especially true in Heerlen and other places on the German border from where large numbers of troops were sent into the enemy's den, only to return grimy and exhausted. "They arrived as cheerful and carefree boys," one Heerlen adopter observed, "but later returned from the front marked men." An adopter from Kerkrade had not known what to say when in 1945 one of two soldiers her family had played games with during many an evening suddenly returned from Germany. He was missing an arm, was on his way home, and had decided to drop in on his host family one last time.[49]

Adopters in southern Limburg also recalled the terrible shape American troops were in when they arrived for rest and recreation at the end of the Battle of the Bulge that had raged in the nearby Belgian Ardennes. Dirty and exhausted dogfaces had dropped to the floor of every available building in the area, from houses and farms in the hamlet of Vijlen on the Belgian border to schools way back in the city of Maastricht. For a teenage girl from Vijlen, the memory of the sight of seven such soldiers billeted in their home in February 1945 sufficed for her in 1946 to accept keeping eternal vigil over the grave of Robert Mitts, a lieutenant and paratrooper from Michigan.[50]

Some adopters had fought side by side with the Americans on the front line. Most had joined as members of the Dutch *Stoottroepen*, a military unit created from resistance fighters on the initiative of Prince Bernhard in September 1944. They had served as guides in the border area as well as translators and pushed deep into Nazi Germany together with the Ninth Army. One of those who had been up front with the GIs was mining engineer Adriaan Paulen. A former athlete who had run the 800 meters final in the Antwerp Olympics in 1920, Paulen had broken through the German lines in September 1944 and linked up with the American forces even before they liberated his home soil. For his courage under fire with the 2nd Armored Division, the Dutchman was awarded the US Medal of Honor in 1946. Paulen himself considered it an even greater honor to have adopted the grave of Lieutenant Colonel Charles Etter, a Tennessean from the Hell on Wheels division whom he had come to like and admire before the officer was killed in November 1944.[51]

For people in Limburg, most shocking of all had been the inevitable sight of thousands upon thousands of once confident and energetic American soldiers being trucked back as wax-like bodies to the vast burial ground at Margraten. Adopters from as far away as Heerlen and Gulpen remembered the endless series of trucks passing through their towns with corpses stacked like cordwood. An adopter from

Eygelshoven was forever haunted by the sight of bodies, and body parts, being unloaded in a nearby field, sorted, and then reloaded for transport to Margraten. Several of the Dutch civilian men who helped bury the Americans were so moved by bodies mutilated beyond recognition that they insisted on adopting only unknown dead.[52]

The experience at Margraten caused children in particular to grow up fast. Although as a general rule adults tried hard to keep them away from the cemetery, wartime did not always allow such shielding. At least one local boy found himself actively involved at the cemetery for several days after an American chaplain asked him to help out as an altar boy during Masses for the casualties that kept arriving at a ceaseless pace. Soon after, although barely 14 years old, the boy adopted the grave of Major Victor Maleski, the son of a steelworker of Polish origin, seeing it as his duty to comfort the officer's widow in a series of letters to Pennsylvania.[53]

The 14-year-old altar boy had never known Victor Maleski in person. But scores of people in southern Limburg were aghast to learn that among those who had ended up in Margraten's soil were boys they had come to know very well. In one Dutch home, 13 GIs had settled in and built a warm relationship with the owners and their children largely thanks to Max Weller, a Pennsylvanian of Swiss descent who spoke German and thus also understood some Dutch. Upon leaving for the German front, all 13 had signed their names and addresses in the daughter's personal album. Months after the war had ended, the Dutch host father sent a letter to Max Weller's address to find out how the 13 men had fared in Germany. The answer he received came from Max's mother. Max had been killed in Germany and was now buried in Margraten, just a few miles from the home where he and his comrades had so often sat around the glowing stove. Within weeks of receiving the shattering news, Max's host family had signed up as the adopters of his grave.[54]

With heavy hearts, many more Dutch families searched the barren field for the exact location of their friends' final resting places. "Dad and I," a man who was 13 in 1945 grimly recalled, "found him in the Margraten cemetery in plot A – right behind the American flag."[55]

A teenage boy from Nieuwenhagen, a town a stone's throw away from the German border, had an even more harrowing experience. He had struck up a friendship with Donald Diez from Santa Clara,

California, a soldier he sometimes even accompanied on guard duty. During those long evenings, Dan taught the Dutch boy how to play rummy and both merrily discussed their stamp collections. When Dan left for Germany, the boy presented the GI with hundreds of European stamps as a farewell gift.

In July 1945, the Dutch teenager received a letter from someone in Dan's anti-aircraft artillery battalion informing him that Donald Diez had not survived the war. The boy jumped on his bicycle and, propelled by anger and disbelief, easily covered the 13 miles that separated his home from Margraten. There was, however, no Donald Diez in the American cemetery's records. Months later, the boy rode his bicycle to Margraten again to search for his friend. There was still no soldier by that name in any of the plots.

Dan had left behind his address before leaving Nieuwenhagen, but the teenage boy was unsure about how to start a letter to his family on such a sensitive subject and in clumsy English. In April 1946 he finally sat down and drafted a letter explaining his relationship with Dan Diez. Dan's father replied almost immediately with a very emotional letter. His son had been killed not in Germany, but in Belgium, at the end of the Battle of the Bulge. He had been buried in Henri-Chapelle.

Though the Dutch boy had never even heard of the American military cemetery in Belgium, within days he managed to locate the place, covering 20 miles of bad secondary roads on his bicycle. It was at Henri-Chapelle that the boy reunited with his rummy-playing, stamp-collecting friend and vowed to watch over his grave in the manner of Dutch adopters at Margraten.[56]

6

In the course of 1946, more and more people descended on Margraten as adopters haunted by painfully vivid memories of American boys who had once lightened up their lives with a reassuring presence and easygoing manner. Francis Doyle: a medic who had paid regular visits to a family in Heer whose daughters so reminded him of his own children. Wesley Wright: an infantryman from New Jersey who shortly before he left for the front had presented both his host mother and her daughter in Terwinselen with bracelets made from Dutch coins. George Sullivan: a Virginian of the 30th Infantry Division who had amazed a teenage boy in Kaalheide with the art of putting together miniature sets inside bottles. Paul Baker: a Pennsylvania private who in the company of his host family in Hulsberg had not been ashamed to admit how much he missed his mother. Sidney Curtis: a Texan of the 79th Infantry Division whose drink had been kept hot over a tea light for whenever he would return 'home' from guard duty at night.[57]

In wartime mere weeks had sufficed to forge ties between Americans and Dutch that felt as if they had existed a lifetime. The GIs' backgrounds and personalities were as diverse as the American society they came from. But for the Dutch who were shocked to learn that war had snatched them away forever, the pain was always the same.

Jerold Le Hoty was a bespectacled combat engineer from Ohio who was stationed in Brunssum for about a month. At one point, some Dutch girls invited him into their home after having struck up a conversation from their doorstep. Before he knew it, the soft-spoken Ohioan was a favorite guest, addressing the girls' parents with 'Mom' and 'Dad.' Many an evening was spent baking the apple pancakes that the American so enjoyed. Jerold would provide the flour and entertain his Dutch hosts on the piano with a wide variety of American songs.

The staff sergeant from Ohio was killed on a cold night in February 1945 somewhere between Geilenkirchen and Cologne. All that remained of him in the home of his Brunssum adopters in 1946 were warm memories and a photo with a black ribbon on the piano.[58]

Stephen Mosbacher was a staff sergeant from Ohio too. But he had arrived in the American heartland only recently by way of Queens, New York City, and Nurnberg, Germany. In 1938 his Jewish family had fled to the US to escape the growing threats of the Nazi regime. Although Stephen's father had been a leading obstetrician in Nurnberg, the family had fallen on hard times in Great Depression America. Still, by taking on jobs in a paint factory, Stephen, a gifted student, had somehow managed to work his way through college.

A big man called 'Moose' by the comrades in his unit, Stephen's native German made him a member of a specialist prisoner-of-war interrogation team in the 8th Armored Division. His knowledge of German also made it possible for the bookish sergeant to have long conversations with his host mother in Margraten who made him feel as if he was her son too.

Although in his letters home, Stephen was careful to sound ever cheerful, he confided to his Dutch 'Mom' that somehow he sensed he would not make it home to the States again. He was right. In April 1945 a tank shell killed him while he was trying to rescue a wounded soldier in a jeep. For this selfless act of bravery, Stephen was posthumously awarded the Silver Star.

Rather than live out his life in the New World, Stephen Mosbacher remained forever 21 and within walking distance of his Dutch adoptive family in Old World Margraten.[59]

2 A Web of Intimate Relations

Many in the US wished they could have walked to Margraten. To provide American families with some comfort by letting them know that their boys' graves were being watched over by caring Dutch families, the decision had been made some weeks before Memorial Day in 1946 to have Emilie van Kessenich, the mayor of Maastricht's wife, set out on an American tour.

So soon after the war, such an initiative posed major financial and logistical challenges. That it became a reality at all was due mainly to the support provided by the Dutch government. Both the Dutch ambassador in Washington and the Dutch Ministry of Foreign Affairs considered publicizing the adoption program as an ideal way of promoting goodwill for their small and battered country in what was now the world's major superpower. The NWGC in Amsterdam agreed to pay for travel and accommodation overseas. KLM, the national Dutch airline, sensing an excellent opportunity for publicity in a giant postwar market, was happy to offer to fly Emilie van Kessenich to America for free.

In characteristic fashion, the mayor's dynamic wife immediately arranged for an impressive display to be put together showcasing the Margraten cemetery. Limburg photographers donated 30 oversized illustrations showing the burial site from different angles as well as highlights of the Memorial Day ceremony. Margraten's Civilian Committee added a large number of the ceremony's memorial cards. A local engineer created a series of colored photographic transparencies to be projected on a wall or screen. The same engineer also came up with a design that would prove to be a main attraction in the States. A massive drawing on canvas provided an aerial view of the Margraten cemetery in all its minute details, including the numbered location of every single grave. Dutch military personnel presented Emilie van

Kessenich with half a dozen miniature crosses and Stars of David made of oak and filled with earth from the graves of a few selected GIs whose families she was scheduled to meet. Mrs. van Kessenich also gladly accepted a file with documents clearly outlining for an American audience the key role of the Limburg resistance in smuggling downed Allied air force personnel back to their own lines.

On Saturday morning, 8 June 1946, Emilie van Kessenich, seen off by the Limburg governor's wife and accompanied by a journalist, boarded a plane in Maastricht for Amsterdam's Schiphol airport. In Amsterdam she was met by a delegation composed of American ambassador Stanley Hornbeck, the board of the NWGC, and KLM representatives. Emilie eventually set out on her transatlantic trip, first touching down at Prestwick in Scotland and then making another stop in Newfoundland before arriving at La Guardia airport in New York.[1]

1

By all accounts, the month-long American tour showcasing the special care for the boys at Margraten was to prove a resounding success. With the memory of the war's tremendous sacrifices still raw, the response was often very emotional, as Mrs. van Kessenich immediately learned at La Guardia. Airport officials were obliged to inform her that she would have to pay a rather large sum of import duties on the display materials she had brought with her. When they learned about the exact nature of the materials, however, American customs officers spontaneously passed round a hat and insisted on paying the duties for her on the spot.

Mrs. van Kessenich's trip was meticulously planned with the help of staff from the Dutch embassy and the Netherlands Information Bureau on New York's Rockefeller Plaza who provided much logistical support. Most emotional of all, of course, were the many contacts that the Dutch mayor's wife had with bereaved American families of loved ones buried in Margraten. Some were already waiting for her when she arrived at La Guardia and more were eager to meet her at a reception that evening. During the next few days in New York and Washington, Emilie van Kessenich took calls from parents from across the country, had lunch with a mother from New Jersey, and pored over the Margraten photographs with another Gold Star mother who had boarded a bus in Detroit, Michigan, for a trip of more than 20 hours.[2]

Ten days after her arrival in New York, Emilie flew to Dallas for the southern leg of her tour. From Washington, Congressman Lyndon B. Johnson instructed aides in Texas to meet Mrs. van Kessenich at the airport and provide her with a place to stay. More grieving families were waiting for her at Dallas airport and three exhausting days were spent in the Lone Star State giving one presentation after another to next of kin. The main objective of the whirlwind tour through the South, however, was the unlikely town of Demopolis, Alabama. This was where, in the summer of 1945, Mabel Rose Feil, Private Robert Feil's widow, had unwittingly set in motion Mrs. van Kessenich's involvement in the adoption program. The meeting between Emilie and Mabel Rose was a major event, with the town mayor putting at Emilie's disposal a Highway Patrol car for the next two days. On the final evening in Demopolis, her American hosts almost reduced her to tears when they surprised her with a performance of the Dutch national anthem.[3]

Loaded down with gardenias and peaches given to her as presents from the Georgia Gold Star Wives in Atlanta, Mrs. van Kessenich returned to New York at the end of June. On the first day of July, she was surprised and very pleased to be able to meet with what she described as "the first Colored mother in my audience." The audience was all white again, however, when the mayor of Bridgeport, Connecticut, invited her over for a talk and presented her with a finely crafted silver rosary as well as an Underwood typewriter for the adoption's administrative work.

American politicians high and low were impressed by Mrs. van Kessenich's persona and the Dutch message from Margraten. If in Alabama Governor Chauncey Sparks insisted on shaking hands with her, in Washington, DC, the reception was even more impressive, with lunch in the presence of the Dutch ambassador and a delegation of Congress made up of the powerful Senator Richard Russell and Representatives William Whittington, George Dondero, and Lyndon B. Johnson. The American politicians expressed their sincere admiration for the adoption program and, after lunch, Mississippian William Whittington graciously offered his Dutch guest of honor a guided tour of the Capitol.

It was the grace of the Dutch mother of eleven as much as her unstinting effort in promoting the Margraten adoption program

6–7. The mayor of Montgomery, Alabama, welcomes Mrs. Michiels van Kessenich. Mrs. Michiels van Kessenich is accompanied by the grandfather of Lt Harte. Frank Harte was the pilot of a B-17 Flying Fortress that was downed by German fighters and one of many airmen buried at Margraten. (Courtesy Regionaal Historisch Centrum Limburg and photographer Johan Martens)

that also made her a darling of the American media. One of her first visits in the US was to the New York office of *Life*, the magazine that, by publishing the story of Mrs. Mabel Rose Feil, had done much to publicize the Margraten adoption. In between talks with next of kin and presentations, Emilie van Kessenich was dragged from one press conference to another, addressing journalists from dozens of newspapers, including the *New York Times*. Journalists were impressed. The *Bridgeport Telegram* described her as a "calm, gentle-faced woman" whose figure, despite raising eleven children, "is as slim as a girl's and whose face has no line in it." "Mme. Van Kessenich," the *Atlanta Journal* wrote, "a quiet, dignified figure dressed in black, made her audience, by turn, weep and laugh as she talked in a warm, British-accented voice."

On Monday, 17 June, Mrs. van Kessenich appeared live on ABC's *Headline Edition*. To a nationwide audience she explained how the purpose of the adoption program was to bring some measure of solace to the liberators' next of kin. She also made it abundantly clear that the Dutch were footing the bill for this program and that it "was not to cost American families one penny." The interviewer thanked her for "a warm-hearted message and a sympathetic invitation from the people of the Netherlands to the people of America." By midnight, ABC in response to the story had received more than 200 phone calls from all over the US.

A week before she was to return home, another invitation came, this time for an appearance, together with the widowed Mabel Rose Feil, in the hugely popular CBS program *We, the People*. After several rehearsals with an audience and an orchestra in a Madison Avenue studio during the day, the two women were ready for the radio broadcast on Sunday evening. Both talked up the importance of the adoption program and advised American families that the best thing to do was to contact the Dutch embassy in Washington, DC, with any queries they might have. By Monday, however, another deluge of telegrams and notes from phone calls was coming Emilie's way from the offices of CBS.

Exhaustion eventually made Emilie lose her voice, causing her to cancel various final appearances in Connecticut and Boston. In one small Massachusetts town, however, this did not prevent her from agreeing to an impromptu presentation on the Margraten cemetery for the benefit of the local fire brigade. The men had lost several

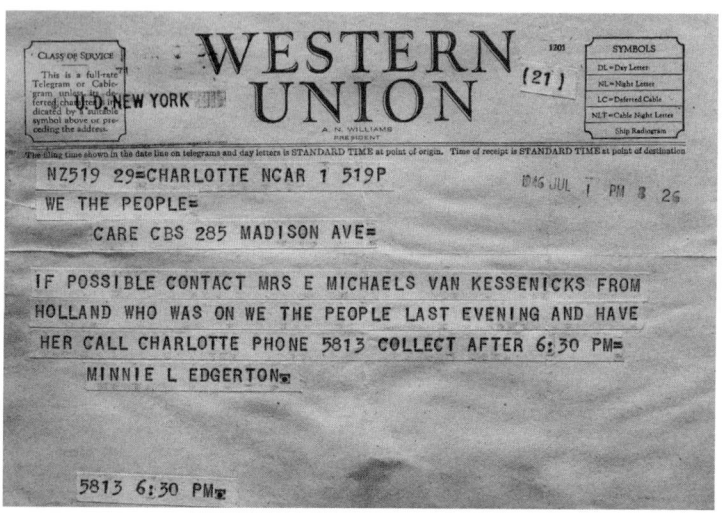

8. The mother of a Margraten boy from North Carolina tries to get in touch with Mrs. Michiels van Kessenich following her talk on CBS's *We, the People* in 1946. Hers was just one of many attempts by grieving American parents and siblings to find out more about the faraway resting places of their loved ones. (Courtesy Regionaal Historisch Centrum Limburg and photographer Johan Martens)

colleagues in the war but, because of the nature of their work, had not been able to attend any of her scheduled meetings. Aware of the grease and oil inside, firefighters helped Mrs. van Kessenich set up her displays on the lawn in front of the building and then bunched together to listen to her presentation in hushed silence.[4]

2

Mrs. van Kessenich's return to Maastricht on 11 July took place amidst much fanfare. Journalists from the region's radio station and newspapers were waiting for her at the local airport in Beek with questions about her trip, her radio appearances in New York, and her visit to the Capitol in Washington, DC. In the weeks that followed, organizations in Limburg bombarded her with requests for a talk on her American experiences and impressions. At the end of July, Emilie van Kessenich even agreed to undertake a trip to Hilversum at the invitation of the leading Catholic radio broadcaster for an interview about her American tour for a nationwide audience.[5]

Meanwhile, letters were arriving at the Dutch embassy in Washington, DC, praising Mrs. van Kessenich for her fine work. "Her extreme friendliness and charm, her nobility of character, her kind heart and sympathy and her Christian love for all those bereaved," wrote Mabel Rose Feil's father, "have made a great impression on us." The Demopolis Rotary Club readily concurred and was convinced that "her speaking tour in the United States must have done a great deal to cement the close ties which should always exist between the Netherlands and the United States." Mrs. van Kessenich on her part was quick to cultivate some of the newly forged political connections, as is obvious from the personal and warm letter from Lyndon B. Johnson, thanking her and her husband for congratulating him on his re-election to Congress.[6]

Not surprisingly, in the autumn, the Dutch ambassador to the US, referring to the many messages he had been receiving, sent a word of sincere thanks to the mayor of Maastricht's wife. "From the perspective of creating goodwill," he wrote, "your trip has without a doubt proved to be a tremendous success; your American acquaintances can now be counted on as staunch friends of the Netherlands." Still in the autumn, the international desk of the Dutch Radio Institute in Hilversum passed on to Emilie van Kessenich a request from the Canadian Broadcasting Corporation for a pre-recorded radio talk about postwar Holland "by some prominent Dutch woman speaking in English." She was the ideal person for this, they insisted, as contacts in New York had assured them of her earlier success with an American audience.[7]

As more and more of the spotlight was being directed to Mrs. van Kessenich in Maastricht, however, dark storm clouds were gathering over Margraten. Against the backdrop of rural Limburg's age-old suspicions of the city of Maastricht, Margraten from the very start had jealously guarded its unique relationship with the American military cemetery that had claimed so much of its richest soil. But ill feelings between Father Heuschen and Mrs. van Kessenich in particular had begun to surface even in the weeks preceding Memorial Day 1946. Indeed, one regional newspaper in May had been forced to print a rectification in response to an earlier claim that the adoption program had been Emilie van Kessenich's brainchild. It had hurriedly withdrawn the comment, emphasizing that the true adoption pioneers had been the members of the Margraten Civilian Committee early in 1945, and that Mrs. van Kessenich had begun to propagate adoption from Maastricht separate from the committee only half a year later.[8]

Even then, however, much of the public relations surrounding the Margraten adoption had irrevocably shifted to Maastricht as soon as it had become clear that the city mayor's wife would be the one publicizing the adoption program in a tour of the US. Proof of that appeared with the publication of a two-page article in *Libelle*, one of the Netherlands' most popular women's magazines. Early in June 1946, prompted by the massive media attention for Memorial Day, a journalist for the women's weekly had traveled to Margraten to find out how a village of barely 1,500 people had managed to acquire such a "world reputation." The female reporter had started out in Father Heuschen's office but, after hearing about Emilie van Kessenich's upcoming American tour during a visit to the cemetery, had rushed to Maastricht to hear all about Margraten from the mayor of Maastricht's wife. Published while Mrs. van Kessenich was in the States, the women's weekly naturally played up the busy role of an enterprising mother of eleven, with a photograph of her husband and children juxtaposed with one of herself making a phone call at a desk covered with piles of paperwork.[9]

For Father Heuschen, however, it must have been galling to find only one paragraph in *Libelle* on the hard work put in by the Civilian Committee and his loyal volunteers, and to read that Margraten was now responsible only for the "technical part" of the adoption program. This for Heuschen summed up all that was wrong with the relationship with Mrs. van Kessenich: people in Margraten were quietly doing the hard work, while the mayor of Maastricht's wife was triumphantly garnering the honors and praise. Mrs. van Kessenich's American tour further poisoned an already loaded atmosphere. In a radio interview after her return from the US, van Kessenich claimed that she had suggested sending Heuschen in her place, but that parish duties had forced him to decline, and that official authorities "wiser and better than I" had urged her to accept their request. Those authorities from the outset might well have judged the goodwill potential of a graceful and worldly mayor's wife much more promising than that of a hard-working village priest. Whatever the case, during Mrs. van

Kessenich's media junket on the heels of her trip, Father Heuschen became incensed at how he and his flock in Margraten were being marginalized in the adoption work for the boys who had always been so close to their hearts.[10]

Though lauded in one American newspaper in June for the "modesty that held her own doings in almost-Rembrandt shadow," by mid-July Father Heuschen was convinced that Mrs. van Kessenich possessed no such quality whatsoever. Indeed, he had just learned that she was now trying to persuade the Margraten Civilian Committee to have him hand over all of the files on the cemetery graves that he and his team of volunteers had so painstakingly collected. Included in those files were the grave locations and military details of all American dead buried in Margraten, which his volunteers had begun copying from American records in Liège, Belgium, in November 1945.[11]

Heuschen feared that van Kessenich, buoyed by her reception in the US, was plotting to seize total control of the adoption program and to have it administered from Maastricht. Determined to put a stop to this, Heuschen traveled to Liège to see Colonel Johnson, Commanding Officer Sector II of the AGRC. It was Colonel Johnson who had given permission for Heuschen's volunteers to copy the American files. In the past half year, Margraten's priest had built a relation of trust with the American officer. For a man of the cloth, Heuschen now showed himself to be quite unforgiving and not averse to a shrewd game of character assassination. He managed to convince Colonel Johnson that handing over the files would be against American interests and that "a racket was going to be made out of this, in order to obtain money and parcels from the next of kin."

The American colonel took to heart the priest's concerns. He immediately had a letter drawn up for Heuschen to take back to Margraten. In it, the commanding officer emphasized that it was important that "these valuable data shall in no way be exploited," that they had been entrusted to Father Heuschen "as we saw behind your person the Church as a sure guarantee," and that it was "therefore our express desire that the mentioned files remain under your personal management."[12]

The letter caused a fierce fight to erupt between Mrs. van Kessenich and Father Heuschen in which no holds were barred any longer. When people in the camp of van Kessenich also traveled to Liège to reason with Colonel Johnson, the American ordered Dutch liaison officer

Captain Loudon at the AGRC headquarters in Versailles to Margraten for an investigation. Loudon first had a talk with Heuschen. The priest told him that after the failed attempt to obtain the Margraten files from Colonel Johnson's office, Emilie van Kessenich had sent him "an extremely disagreeable letter, in which she had even cast a slur upon his conduct as a priest." Infuriated by nasty insinuations of behavior unworthy of a priest, including financial improprieties, Heuschen now saw a chance to vent his spleen. "She was always," he lamented to Loudon, "using her trip to America as a means of propaganda for herself, both here and in the States." And there was more, he whispered viciously; she "was receiving parcels on a large scale" and had "her whole family of thirteen newly dressed and presented with thirteen gold fountain pens."

Captain Loudon's next stop was the US military cemetery. The American superintendent there vouched for Father Heuschen, whose devotion to the adoption program, he claimed, was most sincere. The liaison officer then traveled to Maastricht. There he talked with several officials who clearly had reasons of their own to try and damage the van Kessenichs. They agreed with Father Heuschen that Emilie van Kessenich had "a tendency toward self glorification." But they were also quick to point out that she was using "her position on the war graves Committee to ameliorate the position of her husband whose reputation during the war had been none too good."

Inexplicably, Captain Loudon returned to Versailles to draw up a report on the matter without having talked with Emilie van Kessenich herself. Indeed, although he warned in his report to the AGRC that "much of the whole trouble is based on personal ill feeling between Mrs. van Kessenich and Father Heuschen" and advised that "at all costs Headquarters should keep out of this," Loudon in follow-up correspondence with Heuschen appeared to be siding with the priest and condoning the actions he was taking. Those actions, aimed at sidelining van Kessenich in the adoption program, were proving to be increasingly damaging to the mayor's wife at home and abroad. Because of her growing influence in Margraten's Civilian Committee, Heuschen early in September 1946 decided to resign as secretary and member, a decision that made several volunteers quit too, albeit with much pain in their hearts. Then Heuschen diligently proceeded to undermine Mrs. van Kessenich's reputation at the American embassy in The Hague, the Gold Star Wives Association in the US, and the NWGC in Amsterdam.[13]

Although officials in Amsterdam were by no means happy with the independent course that the ambitious Mrs. van Kessenich was steering in Maastricht, they deemed it wise to let the case rest to prevent her from mobilizing her "many powerful relations." But by the end of October 1946, it was too late for that. Emilie van Kessenich had just participated as a special guest in a transatlantic telephone talk on the Margraten adoption for an NBC *Special Salute to the Netherlands* in honor of United Nations week. The live radio broadcast in the US had included contributions from none less than General James Gavin, hero of the 82nd Airborne Division, and Dutch Royal Highness Princess Juliana. Stung and flabbergasted by the various allegations that were coming her way at this crucial time, Emilie van Kessenich fired off letters to the Dutch ambassador in the US and to American contacts she had made during her overseas tour. In a letter to Major General Thomas Larkin of the Quartermaster General in Washington, DC, she complained that in the last three months the attitude of American authorities towards her had markedly cooled. Her letters were no longer being answered, she claimed, and she had learned that both the US War Department and the Gold Star Wives Association had received information alleging her involvement in the adoption program for material benefits.[14]

Mrs. van Kessenich also contacted high-ranking officials within the Dutch Ministry of Foreign Affairs, demanding an investigation into this intrigue both to clear her name and to avoid damage to Dutch-American relations. By the start of December, the charges against Mrs. van Kessenich had been thoroughly investigated by the Dutch Ministry of War instead. The charges were found "to be entirely without foundation." Moreover, Captain Loudon was severely reprimanded for the way he had handled the investigation in the summer. "The matter," the Dutch Ministry of War concluded, "had been blown out of proportion and was characterized by the jealousy and backbiting typical of a provincial town and motivated by personal and political enmity." In a matter so important to the prestige of the Netherlands in American public opinion, a relieved Dutch ambassador in Washington was quick to report the findings to Major General

Larkin at the US War Department and to John Morgan, Assistant Chief of the State Department's Division of Northern European Affairs.[15]

Earlier in 1946, the investigation into the conduct of Emilie van Kessenich's husband during the occupation had led to the mayor receiving a written reprimand from the Minister of the Interior. For Mr. Michiels van Kessenich this meant the end of any ambition of a national career in politics. But, together with the clearing of his wife's name in the adoption affair, it now at least allowed him to remain firmly entrenched as the mayor of Maastricht. Just as deeply entrenched by the end of 1946, however, were those in Margraten determined to protect their adoption program from outside control. Shortly after resigning from the Civilian Committee in September, Father Heuschen had taken one last step to block any attempt at interference from Maastricht. The tens of thousands of alphabetically organized index cards on the American dead and their adopters were transferred from the priest's home office to Margraten's town hall. The Civilian Committee immediately ordered a large wooden chest of drawers to be built for the special purpose of safely storing away the index cards. Henceforth the robust piece of furniture would sit and remain housed in the town hall under the watchful eye of Margraten's mayor.[16]

3

The rank and file of adopters were blissfully unaware of the tug of war over who was to have control over the increasingly successful program. To them what mattered was that such a program existed, allowing them to express their gratitude in a deeply meaningful way. Adopters who registered with the Civilian Committee pledged first and foremost that they would pay visits to the cemetery on special occasions and adorn the assigned graves with flowers. This they did with increasing abandon in 1946 as the cemetery was completed and opening hours extended to most of the day. People undertook pilgrimages to the cemetery regardless of the weather, but police reports noted that during spring and summer in particular very large numbers of visitors from all over the province and beyond were flocking to Margraten. With motor vehicles scarce so soon after the war, many people arrived in horsedrawn carts or on bicycles. Or they took the train to the station nearest to Margraten and then proceeded to cover the remaining distance on foot. A couple in Maastricht who had harbored Jews during the occupation and adopted an infantryman from Connecticut made a point of regularly walking the five miles to and from the burial ground with all of their seven small children.[17]

Adults and children alike walked through the cemetery gate clasping baskets weighed down with flowers from gardens and fields. Scores of photographs have been preserved that show mothers, girls, and children standing, squatting, or kneeling besides graves decorated with fresh flowers and adorned with petals forming the words 'Rest in Peace.' Dutch war brides on their wedding day were known to make trips to Margraten to place their bridal bouquets on the graves of GIs who had died liberating their country.[18]

Brightly colored tulips were 15-year-old Aggie Schroeders' favorite flowers. She and her brother would start out on their bicycles in the morning, have a rest at a convent to eat their sandwiches and drink some coffee offered by the nuns, and then continue the ten miles from their home in Heerlerbaan to Margraten. The flowers, paid for with a portion of their small weekly allowance, were intended for William Sievers about whom these Dutch children knew no more than that he was a liberator from Michigan.[19]

Amidst the hustle and bustle in Margraten, an awkward silence cloaked the cemetery's German section. In addition to the nearly 18,000 GI graves, the American military cemetery had become the resting place also for more than 1,000 soldier dead from various Allied nations. But another 3,000 graves were laid out separately from the combined Allied plots in the field of honor. They were discreetly hidden away behind a screen of greenery and a grim sign at the section's entrance warned people that here were buried 'Enemy Dead.' Still, the families of the defeated, too, were desperate to learn more about loved ones who had vanished in the war. Mixed in with the growing mail from America that arrived at the Margraten mayor's office, and was passed on to the Civilian Committee, were scores of German letters in envelopes opened and stamped by censors in American, British, and French zones of occupation. Indeed, this continued long after the German dead had already been transferred from Margraten to their own military cemetery on Dutch soil at Ysselsteyn near Venray in the autumn of 1946, a fact that remained unknown to countless grieving families in Germany.[20]

For the next of kin to request more information from a Dutch mayor about the fate of those who had once occupied and terrorized the Netherlands was an exceedingly difficult and embarrassing thing to do. Many Germans preferred to operate through the International and German Red Cross or through the *Volksbund Deutsche Kriegsgräberfürsorge*. Others thought it more diplomatic to use Dutch contacts as intermediaries. On behalf of a German mother, a woman from Amsterdam inquired about the presence of the grave of a Luftwaffe NCO thought to have been wounded and captured at Arnhem and to have died in a British prison camp. "I sincerely hope," the Dutch correspondent wrote in closing, "that although this concerns an enemy, you might be willing to provide some information."[21]

Still, dozens of Germans in an act of desperate grief took the initiative to write to the Margraten mayor directly. Some were women with children who knew only that their husbands had gone missing but now needed proof of their deaths in order to qualify for urgently needed government allowances. Others had received official notification and knew for certain that their husbands and sons were buried in Margraten. Among the latter, there were those who simply refused to believe the news and begged to be sent a photograph of the cross showing the name of their beloved and other details. There were those too who wanted to know more about how their boys had died and if there were any personal belongings that could be mailed home to have at least something fill the dreadful emptiness. In one letter, German parents pleaded with the Dutch mayor to let them know what forms and costs were involved to have their 19-year-old son disinterred and brought home to Homberg in Oberhessen.[22]

Most Germans accepted that the Netherlands would be the final resting place of the fallen soldiers. A very few, like a man from Hagen in North Rhine-Westphalia, even dared to hope against hope that, "despite the terrible chasms that the unfortunate war has caused between peoples," there might be "loving hands" in Margraten willing to take care of the German graves. "If among you," the heartbroken mother of an 18-year-old casualty wrote in a letter from Vienna, "there might be a sweet little mother willing to visit my child's resting place and say the Lord's Prayer or light a little candle, it would provide some comfort."[23]

In Margraten the desperate requests for information about the German dead were answered in detail and with formal politeness. But for the German bereaved to expect more compassion so soon after the war was to underestimate the true depth of the chasm now separating them from the Dutch. Information released through the Margraten American Cemetery Headquarters in August 1946 poignantly captured the feelings of the Dutch in adoption statistics: "Number of adoptions in American plots: all 17,738 graves; number of adoptions in Allied plots: all 1,026 graves; number of adoptions in German plots: none."[24]

If there were no Dutch gestures to comfort German families, in 1946 people in Limburg were all too eager to reach out across the ocean to express heartfelt sympathy to as many American families as possible. Indeed, by the spring of that year, the Civilian Committee in its statutes had enshrined that adoption should entail much more than regular visits to the cemetery and flower offerings. Increasingly aware of the great need of families to feel closer to the faraway dead, a key part of the adoption pledge now came to consist of actively seeking contact with the next of kin and keeping up regular correspondence. All this was aimed at assuring relatives that their loved ones were not being forgotten and that their grief was being shared.[25]

Ironically, however, by the spring of 1946 it was becoming obvious to those running the program that American authorities were unwilling to go along with this increasingly popular part of the adoption program. In fact, Memorial Day in 1946 appeared to be the signal for the US military to considerably tighten the rules regarding America's war cemeteries overseas. In May a storm of protest erupted when authorities issued orders from Frankfurt prohibiting visitors from placing flowers on American soldiers' graves until after the official commemoration on Memorial Day. The Limburg press was offended and reported that the *New York Times* too had responded with indignation. Meanwhile, the Gold Star Wives sent emotional telegrams to President Truman and General Eisenhower and succeeded in their appeal for the orders to be rescinded.[26]

American military authorities remained adamant, however, in their refusal to give up control over communications between adopters and relatives of the fallen soldiers. In June the AGRC announced that the photographing of any graves "outside the continental limits of the

US" was "absolutely prohibited." The order was soon made public on large signs near the entrance to the Margraten cemetery, abruptly calling a halt to a phenomenon that had become widespread among adopters because a photo of the grave was often what American relatives longed for most.[27]

Yet, by far the most serious frustration for the Civilian Committee was that the large majority of adopters were also unable to send to the American bereaved letters or any other token of comfort. In fact, the AGRC had already taken steps to block the release of home addresses of deceased personnel to civilians as far back as the autumn of 1945. These measures were prompted by various concerns. The greatest worry was that civilians in a war-torn country might abuse their position as adopters for material benefits. "Although a majority of such communications would undoubtedly be of a proper nature," an order from the AGRC European Theater headquarters had clarified on 31 October 1945, "some few individuals may use information as a basis for requesting funds or articles of clothing, food, etc." Shortly after Memorial Day 1946, Father Heuschen traveled all the way to the AGRC headquarters to try and persuade military authorities that to release the home addresses would only benefit American next of kin, who stood to derive tremendous spiritual comfort from communications with adopters. But even his status as a man of the cloth got him nowhere in Versailles, and the priest was frustrated to have to return to Margraten empty-handed.[28]

Developments in the months that followed only caused the American military to tighten their grip on the home addresses. American and Dutch investigations into the alleged attempts by Mrs. van Kessenich to use the program for material purposes, although unearthing not the least bit of evidence, did much to make authorities in Versailles even more suspicious and protective. Lacking clear information about the nature and purpose of adoption, some in the US gradually also raised the question of why civilians abroad were having to take care of American graves in the first place. "This situation became so serious at one time," AGRC headquarters reported, "that it was necessary to issue several press releases to reassure American next of kin that the intervention of no third party was necessary to assure that the graves were receiving proper care from the US Army." To add to the sensitivities surrounding the GI home addresses, there was a constant worry that Dutch adopters might be sending photos or other information regarding deceased soldiers to the wrong families. Such errors were not unlikely in a massive military where many soldiers had similar surnames and numerous corpses remained missing or unidentified.[29]

In this uncooperative climate it became clear to the Civilian Committee that the only American home addresses they would be adding to the index cards uniting the Margraten boys and their adopters were those revealed by the American families themselves in letters sent to the village mayor or to Mrs. van Kessenich in Maastricht. But by the end of 1946 these amounted to no more than a small percentage of the total. It necessitated the committee creating a standard letter to be sent in response to an endless series of inquiries by Dutch adopters impatient to obtain the home address of their boy. In this letter, the committee regretted that they had failed to obtain the requested information from the American authorities and encouraged adopters to try their luck with the Adjudant General's Office in the US War Department. The standard response provided the adopter with an office address in the Pentagon Building as well as a model letter of inquiry. This sufficed for scores of letters from Limburg's rural villages to find their way to Washington, DC.

The nature of the reply from Washington appeared to depend much on whose inbox in the Pentagon the request for home addresses had landed in. It was routine for requests from adopters to be forwarded to the Quartermaster General's Memorial Division. After weeks of anxious waiting, most adopters were gravely disappointed to receive yet another standardized letter. "While it is regarded that your interest in this matter is motivated by an unselfish desire to assist in perpetuating the memory of an American who made the supreme sacrifice in behalf of his country," the Memorial Division's formal reply read, "existing regulations preclude transmittal of your letter to the next of kin. Also this office is not permitted to furnish addresses of next of kin. Your inquiry is therefore returned without action." Some kindly officials within the Memorial Division, however, could not be prevented from taking action. Bending the existing regulations, or choosing to interpret them differently, they informed more fortunate Dutch adopters that their letters and photos had been forwarded to the families in question. A few actually flaunted the rules, slipping American addresses into envelopes bearing the Pentagon letterhead.[30]

4

Neither the trickle of home addresses from the War Department nor the steady stream of addresses arriving in Margraten and Maastricht in letters from next of kin sufficed to have the adopters reach out to all of the bereaved. As a result, and despite the publicity created by *Life* and Mrs. van Kessenich's American tour, countless relatives of the Margraten boys continued to be wholly ignorant of the existence of the adoption program and the much-sought-after comfort it offered to bring. In the autumn of 1946, the public relations director of the *Toledo Blade* in Ohio wrote a letter to the commanding officer of the US military cemetery with a request for more information about boys from the area buried in Margraten. The letter was forwarded to the Civilian Committee. They drew up a long reply to the newspaper informing them of the existence of the adoption program and its purposes and lamenting that, because they knew so "few addresses of the relatives of the heroes buried in Margraten," they were unable to contact the many families in America. In closing, they asked for the newspaper to print a short notice about the adoption program together with a contact address.[31]

Meanwhile, in letters from all over the US, relatives and friends continued to plead for more information about the appearance of the cemetery and particular graves. Almost all letters contained urgent requests for photographs or for someone in Margraten to be kind enough to place flowers at a cross. Most Americans responded with utter surprise and deep emotion to letters from the Civilian Committee assuring them that Dutch people were already watching over the final resting place of their loved ones and that local families would be happy to get in touch with them so as to take care of any other wishes they might have.

Great was the gratitude in response to the unexpected news that a mother in Heerlen and her two daughters were lovingly caring for the grave of Don Smith of the 84th Infantry Division. The lieutenant's family in Bonham, Texas, had the first adopters' letter published in the local paper together with their Dutch address. Before long, the Heerlen family was corresponding not only with the officer's parents and other relatives, but with numerous American friends and neighbors as well.[32]

American appreciation for the kindness of the Heerlen family was nothing, however, compared with the sudden deluge of praise and thanks befalling a young woman in the small village of Gronsveld. Lucie van den Boorn was 22 in 1946 and the oldest of eight children. Like so many other families in southern Limburg, the liberated van den Boorns had befriended several American soldiers who had been all too happy bringing coal and coffee and spending evenings chatting around the kitchen stove. Like so many other GIs, they too had eventually moved on to Germany, leaving only their home addresses. In the spring of 1946, Lucie decided to write a letter to the California address of Miles Strand to find out if the GIs she had known had arrived home safely. She also mentioned that a huge American cemetery was located some four miles northeast of her home and that she would be happy to look after the graves of their comrades should any have been killed and buried there.[33]

It would have been impossible for Lucie to foresee the chain of events that her letter was to set off. Many weeks after she had sent the letter, Lucie had still not heard from the soldier in California. But then, early in July, the first envelopes from America began arriving in Gronsveld. In the weeks and months that followed, the numbers swelled. Letters poured in from California, but also from the Great Plains, the Midwest, New England, and the mid-Atlantic coast. At first, Lucie could not quite comprehend what was happening. A man from Roxbury, Massachusetts, said she had "the heart and mind of an angel of love and kindness." A 17-year-old girl from a small village in Virginia, whose main buildings were the post office and a Baptist church, wrote: "Your kindness will be returned to you and God will remember you for the deeds you have done." A 20-year-old sent a letter from Rhode Island on behalf of all the sailors on the USS *Yellowstone*: "We want to say, we think it is really wonderful for you to tend one of our soldiers' graves. May the Lord bless you & your family & others like you."

It took until September for an explanation to arrive from Miles Strand. The American veteran had not been able to write to Lucie any sooner because of a move to Los Angeles, the tragic death of his wife's father, and the joyous birth of their baby girl. By the time she received his letter, however, Lucie had already pieced together what had happened as scores of the envelopes she received contained clippings from newspapers from across the country. Miles Strand had thought Lucie's offer to care for American graves so uplifting that he had passed it on to a California newspaper. They had printed it and somehow the article and Lucie's address had been picked up by Associated Press and published by scores of American newspapers.

The emotions coming Lucie's way from America were overwhelming as unspeakable grief alternated with deep gratitude. Few if any correspondents appeared to be aware that there existed an adoption program created with the express purpose of providing them with some consolation. Indeed, more than a year after the end of the war in Europe, many inexplicably did not even have a clear idea of where exactly their loved ones might be buried. That is why they latched onto the Gronsveld girl, imploring her to find out all that she possibly could on their behalf. "Our brother, whom we loved very dearly, and will never cease grieving for," the sister of Lieutenant William House wrote from Massachusetts, "was killed in October 1944, in Holland. We are not sure where he was buried. The commanding officer wrote, somewhere in Belgium."

The situation was compounded by the fact that the newspaper article described the cemetery near Lucie's home as that of the First and Ninth Army, but did not mention Margraten by name. Several failed to find Lucie's small village on any map and therefore remained in the dark about the exact location of the cemetery she had mentioned. Some hoped that the Dutch girl could travel to neighboring countries and visit the American cemeteries of Henri-Chapelle and Neuville-en-Condroz in Belgium or that of Hamm in Luxembourg. It hurt Lucie to have to disappoint them and tell them that she owned no more than a bicycle and could not reach these places.

Still other correspondents Lucie reluctantly had to set straight on European geography. A woman whose son had gone down in a bomber over France on the way back from a raid against the German city of Solingen asked the Dutch girl to visit his grave in a place "48 miles west of Paris." "My husband's brother was killed in England," a woman from Texas wrote. "Would you by any chance have happened to have ever seen the boy? He was then Sgt. Roy A. Miller of the Signal Corps. I would certainly really appreciate any information that you might give us." A girl from Pennsylvania informed Lucie that her brother was "in grave 51, row 5, 19 miles south of Naples." "If he is near you," she begged, "I would love to have a picture of his grave."

Those who knew for sure that the cemetery near Lucie was that of Margraten and that this was where their relatives or friends were laid to rest, hurried and asked the girl to tell them all there was to know about the cemetery and grave. They wanted her to send them photos and preferably even the negatives so that copies could be made for others in the family and the neighborhood. The mother of 18-year-old Benjamin Anderson, "one of the finest boys that God could give a Mother," asked Lucie to make inquiries at the cemetery "about the way our boys were buried out there, were their bodies put in anything to protect them?" Still another family was impatient to learn when the body of their loved one would be returned and urgently wanted Lucie to find out.

Veterans who had seen buddies killed but had never had the opportunity to visit their graves before being sent home now asked Lucie to perform the ritual on their behalf. One of them had lost three close friends in Germany and possessed only a few pictures of some officers and a chaplain attending their burial. He sent the original pictures to Lucie, imploring her to return them to him as he cherished them more than anything else. "All the people thought the world of Ernest," another veteran reminisced about his good friend in the 2nd Armored Division, killed on Easter Day 1945 just a few feet from where he had been. "I read in our paper that your family wept when this friend of yours moved to the front. Hundreds and hundreds of American soldiers cried too. I did, and I'm not ashamed to say so."

Relatives had equally heartbreaking stories to tell about boys now thousands of miles removed from their homes. The sister of John Gallion recounted that 'Buster,' the only boy of four siblings, had been 19 when he was sent overseas with the 115th Infantry in July 1944. They heard from him twice after he went over. The next communication was from the War Department telling them he was no more. All the letters and Christmas packages that his family had sent were returned to them unopened shortly after that. Could Lucie please find his grave in Margraten?[34]

Captain Ernest C. Lacy Jr. of the 327th Engineer Combat Battalion was killed about a week before the war in Europe ended. German machine-gun fire cut him down while on a patrol across the Elbe to prepare a crossing aimed at establishing contact with the Russians. Ernest's father, a clerk at the Halifax County circuit court in Virginia, in an envelope to Gronsveld enclosed letters from the commanding officer, from a classmate at West Point, and from the Adjutant General's Office awarding his son the Bronze Star. Ernest's mother some time later wrote: "In our little town of 500 inhabitants he was the only one who lost his life. It was sad to see all of his friends coming home and know we would never see him again." Could Lucie send them a letter "and if possible a small photograph of the grave?"[35]

Gene Tyler from Clarendon, Texas, described herself to Lucie as "just a typical American girl who has led a normal life." She lived in a small ranch town, had married her sweetheart at a young age, and had made an effort to complete high school. But then the war had come and devastated her life. Her husband Harry had been drafted and for two years she had followed him to every training camp he was sent to. In October 1944 he had suddenly been whisked away on a troop transport to Europe. In March 1945 his life had just as suddenly been snuffed out during a night patrol. "It was hard for me," she confided to Lucie, "to realize that I was a widow at the age of nineteen. But yet, I had three years of perfect happiness that no one can take away from me. Very few people have had the happiness that we had in a lifetime." "But I," she continued, "like all the other Americans who have loved ones buried in Holland, can only plead that you might adopt my Husband's grave. Please, please, please, write to me and tell me of your decision."

Urged on by scores of similar heartbreaking pleas, Lucie set to work, apparently not realizing that she was replicating much of the Civilian Committee's activities in Margraten. She compiled long lists of soldiers' names and on her bicycle traveled back and forth to the cemetery to determine who was in effect buried there. With a girlfriend on several occasions she even pedaled the long road to Henri-Chapelle in Belgium to make inquiries. As Lucie's family did not possess a camera, that same girlfriend lent her hers so that dozens of photos were taken of graves until they ran out of film and were unable to find any more even in the city of Maastricht. From Lucie's home, letters went out to the headquarters of the AGRC in Versailles and to the War Department's Office of the Quartermaster General in Washington, DC. In the evenings, Lucie with the help of her brothers wrote hundreds of letters to American families, first making sure to draft the texts in pencil to get the tricky English right. For a family of ten in a war-torn country, the cost of stamps was no laughing matter, but with the support of her parents Lucie managed to cross this hurdle too. "If you have a bit of a heart," she commented much later, "that is what you do."

It made it all the harder for Lucie to understand why, early in December 1946, she received a letter from the NWGC in Amsterdam exhorting her in strong language to halt the work she was doing. Lucie van den Boorn was told that Allied authorities prohibited any individual initiative of civilians locating graves and passing on information to next of kin. If she did not immediately cease such activities, the NWGC warned, they would have no other choice but to inform the Dutch Ministry of War of her activities. But Lucie was in no mood to be ordered about by pitiless bureaucrats in faraway Amsterdam. "You threaten," she bit back in writing, "to put this question before the Ministry of War? Well, I will not let this scare me because I have no reason to be scared. We have done this out of humanitarian consideration because we consider them to be people with a heart like ourselves."

Lucie's emotional letter apparently sufficed to make authorities in Amsterdam back off. She continued her good work for quite some time until more and more American families were happy to inform her that they were now receiving letters from adopters registered with the Margraten Civilian Committee. Lucie, too, eventually registered as an official adopter, now accepting care of a single grave, that of Sergeant Thomas Steele Jr. of the 9th Armored Division. More than 60 years later, Lucie could still be found keeping staunch vigil over the grave of the liberator from New York.[36]

5

The gratitude that came the adopters' way from America was immeasurable. An occasional envelope contained cash dollars to recompense the good Samaritans for the postage and pictures. But mostly, Dutch families were inundated with parcels containing clothes, food, toys, and a wide variety of unique presents. In a package that arrived in Heerlen there were a porcelain salt-and-pepper set and a fruit bowl made of sequoia hardwood. One box shipped to Margraten contained stockings and some dresses so revealing that the parents of the strict Catholic household thought it wise to prohibit their daughters from wearing them.[37]

"My heart is broken," a mother in Dallas, Texas, told Lucie van den Boorn, "and will be until I meet my Darling Boy in the great beyond." But she said she would love Lucie eternally for what she had done, and she and her four daughters all put a little something in a box bearing the Gronsveld address. "I sent the fountain pen," the Texan mother clarified. "Ada the stationary. Mary the gloves. Barbara the little pin. Annie the handkerchief."

Correspondents tried to wheedle out of Lucie what more it was she might be needing: tea, coffee, cacao, nutmeg, soap, combs, toothbrushes, ice skates, comic books, movie magazines? Would she perhaps like, someone from Seattle suggested, a pair of cowboy boots? Most women simply figured that what a girl would want most was clothing. With new clothing still very expensive in the US, too, they stuffed boxes with second-hand items as well as rolls of fabric. With the latter also came tape measures, knitting needles, crochet hooks, buttons, and sewing and embroidery thread. Others decided to do the work for her. "We lost a neighbor boy in your land," a family wrote from New England, offering to knit a sweater for anyone she knew was expecting a baby. In other American towns, mothers and daughters sat down to knit clothing for Lucie's hope chest. A woman in Sacramento, California, called on her Jewish neighbor. Mrs. Goldberg had fled Nazi Germany by way of the Netherlands and was all too happy to give advice on European measurements and provide her with a tape measure in centimeters.

But for Lucie perhaps the most valuable present came from the Steiners in Plymouth, California. They had only two children, two boys, and they lost them both. The younger, Cecil, was killed at Groesbeek in September 1944 during Operation Market Garden with the 82nd Airborne Division and was given a final resting place in Margraten. His older brother, Walter, crashed with his fighter plane six weeks later and was buried in France. Prompted by the publication of Lucie's letter, Mrs. Steiner had asked the Dutch girl if she "could find out anything about her Son, how he was killed, or anything at all that would help to satisfy all the things a Mother wonders about when she loses a boy in the war." In the autumn of 1946, Mrs. Steiner stuffed some clothing that had belonged to her boys in a big box. Then she took a black dress of hers that she wanted Lucie's mother to have. In it, she wrapped Cecil's Kodak and several rolls of film. The Kodak was hers to keep, Mrs. Steiner assured Lucie, on the condition that first she used Cecil's camera to snap some close-ups of his own grave.[38]

All the Dutch families could send to America in return were pictures of themselves kneeling and praying at the crosses and arranging flowers on the graves. Despite the prohibition against taking photographs, adopters continued to sneak cameras onto the grounds, smuggling pictures of graves out to be sent to grateful American families. Still others scooped up dirt from grave mounds and sent it to relatives who deposited it in urns at home. As presents, Lucie's family and countless others could send only the one thing that was still abundant in the Netherlands after the war. Tulip bulbs were shipped out by the thousands and were to brighten many a Gold Star Mother and Gold Star Wife's garden as long-lasting symbols of the unique ties between families on opposite sides of the ocean.

There was, however, only so much that could be written about the haunting stillness of cemeteries and graves. And so adopters gradually began sending pictures of their families and homes and more lively descriptions of who they were and what they did. In response, and also because Dutch families expressed a keen interest in learning as much as possible about the boys they had adopted, many American families began to do the same. Pictures arrived showing soldiers' parents, brothers and sisters, even aunts and uncles, posing in front of porches. They showed Margraten boys holding hands with their wives in parks and being hugged by children in back yards. Quite often, American families insisted on sending adopters photographs of their boy's very last visit home.

Some of the items that arrived from America were almost painfully intimate, as if families there were determined to involve adopters in recreating some of the home warmth closer to where their boys lay. Lieutenant Thomas Sidney Machen had been killed in Germany on 25 March 1945. Riet, a young woman in Schaesberg, had adopted his grave and learned of the officer's Norfolk, Virginia, address via the War Department. After some letters back and forth, a larger envelope arrived. In it the lieutenant's widowed mother, Florence, had put copies of some of her most treasured photographs. One showed a smiling Thomas with the insignia of the engineer corps on his collar. "He was 6 feet tall, dark hair and big blue eyes," it said on the back. "He will be 26 years old Nov. 26, 1945." Arrows pointing to a sailor in a group of uniformed men in another picture explained: "This is Frank, the only child I have left." In a pocket-sized, transparent folder was a portrait photo of an elderly-looking woman wearing wire-rimmed glasses, a pearl necklace, and a brooch pinned onto a Sunday dress. In the frame on the left were the words: "To my niece Riet from Aunt Florence. With all my love and appreciation. This picture was taken for Thomas in the year 1942."[39]

In letters written from Madison Avenue in New York City, the well-to-do father of another officer likewise expressed "deep gratitude" for the "tender care" for the grave that a family in Heer was providing and the "tremendous consolation" that this was giving him and his wife. In the summer of 1946, various parcels arrived from New York containing cartons of cigarettes and "sugar for your children." "I have today ordered sent to you," a letter dated 9 July said, "a 49 lb. scientifically proportioned food package through the Cooperative for American Remittances to Europe, delivery guaranteed, duty free and tax exempt."

But the gift most treasured by the adopters in Heer arrived some time later. It was a "brief book, which gives the record of Lieutenant John A. Larkin, Jr., whose life was short in years yet long in accomplishments." A copy was to be presented by Princeton University each year to the winner of the Memorial Scholarship for freshmen established in 1945 in their son's name. The booklet offered the Dutch family a unique insight into the life of the young American they had adopted. There were photos of the lieutenant as a chubby baby in a sun-drenched garden and as a vivacious child dressed in a cowboy outfit; eulogies from the deans at Phillips Exeter Academy and Princeton University; and a contribution from a fellow soldier citing "his love of reading."

In a rushed letter from the front dated 25 March 1945, John had assured his much younger only brother that "there will be plenty of time for us to get to know each other when our difference in age will make little difference." Two weeks later, John was dead, mowed down by a machine gun during the assault on the German town of

Kirchlinde. The document that posthumously awarded John Larkin with the Silver Star described how, as a forward artillery observer, he had fought "with complete disregard for his own safety."

John's father closed the memorial booklet with the words: "He never liked to say good-bye. So we did not say good-bye. And never will."[40]

3 Saying Goodbye

In 1948 the grieving parents of Lieutenant John Larkin made the decision to have their boy repatriated to the US. With much pain in their hearts, Dutch adopting families would soon be saying goodbye to many more American soldiers whom they had come to think of as their boys too over the years.

Rumors about the uncertain future of the American cemetery at Margraten had begun to circulate almost as soon as the adoption of most of the close to 18,000 graves had been accomplished around Memorial Day in May 1946. There were claims even that the remains of the soldiers would be transferred to cemeteries elsewhere in Europe and that the cemetery in Margraten ran the risk of disappearing altogether. This caused disbelief and consternation in the adoption community as well as in the media and among Dutch authorities.[1]

Since its creation in 1944, the burial site had taken on deep meaning and significance for many in the region and the country. Some adopting families had known Margraten boys in person during the final offensive against Nazi Germany; many had grown familiar with them and their families after the war through transatlantic correspondence and exchanges of photos and token gifts; all were compulsively drawn to the site of memory to give thanks for the liberation and to try and make sense of the horrific suffering that the war had wreaked on Europe and the world.

So proud and protective of their special relationship with the Margraten boys was the adoption community that in the summer of 1946 they took offense at the many tourists descending on the cemetery from all over the country. Complaints were leaked to the national press and the Dutch Ministry of War of the "cheap" behavior of tourists and the "brisk" business of commercial entrepreneurs sullying the memory of the fallen. Neither Dutch nor American investigations could find much evidence of this. Indeed, the Dutch Ministry of War reported that whereas locals had suggested "allowing access only to relatives and adopters and not to tourist groups and such," American military authorities indicated that such restrictions could not be enforced, and that they "were very keen to have as many people as possible visit the cemetery."[2]

The position of the Americans can be seen as an early sign of the strategy to regard the overseas cemeteries of World War II as instruments of public diplomacy. The cemeteries became symbols which, in the words of historian Ron Robin, "strove to win the sympathies of, or induce awe among, foreign beholders." But if that was indeed the case, then Dutch authorities signaled that they understood the value of memory diplomacy just as keenly, especially where it concerned the Margraten adoption program.[3]

It was clear that the United States had risen to the status of superpower as a result of World War II and that it had no intention of reneging on its leadership position as had happened after World War I. It quickly became clear also to the Dutch government, however, that this New World Order would bring benefits as well as constraints. Nothing illustrated this better than the crisis over the Dutch East Indies. Japanese occupation had robbed the Dutch of the pearl in their imperial crown and, when the end of the war came, an emboldened indigenous population declared the independence of what they now called the Republic of Indonesia. The Dutch government refused to accept this and by 1947 was sending large numbers of troops to the islands in a war that would last until 1949. Fearful of being seen as in league with Western colonialism and concerned that Indonesian instability might strengthen local communist forces, the US clamped down hard on the Dutch, threatening among other things to withhold vital Marshall aid if they did not agree to a ceasefire.[4]

It is in this context that the demarche of the Dutch ambassador in Washington should be understood. Prompted by correspondence from Americans thanking him and his government for the unsurpassed reverence of the Dutch people shown at the Margraten cemetery on Memorial Day in May 1947, in August the ambassador advised the Dutch Minister of Foreign Affairs: "At this moment in time when, as a result of the Indies affair, sympathy for the Netherlands has unfortunately dwindled significantly, it appears of utmost importance to me that this is again rekindled by all means possible; what is taking place at Margraten perfectly suits this purpose."[5]

In the same letter, the ambassador suggested having the Governor of Limburg informed of this and to have him encourage the continued involvement of Dutch citizens at the cemetery. This apparently happened. In October 1947 members of the Margraten adoption committee thanked the governor for letting them know that their work was being appreciated "also from the point of view of the national interest." "Although this cannot be our main purpose," the committee members cautioned in some diplomatic wording of their own, "it is undoubtedly an incentive for us to continue along the road taken."[6]

Meanwhile, as the total number of Dutch boys who volunteered or were drafted for service in the Dutch East Indies rose to an astounding 140,000, including dozens from the city of Maastricht and several also from the village of Margraten, affinity with the American boys who had fallen victim to war grew stronger still. Parents volunteered for adoption as soon as their sons had left with the troop transports and local boys in the front lines vowed to adopt American graves should they return home from the tropics safely.[7]

The Dorscheidt family from Kerkrade had adopted the grave of Peter Evancho from Pennsylvania long before the Dutch war in Asia erupted. But when, at the end of his military training, Grada's brother and only sibling visited his home in Kerkrade one last time before going to war in the East Indies, the two decided they should pay a visit to Peter Evancho's final resting place. Amidst the quiet and peace of the Margraten cemetery, 19-year-old Grada and her brother had "a long, good talk." It was to be their last. The life of Grada's brother would be cut short overseas just four years after what ought to have been liberation for the Dorscheidts.[8]

1

As early as October 1946, the Netherlands Liaison Section of the AGRC headquarters in Versailles informed the Dutch Ministry of War that a decision had been made to designate the Margraten site as one of the permanent American cemeteries of World War II in Europe. This was greeted with relief in the adoption community. By April 1947 the Dutch and American governments in an exchange of notes had already reached agreement on the rules governing the military cemetery and the American personnel watching over it. The Dutch government, the notes read, was "pleased to grant to the United States of America" the use of the site "in perpetuity" and without payment or compensation.[9]

While it became clear that the American cemetery at Margraten was now there to stay, however, it was also brought home to the Dutch that this would by no means be the case for all of the graves. The Americans had already gone through an agonizing debate over what to do with the overseas dead after the World War I armistice. In the end it had been decided to allow the next of kin of the fallen the final say. This had resulted in the return of 46,000 of the 77,000 dead for interment in the US or a ratio of four homeland to three overseas burials. Under terms of legislation passed by Congress in May 1946, next of kin were again accorded the opportunity to request the return of the dead for burial at home. Moreover, as early as August 1943 the trend toward return had seemed even more overwhelming than after World War I, with an expected ratio this time of four returns to one foreign burial. As in World War I, however, the American government, for reasons that ranged from logistical concerns to opportunities for public diplomacy, was more in favor of letting the soldiers rest overseas. President Truman assured Americans in May 1947 "that if they could see for themselves the care which is devoted to the graves of those who died in the First World War, and to the temporary cemeteries in which their own dead lie buried today, many of the next of kin would prefer that their loved ones should rest forever in the countries where they fell." The president even promised to look into the possibility of providing government support to enable relatives to go on pilgrimages to America's overseas cemeteries.[10]

It remained everyone's guess how many of the Margraten boys would stay once the repatriation program had run its course. Already in the spring of 1946, the Dutch ambassador in Washington had warned the Minister of Foreign Affairs that the number of requests for repatriation would be "high." The minister in turn alerted the Ministry of War to an American document that had arrived at the Dutch embassy in Washington. In it was mentioned "that current plans call for the evacuation from the Netherlands and the return to the US of approximately 16,000 remains."[11]

Meanwhile, some of the key players in the adoption program appeared in denial that this might happen. Mrs. Michiels van Kessenich was certainly one of them as she insisted during her American goodwill tour in the summer of 1946 that among the thousands of letters she had received in Maastricht from relatives of the fallen no more than a handful had mentioned repatriation.[12]

The debate turned ugly in the summer of 1947 when a journalist from the *Chicago Sun* reported having visited Margraten and uncovered evidence showing that much of the adoption program was a racket. He went so far as to claim that the scam had been set up by "this thrifty, prosperous farm community – with the fattest children" with the express purpose of wheedling money and gifts of food and clothing from "bereft mothers and wives." In a scathing report pertaining to the *Chicago Sun*'s allegations, the Dutch Ministry of Foreign Affairs pointed to the extensive investigation that had already taken place the previous year in response to similar accusations at the address of Emilie van Kessenich and that this had unearthed no evidence of a racket whatsoever. The ministry emphasized that the American article had simply stirred up old rumors and pointed out that it had asked the American military attaché to counter this "shady piece of journalism." It was even suggested in the report that it "might possibly have been inspired by American undertakers and manufacturers of coffins who stood to benefit from the return to the US of as many dead soldiers as possible."[13]

Ultimately, of course, the decision about how many of the Margraten boys would be repatriated, and who they would be exactly, was not that of the president or the media or the adopters, but of the American relatives. For most of them that choice had to be pondered in the quiet and calm of their homes in the first half of 1948. That is when they received in the mail many sets of War Department forms as well as a pamphlet clarifying, in the unemotional language of bureaucracy, "the disposition, options, and services made available to you by your Government."[14]

It goes without saying that those relatives who ticked the option of "return" had in mind only one overriding concern: to have their loved one back home as soon as possible and, more often than not, interred in a private plot close to where the family lived. Relatives had been trying to be nearer those they had lost in the European theater of war even in the years prior to repatriation in 1948. Shortly before Memorial Day in 1945, for example, Captain Shomon of the 611th Graves Registration Company already had a visit from one of the Margraten boys' mothers. She was a member of the Women's Army Corps and, accompanied by a young medical officer, had traveled all the way from Reims in France to spend some time at the grave. "For two days she remained with us," Shomon recalled, "weeping and sobbing until it was necessary for her to leave."[15]

Together with two or three others from the class of '45 of Greene Central High School in upstate New York, Clifford Thomas had found his way into the army via the last wartime draft. The first thing he did when he arrived in Europe in 1946 was travel to Margraten. His brother John had graduated from Green Central High in 1941 and worked at a dairy farm before volunteering as a paratrooper. He had survived the furor of the Battle of the Bulge, only to be killed during the jump across the Rhine on the very first day of Operation Varsity. Clifford stood at the wooden cross with the name of his older brother and whispered greetings from his parents and sister. Then he moved on to commence his military service in occupied Germany.[16]

By 1947 the number of people visiting the Margraten cemetery from overseas had grown so large that Mrs. Michiels van Kessenich signaled to the Civilian Committee and the Limburg governor that, even with the part-time help of a secretary from her husband's mayor office, she could no longer shoulder the burden of correspondence, hotel bookings, and travel arrangements.[17]

Even then, however, these visitors represented only a fraction of the tens of thousands of grieving relatives. Most Americans did not have the means to travel all the way to the Netherlands so soon after the war and this made them feel the hurt all the more. "I'll never get over this cruel war," a despairing Mrs. Anderson confided in Lucie van den Boorn in the summer of 1946 in a letter posted in Scottsville, Virginia. She thanked the young Dutch woman from Gronsveld for the photos of Benjamin's grave and the flowers on it, but then pined, "I wish I could have visited my son's grave with you." Later that year, an increasingly bitter Mrs. Anderson complained, "I was in hopes we would get his body home before Christmas, but it seems they have forgotten about it." Benjamin had been killed in Germany as an 18-year-old and neither his mother nor his four brothers and one sister could feel complete again before he was returned to them. "He loved Virginia," his mother told Lucie, "and I want him buried here."[18]

For obvious reasons made abundantly clear, Benjamin Anderson was one of the many Margraten boys that adopters were made to say goodbye to in the late 1940s. The reasons why American relatives decided not to have the bodies returned, on the other hand, appear less obvious and they were certainly more complex. Some may indeed have been swayed by American authorities that interment in an official military cemetery near the overseas battlefield was the patriotic thing to do. Historian Roy Robin has pointed out, for example, that some of the persuasion in this regard entailed subtle bureaucratic manipulation, like making burial in a permanent overseas cemetery "Option 1" in the War Department's form, thereby suggesting that this was the most appropriate and common choice. But much of what Robin has labeled "moral pressure" was decidedly more blatant. After all, in 1947 even President Truman, who had fought in Europe during World War I, had openly spoken in favor of letting the boys rest in peace overseas. American media also made much of the fact that high-ranking military commanders like the much-admired General Patton lay buried under simple markers among their men in the overseas cemeteries. Perhaps as part of that media campaign, the *New York Herald Tribune* in 1947 published a story on the recent visit that a professor of history and his wife had paid to the grave of their son in Margraten. They were in the company of the boy's two brothers and at peace with the thought that this Dutch cemetery would be his final resting place. In the article, the father from New England said he was particularly struck by the fact that the boys were "separated neither by rank nor decoration." He was also quick to add that, as a Protestant, he saw no problem in the fact that this was a predominantly Catholic region where no Protestant church could be found. After all, he remarked, what spoke more forcefully than religion was "the love with which the people keep vigil over the cemetery."[19]

Others simply thought it would be inappropriate to have the peace disturbed of those who deserved it so much after the horrors of war. "I do not desire to bring my son back to the States," the father of Warren Miller of the 437th Troop Carrier Group said in a letter from Charlotte, North Carolina, to the Office of the Quartermaster General in Washington, DC. But he stressed that this was conditional on whether they could indeed confirm that Margraten was to be a permanent cemetery. If not, he specified, "please advise me as in that case I would want my boy brought back to America and buried in our own cemetery or if you find, that he is to be moved from this cemetery to another United States military cemetery in Europe, I would like him brought back here instead of that."[20]

There were those also who reasoned they could not bear the strain again of having to experience the unspeakable heartbreak and grief that the arrival of the War Department's dreaded telegram had already caused years earlier. For many, the image of a train returning a coffin to the station where once a sprightly young man in uniform had waved goodbye was too harrowing even to contemplate. Early in 1948, one of the 117 fallen from the town of Bedford, Virginia, was among the dead being repatriated from American cemeteries in Britain. The day after her son's coffin arrived in the small Southern town, Rose White suffered a massive stroke and slipped into a coma. Several days later, family members keeping vigil at Rose's bedside briefly disappeared from the room to attend the funeral she would never know about. With stories of such tragedies rife, children, doctors, and even clergymen cautioned parents whose health had suffered much already against putting themselves through the ordeal. "She had lost her husband before the war," Ruth shrugged when asked much later why her mother had decided not to have the body of Donald repatriated from Margraten to Michigan. "Then, shortly after that, her only son. It had taken quite a toll."[21]

More tragically still, some of the Margraten boys were orphaned or came from broken homes. In such cases, uncles, aunts, step-parents, and guardians in America often reasoned that the deceased soldiers might just as well remain in Europe in the company of thousands of men their age. Much more numerous, however, were the widows who chose to leave the remains of beloved husbands overseas. In most instances, they did so because by the time the forms arrived with the boxes to be ticked, these young women had been forced to move on and had decided to make the best of what remained of their shattered lives. By 1948, many of them, with or without children, were involved in new relationships or had remarried. They sensed that to go through the process of repatriation and reburial would pose unnecessary threats to the fragile stability they had rebuilt for themselves. Some even informed the adopters of their former husbands' graves that it would be better for them not to receive letters any longer. On occasion this caused tension nevertheless, as parents and siblings of the fallen, who had no legal say in the matter, deeply deplored the widows' decisions not to have the bodies returned. Some refused to leave the past behind, picking up correspondence with adopters where daughters-in-law or sisters-in-law had left off.[22]

2

As families in America began to seal the fate of the remains of their loved ones with their signatures on the War Department's forms, Margraten prepared for yet another Memorial Day. The previous year the commemoration on the American field of honor had been conducted in the presence of massive crowds and of no one less than Her Majesty Queen Wilhelmina. In May 1948, visitors again descended on Margraten en masse. They did so in the company of countless civil, military, and church dignitaries from the US and the Netherlands, and a diplomatic corps with representatives from at least 22 different countries, including Australia, China, Peru, and the Soviet Union.[23]

But on this occasion, what made Memorial Day at Margraten special was that it would be the last one for a very long time. American authorities had announced that, immediately following the ceremony, no more access would be granted to the public until both the repatriation program and the permanent re-interments had been completed. Neither the adoption committee nor Dutch authorities had the slightest idea of when that would be.

Even while the adoption program was taking shape, work at the Margraten cemetery had continued at a feverish pace. According to official records, John Singer, a 25-year-old infantryman from Maryland, killed at Geilenkirchen, was the very first soldier to have been buried at Margraten on 10 November 1944 in Grave 1, Row 1, Plot A. Rows upon rows and plots upon plots had been added since that day. When in June 1945 the 603rd Graves Registration Company had taken over from Captain Shomon's 611th, they had continued the expansion until March 1946. They had done so mainly to add to the Margraten boys the American dead that were being exhumed in Germany at the express order of General Eisenhower, who had decided he did not want them to rest in enemy soil. By the time they were done, some 17,740 American soldiers had been laid to rest in Margraten, making it the largest American cemetery on the European mainland after Henri-Chapelle in Belgium.[24]

Moreover, although firmly under the authority of the US military, the cemetery in the Netherlands in the early stages had never been exclusively American. In the chaos and urgency of the war, American authorities had rushed military dead of many other nations, allied and enemy, to Margraten. In 1946, however, these same authorities signaled to the Dutch government that they now thought it time to have the foreign dead removed. This set in motion a whole new series of re-interments. By early 1947, for example, many of the approximately three hundred western allies had been reburied in British and Canadian cemeteries in the Netherlands or repatriated to Belgium and France.[25]

The problem of what to do with the more than seven hundred dead that belonged to other nations of the former alliance of World War II caused more serious headaches, however. Some of them were from eastern and southern Europe. But the overwhelming majority were soldiers from the Soviet Union. They had been prisoners of war of the Germans and most had died from tuberculosis at the end of the war. This made the problem particularly sensitive in a year when the Cold War was dangerously heating up. The Dutch government was aware that Soviet authorities regarded soldiers captured by the Nazis more as traitors than as victims. But it was aware also that any hint of American ill will towards Soviet compatriots might spark a political row. To make matters worse, the Soviet embassy in the Netherlands demanded to know if the decision to remove the bodies from Margraten had anything to do with the reluctance of Catholics to have Soviets buried in their soil. It was enough for the Dutch Minister of Foreign Affairs to instruct his staff to inform his colleagues at the Ministry of War carefully about what exactly they could and could not say to the Soviets regarding this matter. "I do not in the least," the worried minister scribbled in the margin in March 1947, "trust the military people in this area."[26]

The potential for a diplomatic incident was successfully defused when, after some scouting for an appropriate location, a separate field of honor was created for the Soviet dead in Leusden near the

Dutch city of Amersfoort. Ironically, the solution for the former enemy proved a lot more straightforward as the Dutch government was firmly committed to creating a single massive cemetery for the Germans who had fallen on or near their territory. The location for this cemetery was the small village of Ysselsteyn in northern Limburg where, as early as the autumn of 1946, all of the 3,075 Germans from Margraten had been laid to rest in the company of no fewer than 28,000 other comrades.[27]

Still, even when compared with the massive operations that had gone before, what was to happen at the Margraten cemetery once the gates swung shut at the end of Memorial Day 1948 appeared mind-boggling in scope. The repatriation of thousands upon thousands of American bodies commenced on 11 June 1948 and continued ceaselessly for many months. One by one the remains of the soldiers were dug up, removed from the linen covers, and placed in sturdy caskets that in turn were encased in rectangular wooden crates draped in American flags. The crates were lifted onto trucks that headed for Liège in Belgium, where they were loaded onto barges that slowly made their way along the quiet canals to Antwerp.[28]

At the Belgian port city the Margraten boys joined tens of thousands of other American dead from all over Europe for the start of the sad transatlantic journey home. They were part of the 405,399 GIs killed in World War II and of the more than 170,000 dead to be repatriated from across the globe at the request of American next of kin. The vanguard of the dead had already arrived in Antwerp from the Belgian cemetery of Henri-Chapelle as early as October 1947. The occasion was marked by a moving ceremony that centered on the flower-strewn casket of a soldier designated 'John X.' The casket was put on display in Antwerp's ancient Grand Place. The Stars and Stripes were draped from windows and balconies and 5,000 Belgians drummed together to pay their respects, many of them bearing chrysanthemums. Lucius D. Clay, the American general who a year later would be overseeing the Berlin airlift in defiance of the Soviets, spoke a few solemn words. Belgian Cardinal Van Roey said a brief blessing. Then the massive bells of the Notre Dame Cathedral began to toll. Hundreds of Belgians fell in behind the caisson as it carried the casket to a pier on the Scheldt. Here John X joined 5,599 other soldier dead in the hold of the US Army transport *Joseph V. Connolly*. "While U.S. Thunderbolts from

Germany dipped aloft," *Time* described the scene for its American audience, "the *Connolly* steamed down the Scheldt, its banks lined with thousands of silent Belgians."[29]

An eerie silence descended on Margraten too as the cumbersome operations continued throughout 1948 and 1949. Even while countless crate-packed caskets were leaving the cemetery for transport to America, more soldier dead were arriving for a permanent home in the Netherlands. They were mostly paratroopers who had been killed in the Netherlands during the daring but disastrous Operation Market Garden in the autumn of 1944. Those from the 82nd Airborne Division came from a temporary military cemetery at Molenhoek near Nijmegen. The dead from the 101st Airborne Division had been exhumed at Son near Eindhoven. All became Margraten boys as the permanent re-interments began on 1 December 1948. The digging once again took long months of hard work, involving American military personnel as well as civilian labor recruited in Margraten and from across Limburg. As the work progressed, more and more letters went out from the Quartermaster General informing next of kin in the US that the remains of their loved ones had been permanently interred at last. "You may rest assured," the standard letter concluded, "that this final interment was conducted with fitting dignity and solemnity and that the grave-site will be carefully and conscientiously maintained in perpetuity by the United States Government."[30]

3

Dutch authorities found the American government to be less conscientious about keeping them informed of their future plans for the Margraten cemetery. As the American enclave became hermetically sealed for the complex operation of repatriation and re-interment, local mayors and the Limburg governor were in the dark about the exact size and boundaries it would have once it was reopened. The Margraten mayor reported to the governor that some sources claimed that, depending on the funds to be appropriated by the US Congress, the final field of honor might end up being three times the size of the wartime one. There was talk also of the creation of a large exclusion zone around the actual cemetery, a zone where residential building and commercial activities would be severely restricted or outright prohibited. To ensure the typical image of a Dutch landscape, American authorities were even having Dutch authorities intervene to guarantee the preservation of a windmill that from the cemetery could be seen in the far distance. The most urgent problem in all of this was that several dozen farmers had seen their rich soil expropriated in 1944. Because of the continued uncertainty surrounding the exact shape and size of the American cemetery, none of these farmers had as yet received compensation; more feared that they too might have to give up valuable acreage that had been in the family for generations.[31]

If this uncertainty was causing irritation and tension among some in the farming community, the loyalty of the locals for the Margraten boys remained unaffected, however. In the summer of 1949, when most of the cemetery's reorganization was nearing completion, the cousin of Robert Pegues was allowed entry to the still-closed site when he told American personnel he was related to Sergeant Pegues and had traveled all the way from his base in Germany to visit the soldier's grave. The American's cousin had perished over Germany with all of the crew when their B-26 Marauder was downed in February 1945. In a letter to Robert's mother after the visit, the soldier said he had placed "a bouquet of gladiolas" on the grave of the young man who had always "seemed more like a brother to me." "I've noticed," he also mentioned to his aunt in the same letter, "and others have told me, that the Dutch are the nearest like Americans of all the Europeans. They certainly did seem fine to me, and they seemed so grateful to us for what we have done for them."[32]

Meanwhile, adopters were showing increasing concern about what was happening with the graves of the boys that had been assigned to their care. Letters flooded the office of the Civilian Committee with urgent and often emotional queries about whether or not this or that American soldier would remain at Margraten. Still other adopters said they were being besieged by anxious American relatives who wanted them to visit the cemetery to make sure that the procedures were carried out with respect and that no mistakes were being made with the caskets for those to be returned to America. In a letter from California, the mother of the Steiner boys informed Lucie van den Boorn of her decision to have the remains of fighter pilot Walter transferred from France and buried permanently beside his younger brother and paratrooper Cecil in Margraten. "I wondered," she asked Lucie, "if you could sort of keep in touch with the cemetery and maybe be there for the service if they have one. Do you know anyone who has a 16 mm movie camera? I would like to have a roll of the graves and surrounding country after they have buried our other son there."[33]

As early as December 1948, seven months after the cemetery had been sealed off, the Civilian Committee put out a communiqué. It said that they had become overburdened with queries and appealed to adopters "to refrain from corresponding as much as possible for the time being." Such an appeal was necessary as the adoption committee's 'office' by this time was made up of no more than one person who was made to operate from a space in the town hall's attic. Lies Köster, a 27-year-old woman from Margraten, had been hired in 1946 by the NWGC in Amsterdam to manage the local adoption administration and now found herself valiantly trying to keep the program afloat amidst chaos and uncertainty. Meanwhile, the reopening continued to be postponed. For a long time it was rumored that the cemetery would open its gates for visitors again in September 1949, around the time of the fifth anniversary of the liberation of southern Limburg. But that date too came and went again, heightening the adoption community's agony. Lies Köster eventually put together a standard form designed to address the most frequent questions from adopters during the time of repatriation. It stressed that the committee did not know which soldiers were to leave Margraten, was still not in a position to obtain home addresses of American relatives, and could not at this stage assign new adopters to graves of American paratroopers who people had already learned were being brought to Margraten from the battlefields of Operation Market Garden.[34]

The fear within the Civilian Committee was that if they failed to obtain as soon as possible the full details and new grave locations of the soldiers remaining at Margraten, the cherished adoption program might collapse. As early as the summer of 1948, attempts were made to have the regional headquarters of the AGRC in Liège release the names of GIs being repatriated, but all to no avail. Impatience and frustration were palpable in correspondence with the NWGC in Amsterdam. A letter from Margraten late in 1949 reported that, "for whatever possible reason," American officials were showing themselves to be "highly reluctant to provide us with information of any kind." Having tried their luck higher up the hierarchy, the NWGC in January 1950 had to admit that at the central headquarters of the

AGRC in Versailles, they too had run into "a wall of inexplicable suspicion or obstruction of a kind that was hard to gauge."[35]

A month later, however, it appeared that the long wait was finally over when the NWGC was happy to inform the Civilian Committee that an organization called the American Battle Monuments Commission was now looking into the matter. The US Congress had established the ABMC in 1923. As an agency of the federal government it was to serve as the "guardian of America's overseas commemorative memorials and cemeteries." After World War II this charter was extended to the new generation of burial grounds overseas. Indeed, in the afternoon of 28 December 1949, a simple religious ceremony at the Margraten cemetery had already marked its official transfer from the AGRC to the ABMC. Even then, however, it took until the autumn of 1950 for the rosters of "the decedents now permanently interred in the cemetery" to make their way from the ABMC in Paris to the adoption committee in Margraten. The committee accepted the rosters with "exceptional pleasure" and "heartfelt thanks." This, they pointed out to the NWGC in Amsterdam, "was the most important condition for us to be able to continue our work." Much of that work was the full-time job of Lies Köster. She now commenced the gigantic task of informing every singly adopter mentioned on the thousands of index cards compiled by Father Heuschen and his team as to whether their soldier was still among the remaining Margraten boys and where exactly his grave could be found. Nothing changed, meanwhile, with regards to the problems the Civilian Committee had been experiencing in having the adopters establish transatlantic contacts. Indeed, in 1950 the ABMC warned that their superintendent at Margraten had been advised that he "may not release to any one the names or addresses of the next of kin of any of the deceased in his cemetery."[36]

In the spring of 1950, the Dutch were excited to learn that General Omar Bradley, one of the heroes of World War II and now the first chairman of the NATO Military Committee, had made a surprise visit to Margraten. Bradley and his military entourage had first circled the cemetery in a Dakota to inspect it from the air and had then been rushed to the site in a six-car convoy. The general had placed a large wreath of white flowers at the entrance to the cemetery and had walked pensively between the graves for some time before being whisked back to his aircraft. Even then, however, the impatient adoption community was made to wait for almost another year before being admitted to the reshaped field of honor themselves.[37]

In May 1951, a few months after the cemetery had at last reopened for the general public, the first Memorial Day was held again after a hiatus of three long years. The overhaul of the field of honor was by no means complete at that stage. The architectural embellishment was still in progress and the marble headstones had not even begun to arrive. Indeed, the painstaking work would take until 1960 to be completed. But that did not in any way affect the solemnity of the moment. In his speech, US ambassador Selden Chapin regretted that the ceremony had to take place at a time when the war with communist forces in Korea was making clear that world peace was still a faraway dream. But he lauded the Dutch for having sent troops to Korea that were now fighting side by side with American soldiers and many other United Nations forces. Such concerted and determined forward defense, the ambassador reasoned, was the best way to ensure security for the Dutch at home. "We do not want," he emphasized, "Europe to be a war theater again and we do not want the digging of new graves here."[38]

Frightening and discouraging as the Korean War was for the thousands of Dutch adults and school children attending the ceremony that spring, for the adopters of the fallen of World War II the return to Margraten was all about reconnecting with a site of memory that had loomed large in their lives for many years. The predictions of a significantly higher repatriation rate for Word War II were shown to be unfounded. At 61 percent the return rate stood at almost the same level as that of World War I. Still, with more than half the American graves gone now at Margraten, too, thousands of adopters could be seen wandering forlornly between the wooden crosses and Stars of David, deploring the loss of 'their' boy. Even at the start of the new millennium, many of these families could be found clinging to their old adoption certificates and to letters and photographs sent to them by American relatives before the start of repatriation in 1948.[39]

For the woman who in 1946 had volunteered to watch over the grave of Private Ralph Jones of the 84th Infantry Division, the memory of adoption would remain even more poignant. In the two years before Ralph was repatriated, the young woman from Maastricht had learned much about the American from his mother Ruth in Colorado. Both his brothers had returned safely from the navy and war in the

Pacific. The Dutch woman was struck by the fact that Ralph had been accepted into the infantry despite having suffered a mild case of polio that had slightly affected his left arm. She was touched even more by the fact that he shared her birthday and had married his sweetheart just six weeks before being sent overseas. The young woman promised Ralph's mother that if she would ever give birth to a boy she would name the baby after her deceased son. The remains of Private Jones were returned to Colorado at about the same time in 1948 that his adopter and her Dutch husband made the decision to emigrate to Florida. In America the young woman kept the promise she had made. On several occasions, the parents of the American infantryman who had been killed in Germany in December 1944 drove all the way from Colorado to Fort Lauderdale in their Cadillac to meet up with their son's former Dutch adopter. And to steal a glance at a small boy called Ralph. Almost seven decades after World War II, both families still remain in close touch.[40]

With the cemetery's blueprint completely redrawn and all of the remaining graves relocated, there were several adopters also who wrongly assumed that the graves of their soldiers had disappeared, despite the massive campaign by the Civilian Committee to provide all of them with the correct information. For some of these adopters it would take until the creation of a computerized adoption database in 2003 to make the appalling discovery that in the past decades they had been visiting the cemetery time and again only to pass their lost soldier by at a distance of no more than a few feet.

In the spring of 1951, however, most of the adopters of the 8,301 American soldiers who remained at Margraten successfully reunited with them and were happy and proud to do so again after three long years of separation. One of them was Grada Dorscheidt. She was 24 now and the last time she had paid a long visit to the cemetery she had been in the company of her brother just before he was sent overseas to the war in the East Indies that had claimed his life in 1949. Grada had been much relieved to receive a notice from the Civilian Committee informing her that infantryman Peter Evancho from Pennsylvania had found a permanent home at the Margraten cemetery. But she was even more honored to find at his side now his brother George whose final resting place she had just recently volunteered to watch over too. Lieutenant George Evancho had been killed when his B-17 crashed into another Flying Fortress during a raid

From Left to right seated: George (3), Mother Mary (38) and Father Michael (43), Helen (baby on lap), Peter (5)
Standing back row from left: Jospeh (7), Anna (12), Mary (16), Godmother Mary Yeager, John (14) and Michael Jr. (10)

9. A studio photo of the Evancho family in Pennsylvania around 1920. World War II would take the lives of brothers George and Peter, here seated left and right of their parents at ages three and five respectively. Both lie side by side in Margraten. Baby sister Helen (here on her mother's lap) made contact with her brothers' new adopter, a Belgian, shortly before her death in 2008. (Courtesy Mary Anne Fedor and Erik De Bruyne)

against an oil refinery in Merseburg near Leipzig in November 1944, less than five months before the death of his brother Peter in Germany. In July 1946 the bodies of George and 21 other American airmen had been found in the civilian cemetery of Raschwitz in a mass grave that the Germans had taken good care of and marked with a large white cross. After identification, George's remains had been transported to the American military cemetery in Neuville-en-Condroz in Belgium. With the soldiers' parents deceased in 1948, Peter's oldest brother and George's wife had agreed to have both brothers rest in peace overseas. But they had carefully instructed the Quartermaster General to have them buried next to each other in accordance with the wish of their mother, who had passed away not long after learning of their deaths.

In 1951 Grada Dorscheidt was still having much difficulty coming to terms with the loss of her brother. But she was happy to see that Peter Evancho had been reunited with his.[41]

4 The War Turns Cold

In October 1951 Harry Cook learned that John Butler, the Republican senator from Maryland, was to be part of an American delegation soon to depart for Europe on a special mission. The well-to-do Mr. Cook, scion of a Baltimore family of food brokers who knew the senator on a first-name basis and counted high-ranking State Department officials among his friends, immediately sat down to write a letter. He tried to convince his powerful connection to have the delegation pay a visit to Margraten should they happen to make a stop in the Netherlands too. "As I told you in person a couple of months ago," Mr. Cook reminded the senator, "those American families who finally determined to leave the remains of their loved ones to stay with their Dutch friends were much comforted because of the interest of these same Dutch friends. Again, the Dutch people deeply appreciate the fact that 8,000 American families have entrusted their loved ones to their care, and they are accepting the challenge so presented."

Harry Cook should know. His son was buried in Margraten. In 1950 he and his wife had paid a visit to say goodbye at what they had decided would be their son's final resting place. That decision had been made a lot easier knowing that a butcher's family in Heerlen was taking good care of the grave. Meeting the adopters at the cemetery had been a deeply comforting experience.[1]

The Maryland senator and the American delegation most likely never made it to Margraten in 1951. A year later, however, Harry Cook and other well-connected Americans made it possible for Baron Michiels van Kessenich, the mayor of Maastricht, to travel to the US. The idea started with an official invitation from the president of the veterans' association of the 30th Infantry Division, the unit that had liberated Maastricht and much of Limburg, for the mayor to attend their convention in New York early in July 1952. His good friends of the Old Hickory Division offered to put him up in a suite at the Roosevelt Hotel on Madison Avenue for a long weekend. Speaking fees and private sponsoring by people like Harry Cook and others in New York, Philadelphia, and Chicago enabled the 49-year-old mayor to extend the invitation into a month-long tour reminiscent of his wife's goodwill trip in 1946.[2]

Like his wife's visit, the mayor's tour through America's northeast and Midwest in 1952 was prompted above all by the special relationship of his family with the Margraten adoption program. Mindful of that, those in the Netherlands who organized his program for the period of 8 June to 5 July made sure to leave enough room for contacts with relatives of the Margraten boys. In Philadelphia, the mayor was to talk with the Goldsmiths who had lost one son in the Pacific whose body had never been recovered, and another son who was buried in the Netherlands where Mrs. van Kessenich took care to pay regular visits to his grave. At the request of Harry Cook, the Dutch mayor was also scheduled to meet in Boston "a young man who was in the Army with my son and who suffered the loss of his leg at the same time my son lost his life."[3]

But Michiels van Kessenich set out for America with other things on his agenda besides Margraten. The adoption program with its emotional resonance represented the perfect key for opening important doors in Washington and beyond. Making the ties between the US and the Netherlands still stronger certainly was a core objective of the mayor's trip. With an eye to this, both countries' embassies as well as the Netherlands Information Service in New York did what they could to publicize the mayor's visit and his Margraten involvement, including drafting press releases and arranging visits with leading figures. In a letter to Cardinal Francis Spellman, the American embassy at The Hague requested the privilege of an audience for the mayor, who had shown himself to be "a great friend of the United States" through his and his wife's "devoted work" for the American cemetery in the Netherlands. Among the many guests who had accepted the invitation to a cocktail party at the Washington residence of the American ambassador to the Netherlands in honor of the mayor was General McAuliffe, the celebrated hero of Bastogne. But Dutch ambassador Herman van Roijen in Washington was particularly pleased to let the mayor know shortly before his departure that an agreement had been reached on a meeting with no one less than the

American president himself on Friday, 13 June, at noon. Michiels van Kessenich later was to wax triumphantly about "my visit to President Truman who was kind enough to give half an hour of his precious time to a simple Dutch burgomaster."[4]

Later that same Friday, the Maastricht mayor had dinner at the Dutch embassy with officials from the State and other departments, and his schedule for the Washington area would further include lectures at Catholic University of America and George Washington University. Unlike Mrs. van Kessenich, however, who had been loaded down with photographs and maps displaying the Margraten cemetery, her husband arrived in the US with stacks of printed material selling nearby Maastricht as an ideal investment opportunity. Seven years had now passed since the end of World War II, and the American press clearly saw no bones in a mayor's attempts to, as one newspaper put it, "sell his town." Certainly not at a time when the Netherlands was engaged in reconstruction, much of it financed by the Marshall Plan, presenting exciting business opportunities on both sides of the ocean.

A Michigan newspaper journalist described the mayor's arrival in his state as "one of a score of stops he is making in this country in search of industry for his home town." If Margraten was "a spot of common grief," the *Baltimore Sun* quoted the mayor as saying in a speech before the city's Kiwanis Club, "Maastricht itself is an international crossroads, a center of industry and transportation between Cologne and Brussels." Too many people in and around Maastricht were working in Belgium where the economy had recovered much more quickly, the American press reported. The Dutch mayor was determined to halt this trend by improving infrastructure in his city of 80,000 people and attracting industries that were forward-looking. And where better to find the future in 1952 than in America? Now that the Dutch East Indies, the country's colonial pride, had been irretrievably lost, Michiels van Kessenich reminded himself in a notebook during his travels, it was important for him to gain knowledge about the US instead and forge connections in this giant country. And so he toured a Ford factory in Detroit, shuttled between Kiwanis and Rotary Clubs, and attended a luncheon organized by the *New York Times* for, among others, the chief Dutch trade commissioner in the US, the director of the Dutch Economic Information Service, the president of the Netherlands Chamber of Commerce in the US, and representatives of KLM airline and the Dutch tourist industry.[5]

In all of this, the Dutch mayor at times played the Margraten card rather brashly. "Come visit us," he urged his Kiwanis audience according to the *Baltimore American*. "You will find that in Holland, at least, the war's effects are not entirely evil. You will find that the feeling of kinship, of friendship for America, which was created during the war, lives on." But in an editorial on the same Kiwanis speech, a Baltimore journalist who said he had friends buried at Margraten appeared to take not the least offense. "In this day of tensions and dissensions among nations whose men died in a common cause," he reminded readers in a reference to the Cold War that had now spread as far as Korea, "these were comforting words, too rarely heard."[6]

1

By the early 1950s Dutch politicians and business leaders might have been tempted to use Margraten as an instrument of leverage in the US, and in September 1952 the mayor of Maastricht was keen on explaining before the Limburg branch of the Dutch Society for Industry and Trade what he had learned during his goodwill trip about "the American people that now play such an important part in world affairs." But for ordinary adopters in villages and towns across Limburg, the feelings of kinship with Americans created during the war remained untainted by power politics and economic calculations.[7]

Their feelings were perhaps best captured in the war monument that was unveiled in Maastricht a few days after the mayor's America talk before the region's business community. The sculpture represented all of the people who had played a key role in the war's various stages. The resistance man breaking his chains, the laborer engaged in rebuilding, women protecting children cheering at a new dawn. An American soldier stood symbol for the liberation. Veterans from the 30th Infantry Division watched the unveiling, and the artist in a statement emphasized that he had taken care not to portray the GI as "the merciless warrior," but rather as "the human soldier" the Dutch had encountered behind the lines.[8]

This is how adopters too preferred to remember the GIs. A web of intimate relations between American and Dutch families did much to sustain that memory. As many of the girls who had adopted graves

10. Women and girls jostle to have their picture taken with American liberators in Maastricht in 1944. Females of all ages would play a crucial role in Margraten's adoption program. (Courtesy Regionaal Historisch Centrum Limburg and photographer Jef Naseman)

immediately after the war now were getting married, Americans were happy to send them presents and fabric for dresses. A 27-year-old bride-to-be from Groot Welsden vividly remembered receiving a box from New York. The sender was Mrs. Jacob. Her only child, Robert, was one of the Margraten boys. To the girl's astonishment, the box contained not just any fabric, but quality silk of the purest white.[9]

And as these young women were having their first children, names that would have sounded most familiar to the Margraten boys were added to Dutch baptismal records across the region. The adopter of an Illinois lieutenant from the 323rd Bomber Squadron through intense correspondence had developed such close ties with Alfred Zwicky's family that she named one of her daughters after Alfred's mother and another after his sister.[10]

An adoptive family in Eindhoven received pictures of Hale Watson, another airman, not only from his family in New England, but also from his fiancée in the old country. The girl was a nurse and had fallen in love with the lieutenant at an English air base. It was hard for her to let go and she found much consolation in contacts with the Dutch family watching over his grave. In the 1950s these contacts became ever closer, with the adoptive father making a trip to England and meeting her family, and the nurse paying a visit to Hale's grave in Margraten just in time to help the adoptive father's sister deliver her first child.[11]

Intimate contacts remained even with families that several years earlier had decided to have the body of their boy brought home. Upon learning from the Haskins family that their son James had now at last been given a final resting place near his home in North Carolina, his former adoptive family carefully packed a box with tulip bulbs to be planted on his grave. Mrs. Bell thought of an even more personal gesture appropriate for the family in Maastricht that had taken such good care of the grave of her son Richard. War in an ironic twist of fate had given Mrs. Bell her son and taken him away again. She had met Richard's father in France at the end of World War I and had left for America as a war bride. World War II had made her son return to the Old World and end up at the cemetery in the Netherlands. Even before repatriation, Mrs. Bell had stood at his grave. She had been given much support then by Richard's adopters, who had not only welcomed her into their home in Maastricht, but had also accompanied her while she was staying with her family in

France. Now that Richard had been laid to rest in America again, Mrs. Bell thought the moment right for the Dutch family to have something special as a memento. After some deliberation, she decided to send them her son's favorite cufflinks.[12]

American feelings of kinship easily spread from the Margraten community to all of the Netherlands when in the night of 31 January 1953 a violent storm caused devastating floods in the low country's coastal areas. The mayor of Maastricht in a letter to an American contact in Florida ten days later spoke of a "terrible calamity" that had already claimed the lives of more than 1,400 people and caused more than 50,000 Dutch to be evacuated. But he emphasized that Limburg province was situated far from the sea and "did not suffer at all from the cruel waters."[13]

That did nothing, however, to stop Americans with contacts in Limburg from sending aid. From Florida the father of a Margraten boy sent a generous contribution of $500 to relieve the suffering of the flood victims. Michiels van Kessenich had pictures taken of himself and the Limburg governor to whom he presented the check. "It is so wonderful of you," the baron told the father, "that in spite of your own grief you wanted to help people in a faraway country."[14]

In New York City, Jacob Singer, lawyer and president of the 30th Infantry Division Association, upon hearing "the doleful news" on the radio, immediately called upon members "to send checks and clothing to the Netherlands Consul." "The response," Singer noted in a letter to Michiels van Kessenich, "was tremendous." It did not in the least surprise the president of the veterans responsible for the liberation of much of Limburg. "The English and the Americans have often been referred to as cousins," he told the baron, "but I am happily inclined to believe that the relationship that exists between the Dutch and the Americans may be confidently referred to as brothers ready to assist each other abundantly and unselfishly, and more importantly, without being asked."[15]

The memory of America's role in the liberation continued to engender equally warm gestures on the Dutch side. In the run-up to Memorial Day in May 1953, the US ambassador to the Netherlands sent sincere thanks to the Limburg governor's staff and the province's inhabitants for "the participation of the school children, flowers, music, traffic control, etc." and for being "as helpful and cooperative with we Americans this year as in previous years." On 5 May 1954, exactly nine years after the war had ended for the Netherlands, in Washington, DC the president of the Dutch parliament's Lower House presented his counterpart, the speaker of the American House of Representatives, with a special gift from the Dutch people to the American people. The majestic and artfully designed carillon had been crafted in the Netherlands and consisted of 49 bells, one for each American state and one for the District of Columbia. The Dutch parliamentarian paid a visit to President Eisenhower at the White House and in a speech afterwards reminded his American audience that Dutch freedom had been bought "with the blood of thousands of your boys," blood that "has drenched our national soil." "I wish," he said in a nod to the work of the adopters, "that you could see the graves of your loved ones covered in flowers."[16]

2

Meanwhile, however, for those who had survived the war, life ran its usual course, making it difficult even for the powerful Margraten symbol not to be tarnished on occasion by economic calculation. By the early 1950s, more than 30 farmers whose land had been appropriated to make room for the giant cemetery were still waiting for financial compensation to be finalized. They were dissatisfied and increasingly impatient with the endless commissions and procedures with which the Dutch government was trying to settle the issue once and for all.

In September 1954, on the tenth anniversary of the ferocious battle for Arnhem, some 40 'Screaming Eagles,' veterans of the 101st Airborne Division, traveled to the Netherlands for a solemn ceremony commemorating their fallen comrades in Margraten. They arrived at the cemetery by way of Eindhoven, a grateful city in the Arnhem corridor, but home too to the electronics giant Philips whose board's marketing instinct had told them that it would be a smart move to be seen hosting the Americans.[17]

That same month, the former commander of the Old Hickory Division, Leland Hobbs, attempted to use his war ties for business purposes just as unashamedly. In a letter to the Maastricht mayor, he announced that he had just been made vice-president of a major bank in New York City. "It would be a most appropriate ten-year celebration, and a great help to me," he suggested, "if you could persuade some of your prominent banks to do business with Colonial Trust Company." Hobbs hinted that it would be "a fine continuance of our war-time associations." "We will," he assured, "afford the same efficiency in all banking matters as you saw displayed by the 30th US Infantry Division."

Not wanting to be seen as disloyal, Michiels van Kessenich sent a somewhat awkward letter to banks and businesses in Maastricht and as faraway as Amsterdam and Rotterdam. The postwar business overture ended in embarrassment for all when the mayor's contacts refused to take up the offer and a banker in Amsterdam warned him that Hobbs' institution had experienced "a number of ups and downs" and could in no way be called a first-rate bank.[18]

A decade after the war, financial woes also had a reluctant Civilian Committee in Margraten terminate the employment of the now 34-year-old Lies Köster, the adoption program's full-time administrator. It was the NWGC in Amsterdam that had been financing Ms. Köster's salary all along. As they now announced serious cutbacks and Margraten's modest town hall did not have the budget for an extra employee, the burgomaster had no choice but to let her go as of 1 January 1954. Indeed, the NWGC's slashed budget placed the Civilian Committee in a "precarious financial situation," and in Margraten they now scrambled to have the organization in Amsterdam assure at least limited annual financing for such costs as telephone, stamps, and stationary.[19]

The financial crippling of Margraten's Civilian Committee in 1954 was followed almost immediately by the death of the village's burgomaster. Ronckers had been not only one of the committee's founders, but also their honorary president and staunchest defender. With his passing and the committee's now wobbly finances, some in Maastricht sensed that the time had finally come for Limburg's capital to take over a program too important for the province and Dutch-American relations to be left in the amateur hands of a small rural community.

Emilie van Kessenich had always been of that opinion. She was still an influential member of the NWGC and therefore instrumental in having the organization approach the Limburg governor with a request for a drastically new approach to the Margraten cemetery. The governor thought it appropriate to hold off at least until Margraten had a mayor again. But once Mr. Vrouenraets had been installed as the new burgomaster, things were moved forward in a hurry. With Vrouenraets' acquiescence, by 1955 the Limburg governor, in tandem with the NWGC, had accomplished what some in Margraten regarded as nothing less than a Maastricht coup.[20]

Where the statutes of the Civilian Committee in 1946 had ruled that members had to be inhabitants of Margraten, the original committee, now renamed Limburg Committee American Military Cemetery Margraten, for practical purposes was split up in two. An executive committee for day-to-day operations accepted Margraten's new mayor and two of his clerks as members. But Limburg's governor, with his seat in Maastricht, now was to head the executive committee and Mrs. van Kessenich, wife of the Maastricht mayor, was added as another core member. In addition to that, a separate honorary committee was created made up of notables and dignitaries from across the province. Leading figures in Maastricht made no secret of the fact that from now on they were to be the ones handling contacts with the Dutch royal family and high-ranking American and other foreign officials in ceremonies at the cemetery.

During preparations for Memorial Day in March 1955, even the American ambassador was informed of this shift rather bluntly. Until his death the year before, the American embassy had always been happy to invite Margraten's burgomaster Ronckers for a short address at the annual ceremony. But in response to a US embassy inquiry as to whether the new Margraten burgomaster might be willing to serve as "the Netherlands speaker," the Limburg governor was now quick to assert his authority. In a letter to American ambassador H. Freeman Matthews, he announced his firm intention to assist the burgomaster by saying a few words too, "in order to express that the people of the whole of Limburg Province commemorate this day and not only the local people of Margraten."[21]

As Margraten's grip on the ceremonies weakened in the 1950s, so too did the active involvement of some of the Limburg rank and file in the adoption program. Indeed, economic calculation forced quite a few to emigrate and thus to break their ties with the Margraten graves. On the heels of the 1930s depression, war and Nazi occupation had devastated the Dutch economy, and the loss of the Dutch East Indies had made prospects look even bleaker. High unemployment, the lack of proper housing, and a shortage of agricultural land would push more than 400,000 Dutchmen into exodus in the period between 1947 and 1963. The large majority of these went to Australia and Canada because of their more flexible immigration policies. Some 76,000 Dutch managed to enter the US, however. Indeed, quite a few of the latter, especially in the early 1950s, were adopters who found family of the Margraten boys more than happy to function as sponsors providing the required guarantee of housing and work.[22]

One such sponsor was the wife of Joe Dziesulski in Chicago. Joe, a sergeant in the 101st Airborne Division, had been killed early in October 1944. It had been impossible for his wife to come to terms with the loss. She had married Joe in 1941 and followed him all the way to training camps in Texas. Shortly after he had been shipped to Europe, she had discovered that she was pregnant and a little later had suffered a miscarriage. As early as 1950, she made the expensive trip to Europe to convince herself of the cruel fact that her husband was dead and would never return. At the cemetery, however, she derived much consolation from the presence of the Limburg family watching over Joe's grave. So much so that the lonely widow after her return home managed to convince one of the family members to emigrate to her country with her husband and two children. In Chicago the Limburgers had another child, a daughter whom they gladly named after Joe's wife.[23]

Relatives could replace emigrants as caretakers of the graves. But nothing could prevent marriage, the arrival of children, and the demands of work from grinding down active involvement in adoption. A family in Wittem that in 1946 had proudly accepted their certificate of adoption later regretted how life had forced their pledge to become hollow. "I got married," a daughter who turned 20 in 1955 explained, "had a child, my parents died young, and a sister had a bad fall and remained an invalid for the rest of her life. Adoption was placed on the backburner."[24]

By then also there was no more network of so-called correspondents who, as they had done right after the war, helped adopters draft letters in English. A family in Heerlen forever treasured the memories of American soldiers from a nearby rest center dropping by on weekends to talk and listen to some music. The well-behaved boys had made sure to bring not only alcohol and chocolate, but even polish with which to wipe the floor clean after they were done dancing. The Dutch family had accepted adoption of a soldier from New Jersey from the bottom of their hearts. But by 1952 the correspondence with the boy's family was limited to a Christmas card for which the busy father of four daughters had to sit down at the table and study a dictionary.[25]

That correspondence with some families in the 1950s became less intense, or ended altogether, just as often was the result of waning interest on the other side of the ocean. Here too families had to get on with their lives. For the same reason that some American women had decided not to have the bodies of husbands brought home, others now made clear that it was better for them and their new partners not to continue to dwell on the past in letters with adoptive families.

In 1950 the brother of a woman from Valkenburg made sure to make a stopover in New York. He had been active as a priest in American parishes for years and now was on his way for a visit to his family in Limburg. His sister for several years had been corresponding with the family of Herbert Feldman, a private of the 30th Infantry Division. She wanted her brother to give them a recent picture of the boy's grave and have a talk with them in his fluent English. The priest had a long conversation with the soldier's parents. And Herbert's sister too embraced him warmly. But he never got to see the soldier's widow. She had remarried, Herbert's embarrassed family explained, and now wanted nothing further to do with them.[26]

3

After more than a decade of depression and war, people were impatient to get on with their lives. And they desperately wanted to do so in a world that was stable and at peace. These hopes were cruelly shattered when three years of war in Korea caused deep fears of the conflict escalating into World War III. The Korean War would eventually end in an uneasy stalemate, but not before setting in motion a global nuclear arms race more nightmarish in its implications than any known war. On Memorial Day 1954, the Limburg governor amidst the more than 8,000 American graves appealed for the Christian commandment of love for one another to prevail over the climate of hatred and the threat of annihilation. The call came in the wake of the detonation of a frighteningly powerful American hydrogen bomb in the Pacific. Dutch newspapers were carrying reports about abnormal levels of radioactivity and the potential increases in cancer tumors and leukemia even in Europe. It was the beginning of what was to be a long tradition of Dutch officials using the Margraten cemetery as a powerful platform for peace and disarmament.[27]

This by no means caused the original Margraten message to be drowned out. The bravery of the American liberators, the Limburg governor assured his audience on Memorial Day 1956, "fills our hearts with awe and soul-stirring emotion. We hear the lesson taught to us by those unforgettable heroes." Yet the lesson was one that would sound increasingly confusing and contradictory on Margraten's windy plain. The governor, that same Memorial Day, launched an emotional plea for peace in a world "feeling threatened by the power of natural science." But at the same time he could not but acknowledge that there had been and would be times when war was necessary and just. World War II had been such a war and the governor sincerely thanked the Allies for "the struggle for the freedom of all peoples, the Netherlands included." Meanwhile, in the midst of desperate stirrings for freedom in Poland and Hungary, the governor did not shrink from criticizing the world on the other side of the Iron Curtain, where "one people oppresses the other with the force of weapons." The Dutch government had decided to join NATO in 1949 and, whatever the country's misgivings about the nuclear arms race, in the poisoned atmosphere of the Cold War was determined to remain a staunch ally of the US.[28]

The Margraten burgomaster that Memorial Day 1956 arranged for close to 1,000 children to be bussed in from all over southern Limburg with the financial support of the NWGC in Amsterdam. At around the same time, the special relationship with the US was further cemented in Margraten through a series of political and financial accords. The Dutch government agreed to extend the privileges, originally granted to the American military authorities at the Margraten cemetery in 1947, for an additional period of eight years until 1963. In 1957 the Dutch government at last also succeeded in closing the chapter on the sensitive issue of farmers' compensation for the land requisitioned to build the American cemetery.[29]

In addition, with the American construction of the permanent cemetery still in progress, the provincial government of Limburg and the Dutch Queen, in the name of her country's government, proposed to the American ambassador the creation of several ornamental features as gifts. These were to be placed in the main memorial building once completed. "The objects," an appreciative American ambassador assured the Limburg governor, "will serve as further evidence of the kindness which the Dutch people, particularly those of Limburg, have always shown to our American soldiers." By 1956 the Dutch government had commissioned an elegant chandelier covered in plate gold and the provincial government a six-armed candelabra in wrought iron as well as a flower bowl in polished solid silver. The Limburg Committee and the Margraten mayor mobilized press and churches to have adopters and others step forward with donations in order to demonstrate that the provincial government's gifts were indeed theirs too.[30]

Meanwhile, the vagaries of politics failed to impact the adopters' unstinting commitment. Ordinary citizens remained all too aware of the numbing pain that American families continued to suffer. Early in 1957, Emilie van Kessenich through the Limburg Committee approached a woman in Heerlen with the message that a mother in Winslow, Indiana, had complained that she was neglecting her duties as an adopter. The adopter's indignant husband was quick to send Mrs. van Kessenich a long reply. It detailed the numerous letters that had been sent all the way to Winslow as well as the newspaper clippings of Memorial Day and the many photographs taken with a borrowed camera. But the American mother, the Dutch husband claimed, was showing herself more and more unreasonable. In every new letter she was asking for additional pictures not just of the cross with her son's name on it, but also of the entire adoptive family at his grave. It pained him, he said, to have to suggest that grief might have left her "mentally not 100%." Mrs. van Kessenich conceded that this was quite possible. She nevertheless prodded the family to continue to write now and then "out of charity."[31]

The year before, a similar tragic story had played out between Maastricht and Minnesota. In August 1944 an Allied bombardment paving the way for the rapidly advancing liberators had destroyed the home of the Herman family in Maastricht. The family's only son was found dead in the rubble. In 1946 the 17-year-old's mother gladly became the adopter of an American grave in Margraten. It did not bother her that the grave was that of Phillip Barker, a sergeant who had lost his life in the kind of aircraft responsible for the loss of her own son. All that mattered to Mrs. Herman was to show gratitude to the liberators and support for an overseas mother having to endure the pain she knew so well. When in the early 1950s it became clear to Mrs. Herman that Mrs. Barker did not have the money to travel from Mankato to Margraten to experience the comfort of standing at his grave, she was determined to make this possible for her. Having lost everything in the war, Mrs. Herman could not provide any financing herself. Instead she began to solicit money from family members, friends, neighbors, schools, shops, and convents to raise the money for Mrs. Barker's trip from Minnesota. In 1956 even the Limburg governor decided to get on board. He joined hands with the NWGC in Amsterdam and together they provided the rest of the money. By then, however, Ida Barker had been diagnosed with a serious heart condition. The Soviet crackdown in Hungary and the war over the Egyptian Suez Canal did the rest and regretfully made a frightened mother decline the kind Dutch offer.[32]

The gratitude of those who knew that well-meaning Dutch were taking care of the graves of their boys as if they belonged to their own family hardly abated a decade after the war. In 1954 an article appeared in a newspaper in Georgia's Worth County. It was written by a local who during a European tour had stopped in Margraten to visit the grave of Robert Long of Red Rock, the only Worth County soldier buried there. She had also met Mrs. van Kessenich who had managed to get her in touch with Robert's adoptive family, a young couple in Groot Welsden who had just had their first child.

The story sent ripples of approval through the small Southern community and in 1955 a parcel was sent to the address of the Maastricht mayor. Having learned from the author of the article that the van Kessenichs were celebrating their silver wedding anniversary that year, the mayor of Sylvester, Robert Long's parents, and "quite a number of Worth Countians" had thought it appropriate to send "warm best wishes as well as our gratefulness." For some time in one of Sylvester's store windows, a newspaper clipping explained, pictures had been shown of Robert Long, the van Kessenichs in Maastricht, and the adoptive family in Groot Welsden. A globe had been added to show the location of the Netherlands. Also part of the window display had been the presents bought by the local community to be shipped to the Netherlands. The young adoptive family and their baby daughter Claartje were presented with a silver spoon engraved with the Georgia Cherokee Rose pattern. The van Kessenichs received a similar spoon as well as a leather-bound copy of *Aneas Africanus*, a tale set in Georgia and written by native son Harry Stillwell Edwards. "Those who have sacrificed together, learn to pray together," the mayor added. "And we have an old Georgian saying: Those who pray together, stay together."[33]

4

The problem remained, however, that few in the US knew there were Dutch families praying at Margraten cemetery for the boys and their mourning relatives. In the very year that the presents from Georgia arrived, Mrs. van Kessenich once more raised the issue of the withheld American home addresses to give new impetus to the adoption program. Once again, however, the attempt failed. Ambassador H. Freeman Matthews informed the Maastricht mayor's wife that he had taken up the question with General George C. Marshall, Chairman of the ABMC. But the ambassador said he had to report to her that, even after a decade, the ABMC had signaled that it had not changed its stance "with regard to the names and addresses of the next of kin of our Dead" and that it "must continue to withhold such information." "Its reasoning on this point is," H. Freeman Matthews explained, "that it would be unfortunate if the American people came to believe that the graves were not the responsibility of United States authorities." The ambassador to the Netherlands deeply regretted this decision. But, in a slightly veiled reference to the ghost of McCarthyism and rampant accusations of disloyalty, he also told Mrs. van Kessenich that he understood the decision. "You can well imagine," he confided, "that such an impression might be exploited by unscrupulous people for their own 'political' advantage."[34]

Thus it was that American relatives stumbled upon the existence of the Margraten adoption by sheer coincidence more than a decade after it had been created. Lieutenant Bryce Ralston, a fighter pilot awarded the Distinguished Flying Cross, was shot down in his P-47 Thunderbolt over the German town of Kruft two days before Christmas 1944. His mother in Grand Forks, North Dakota, first learned about adoption in 1958 when she happened to read an article about the NWGC in an old magazine of the Veterans of Foreign Wars. She immediately wrote a letter to the Amsterdam address, telling them that she was most eager to learn if anyone had perhaps adopted her son's grave too and "to hear anything you could write and tell me regarding his grave there." The NWGC forwarded Mrs. Ralston's letter to the Limburg Committee and they were happy to inform her that a family near Maastricht had been caring for Bryce's grave for twelve years now.[35]

Mrs. Miller, the mother of a Margraten boy from York County in Pennsylvania, had been more fortunate. In a letter to the NWGC in 1959 she wrote that she had "discovered" the girl who was caring for their son's grave as early as July 1947. She had received photos of the grave from her, and not only the girl but other family members, too, had been sending letters regularly. "Since I have found the girl who has adopted my son's grave and can write to her," she confided, "it has eased the burden of our hearts."

However, this letter was not about her, she told the NWGC, but about another mother who lived not far from their home in York County. "The mother isn't well," she wrote, "and worries about her son." Mrs. Miller had learned that Mrs. Zeigler's son had also been laid to rest in Margraten. Paul Zeigler had been a radio operator on a B-24 when on 7 July 1944 the aircraft was downed over Bernburg in an attempt to take out a German aircraft manufacturing plant. Within a matter of weeks, Mrs. Miller received word from the Netherlands that Paul Zeigler, like most Margraten boys, had been adopted at about the same time as her own son. For want of an American home address, the Dutch adoptive family had never been able to establish contact, the kind of contact that could have made a world of difference to Paul's mother. "I took the letter to the parents about 2 hours after I received it," Mrs. Miller wrote to thank the NWGC in Amsterdam, "and I wish you could have seen their faces."[36]

Dutch adopters did not need to see the faces of American relatives to realize that what they were doing was worthwhile. Indeed, it did not matter to them if anyone in the US knew what they were doing at all. Whether out of deep gratitude or sheer humanitarian concern, caring for the memory of the Margraten boys simply remained the right thing to do for the adopters. A decade after the end of the war, a woman from Schaesberg sent a long letter of apology to the Limburg Committee. She was embarrassed to have to own up to the fact that the past year she had neglected the adopted grave of Private William Dellapenta of the 101st Airborne Division. The woman's husband had suddenly died at the age of 35, causing her to be left behind with four young children. "You may understand," she pleaded, "that I had much on my mind and forgot about Margraten." The woman assured, however, that she would be present at the upcoming Memorial Day ceremony and would visit the cemetery more often to make up for her absence the year before. Her biggest fear was that the grave had already been taken away from her and assigned to someone else. "I would regret that very much," she said, "especially because it would be the result of my not living up to my promise."[37]

The Limburg Committee saw no reason to take the private's grave away from an adopter showing such genuine commitment. Still others proved equally committed to step in and take over when adopters for one reason or another found it altogether impossible to continue carrying on their duties. For a 28-year-old from Heerlen it was only natural to have the committee replace the name of her parents on the adoption certificate with her own in 1958. Her parents had cared for the grave of Henry Coker, an infantryman from Missouri, with great tenderness. But she too would never forget the encounter with Henry's brother early in 1945 when the GI was forlornly walking the cemetery while on leave from the front. She owed that much to Henry in Margraten. And to his brother in America.[38]

Johan Vrancken in Meerssen made a similar vow at about the same time. He made the vow as much for his sister as for the farm boy from North Carolina. Betty Vrancken had adopted Eddie Hart's grave as a young girl immediately after the war. She had managed to get in touch with Hattie, Eddie's sister, and from her had learned that he had joined the 329th Infantry as a replacement after the Battle of the Bulge had wreaked havoc with the unit. Private Hart had been part of the drive to the Rhine in February 1945 and had begun dreaming of his return to the farm when in April the house in the German town of Barby, where his platoon had taken shelter, received a direct hit. "I hope, dear Miss Hart," Betty wrote to Eddie's sister in her very first letter, "that this will be a little better for you to know that your brother's grave is not lonely and forgotten." The young women continued to exchange letters. But then life caught up with Betty too. She married, and in 1957 she and her husband decided that they would be better off emigrating to America. Johan was sorry to see his sister leave. The least he could do was to promise that he would continue to watch over her soldier in Margraten. Forty-five years later, Johan, leaning on a cane, would lead Hattie and her family to Eddie's grave. "After so many years, like I tell her," he said in the presence of a film crew capturing the moment, "I kept my promise."[39]

Not only the adopters continued to be drawn to Margraten in the 1950s. Even at the end of the decade, the schools of southern Limburg were still making sure that some one thousand children, the memory of a future generation, were present at the cemetery for the Memorial Day ceremonies. "I still feel," US ambassador Philip Young said in a note of thanks to the Limburg governor in 1960, "that the laying of flowers on the graves by children is the most effective part of the ceremony."[40]

Each year on Ascension Day, members of the Globetrotters, a regional club of hiking enthusiasts, designated the American cemetery a place of pilgrimage. Two thousand men and women wound their way to Margraten in 1956. A year later, the number of people marching on Margraten to pay tribute to the fallen heroes had swollen to 3,000.

Also in 1957, the Dutch section of the International Prayer Union of Our Lady of Banneux, one of the most popular Catholic shrines in Europe, announced to the mayor of Margraten their pilgrims' intention to halt on their way to the Belgian shrine to celebrate Mass at the American cemetery. The mayor contacted the cemetery's superintendent and the American was immediately prepared to lend them his full cooperation. As the weather grew milder, ten different journeys were made to Banneux by a total of some one thousand pilgrims from the diocese of Rotterdam. Ten Sundays in a row each group arrived at the American cemetery early in the morning and in their prayers implored Our Lady to keep vigil over the boys in Margraten.[41]

5

By the late 1950s too, however, there were the slow stirrings of a new generation. In a letter to the Margraten mayor, a man from a neighboring province, after a visit to the American cemetery in the summer of 1957, showed himself very displeased. He had been "stunned and saddened," he wrote, to find that several visitors in their dress code had not shown "the respect befitting the honoring and beholding of the sacrifices made for our freedom." There had been men, he detailed, who had thought nothing of entering the premises with their sleeves rolled up. And he had seen quite a few women in dresses fit for a fashion parade, but not for Margraten's "sacred soil."[42]

But there were gradual changes in political sensitivities as well as mores. During Memorial Day ceremonies the traditional message continued to reverberate across the graves of the fallen heroes. "The army of the US," the Limburg governor said in 1959, "in the twentieth century has shown the courage to accept the greatest risks at a time when tyranny threatened Europe and the world." That past demanded undiminished "gratitude for the sacrifice." On the other hand, however, the future with its threat of mutually assured nuclear destruction warranted a clear and urgent "siding with peace and against the horrific forces of technocracy." And the most fundamental way of ensuring such peace, the governor pointed the way, was to champion justice for "all people, white and brown." The governor was assured of a receptive audience for his message of social and racial justice at a time when Dutch newspapers teemed with headlines of wars against colonial oppression, protests against apartheid in South Africa, and civil rights struggles in the US.[43]

At the same time, hints of rapprochement were in the air in the Netherlands even where it concerned the arch-enemy. In the spring of 1958, in the center of Maastricht, a long peal of horns suddenly sounded. Pulled by six magnificent horses, an antique traveling coach swept into the square and drew up in front of city hall. Out of the coach stepped four young people dressed like characters from a Dickens novel. One of the young men approached mayor Michiels van Kessenich with great dignity, slowly unrolled a long parchment scroll, and then proceeded to read a text in German. They were on their way, the messenger proclaimed, from Hamburg to the World's Fair in Brussels and had halted in Maastricht bearing gifts and good wishes from the mayor of their city. At the end of the brief ceremony, the coachman blew his long silver horn again and the horses whisked the German delegation off to Belgium.[44]

By the late 1950s, a détente in relations with West Germany, which had been admitted to NATO in 1955, brought a different climate even to Margraten. Mistakenly assuming that their loved one was still buried there, early in December 1958 a German family appealed to the mayor, asking him for a picture of the soldier's grave. Günther Klinkisch had been 19, they wrote, when the war – "that none of us wanted" – had taken him away forever in 1944. "All over the world," the letter said, "there are people with a heart and for sure there must be someone in your town who might be willing to send us such a picture." There had been many such requests in the late 1940s. But by now the response from Margraten was not just polite and efficient, but decidedly warm. The Limburg Committee notified the family in Bayreuth that their loved one had long since been transferred to the German cemetery at Ysselsteyn. They had nevertheless arranged at their own expense for several photos to be made of his grave there and added that they were enclosing them as a Christmas gift for his mother. An elated Klinkisch family immediately replied, thanking the Dutch committee profusely for the photos that now had been given a special place by the Christmas tree. "We also want to thank you," Günther's sister-in-law wrote, "for the beautiful wreath that you placed on his grave."[45]

The Klinkisch family closed their letter with the profound wish "that peace on earth would be for all times and that our children will never have to know war." Eight years earlier that same wish had prompted Italian war widows to start a movement of reconciliation. With the support of Italian veterans' organizations, they had invited family members of the fallen of all nationalities to their country and together had visited a Commonwealth cemetery at Anzio and a German cemetery at Pomezia. Their final visit had been to the Benedictine monastery at Monte Cassino, where a small 'lamp of brotherhood' was placed symbolizing shared suffering and hope for a peaceful future. By the late 1950s, the Italian widows' initiative had grown into an International Organization of the Brotherhood of the Lamp with the support of the World Veterans Federation, which represented 20 million veterans in 35 countries across the world. The Lamp of Brotherhood was brought from Italy to various cemeteries and in 1957 a small lamp was lighted at the American military cemetery in Margraten too. Formally installed there by an impressive Italian delegation of war widows and Bersaglieri soldiers wearing black-feathered hats, the Lamp of Brotherhood represented among its many official member countries not only the US and the Netherlands, but also West Germany.[46]

At the end of the decade, the NWGC for its newsletter interviewed the American who had been Margraten cemetery's superintendent since the end of World War II. Johannes Staarup himself had lived through many a battle in that war. He walked with a slight limp and was all but deaf in his left ear. "The number of Germans visiting the cemetery increases each year," he remarked with a dour face. "I can't completely understand that."[47]

German visitors at Margraten may have caused Dutch frowns, too, barely a decade and a half after the disastrous war. It was clear nevertheless that, as part of the Dutch economic strategy for the future, tourists from all over the world were to be seduced to visit the country of windmills and wooden shoes. Particularly interesting in that regard was the rapidly growing market of American tourists willing to spend a very strong dollar. And it was equally clear that the American military cemetery in Margraten, besides functioning as a memorial and stark message, was to serve also as a powerful tourist magnet.

In April 1958 a group of travel agents from the states of Louisiana, Texas, and Oklahoma boarded a plane for Amsterdam. The original goal of their trip had been the World's Fair in Brussels and in particular the American pavilion with the Russian building directly opposite. But then the National Tourist Bureau of the Netherlands had stepped forward with an offer the agents had been unable to refuse: a sightseeing tour of their country, all expenses taken care of, before continuing on to Brussels. The agents made the transatlantic trip with KLM Royal Dutch Airlines in their First Class Deluxe section. By the time they arrived in Amsterdam, they had been spoiled with champagne, assortments of delicious cheeses, and canapés of lobster, crab, and smoked salmon.

Apart from Amsterdam itself, the itinerary contained visits to the obvious places: Rotterdam, The Hague's Madurodam, and Delft. But the organization had gone out of its way to fit in a train trip also all the way down to the much smaller city of Maastricht for the sole purpose of visiting its nearby American cemetery. First the American travel agents were entertained at the residence of Mr. and Mrs. van Kessenich, where they heard all about the adoption program. Then they headed off into the countryside on their way to Margraten. In some places, they could see farmers plowing the fine black soil with the aid of horses and oxen. On other farms, brand-new mechanized machinery was speeding up the work. But later that day, the travel agents left the Margraten cemetery with just one single powerful impression. "The Dutch in this part of Holland," a Texan agent noted in his travel journal, "where you can see Germany and Belgium from the top of the nearest hill, are, I believe, the staunchest and most enthusiastic friends of America you will find anywhere in Europe."[48]

At the end of the decade this special relationship was re-emphasized by a series of politically potent gestures and ceremonies. In the same month that the American travel agents visited Margraten, Limburg governor Houben announced that his daughters, Annemiek and Carla, were each to take over the care of an American grave no longer tended by the original adopter. Two years later, Margraten and Limburg were buzzing with the news of the official opening of the American cemetery in its final form. The wait had been very long. The first 200 crosses and stars in pure white marble from the Italian quarry of Lasa had arrived by train in Maastricht in 1953. The construction work and landscaping had continued almost nonstop since. The ABMC in Paris in the spring of 1959 informed the Limburg governor that the formal dedication of the cemetery was now scheduled for 7 July 1960. It immediately prompted workers to install the electrical wires for the Dutch government's chandelier in the memorial building's chapel and the province's altar furnishings too were now put on display. The gifts, General Jacob Devers told the Limburg governor as chairman of the ABMC, "were enduring testimony to the appreciation of the people of the Netherlands for the sacrifice of those Americans who rest in the cemetery, as well as to the centuries of friendly association of our two peoples."[49]

These sentiments were given an even more exalted expression during the formal dedication on 7 July 1960. "For the community of Margraten," mayor Vrouenraets told the governor, "this day will be of exceptional significance." That Thursday people thronged the Rijksweg leading to the cemetery to see their mayor, governor, and ministers as well as high-ranking American officials such as Generals Jacob Devers and Carl Spaatz and Secretary of the Army Wilber Brucker. Above all else, however, they wanted to catch a glimpse of their beloved Queen Juliana. She had arrived at the nearby airport in a red-white-and-blue royal Fokker Friendship and with a police escort headed straight for the Margraten cemetery in an open Rolls Royce. An audience of tens of thousands at the cemetery listened as the Queen in a brief speech caught the essence of the beautiful and haunting place in a single sentence, "They met death, that we should be granted life anew."[50]

In a smaller ceremony that weekend, the people of Margraten just as enthusiastically embraced a less conspicuous guest whom the mayor had insisted should be there at this special time. Joseph Shomon, the American officer who in 1944 had selected the cemetery's location and won over the hearts of the villagers with his men, had flown in from Richmond, Virginia. Margraten made the 45-year-old American its first honorary citizen and named a street after him too.[51]

It must have pleased Joseph Shomon to see the proud wooden chest of index cards at town hall and to learn that the adoption program continued to be in safe hands. For some time in the mid-1950s it had seemed to the NWGC in Amsterdam that the administration of the very adoption program that had served as the national organization's model was about to collapse. The reorganization of the Margraten Civilian Committee into a broader Limburg Committee had made sure to transfer to Maastricht public relations tasks such as organizing memorial ceremonies and foreign visits to the cemetery. But the adoption program's secretariat had remained at Margraten's town hall and, with it, all of the painstaking administrative work involved in keeping track of and corresponding with thousands of Dutch adopters and American families. Without further NWGC funding for a separate employee, town clerks and even the mayor himself had been forced to take care of the adoption administration in addition to their many regular tasks. At the start of 1958 it had taken town hall so long to answer phone calls and written requests from Amsterdam for information on adoption that the NWGC had complained to Mrs. van Kessenich that the situation in Margraten had become "untenable."[52]

In the spring of 1958, however, possibly as a result of these alarm bells, the adoption's worrying downward spiral had been abruptly halted after Mr. van Mulken, town hall's experienced and meticulous secretary, had assumed full control of the program's administration. From that time on, Mr. van Mulken had been spending not only many an office hour, but also much of his spare time, on ensuring the adoption program's continuity.[53]

6

"The history of the fallen who rest here," US Secretary of the Army Wilber Brucker declared during the formal dedication in July 1960, "is written not only in stone. It lives on in the lives of others." That was as true of the families in America as it was of the adoptive families in the Netherlands. And with the waning of the 1950s, Margraten's web of connections had become still more intimate as international travel had gradually begun to present itself as another defining feature of the postwar world.[54]

Although hundreds of thousands of Dutch emigrated overseas in the 1950s, only very few were lucky enough to visit the US for purposes of leisure. One such exception was the 19-year-old adopter of Ben Tisinger. In 1952 Ben's parents in Texas insisted on having the young Dutchman over for a visit to say thanks to him and perhaps also to be reminded of their own son. Ben, a PFC of the 405th Infantry, had been 19 in 1944 when he was killed near Aachen, the German city at the end of the Rijksweg besides which lay the Margraten cemetery. At the start of the 1950s, the Limburger's visit was considered so special that the event was covered in Dutch and American newspapers and resulted even in an interview for a Dallas radio station.[55]

But the 1950s would see the novelty of American relatives visiting Margraten gradually wear off. In August 1952 the presence of Richard Anderson's uncle from Napa, California, at the cemetery sufficed to have the *Gazet van Limburg* devote a large article to the visit. The Californian said that he was glad to be able to pay his respects to the sergeant of the 17th Airborne Division and that he had promised to do this as a favor to his devastated parents who had lost their only child. But he added that it might never have happened so early had he not been at Helsinki for the Olympic Games earlier that month. Already two years later, at a time when during the summer several thousand visitors were said to be flocking to Margraten each day, an estimated 50 Americans were finding their way to the cemetery each week. And the number of visiting Americans climbed steadily with each new year. More and more Americans had the means to make the trip as the economy boomed at home and the dollar reigned supreme abroad, but US military personnel stationed in West-Germany accounted for much of the increase as well.[56]

In 1955 the parents of Richard Hewitt, a private in the 84th Infantry Division, arrived in Waubach, Limburg, from Hanover, New Hampshire. They were to attend Margraten's Memorial Day services together with their son's adoptive parents. They had been corresponding since 1946 and had developed "an intimate understanding of family relations and problems as the two mothers have shared confidences with each other." As a special gift for Mr. and Mrs. Meerten in Waubach, the Hewitts carried a letter from none other than President Eisenhower. "The opportunity to visit the grave of their son Richard in company with the Dutch family who have cared for it since the war means a great deal to them," the former Supreme Commander assured them. "Possibly the Hewitts can convey to others in the Margraten area some of the gratitude felt by thousands of Americans whose loved ones at Margraten are being watched over by people in the area they helped liberate." "It is enheartening indeed," the American president concluded, "to know of such humanity and kindness as you and your neighbors have displayed."[57]

Still, even by the late 1950s, for many Americans the dream of a trip to the Margraten cemetery remained hopelessly out of reach. This was true also for Justine, Thomas Steele's widow. Her husband's grave had been adopted by Lucie van den Boorn, the girl who in 1946 for some time had been watching over several dozen GI resting places. In 1950 Justine, after talking it over with Tom's mother and dad, had remarried and become Mrs. Keller. But although Justine told Lucie that Warren Keller was "a wonderful fellow," Tom Steele's ghost was never far away. "They have never recovered from Tom's loss though," Justine wrote about her first husband's parents in 1959, "and still talk about him as though it happened yesterday." But so did Justine. She thanked Lucie once more "for all you have done for me in caring for my Tom's grave as you did" and told her she was excited that a colleague of hers was to visit the Low Countries later that year. Although the colleague had never even met Tom, Justine gave her Lucie's phone number and forwarded the woman's itinerary and list of hotels. "I certainly hope she can get through to you and say one big hello for me," Justine wrote wistfully. "Some day, when my ship comes in, I will most certainly make the trip myself."[58]

It was the heartache of people like Justine Keller that had made the NWGC decide earlier in the decade to help finance the trip for at least some of those needing assistance. Funding came from the annual 'Poppy sale,' a nationwide campaign organized around Armistice Day. The money was used only to provide for the next of kin's travel within the Netherlands and for up to a week's accommodation. In 1959, for example, such assistance made it easier for two of the Margraten boys' mothers to visit their graves at last. It had taken Mrs. Ross ten years to put aside enough money each month from her salary as a sales clerk in a Richmond, Virginia, department store to save up for the transatlantic trip. But now, on the eve of Memorial Day, Eugenia Ross arrived in Amsterdam to be welcomed by members of the NWGC and Mr. van Lennep, the adoptive father of her son George. Several days later, she was walking between the crosses and stars arm-in-arm with Netty Olivers from California whose son Lynn had been George's co-pilot when their plane had been shot down by flak on a bombing raid over Münster on Armistice Day 1943.[59]

Meeting the adoptive families and getting to know them up close and personal did much to strengthen already strong bonds. Hugh Ratchford, a flight engineer on a B-24 Liberator, had also been shot down by flak over Münster, but in March 1945 when the war was almost over. He too was laid to rest in Margraten. His widowed mother Jessie in North Carolina kept up a steady correspondence with the adopter of his grave, an English teacher who was in her thirties when she accepted the responsibility at the end of the war. Hugh's mother never made it to Margraten. But his brother Lenny finally had a chance to say thanks to the adoptive lady at her home in Linne in 1960. The meeting made such an impression on Lenny that for the rest of his life he insisted on paying the teacher's subscription to *National Geographic* magazine. And when Lenny died in 1996, in his will he had made sure to bequeath one thousand dollars to the kind lady still watching over his brother's grave at age 84.[60]

As the 15th anniversary of Operation Market Garden came up, a group of some 90 American veterans of the 101st Airborne Division combined a tour of the Arnhem corridor with a visit to the Margraten cemetery. Mrs. Cyrus Miller from Dallas, Texas, was the group's guest of honor. She was a Gold Star Mother whose son had been one of the many paratroopers killed during the ill-fated airborne campaign in the Netherlands in September 1944. Mrs. Miller carried with her a container filled with soil collected in the capitals of all 50 states and at the White House in Washington, DC. Arrangements were made to have her fly over Margraten in a Piper Cub and release the contents of the container over the American cemetery.[61]

The ceremony, symbolizing that henceforth the Margraten boys would rest in American as well as Dutch soil, made a big impression on many within the American Gold Star Mothers Association. So much so that early in 1962 key members of the organization approached the new Margraten mayor, Mr. Kuijpers, with a plan to have more mothers visit the cemetery in September of that year. "We want," one of them told the burgomaster, "the Gold Star Mothers of America to have the feeling of peace that came to Mrs. Miller."[62]

The effort centered on mothers who lived on small pensions and old-age benefits that did not allow them to make such a trip on their own. Sponsoring offered by KLM airline and others in the travel industry as well as American churches and veterans' organizations helped to reduce the cost of transatlantic travel for some 70 Gold Star Mothers and half a dozen Gold Star Dads. Adoptive families in and around Margraten were happy to offer all of them accommodation for free and even Mayor Kuijpers wrote a letter offering to host several American mothers in his own home.

The Americans spent five nights with Dutch families in and around Margraten. The simple ceremony at the cemetery in the presence of so many grieving mothers and fathers was more impressive than any Memorial Day had ever been. "May the horrors of war never again strike households," the president of the Gold Star Mothers said in a brief speech. "That is the sincere wish of all mothers." A month later a Gold Star Mother from Maryland thanked the burgomaster and the people of Margraten for "the many courtesies and kindnesses shown." "I feel so much better about my son now," she wrote in closing, "knowing he helped to liberate such kind and sincere people. I feel he did not give his life in vain."[63]

7

One of the reasons for the trip in 1962, according to an American organizer, was "the advancing years of the Gold Star Mothers." Both in Washington and in Margraten there were unmistakable signs now of an older generation passing on the torch. In 1961 Father Heuschen passed away. Obituaries in the Limburg press remembered him as the "driving force" behind the adoption program, as indeed he had been even after his fallout with Mrs. van Kessenich and his resignation from the Civilian Committee in 1946, after which he continued to correspond in his own name with scores of American families until his death. In 1962 the NWGC in Amsterdam was saddened by the death of Mr. Blom, the organization's secretary and the man who had been their driving force since the end of the war. Another year later, health problems forced even the indomitable Mrs. van Kessenich in Maastricht to announce her resignation from both the NWGC and the Limburg Committee.

The death of their dynamic secretary forced the NWGC to rethink their approach to the management of the war graves of World War II. They were most keen on devising better forms of communication with their members for fear that otherwise these might begin "to question whether the war graves work, more than fifteen years after the war, still holds any real significance." The NWGC certainly believed so and promised to continue funding local committees like the one in Limburg overseeing the adoption and commemorations at Margraten. The Limburg Committee itself that same year was happy to note that further funding provided by the province's municipalities meant that the tradition of having some 1,000 children attend Memorial Day with flowers for the American soldiers' graves was secure.[64]

Around the same time, the significance of the Margraten cemetery appeared to be recognized with renewed vigor by the American press too. A journalist writing an article on the ABMC for the *Rotarian* early in 1963 was told by officials in Paris to contact people in Margraten as the cemetery there was, in their view, "outstanding," not in the least because of its program of adoption. "This, indeed," the journalist noted, "is a mark of recognition that American readers know all too little about, and I hope that my article will, in some degree, correct the situation."[65]

That same year, 50-year-old George Kent was about to correct the situation to a much larger degree. Now a journalist for the *Christian Herald*, the American had spent some time in Maastricht as a correspondent after the city's liberation in 1944. He was glad to be back for an in-depth article on the Margraten cemetery and even gladder to see that people in Maastricht no longer looked "poorly dressed and hungry" and that the city, like the rest of the country, had become "busy and prosperous." His report on the Margraten boys and their Dutch adopters made such an impression in the US that the *Reader's Digest*, one of the country's largest-circulation magazines, decided to republish it in its trademark condensed form in June 1963.[66]

As Dutch and Americans reaffirmed their commitment not to let the Margraten boys and their message of sacrifice for freedom fade away, a dramatic transition in the White House renewed hope on a much larger scale. Like many Americans in the election of 1960, the Dutch during the formal dedication of the Margraten cemetery that year had come to believe that it was time for the promise of youth when President Eisenhower disappointed by declining to make the demanding trip himself and sending an envoy with a friendly message instead. The suave charm and youthful vigor of America's first Catholic president took the Netherlands by storm and made Catholic Limburg forget even their beloved war hero Ike.

With the abrupt change in style came a transformation also in the message on America's future relations with the world. After more than a decade of Cold War and the threat of nuclear annihilation, John Stanley Rice, the new ambassador to the Netherlands, set the tone in his Memorial Day speeches at the Margraten cemetery in 1961 and 1962. Like the ambassadors of the past decade, Rice strongly emphasized the importance of military preparedness and alliances to prevent "certain forces in the world from imposing on us a way of life" that made a travesty of the freedoms for which the Margraten boys had given their lives. But at the same time, the American ambassador now just as strongly heralded the importance of "fundamental human rights" and of a world in which "the rule of law, peace, and justice" were to be central tenets. The words of President Kennedy's ambassador stirred the audience at Margraten, especially the younger generation. Like their peers in America, they too had been waiting impatiently to embrace new frontiers at home and abroad.[67]

5 A Long and Dark Shadow

The shots that killed John F. Kennedy and the promise of his generation on 22 November 1963 were heard around the world. It took those assembling on the Margraten plateau, too, a long time to accept the cruel reality of the Dallas assassination. So many questions that people had hoped would be addressed by Kennedy's best and brightest now lingered hollow and unanswered. "Have we," the Limburg governor asked on Memorial Day 1964, "made progress on the road to a more humane society? Here in Limburg, in the Netherlands, in Europe, on our planet? Our earth is still not without war – cold or hot." "We claim to be brothers," the governor continued, "but do we act accordingly? There is still tension between black, brown, and white."

Governor Charles van Rooy then called on his audience to be inspired by the late American president's "luminous example" and to bring the planet, through their own efforts, "a little nearer to the ideal for which he struggled and died." "Is not peace, in the last analysis," the governor reminded his audience, quoting President Kennedy himself, "basically a matter of human rights – the right to live out our lives without fear of devastation, the right to breathe air as nature provided it, the right of future generations to a healthy existence." "For the moment," the governor concluded with sadness, "our thoughts go out to that other military cemetery where he rests now."

On Memorial Day a year later, the governor's thoughts again drifted off to Virginia's Arlington National Cemetery and the ideals so eloquently expressed by the late American president. Van Rooy urged his audience to continue to be inspired by his example and for the second year in a row reminded them of the ringing promise John F. Kennedy had made in the name of America: "We shall do our part to build a world of peace where the weak are safe and the strong are just." "May the sacrifice of those whose bodies rest here," the governor solemnly closed his speech, "strengthen us when going the way your President pointed out."[1]

1

With the liberation of his country now 20 years in the past, Governor van Rooy was keen also to protect the legacy of the Margraten boys. "The further the war recedes into the past," he warned American and Dutch visitors in 1964, "the more important will be this commemorating." At the US embassy in The Hague, standard procedures were in place by the early sixties to ensure the continuation of the annual Memorial Day services at Margraten regardless of who was in power in Washington. But the standardized approach lacked the emotion and conviction of older Memorial Days. "Almost all of the arrangements," the US embassy guidelines said, "are repetitive each year, as are the contents of the various letters transmitted in conjunction therewith. To avoid the appearance of forwarding 'form letters,' separate drafts are prepared from year to year in which the contents are rearranged slightly and expressed in different fashion."[2]

No such atrophied treatment of the Margraten legacy threatened to take hold of the adoptive community, however. Although organized tours of American relatives and comrades were taking place quite regularly now, Dutch families in and around Margraten continued to be honored and excited by each new visit. For the twentieth anniversary of their part in the liberation of Europe, the 82nd Airborne Division carefully planned a ceremony at the cemetery for veterans and their wives in close cooperation with Margraten burgomaster Kuijpers. "It goes without saying," the association's appreciative secretary emphasized, "that we extend an invitation to the citizens of Margraten to attend these services." A year later, burgomaster Kuijpers himself extended an invitation to his fellow citizens to open their homes once again for a group of more than 40 Gold Star Mothers. As many bonds of friendship had been formed during the 1962 visit, the response to the new call was decidedly warm. "I must say," Major General William Baker complimented the Margraten mayor on behalf of the

ABMC, "that I have never seen anything equal to it. We are all grateful for what you have done and are doing."³

More and more American relatives began to find their way to Margraten on their own too. From New York the parents of Vincent Stabile, a sergeant in the 8th Infantry Division, had sent their son's adopters parcels with clothing and toys several years in a row after the war had ended. But they had never been able to save enough money for a transatlantic trip. In the early 1960s, Vincent at last received a visit from his brother and sister. Vincent's siblings in turn were given a warm welcome in the home of their brother's adopters in Margraten. Vincent's adoptive father was one of the men who had helped dig the cemetery's graves in the late 1940s and he embraced the American next of kin firmly and with heartfelt emotion.⁴

Bill Driver had been a tall and lanky farm boy who had been very good at basketball during his time at Quenemo high school in Kansas. He had been drafted in 1944 and sent to the 1st Infantry Division as a replacement early in February 1945. He was found dead in his foxhole somewhere in Germany less than two months later. Bill was one of six Driver sons to serve in the military during the war. He was the only one never to return back home. In 1963 two of his brothers and their wives started out on the family's very first pilgrimage to Bill's grave and his adoptive family in Heerlen. One of Bill's sisters-in-law later said in a poem: "Sometimes I try / To picture him / As he would be now / If he had lived / His hair turned gray / A furrowed brow / But the picture always fades away."⁵

In the eyes of his father, Harold Shroka, too, would remain forever young. A pilot from Ohio in the 305th Bomber Group, he had been killed over Europe even before the first anniversary of the attack on Pearl Harbor. By the time his father made it to Harold's grave in 1964, he was 72. He arrived at the cemetery accompanied by Harold's brother and the young Dutchman who had taken over the grave's care from his parents in 1960. Onto the grass at his son's cross Mr. Shroka sprinkled soil from the grave of his wife and Harold's mother. Then he bent down and scooped some soil from their only child's grave to take back with him across the ocean.⁶

To help soften at least somewhat the searing pain that lingered in so many American households, in 1964 two Limburg priests decided to travel to the US to pay a visit to some of the next of kin of the boys buried in the local American cemetery. One of them was Father Heijnen who had said prayer upon prayer amidst the ceaseless burials at Margraten in 1944–45. The other was Father Janssen who had arrived as a new priest in Margraten parish at the end of the 1950s. Almost half a century later, an ageing Father Janssen would still be persisting in his annual transatlantic pilgrimage to those who had never stopped mourning their relatives in Margraten.[7]

By the mid-1960s, years of dutiful caring for the graves had led many Dutch adopters to think of the American boys in Margraten as part of their families too. Such feelings made it seem natural for a younger generation to take over from parents and aunts and uncles whenever illness, old age, or death put an end to their pledge. For Private Roy Gorham from Michigan and Sergeant Bernard Mathew from Indiana nothing changed when their original adopters could no longer make the trip to Margraten. In 1965 the adopting couple's son appeared at the graves with flowers and silent thoughts. The young man had been only five at the end of the war. But the memory of the liberation's happiness and joy had never left him. He had accompanied his parents to the cemetery from when he was a child and knew how much the visits had meant to them. He too could never forget the first Sherman tank in their street. Nor the first slice of soft white bread handed him by a kind American cook who a little later had tragically perished when his kitchen caught fire.[8]

By the mid-1960s too, changes in adoption certificates as well as all administrative tasks regarding visits and commemorative services were being handled by a new and experienced clerk at Margraten's town hall. On the first day of 1964, Felix Prevoo officially took over from van Mulken as secretary of the Limburg Committee with the approval of the Margraten mayor, the Limburg governor, and the NWGC. Prevoo had been one of the half-dozen young volunteers assisting Father Heuschen who by Memorial Day 1946 had managed to have adopters registered for almost all of the Margraten boys. Not only was he highly motivated to keep the adoption register updated and in good order, he was especially keen also to restore and safeguard the Margraten roots of the organization. Within months he had new letterhead printed reviving the name of the old Margraten Civilian Committee. In no time too, Prevoo was chastising journalists for daring to suggest that the adoption program had somehow originated with Emilie van Kessenich, the wife of the Maastricht mayor.[9]

This personal crusade in no way diminished what the committee's new secretary understood would be his first and most important task: to serve as a bridge between the local Dutch community and the boys' relatives in the US now that World War II threatened to be drowned out by history's accelerating maelstrom.

2

Governor van Rooy's Memorial Day speech in 1965 did not mention a single word about the war in Vietnam that was now rapidly escalating under President Lyndon B. Johnson. Instead, much of the emphasis was on those developments that promised hope, if not for a peaceful world, then at least for a peaceful Europe. The Limburg governor was happy to point to British Queen Elizabeth's recently completed "glorious tour of West Germany," which heralded some form of closure to one of the Old World's darkest chapters. And he announced that this year he would be leaving the Memorial Day service earlier than usual because of a special event elsewhere in the province later that afternoon. He was expected in Venray, together with a representative of Her Majesty Queen Juliana and the US ambassador, for the consecration of a new church dedicated to peace. The church had been jointly built by Dutch, Americans, British, Canadians and Germans, and was now to serve as a powerful symbol of reconciliation on the very spot where once had been fought a ferocious battle for the Siegfried Line.

Ironically, however, as the rapprochement with West Germany was made increasingly explicit, strains in relations between the Dutch and the US over the latter's role in Vietnam failed to stay hidden much longer even on Margraten's sacred soil. Turnout for the Memorial Day ceremony in 1966 was huge once again and traffic became hopelessly jammed on the main road to the American cemetery. But in his speech on this last day of May, the Limburg governor felt he could no longer remain silent about the conflict that was occupying the minds of so many worldwide and in his own country. Unfazed by the presence of the US ambassador and many other American officials and visitors, he stood up for a speech expressing his deep concern about the war in Vietnam and the sincere hope that it could be brought to an end as soon as possible.

Charles van Rooy no doubt felt obliged to speak out in 1966 because, even as the governor of a predominantly rural and traditionally quiet province, he could sense unrest building up. During the Memorial Day weekend that year, the 3rd US Armored Division band had come all the way from Frankfurt, Germany, to give concerts in several towns across southern Limburg. In all of these places, the American musicians were a big success and, according to the press, both their renditions of Dixieland and musicals like *West Side Story* were met with "wild enthusiasm." But those on the dance floor were decidedly out of tune with the more radical, leftist elements of a younger generation that considered American militarism an increasing threat to peace, not only in Europe, but also in a Third World where the superpower was seen as attempting to stifle legitimate social revolution.[10]

During the weekend of 14 and 15 January 1967, some 50 young radicals descended on Maastricht to create havoc and provoke authorities. Known as Provos, a Dutch movement with its origins in anarchism and radical anti-nuclear pacifism, their objective was a barracks in the city that belonged to AFCENT. AFCENT, short for Allied Forces Central Command, was one of a handful of key NATO area commands in Europe and was in the process of moving from Fontainebleau to the Limburg town of Brunssum as a result of France's decision the previous year to leave the NATO command structure. Throughout the weekend, police forces were engaged in a running battle with youngsters throwing bricks at the barracks windows, setting off smoke bombs, and torching leftover Christmas trees. As the Provos shouted "Charles van Rooy has sold us to NATO!" and "Vietnam!," police snapped pictures of the agitators and made several arrests.[11]

Things quieted down again until spring and the eve of yet another Memorial Day. Early in May, on the day when the Netherlands officially commemorates the end of World War II, a group of some two dozen Provos from Maastricht tried to provoke the authorities again when they marched on Margraten with the intention to place a wreath at the American cemetery's Memorial building. Dutch police forces blocked their way and American cemetery officials eventually managed to dissuade the Provos from forcing their way in, arguing heatedly that the thousands of American soldiers there "had died for the freedom of their country and not for politics."[12]

That same May, as 10,000 people of all ages and backgrounds descended on Amsterdam amidst much media attention to protest the massive and indiscriminate bombing of Vietnam, things further heated up in Limburg too. On Monday, 15 May, some 1,000 young people steered what one local newspaper called "a communist-inspired march" towards Brunssum. They had started in the north of the country and protested the presence of military installations in more than a dozen places before setting out for AFCENT. Here they taunted soldiers guarding the NATO headquarters, damaged several vehicles, and through loudspeakers called for the resignation of the West German commander of AFCENT, whom they denounced for playing a key role in the nuclear build-up in his own country.[13]

Not surprisingly, on Memorial Day at the end of May 1967, the Limburg governor again felt compelled to address the burning issue of war. Although he did use the Margraten platform to point also to the war that now threatened between Israel and its Arab neighbors, most of his attention went to the escalating conflict in the Far East. A good listener could not fail to detect criticism of the American intervention there when the governor said, "in Vietnam day by day people die in a fight between brothers" and "peace is a matter of the mind, of justice, and also of mercy." At the same time, however, his tone as an official from a tiny European country was one of frustrating impotence too. "We stand by helplessly," Governor van Rooy lamented, "and we are only able to pray that a peace of justice may be attained soon."[14]

The Vietnam War was so much more confusing than the war that the Americans soon would be referring to as 'The Good War.' World War II had been a war of moral clarity that, in large part thanks to the American military, had resulted in a peace of justice for the Netherlands and Western Europe. This conviction ran deep in Dutch society and allowed the loving care for the Margraten boys to continue unchallenged even as the criticism of America's Cold War policy in Vietnam gained force. Immediately after his wedding in 1966, a man from Heerlen took over from his parents the care for the grave of Hans Burkhalter. The American had been a merchant seaman from Wisconsin and in no way had been part of the liberation of Limburg. But the new adopter remembered how, as a teenager, he had seen his father and older brothers live in constant fear of being sent away as forced labor to Germany and how, after the liberation, the corpses of GIs had been brought back from Germany and laid out at the coalmine depots in his town. For the newlywed, the Wisconsin seaman too stood symbol for the American sacrifice that had restored peace and now enabled him to live the contented life of an ordinary family man.[15]

American family visits continued also as the introduction of tourist and especially economy airfares brought down prices for transatlantic travel considerably in the 1960s. Alvin Brodbeck, a mechanical engineer from Louisville, Kentucky, had been a married man with a two-year-old son when he was rushed to war aboard the *Queen Mary* late in 1944. In April 1945, Al was killed in the German town of Groitzsch, south of Leipzig, during a night patrol for which he had volunteered. The telegram with the dreaded news had caused his wife Mildred's world to collapse. She was left behind with their infant son, a piece of land they had bought in Louisville, and the blueprints for a home drawn up by Al himself.

Mildred had eventually left Kentucky, but year after year she went back to Louisville for the Memorial Day service honoring those of the city who had not returned from the war. Then, on Memorial Day 1967, Mildred at last had a chance to visit her husband Al's grave in Margraten. She must have heard the governor's barely veiled criticism at the address of the American government's policy in Vietnam. But she must have felt secure too in the knowledge that the Dutch in no way intended to aim such criticism at Al and the other Margraten boys. Any doubts about this were easily dispelled by the Dutch woman by her side. Liberthe de Graaff was 14 when an initiative at school had made her adopt Al Brodbeck's grave 20 years earlier. A grown-up now, acutely aware of the momentous changes and challenges facing her country and the world, she was determined to stand by Al's wife and his memory, no matter what.[16]

3

Criticism of the American war in Vietnam steadily spread to broader segments of Dutch society. In Limburg in October 1967, the Provo movement organized a Peace-In addressing the issues of Vietnam as well as the nuclear arms race. The happening appeared to appeal not just to leftist radicals, however, and the local press described it as "a giant success." In December of that same year, a peace march in Maastricht was composed of hundreds of people from all walks of life, including older people and clergy. The mayor of Maastricht addressed the crowd at the end of their march. "This year, Christmas is not a quiet time," he remarked. "Your presence here is a manifestation of the unease that many of us experience, an unease that is now being aired in Maastricht too." "That," the mayor said, "is a good thing."[17]

As was the case in the US, protests in the Netherlands escalated in the wake of the devastating Tet Offensive early in 1968, rocking even the political backwater that was Limburg. On Easter Monday in April, some 300 leftist radicals from the urban heartland around Amsterdam once again descended on Brunssum. They loudly denounced the US role in Vietnam and shocked bystanders by setting alight American flags. When, at one point, protesters threatened to storm NATO buildings, police decided they had had enough, drove them out of town, and banned any further manifestations. This caused the agitators to pull back to Maastricht. Police forces there managed to prevent protesters from across the nearby Belgian border from linking up with their Dutch brethren, and then engaged in a series of running battles that resulted in several arrests and left quite a few wounded.[18]

During this crucial time, Dutch Foreign Minister Joseph Luns met regularly with Secretary of State Dean Rusk and Ambassador William Tyler to discuss how the growing criticism of the US could be kept in check so as to prevent it from affecting relations between their governments. Indeed, during the Memorial Day ceremony at Margraten a month after the violence in nearby Brunssum and Maastricht, Ambassador Tyler and Governor van Rooy seized on the occasion to attempt a calming of the waters. The Limburg governor went out of his way in his speech "to testify of our loyalty." Without the Americans, he emphasized, we would have been "the slaves of Nazism." And without the Marshall Plan, the economic reconstruction of Western Europe would never have succeeded as it did. "They – the Americans – have to know that we have not forgotten that," van Rooy said, expressing satisfaction that peace negotiations on Vietnam had now at last started in Paris.[19]

Despite the governor's efforts, however, Memorial Day 1968 was one of confused and volatile emotions at the American cemetery. "They died defending peace," Ambassador Tyler said of the Margraten boys, "just like the American soldiers dying in Vietnam today." But Sergeant George Smith from Pennsylvania was well aware that Dutch public opinion was not that easily swayed to subscribe to such facile logic. He was present at this particular Memorial Day service to visit the grave of his father James. James Smith had been a 27-year-old private in the 14th Tank Battalion when he was killed in World War II, leaving behind a wife and four children. Glancing at the cemetery's sea of flowers and the countless adopters among the crowd, there was no doubt in George's mind that the Dutch had lost none of the love and respect for his father and the other Margraten boys. But as a member of AFCENT in nearby Brunssum, he had seen enough angry protests at the gates of the NATO compound to know that there were no such feelings for the Americans responsible for the Vietnam fiasco.[20]

Cold War emotions became even more tangled when, at the end of August 1968, Soviet troops in a most brutal fashion snuffed out the Prague Spring and with it any hope of a relaxation of relations with and within the Eastern Bloc. For several days, the Limburg press too headlined nothing but the shocking news from Czechoslovakia. Silent marches were held in protest across the province and thousands of high school students gathered in Weert to protest the Soviet outrage.[21]

On a Sunday morning at the end of September, some 100 men and women walked from Meerssen to Margraten. They were young, but far from leftist radicals. Many of the men were dressed conservatively, sporting a suit and tie, and in Groot Welsden a local priest celebrated Mass in their presence. They did not shout slogans against anyone or anything, but instead dedicated their silent march to a world of peace. The priest accompanied the marchers all the way to the Margraten cemetery, where they gathered at the Memorial chapel, took time out for quiet reflection, and then calmly raised their voices singing 'We Shall Overcome.'[22]

Earlier that month, another 130 Gold Star Mothers and relatives, the largest group yet, had arrived to visit the fallen of World War II. This time too the NWGC in Amsterdam had provided generous financial assistance, and this time too all of the Americans had been offered a warm welcome in households across Margraten and Limburg.[23]

John Klein was also given an emotional reception that year. He traveled to Maastricht on his own to relive the time of the liberation with the family who owned one of the city's hotels. Their hotel had housed the headquarters of General Simpson's Ninth Army. The high-ranking American officers had been courteous and generous, and the family had become good friends with John, then a lieutenant colonel. Now the Dutch family proudly took their American friend to Margraten where they too had adopted a soldier's grave right after the war. At the entrance to the cemetery, John came to a halt by the large wall maps. Arrows of inlaid bronze memorialized the Allied progress in the war against the Nazis, and with his finger John began tracing the Ninth Army's advances and regaling his host family with stories. As he talked and talked, several scores of visitors gathered behind him, hanging on to the American veteran's every word.[24]

4

The Dutch Ministry of Foreign Affairs considered the 25th anniversary of Limburg's liberation by American troops in the autumn of 1969 too good an opportunity for memory diplomacy to pass up. Though by now Richard Nixon had taken over from Lyndon Johnson as president of the US, relations with the new administration remained tense as a result of Vietnam. More and more, it was World War II that presented itself as the perfect conduit for highlighting shared values and causes in a manner that was not contentious. As early as mid-March, the head of the Dutch ministry's North American Bureau was sounding out provincial authorities with regard to possible commemorations.[25]

At the end of March, news came that former American president and hero of World War II, Dwight D. Eisenhower, had passed away. This made liberation's anniversary even more poignant, and immediately arrangements were made to have the Memorial Day service at Margraten preceded by an elaborate Mass dedicated to the popular general who had led the crusade against fascism. Early that afternoon, Prince Bernhard himself arrived in Limburg to attend the service at the American military cemetery.[26]

Less than four months later, yet another elaborate ceremony took place, this time commemorating the liberation of Margraten and southern Limburg. Plans had been made for close to 3,000 children to assemble at the cemetery on 13 September with enough flowers to put a bouquet on each grave. Several days earlier, runners had set off from Caen in France. They were expected to arrive in Maastricht with a torch symbolizing the light that the liberators had brought to the region all the way from the Normandy landing beaches. A large American delegation had been invited, including officials from the embassy and AFCENT headquarters. A special welcome was extended to those at AFCENT who were veterans of World War II. But Dutch and American visitors that day were especially delighted and honored to be in the presence of no one less than Her Majesty Queen Juliana for her second visit to the Margraten cemetery.[27]

Limburgers in 1969 were relieved to be able, in their relations with the Americans, to focus not only on World War II, but also on a brave new future symbolized by the awe-inspiring American endeavor to reach the moon. Mike Dawkins, a civil engineer from North Carolina, in an interview with a Limburg newspaper on Memorial Day, waxed triumphant about the landing on the moon soon to take place. Mike had been nine when he lost his father in World War II. He was especially sad that Private Edgar Dawkins had not lived to see the moon conquered, because he always remembered the story of how awestruck and excited his dad had been upon seeing his first German jet fighter shortly before he was killed at the end of the war.[28]

In the summer of 1969, the new US ambassador in The Hague, J. William Middendorf II, thanked the Limburg governor for his congratulations on the success of Apollo 11. Indeed, Governor van Rooy during the commemoration on 13 September made the heroic American cosmonauts one of the central themes of his speech, reveling in the mind-boggling wonders of technology that had allowed half a billion people to witness live on their television screens at home Armstrong and Aldrin walking the moon.[29]

Yet, despite all the lunar excitement, Vietnam kept pulling public opinion back to earth. Nixon in his presidential campaign had promised to bring an honorable end to the war, but as months went by doubts about the pledge grew. On Memorial Day 1969, the Limburg press had also interviewed a Mr. Collins from Houston, Texas. Like his brother, he had been a pilot during World War II. His brother had failed to return from a bombing raid against Düsseldorf and now rested at Margraten. "It is the same as 25 years ago," the oil executive said when asked about his view on Vietnam. "We did not fight the Germans, but the people who wanted to impose a system on other nations. Later in Korea it was similar, and in Vietnam too this is the case. That is why, despite all the suffering, you have to continue fighting."³⁰

The Dutch government appeared to agree and in May 1970 was the only NATO ally to openly express understanding for President Nixon's invasion of Cambodia aimed at destroying the North Vietnamese bases there. But Dutch public opinion strongly disagreed and widely criticized their government for its stance. So frustrated and angry were young people on the left that some 300 of them took to the streets in Maastricht that same month. They carried banners decrying the invasion of Cambodia, the bombing of Vietnam, and the killing of student protesters at Kent State University in Ohio. Many were hoarse from shouting 'Nixon Murderer!'"³¹

Despite the accumulating tension, relations between Americans and Dutch remained largely unaffected where it concerned the Margraten boys. Barely a week after the start of the Cambodian campaign, Dutch Foreign Minister Luns and American Ambassador Middendorf signed an agreement giving permanent character to all former temporary agreements that had been concluded with regards to the establishment and maintenance of the Margraten cemetery and the commemoration of American personnel buried there. Although the title to the slightly more than 26 hectares was to "remain in the name of the Government of the Kingdom of the Netherlands," the Dutch now granted the Government of the United States of America "the full and free use in perpetuity, without taxation or other compensation." The Dutch government also pledged to "further the conservation of the existing rural aspect of the area surrounding the cemetery and the preservation of the dignity and aesthetic character of the cemeterial site from unsightly or inappropriate structures or activities."³²

In September 1970, yet another group of relatives of the Margraten soldiers were welcomed into the homes of Limburgers with the support of the NWGC. The group was made up of some 110 Americans from all walks of life: bank tellers and dairy farmers, construction engineers and mailmen, housewives and students, real-estate agents and prison guards. Prior to the pilgrimage, the visitors had been asked to indicate their special interests. Their list of hobbies – photography, travel, art, golf, antiques – was a reflection of the kind of affluent society the US had become a quarter century after the Great Depression and the world war. Another list, detailing special requests, showed that the parents of the Margraten boys were slowly getting on in years, and that some were unaware of how much the Netherlands too had changed since the war. According to the organizers, one American lady had expressed preference for a stay in a Maastricht hotel "as she has arthritis and claims most of the homes in Holland do not have hot water."

But the special requests also demonstrated that the memory of World War II continued to haunt those whose loved ones had never returned. One family of four wished to be able to visit Grivegnée across the border in the hope of getting in touch with the Belgian family who they knew had befriended the soldier from Wisconsin shortly before he perished in the Battle of the Bulge. Another family of four also wanted to spend some time in the Liège area in Belgium because, in the words of the organizers, "it was the last place and only place he, Mr. Lynch, saw his brother while overseas."[33]

There was no lack of adopters keen on helping out with whatever wish it was the American visitors might have for the few days they were guests in Limburg. Most had been adopters since the end of the war. Others had recently been handed the torch by an older generation. One of the latter had gladly taken it upon himself to look after the grave of Herbert Reynerson, an Oklahoma sergeant of the 35th Infantry Division. His explanation for volunteering at the height of the Vietnam fallout was as simple as it was terse: "I owe him the life that I now have."[34]

5

At the start of the new decade, the clamor for peace became louder than ever. Governor van Rooy in his Memorial Day speech in 1970 emphasized that in the past quarter-century the Margraten cemetery had morphed into "a far greater Memorial than only a Memorial of the dead." "It has become also," he said, "a Memorial of the living, constantly reminding us of our commitment: peace."

On the same occasion a year later, he repeated this theme and now quoted Eisenhower's words in his first year as president in 1953, when the former general had criticized the excessive expenditures on tools of war: "There must come a time that we can spend this money on those who are hungry and who have no food, on those who are cold and have no clothing to warm themselves." The Americans made sure to signal that they understood growing Dutch concerns by adding to their delegation in Margraten that year Lieutenant General Julian Ewell, described in the Limburg press as a paratrooper veteran of the liberation of the Netherlands, currently deeply involved in the Paris peace talks on Vietnam as a military adviser to President Nixon.

Still a year later, the Limburg governor again harked back to the same message. "We have to," he said, "because the dead of yesterday have a right to ask for the peace of tomorrow." American Ambassador Middendorf on this occasion was happy to reciprocate by calling to mind his president's untiring peace efforts and in particular his breakthrough visit to the Soviet Union just days earlier.[35]

Yet, as Nixon backed up America's peace talks in Paris with an ever more ferocious bombing campaign in Vietnam, outrage and protests spread throughout the world and became more intense in the Netherlands than they had ever been in the 1960s. In January 1972, some 5,000 Limburgers took to the streets to protest the bombing of Vietnam. Later that year, a new Dutch government collided with the Nixon administration over the merciless Christmas bombing offensive. "Political Maastricht united in anti-bombing protest," a Limburg newspaper headlined three days after Christmas, and when on 6 January 1973 a national demonstration in Utrecht drew somewhere between 50,000 and 100,000 people, many of these were Limburgers too. The Dutch government, as late as 1970 characterized by the Nixon administration as a "model ally," now took the remarkable decision of lodging an official protest with the American government.[36]

For people like Baron Michiels van Kessenich and his wife Emilie, both of whom had invested so much in helping to maintain and cultivate good relations with the US, the shift in public opinion was hard to fathom and accept. For many years they had made certain to stay in touch with Lyndon B. Johnson through an occasional card with good wishes as the Texan rose from the congressman Emilie had met in 1946 to senator and vice-president, only to hear student protesters chant "Hey, Hey, LBJ, How Many Kids Did You Kill Today?" when he served as president of the US in the 1960s. "The Atlantic Family of free countries is passing through a very unpleasant era of its common history," Baron van Kessenich deplored in a letter written in June 1968 to someone he knew at the American Legion in New York. "National selfishness and revolutionary unrest seem to prevail," he said in words that Dutch and American student protesters alike would have denounced as reactionary, "and many positive dreams from right after the war are presently fading away."[37]

Although by then the baron had retired as mayor of Maastricht, his wife that same year was still actively involved in organizing the pilgrimage of 130 Gold Star Mothers and other American relatives to Margraten. It was these activities, together with her involvement in the adoption program, that had "endeared her," an American general wrote to her husband when Emilie van Kessenich passed away two years later, "not only to the American Battle Monuments Commission, but to the people of the United States."[38]

As late as the winter of 1972, Baron Michiels van Kessenich was lobbying hard, but without result, to have Harvard University select Limburg as the site for its Business School's overseas program. In the summer of the same year, he confided to the author of a biography on General Simpson, the commander of the Ninth Army whose headquarters had been stationed in Maastricht at the end of World War II: "Unfortunately, today the word 'Atlantic' no longer has the glamour of those days. I will never indulge in criticizing the Americans if they go somewhere to help restore freedom."[39]

But by 1972 for many in the Netherlands it had become impossible to see any parallels between The Good War's liberators and Vietnam's ugly Americans. Worse, by then, political fallout from the Vietnam War was beginning to have an impact even on the commemoration of World War II in Margraten. Early in 1972, Felix Prevoo, the adoption committee's secretary, sounded the alarm at the NWGC. He urgently needed more financial assistance, he signaled, to continue the annual Memorial Day procession of children carrying flowers. The reason for this was, he explained, that more and more of the Limburg municipalities were reneging on the contributions they had been making for this purpose without fault since 1957. Prevoo indicated that this situation was presenting itself because of the deteriorating economic climate. But the Civilian Committee's bookkeeping showed that the trend had in fact started in 1969, a time when it was not so much the world economy, but rather the image of the US that had plummeted.[40]

By the early 1970s it was clear also, however, that World War II was slowly receding into the distant past and that this was now somewhat dulling the public's emotions about the conflict. In September 1972, a group of some 60 American relatives of the fallen arrived in Limburg once again at the invitation of the NWGC. The NWGC that same year took care of similar pilgrimages in other parts of the country for three groups of British relatives and one group of Canadians.[41]

But it was the very last time that such events were to take place. The NWGC announced that as of 1 January 1973 it would close its headquarters in Amsterdam and stop organizing pilgrimages. The reason was, the NWGC explained, that too many of the parents of the fallen had either passed away or become too old to travel long distances. In addition, the organization noted, "the need among other relatives to visit graves in the Netherlands clearly diminishes." The NWGC would not cease to exist. But it would henceforth limit its activities to providing information about grave locations and the participation in commemorative services. This could now happen with the help of no more than a handful of people operating from town halls and their own homes.[42]

Even among the veterans themselves there were striking signs of a change in attitude about the war that had come to an end almost 30 years ago. On 27 May 1973, the 116th Panzer Division was to hold a commemorative service for its former soldiers and their relatives. Known also as the *Windhund* or Greyhound division, the German veterans of this elite unit had fought ferociously against American troops in the battles for Normandy, Aachen, and the Hürtgen Forest as well as in the Battle of the Bulge. At 1400 hours that Sunday in May, they were to arrive punctually at the American military cemetery of Margraten for the service. There they were to meet with what in correspondence in the preceding months they had referred to as "the comrades of the 1st USA Division," the American veterans of the equally elite Big Red One.[43]

But as time caused many things to change profoundly, the legacy of interconnectedness between Americans and Dutch adopters only deepened. In 1973, a 33-year-old Dutchman, who had gone to university in the US and met his American wife there, decided to adopt the grave of Sergeant Donald Forein as soon as he returned to the Netherlands. Donald, a paratrooper in the 82nd Airborne Division, had been killed near the Dutch town of Nijmegen on the very first day of Operation Market Garden.

But what really compelled the Dutchman to become Donald's adopter was that his wife had known the sergeant. She remembered him as a child from the time when he had accompanied his mother who was a hired help in their home in one of Chicago's suburbs. Even in the 1970s, Donald's family did not have the means to pay for a trip across the Atlantic. For the sergeant's Dutch adopter, it was little trouble to travel down to Margraten from Amsterdam from time to time, and even less trouble to correspond with all of the only brother's three sisters.[44]

The mother of Johnny Riddell in many ways resembled Donald's mother. From correspondence that had started in 1946, his adoptive family in Heerlen had learned that Johnny had been raised by a single mother who took him with her each time she went to take care of the household of a well-off family near where she lived in New Jersey. Her employers were kind and Johnny became part of their family and a good friend of their two sons. As he came of age, Johnny met a girl who everyone agreed was a stunning beauty. They got engaged and Muriel promised she would wait for Johnny until he came back from the war.

In June 1944, however, Lieutenant Riddell failed to return from a mission with the 447th Bomber Group. After the war, Muriel married John, one of the two sons Johnny had befriended at the home of his mother's employers. Johnny lived on in the hearts of both in America. And he lived on in the hearts of his adoptive parents in Heerlen too. In 1973, the latter's 31-year-old daughter took over the responsibility for his grave. In the years that followed, she spent eight vacations at Muriel and John's summer residence in Florida. In 2005, she took off from Schiphol airport in Amsterdam to fly to Pennsylvania and be with Johnny's fiancée as she lay dying.[45]

6

In May 1973, after many years of pleading for peace in vain, the Limburg governor in his speech at the Margraten cemetery was happy to cite the signing of the Paris Peace Accords as an indication of a more hopeful future. That same month, in The Hague, a new national government took office that was the most progressive the Netherlands had ever known. With the US retreat from Vietnam formally agreed to, the center-left Dutch government now shifted its attention to other issues of world peace, such as the enforcement of human rights, North-South relations, and the Arab-Israeli conflict.[46]

But American officials were quick to use the Margraten platform to sound dire warnings. On the same day that Governor van Rooy hailed the promise of peace in Vietnam, General Michael Davison, Commander-in-Chief US Army Europe, took to the stand amidst the thousands of crosses and stars. He paid tribute to the long-standing friendship between America and the Netherlands that went back to "the explorations of Henry Hudson in 1609." And he reminded his audience of "the Dutch tolerance of dissent" that had "passed into the fabric of our great nation." But he told that same audience in no uncertain terms that words and pleas alone would not suffice to ensure the privilege of speaking freely. "Sacrifice, of one degree or another," the general intoned, "is the price each generation must bear for its share of freedom. It is a privilege that is granted only to those who are willing to guard it and are prepared to fight for it."

A year later, however, Governor van Rooy continued to be unrepentant and again used Margraten as a bully pulpit for peace. He expressed regret that, 30 years after the liberation of southern Limburg, the ideals of peace had still not been fully realized as war was allowed to fester in several parts of the world. He called it "our human duty to act in due time in the spirit of the United Nations," lauded Henry Kissinger's untiring shuttle diplomacy in the Middle East, and called upon the American Secretary of State to keep his promise to seek not just compromises but "lasting peace."

By now, however, Americans and Dutch at Margraten appeared to be embroiled in their own version of ping-pong diplomacy. At the Memorial Day service in May 1975 it was US Ambassador Kingdon Gould's turn to rebound the ball and lecture the Dutch. He felt he was in a strong position to be frank about armed conflict as "a horrific and torturous experience." He starkly reminded his audience "that most who lie here faced terror and died in agony" and that "few willingly gave their lives, and few deaths in actuality were noble." "This was certainly true," the ambassador noted, "for those eight men of my platoon who perished in 1944 and 1945 and lie in this cemetery today." That is why he was just as concerned as others, he said, "that similar cemeteries will not be needed for the members of our armed forces today or tomorrow."

Yet, despite all that, Ambassador Gould, like General Davison two years before him, urged the Dutch to be mindful of the fact that sometimes war and sacrifice could not, and should not, be avoided. He harked back to the Dutch humiliation at the hands of the Germans in May 1940 to underscore "the fallacy of neutralism." And he went back several centuries when reminding his Dutch audience "that it took eighty years of incredible hardship and valor for the Netherlands to throw off the yoke of Spain."

"Do not," ambassador and veteran of World War II Gould warned, "confuse peace, in the sense of absence of military activity, with freedom." The real question that free societies had to face, he emphasized, and a question he admitted had become problematic in the wake of Vietnam, was "precisely when is it legitimate to commit our military power and risk the individual lives of some of our citizens for the benefit of the nation as a whole?" Or in other words: "How obvious must the national danger be?"[47]

Measured by that standard, there was little agonizing where it concerned America's involvement in World War II. Even in the midst of President Nixon's fall from grace, relatives and adopters of the Margraten boys went about conducting their own quiet form of shuttle diplomacy. It had taken Mary Brown 30 years to save for the trip from San Saba, Texas, to Margraten. During all those years, all that she had learned about her husband Alvin's grave had come from letters and pictures sent to her by his adoptive family in Heerlerheide. Alvin Brown had been a private with the 2nd Armored Division and had been killed aged 32 in November 1944. He had left Mary behind with two children. Alvin had never even had a chance to lay eyes on the younger, a girl named Zudora. Now Mary and Zudora were guests of honor at the home in Heerlerheide, shown around Limburg by Alvin's proud adopters, and accompanied to Alvin's grave in the perfect stillness of the American cemetery. "What I have seen at Margraten," Mary Brown remarked of her first and only visit to her husband's final resting place, "will stay with me forever."[48]

A gratitude similar to that expressed by Mrs. Brown befell a woman from Susteren who in 1974 had a chance to visit the family of John Bariani in America. John had entered the service from California and had fought with the 35th Infantry Division as a lieutenant until he was killed in a car crash in Germany on 5 May 1945, the very day the war officially came to an end in the Netherlands. From day one of the adoption in 1946, both families had been corresponding uninterruptedly and intimately. Still, the adopter from Susteren felt overwhelmed by the warmth of the reception that John's family and the broader community now extended to her. John's sister in particular was very excited. She took the Dutch lady on a tour of the hospital where she worked and proudly introduced her to her church congregation too. Everyone seemed to be aware of who she was and what she had done for John and his family. Even at the local bank people had been informed of her visit and knew about the adoption. "I just couldn't understand what was happening," the flabbergasted adopter recalled much later. "They are very grateful, that has amazed me. And it is such a small thing for us to do. They have done so much for us during the war."[49]

A big article on her stay with John Bariani's family appeared in a local American newspaper on 11 August 1974, two days after the resignation of President Richard Nixon over the Watergate affair. Nixon's resignation, together with the fall of South Vietnam a year later and the images of the last American helicopter escaping from Saigon, signaled the end of a contentious and painful era in American history and American-European relations.

In 1976, Charles van Rooy held his last speech as Limburg governor at Margraten's Memorial Day, and it was the first time in almost ten years that he did so without having to mention Vietnam. In that decade, Vietnam's dark shadow had spread all the way to Margraten. By 1977, exactly 20 years after they had pledged to make financial contributions to ensure the presence of children with flowers at the cemetery on Memorial Day, half of the Limburg municipalities had stopped doing so. It prompted the scandalized former mayor of Groesbeek, a town near Nijmegen where the 82nd Airborne Division had fought hard during Operation Market Garden, to ask in a letter to what remained of the NWGC: "Have they forgotten the suffering of 1940–1945?"[50]

The Vietnam fiasco had not failed to affect even parts of the adoptive community. In 1946 Sereda Feener had been one of the many Americans who had contacted Lucie van den Boorn in response to her offer to care for some of the Margraten graves. Sereda was 16 years old at the time and lived in the small fishing port of Gloucester, Massachusetts. She had told Lucie she didn't know anyone at the cemetery. Still, she had asked the Dutch girl to tend the grave of some soldier with the name of Russel K. in memory of her cousin who had gone missing in the war against Japan and remained without a grave. Twenty years later, both women were still corresponding. Sereda had never left Gloucester. But in a letter to Lucie she now again found herself worrying about the fate of a relative in one of Asia's faraway theaters of war. "My brother's son was home this week for a visit," she wrote in October 1965. "He is in the Marine Corps. I hope he does not have to go to South Vietnam."[51]

It is not clear if Sereda's nephew did indeed end up in Vietnam and, if so, what happened to him. But for one teenage girl in Limburg the fate of American soldiers in Vietnam was brought home in the starkest of terms. At the end of World War II, her parents in Heerlen had adopted the grave of George Williams, a sergeant from Illinois who had served in a quartermaster truck company until his death in December 1944. George was a friend of a soldier with whom the Dutch adoptive parents were still entertaining an active correspondence in the 1960s. In 1964 the web of relations thickened when the adopters' teenage daughter and Judy, the soldier's niece, became pen pals. Judy had one of the Dutch girl's letters read out on a radio station in New Haven, Connecticut, and this led to contacts with an American boy. Those contacts eventually turned into a close friendship when the boy happened to be sent to Germany as a soldier and was able to visit her in Limburg a couple of times. It was the boy's brother who sent a letter to Heerlen some time later, informing the Dutch girl of the soldier's death in Vietnam. It broke her heart. At about the same time, Judy's heart in America was broken with similar news from Vietnam concerning her husband.[52]

7

It was the Vietnam experience more than anything else that strengthened the Dutch impulse to regard the Margraten cemetery as a cry for world peace as much as a memorial for America's liberators. That impulse had gained force during the nuclear arms race in the 1950s and by the late 1970s had turned into a firm tradition, despite regular American exhortations not to lose sight of when wars might be just and necessary.

When Johan Kremers in 1977 took over as Limburg's new governor, he managed to weave his predecessor's peace theme seamlessly into his own speech on Memorial Day the following year. Margraten, he reiterated, was "a far greater Memorial than only a Memorial of the dead." "It also," he emphasized, "stands for a Memorial of mankind, constantly reminding us of our commitment not to war, but to peace." Meanwhile, Dutch public opinion was happy to sense that the Carter administration was ushering in a new era of human rights and nuclear disarmament. In 1979 Governor Kremers, who had studied at the University of California at Berkeley in the early 1960s, was elated to point to the recently signed peace treaty between Israel and Egypt as "a shining example" of President Jimmy Carter's "utmost endeavors in negotiations" that had led to "the almost impossible result."

But if by 1980 the Limburg governor was seeing more such "examples of establishing or rehabilitating peace among people," he remained well aware too that there were "frightening examples of serious disagreements." He again paid special attention to the specter of "terroristic activities," a theme that had first been raised at Margraten two years earlier, when the governor had mentioned what was described as the Western world's "terror psychosis." By then, in a world of ceaseless battle against guerrillas and terrorists, it proved easier to crusade for peace than to define what constituted a wartime hero any longer. The Limburg governor certainly struggled with the issue himself. He made it crystal clear that he regarded visiting Margraten and expressing gratitude to the American boys "our holy duty." But he was found weighing his words when he said, "Personally, I would prefer to call them all heroes, if we did not have to be so careful with the word 'hero.'"[53]

The long, dark shadow of Vietnam had done nothing, however, to obscure the heroic qualities of the Margraten boys in the hearts and minds of the adoptive community. Throughout the late 1970s, Dutch men and women who had been teenagers at the end of World War II stepped forward without hesitation to take over American graves from their parents. They had myriad good reasons for this. One man volunteered for adoption in 1975 because, he said without further explanation, "father was in the resistance and mother was Jewish."[54]

A woman who was 44 in 1976 began looking after the grave of Gussie Knierim of the 106th Infantry Division when her father passed

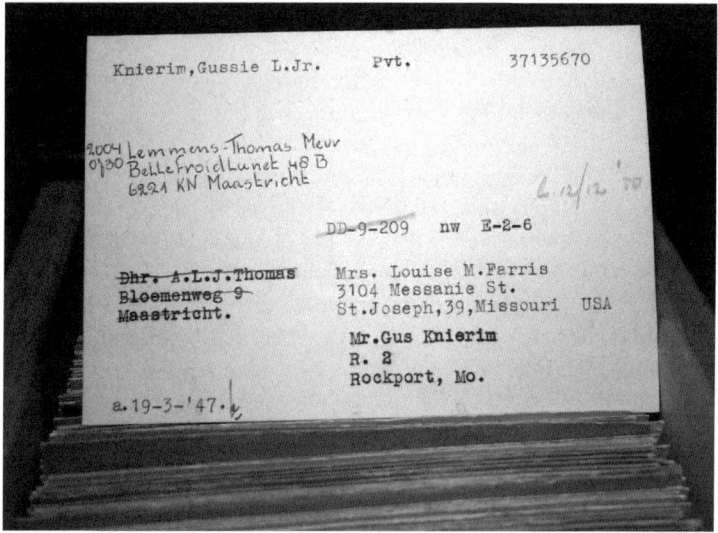

11. One of the thousands of typed index cards in the 1946 wooden chest of drawers linking European adopters with fallen American soldiers and their families overseas. This is the card for Gussie Knierim, an infantryman who grew up on a small farm in Missouri, and his adopters from the Dutch town of Maastricht. Today adoption data are safely stored in computer files and constantly updated. (Courtesy Maria Duizings-Croonen, Reijmerstok, the Netherlands)

away that same year. Her family had never known Private Knierim, but letters and pictures from America had told them that he had been raised in a loving family on a small Missouri farm. Gussie would forever remind his second-generation adopter of the war that had caused her great uncle to join the resistance and perish at the hands of the Germans together with several friends. And he would forever remind her of the American wounded in one of Limburg's local hospitals. Her father once had local musicians brought together to play the harmonica and cheer up the patients. But she also remembered that when the Battle of the Bulge raged and stretchers with badly wounded GIs were jamming the corridors, not even the mass on Christmas Eve had managed to provide the scared boys in the hospital any solace.[55]

In March 1980 a woman who had been 15 when American troops arrived in Limburg began tending the graves of a combat engineer from Maryland and an infantryman from North Carolina immediately after the death of her mother. "The Germans," she said, "had stolen my teenage years and the liberators compensated for that in part." For her, the war had been a time of air-raid sirens, blackout measures, and dashes for underground shelters – a time of constant fear. "The liberation returned to us the life we had so longed for," she noted. "We were able to establish contact again with our family in Halsteren and Amsterdam, we were complete again. Everything changed and it became light again." When asked almost 30 years after having taken over the adoption from her mother why she was so determined to continue the work now that she was almost 80, the woman's reply was quick and firm: "Because they are our boys and no one else is allowed to touch them."[56]

6 The End of History

"Hiroshima is everywhere!" warned the headline of one of Limburg's newspapers on 5 August 1980. The same slogan had been chanted the day before at a rally in Valkenburg staged to protest a frightening flare-up in the nuclear arms race.[1]

By then much had happened since President Carter had come to power promising an American foreign policy with a much stronger moral dimension. If the Vietnam debacle had left the US demoralized, it appeared to have galvanized the Soviets. Soviet conventional and nuclear arsenals had expanded on land and at sea, and when in December 1979 Soviet troops had rolled into Afghanistan for all to see, President Carter had decided to draw a line in the sand to protect American national security interests. It was the end of détente between both superpowers as engineered by Nixon and Kissinger at the height of the Vietnam War, and the beginning of a new arms race more dangerous than ever before.

As early as 1976, the Soviets had started to deploy new and improved intermediate-range nuclear missiles aimed at Western Europe. These SS-20s made the Dutch government and other political leaders in the Old World nervous and keen to look to the New World for answers. Some of the answers came in the form of new and more efficient nuclear weapons. In 1977 the Carter administration suggested the introduction of the neutron bomb into the NATO arsenal. Then, in the wake of the Soviet invasion of Afghanistan, plans for the deployment in Western Europe of nuclear-armed cruise missiles to counter the Soviet SS-20s were speeded up abruptly. On the other hand, however, there had been just as dramatic an acceleration in the Western European protests against the renewed nuclear arms race, and governments and public opinion were quickly shown to be completely out of sync.

1

For the Netherlands and Limburg, protests in 1980 like the one in Valkenburg, a town barely three miles from the Margraten cemetery, signaled the start of a mass movement that was the culmination of a period of unrest and contestation going all the way back to the Vietnam protests in the late 1960s. The movement quickly gained momentum when in January 1981 Ronald Reagan, a proud Cold Warrior determined to lock horns with an evil Soviet empire, was sworn in as America's 40th president. Reagan's unapologetic saber-rattling raised the specter of a nuclear holocaust. When it became clear that the Netherlands too was expected to accept deployment of cruise missiles on its soil, the peace movement burst onto the streets in unseen force.[2]

Already in his first Memorial Day speech of the Reagan era in May 1981, the Limburg governor at the American cemetery in Margraten unapologetically took the side of peace, now lambasting not just terrorism, but also "the growing arms race." Half a year later, Limburgers marched through Maastricht in protest and in November geared up for a national mass demonstration to be held in Amsterdam. On 21 November, a spectacular crowd of over 400,000 descended on the city. Many of the protesters came all the way from Limburg. They traveled to Amsterdam by train and in cars and on more than 100 chartered busses. One Limburg newspaper noted that many of the activists were elderly people. The same newspaper also stated that it wholeheartedly welcomed the Limburgers' decision to take part in the protest despite being known "as generally shy people who were conservative by nature."[3]

With tension over US foreign policy running as high as it had ever been in the Netherlands since the early 1970s, 1982 ironically announced itself as the 200th anniversary of diplomatic relations between both countries. That year, Americans in Congress introduced a House resolution designating 19 April, the day on which Prince William V of Orange had officially recognized the ambassadorial credentials of John Adams exactly two centuries earlier, as Dutch-American Friendship Day. The resolution aimed to commemorate "the longest continuous ties between the United States and any country of the world" and to extol this "as a laudable example for the kinds of relations that should link all the peoples of the earth."[4]

The Dutch government replied in kind and vigorously engaged in some judicious memory diplomacy, again gratefully involving the American military cemetery at Margraten. The Margraten mayor for the anniversary made a special effort to have a sufficiently large number of children attend the Memorial Day service, and he also ordered the design of a pennant commemorating the unique occasion. Queen Beatrix announced that she would be attending the service in person that year, the first time a Dutch queen had done so since 1969.

Governor Kremers on his part made sure to prepare an especially polished and appropriate text for his speech amidst the Margraten boys. In it, on that day late in May, he pointed to the "profound significance" the cemetery gave Dutch-American relations more than any other place in his country. Margraten presented itself not only as "strong evidence" of the sacrifices "a great and magnanimous people is prepared to make," but also as "a symbol of the present and future friendship between the two countries."

Even then, however, as had been the case on a number of occasions during the Vietnam era, words were slipped in between the phrases of praise that could be interpreted as gentle but unmistakable rebukes. "The world of today," the governor reminded his audience, "does not only know gratitude. There is a new threat of war. People take up arms against each other. Let us, however, preserve our belief in a better world. To some extent we can build the future ourselves."

Many Dutch people certainly believed that the Reagan administration was not doing its part to help build a better future. By the autumn of 1982, peace activists in Limburg had gone transnational, linking up in protests with like-minded people from across the border in Belgium and West Germany. As the Dutch government came under increased American pressure to decide in favor of the deployment of cruise missiles, public opinion became ever more outspoken in its opposition to the nuclear arms race. Even Governor Kremers in his Memorial Day speech at Margraten in 1983 reflected this mood when he remarked rather less gently than a year before: "Peace, freedom, justice. We use these words so lightly. They are often not more than clichés, empty of meaning or, ironically, even used to denote the opposite of what they stand for."

"We will not go from here without renewing a promise," Governor Kremers concluded his speech in May 1983, "the promise that we shall all do what we can to promote peace, freedom, and justice. This is what we owe to them who are buried here in the soil of our own Limburg." In October of that same year, the people of Limburg gave a clear demonstration of how much peace was on their minds when more than 12,000 of them traveled to The Hague to join another mass rally that this time took place in an atmosphere described as decidedly "grim."[5]

The Dutch were not alone in their fear of a nuclear holocaust. In the early eighties, similar protests against the nuclear arms race took place in the US and most other NATO member states. Moreover, even at this time of fundamental disagreement over nuclear arms, three quarters of the Dutch population remained in favor of NATO membership. All this served to bring back the dilemma that US Ambassador Gould had raised on Memorial Day at the end of the Vietnam War eight years earlier. Now, in the context of 1983, the core question sounded: for the deployment of new nuclear missiles to be legitimate, "How obvious must the national danger be"?

The poignancy of such dilemmas had always been felt the strongest in the presence of the Margraten boys. That had been true of Ambassador Gould in May 1975. And it was also what a former history teacher from Amsterdam experienced when at the end of October 1983 he decided to go to the American military cemetery instead of the peace rally at The Hague. The former teacher, in a newspaper editorial a few days after the rally, claimed that he had been alone with his thoughts at the cemetery that day. Before the altar in the Memorial chapel, German veterans of the Ruhr front had placed a massive wreath commemorating their own comrades as well as the American opponents who had died or gone missing during the campaign. In the distance, the American flag had hung half-mast, reminding visitors of the new enemies the US and its allies were facing as more than 240 American and some 60 French servicemen had been killed just days earlier in terrorist blasts in Lebanon.

To whom should he be listening, the Dutch teacher had wondered as he sauntered between the crosses. To the more than half a million people in The Hague giving voice to "the most legitimate worry of all times?" Or to people like Andrei Sakharov and Vladimir Bukovsky, courageous Russian dissidents refusing to succumb in "the shadow of totalitarianism?"

The teacher had halted for a few moments at the grave of Jim McCloy. He noted that the sergeant had belonged to the 306th Bomber Group, a unit of B-17s designed for the strategic bombing of another totalitarian regime's industries and cities. The Dutchman had walked away from the cemetery with his dilemma unresolved. "People were right to demonstrate in the capital," he concluded in his editorial. "But you, Jim McCloy, have not died in vain either."[6]

2

With World War II 40 years in the past now, there was a growing concern that the sacrifices of Jim McCloy and the other Margraten boys might be fading into the kind of history too distant for younger generations to have any relevance. In the late seventies, Helen Colijn, a Dutch author residing in California, had begun work on *A Portrait of Holland and the Dutch* for North American readers. She believed that such a book should contain a section on the American military cemetery and approached the Margraten burgomaster with a request for background information and photos of the graves and Memorial Day ceremonies. "And if future American tourists do not want to be bothered by something so sad," she commented, "well, just let them pass Margraten by."[7]

There was some worry too, however, that a younger Dutch generation might stop grasping the continued importance of Margraten and be turned off by commemorative rituals coming across as repetitive and stale. By the early 1980s, the Memorial Day ceremony had been honed to perfection by a succession of military attachés at the US embassy who were the only ones authorized to change the sequence of events at the cemetery or modify the service in any way. Each year, these attachés drew up what they called "after-action reports" and with military precision discussed such things as the number of plastic seat covers, the inferior quality of the name tags on the US VIP seats to those on the Dutch VIP seats, and the fact that the half-step of the wreath bearers was causing the ceremony to be too long.[8]

By 1983 the Margraten burgomaster was complaining that this approach was smothering any possibility of putting across a stirring message. At Memorial Day there were "always exactly the same people present," he remarked in a letter to the governor's office as he offered a number of suggestions aimed at bringing the ceremony closer to the people for the 40th anniversary of the liberation. One such idea, for example, was to invite a different municipality to the cemetery each year and to have them participate with bands, youth clubs, and other local organizations.[9]

The military attachés continued to be rather resistant to innovations with regards to the Memorial Day ceremony. But American authorities did try other ways to address Dutch concerns and breathe new life into the Margraten legacy among younger locals. Indeed, in 1983 President Reagan's newly appointed ambassador to the Netherlands, Paul Bremer III, immediately let it be known that he was interested in running part of the Caen-Maastricht relay himself. The so-called liberation relay had been held every five years since the early 1950s and traditionally wound its way through France and Belgium along the battle route that the 30th Infantry Division, the famous Old Hickory, had covered before its arrival in Dutch Limburg in September 1944.[10]

The ambassador's athletic feat did not fail to make the headlines in the local press. Neither did his decision to issue Felix Prevoo, the secretary of the Margraten adoption committee, with a tribute of appreciation on behalf of the US embassy at The Hague. The tribute thanked Mr. Prevoo for the "untiring liaison" he had provided between the local Dutch community and the American cemetery and for services to visiting American veterans and family members and commemorative initiatives that were "truly extraordinary."[11]

All this was true enough, but the irony was that at about the same time an article in *De Limburger* claimed that the adoption committee had "died a quiet death." Mr. Prevoo, the article explained, was moving mountains to keep the organization alive because he was not just the committee's secretary but, in fact, also the committee's only remaining member. The almost 60-year-old secretary was, the newspaper warned, "the last of the Mohicans."[12]

But even if the organization's structures threatened to crumble, plenty of embers remained within the adoptive community to keep the fire alive and pass it on.

A 31-year-old athlete who joined the American ambassador in the 1983 relay decided to adopt a Margraten grave immediately after carrying the torch of freedom from Normandy to Limburg. He had not even been born when Lieutenant Blanche was killed on 24 March

12. Felix Prevoo says a prayer for Sergeant Ralph Wheeler, a New Yorker who died when his bomber was downed in February 1944. Deeply involved in adoption since the end of the war, Felix at the start of the 1960s stepped forward to run the program's administration single-handedly for the next four decades. (Courtesy Felix Prevoo, Margraten)

1945. And he may not have been aware that this was the day in history when Operation Varsity commenced and joint forces of American and British paratroopers helped establish a foothold across the Rhine River. But the relay runner knew from older people in Limburg how ecstatic they had been to see Nazi Germany crushed. And it was enough for him to know that Edwin Blanche, a glider pilot from Texas, had somehow played an important role in that story.[13]

Two years later, a volunteer fireman from Eijsden of the relay runner's age also accepted the care of an American grave that had come up for adoption. John Vervoort was determined to find out all there was to know about Dennis Venne, a private from Wisconsin who had been killed in the 36th Tank Battalion at the end of the war. In reply to a letter sent to Milwaukee's city hall, the young Dutchman received a copied page from a phone book listing all people in the area who shared the soldier's last name. Dozens of letters and phone calls later, however, John had still not managed to get in touch with any close relative. The breakthrough at last came when the *Milwaukee Sentinel* agreed to lend John a hand and in no time managed to trace Irene Bielinski, Dennis's only surviving sibling and the youngest of eight children.

Irene had named one of her own children after Dennis and was more than happy to have the memory of her brother passed on. Dennis, she told the young Dutchman, had hated school with a passion. He had gone to work on farms in the Tomahawk area at a young age and during the Great Depression had moved to Milwaukee to work in a factory. When war broke out, Dennis tried to enlist but was rejected three times in a row because of physical problems such as poor eyesight. Dennis was allowed to wear the uniform only when the manpower pinch began to be felt most seriously. On 5 March 1945 his tank took a direct hit near the German town of Grefrath. A lieutenant who survived the ordeal but lost an arm in the blast later wrote to Dennis's father that his son had suffered severe wounds in the back. Dennis had been rushed to a military hospital in the Dutch city of Apeldoorn and had died there a month later, a few days before his 35th birthday.[14]

The Dutch adopter's interest in her brother's background meant the world to Irene Bielinski as she had never been able to visit Dennis's grave in person. Dutch adopters in turn were heartened to see that American relatives too refused to let go of the Margraten boys and continued to turn up at the cemetery in large numbers. Frank Berloth had been born in the Netherlands but, like many other Dutch at the time, had emigrated to the US as a young man in the mid-1950s. He had become an American citizen, served two tours of duty in the Vietnam War, and was eventually sent back to the Netherlands as an employee of AFCENT in Brunssum. Now, as the cemetery's superintendent for the ABMC, Mr. Berloth witnessed firsthand every day how emotional a journey the pilgrimage to Margraten could be. In an interview with a Dutch newspaper in 1984, he noted that many relatives were finding their way to the cemetery all the way from the US just to be able to touch the white headstone, gently brush their hands across the grass, and take back home a picture of a name chiseled in marble.

Personnel were always at hand to accompany next of kin to the grave. It was not just a matter of courtesy, the superintendent clarified, but a precautionary measure as well. Just recently, the sister of one of the soldiers had arrived with her husband to visit the grave. On the way from the office to the burial ground, she had to be told that there was no grave for her brother at Margraten and that all they could show her was his name among the 1,721 others recorded on two massive Walls of the Missing. Upon hearing the news, the woman had become unwell and the superintendent quickly had to sit her down on a nearby bench. Her parents had known all along, of course, that their son had gone missing in the war. But they had chosen to keep this hidden from their other children to spare their feelings, preferring to be buried with the heart-rending secret.[15]

3

Shortly after the interview with Margraten's American superintendent, the Dutch peace movement launched a final push and in October 1985 collected nearly 4 million signatures against the deployment of nuclear cruise missiles on home soil. The protests were to no avail, however, and a month later, as other European leaders decided to allow deployment, the Dutch government finally gave its consent too. The fait accompli instantly took the wind out of the peace movement's sails. Ironically, no further storms arose as both superpowers now began to signal a hitherto unseen willingness to engage in serious arms control negotiations.[16]

As the international atmosphere slowly became more hopeful, Margraten's adoptive community quietly continued to renew itself. For an adopter who had been eight when the Germans invaded the Netherlands in May 1940, the war had meant two things. An occupation where you "had to be careful with what you said to whom for four long years." And a liberation that had placed his hometown Brunssum close to the front line along the Siegfried Line and the Hürtgen Forest for six long months. With all that seared into his mind, he knew what was expected of him when by 1985 both his parents had passed away and the grave of Private McBrien of the 8th Infantry Division needed a new caretaker.[17]

That same year, a man who was eight when the Americans liberated southern Limburg in September 1944, had his name registered with the one-man adoption committee and took over the grave of Rocco Zuccarella, a sergeant in the 8th Armored Division, from another family. His own family had never met Sergeant Zuccarella, but they had been close to many other American liberators. One morning one of them had failed to return from a night patrol, and the now 48-year-old Dutchman vividly remembered the horror of scouring the Margraten cemetery with the soldier's comrades and the relief when some time later the soldier had suddenly shown up unharmed and with a hair-raising story of how the Germans had shot his jeep out from under him. But the Dutchman also lived with the memory of how more than a dozen combat engineers who had been billeted in his home were later reported to have gone down with the Ludendorff bridge when on 17 March 1945 it had suddenly collapsed into the Rhine ten days after its spectacular capture by American troops at Remagen.[18]

By 1986 President Reagan's willingness to engage with Soviet leader Mikhail Gorbachev more constructively was causing a collective sigh of relief in Europe. On Memorial Day that year, Governor Kremers felt optimistic enough about the new course in American foreign policy to make "the bonds of friendship" and "mutual alliance" between the US and the Netherlands the core theme of his speech. At the same time, he highlighted the welcome presence in his province of "some hundreds of American families" connected with AFCENT, the NATO headquarters that in the past so often had been the target of angry Dutch protests.[19]

Yet the governor's hopeful speech failed to dispel the nervous tension surrounding the event that year. A month earlier, President Reagan had ordered an air strike against Muammar Khadafi as the Libyan regime was thought responsible for a terrorist attack in Berlin that had killed and wounded American soldiers and European civilians. Protests had flared up again in response to America's perceived tendency to resolve issues with weapons and in Maastricht too a rally had been staged in April condemning the bombing raid.[20]

In the weeks preceding the Memorial Day service, the fear had been that the American military cemetery might form an excellent target for both terrorists and protesters. This had led to a dramatic overhaul in security precautions. Since the Provo incident of 1967, there had been no irregularities at the cemetery to speak of. Exceptions to this had been the theft in the mid-1980s of the silver flower bowl in the Memorial chapel, and a scuffle with a German fashion photographer who had deemed the cemetery an appropriate setting for a lingerie shoot.

Now, however, the American burial ground and the area around it were thrown into virtual lockdown. The number of Dutch security forces was raised dramatically. Bomb squads were sent in to sweep the visitors' stands. Military authorities and VIPs were provided with escorts on their way to and from the cemetery. Patrols were set to scour the premises throughout the service. Detectives stood by in police trucks equipped with everything from Polaroid cameras to fingerprinting equipment, ready to clamp down on any rabble-rousers that might show up. In the run-up to Memorial Day the following year, security guidelines drawn up by the Dutch police "with a view to the American character of the ceremony" were running close to 24 detailed pages.[21]

By all accounts, the Margraten commemorations in the wake of the Libyan crisis were able to proceed in complete serenity. Meanwhile, unperturbed by the ups and downs of global affairs, adopters continued to honor their pledges in the unassuming manner that had characterized their community from the very beginning. A man from Geulle who was 16 at the end of World War II decided to become an adopter in the course of his research into the fate of a B-17 named *Sizzle*, one of many aircraft lost during the calamitous raid against Schweinfurt on 14 October 1943. That Thursday, *Sizzle*, a Flying Fortress of the 305th Bomber Group, had crashed near Amby, a tiny village in southern Limburg. Of the crew of ten, four men saved themselves with their parachutes and were taken prisoner, while another not only landed safely, but succeeded in evading capture. All of the other airmen were killed, however, either because they had jumped too late or, as some Dutch witnesses later claimed, because the Germans had shot their parachutes to shreds.

Whatever the exact circumstances, the teenager from Geulle had been horrified to learn that Thursday in 1943 that one of the unfortunate crew had plunged to earth not far from his home just west of the canal dike. The story had haunted him ever since. Until in 1986 his research revealed that the soldier who had fallen to his death in Geulle was the aircraft's navigator, a lieutenant from California, and that John Manahan had been put to rest at the Margraten cemetery after the war and was now waiting for a new adopter to watch over his grave.[22]

It was research into another aspect of the war that led a much younger man to meet up with American veteran Larry Lucas that same year. Although the Dutchman had been born long after the war and lived in Gelderland, a Dutch province just north of Limburg, he was honored by Larry's request at the end of his visit to take care of the grave of his friend Joe Kukay, one of the Margraten boys. Joe had been a quiet and gentle man who came from a large family with one older brother and several sisters. In peacetime he had been a foreman driller at a limestone quarry near Lake Erie in Ohio.

When the war came, Joe was sent to Europe, and his brother John to the Pacific. In his last letter to his brother at the end of the war, Joe wrote how happy he was to hear that John had already arrived home safely. The next news that reached the family was that Joe was dead. A jeep carrying Joe and two other soldiers had hit a mine near a small village in Belgium early in June 1945. Joe had survived the blast and had been rushed to a hospital in Liège. He had succumbed to his wounds a few days later and more than a full month after Nazi Germany's unconditional surrender.[23]

4

By 1987 hope over arms control negotiations was transformed into euphoria when Reagan and Gorbachev began working their way towards an agreement that promised to ban all intermediate-range nuclear weapons in Europe, a ban that stood to make deployment of the just recently so hotly contested cruise missiles wholly unnecessary.[24]

On Memorial Day, the stunning development caused an elated Governor Kremers to envisage a future for the world brighter than any governor had ever dared imagine at Margraten since the end of World War II. "All of a sudden," the Limburg governor intoned among the crosses, "the dreams for which the young people who lie at rest here were killed so cruelly start to rise up again. All of a sudden we can once again have the dream that weapons be forged into ploughs, the dream that our energy be directed at those who really need it: the poor in the Netherlands and America and Eastern Europe as well as the hungry in the Third World – the needy in the four corners of the world."[25]

On the same spot two years later, with the deafening rumble of freedom rising up from behind the Iron Curtain, Governor Kremers described his hopes for the future even more brazenly when he said he believed "a united Europe" was "approaching day by day." That new Europe, he declared, would be one with "everlasting bonds of friendship" with the United States. And it would, above all, be a continent of peace. He reminded his audience that the Margraten cemetery lay next to the road that 2,000 years ago had been used by conquering Romans, two centuries ago by an ambitious Napoleon, and nearly half a century ago by invading Nazi troops. "Those who lie here have paid the ultimate price," the Dutch governor concluded his speech. "We on this continent have learned our lesson."[26]

With the outbreak of World War II now almost half a century away, however, growing concern that this lesson might not remain evident much longer had Mayor Kaiser of Margraten embark on an ambitious plan. On Memorial Day 1988, he hosted John Shad, the new US ambassador to the Netherlands, at the community's modest town hall in America Square and delivered a speech emphasizing the unique character of the adoption program.

He explained to the ambassador that since the end of the war the Margraten municipality had grown to encompass nine villages and was now made up of some 13,000 souls. Small as it still was, this made it the largest rural community of southern Limburg, a region whose inhabitants, the mayor observed, were "ordinary people with ordinary, everyday cares," many of them farmers, fruit growers, small business owners, and people commuting back and forth to jobs in the nearby city of Maastricht.

But these, the mayor pointed out, were the very people who had never wavered in their commitment to the fallen soldiers of the liberating armies and to their families overseas. "These people," he said to the American ambassador, "have stood at the graves of your bravest sons. Besides feelings of gratitude, they have felt sorrow, and they have shared sorrow." This had been carried on for two generations, the Margraten mayor noted, and it now was his sincere wish to have the torch passed on to the next. "The grandchildren of the generation that grew up during the war," he announced, "now occupy centre stage."[27]

For Mayor Kaiser the speech was part of an effort to convince American authorities that the time had come to solidify the special relationship between their people and his for future generations. In his mind, this could best be done by erecting what he called a Memorial Hall, a building in the immediate vicinity of the cemetery that would consist of a space for commemorative activities as well as an information center documenting the liberation in 1944, the adoption program, and the many friendly relations between Dutch and American families that had sprung from this over the years.

The mayor was particularly keen on having Ambassador Shad assert his influence with the military authorities of the ABMC in Paris and Washington. This the ambassador did late in 1988, describing the Margraten mayor to Major General Adams of the ABMC in Washington as "a good friend of the United States" and the Memorial Hall project as an "entirely non-commercial" venture that would make "a positive contribution to Dutch-American relations."

From the very beginning, however, Major General Adams' response to the project was lukewarm at best. The ABMC had always been extremely protective of America's overseas cemeteries and highly suspicious of any foreign initiatives regarding these sacred spots for fear that the serenity they deserved might become compromised one way or the other. In June 1989, the full board of the ABMC during its annual meeting discussed the Margraten proposal and put it to a vote. In a letter to Herman Kaiser two weeks later, Major General Adams complimented the mayor on the concept of the Memorial Hall, but regretted to have to communicate to him that "because regulations require that our cemeteries operate as separate entities, any addition to a cemetery such as you propose would violate those regulations."[28]

The weight of bureaucratic objections soon caused the mayor's grand vision to collapse. But, as had been the case since the end of the war and the refusal to have American home addresses released, it failed to snuff out what lived in the hearts and minds of the 'ordinary people' in and around Margraten.

In 1988 a 30-year-old woman from Valkenburg took over the grave of a Louisiana airman, who had been killed in a raid against Bremen in 1943, because her mother was now suffering from dementia. Another Limburger, who took over from her parents at about the same time, explained that she accepted responsibility for Pennsylvanian Private Louis Smith of the 104th Infantry Division simply because "That is what you did." For a man from Maastricht who registered as a new adopter in 1988, the decision was even more self-evident. He had been 18 at the time of Limburg's liberation and within days had taken up weapons and joined the American troops in their push towards Nazi Germany. Nothing filled him with more pride, now that he had reached the age of retirement, than to keep vigil over John Aaron, an Oklahoman from the 2nd Armored Division whose crack troops he had once fought shoulder-to-shoulder with.[29]

Similar pride filled an Italian veteran who had also fought on the side of the GIs, but as a soldier in the 210th Italian Infantry Division that had formed part of the US Fifth Army. His son had married a girl from Limburg and now lived on the other side of the Alps. He regretted being so far away from them. But he felt assured they were responsible kids when shortly after their wedding they announced they had decided to adopt the grave of Margraten boy Reuben Mims, an Alabaman from the glider infantry who had been killed in the Netherlands in September 1944. They had done so, they told the approving Italian veteran, "as a kind of tribute to those who died for our country at a moment in time where they themselves were at an age to be thinking of marriage and a beautiful future."[30]

A woman who had been 15 during the liberation of Maastricht in September 1944 had immediately volunteered as an adopter after the war and corresponded with the mother of the soldier until his body had been repatriated to New Mexico at the end of the decade. She had then been assigned the grave of George Knutson, a PFC in a field artillery battalion who had been killed in April 1945. It took the Dutch woman a long time to obtain George's home address, and when she finally did, she learned that the soldier's parents were already deceased. Quite unexpectedly, however, an answer came from George's brother who now lived in La Crosse, Wisconsin, with his wife and children. Still more surprising was the news that George's brother in 1944 had in fact been one of the liberators of her hometown Maastricht. After years of regular correspondence, George's adopter and her family decided to drop by his brother in Wisconsin during a trip to the States in the late 1980s. They stayed at his home for a couple of days and it was a time full of stories about George and the battle for Maastricht. "These folks," the emotional veteran at one point said to his wife, "understand better what I have been through than you people here."[31]

5

As the Iron Curtain lifted in Europe and the wall of shame in Berlin came tumbling down, Limburg's acting governor in 1990 asked the assembled visitors at Margraten to ponder not only the start of World War II in the Netherlands exactly 50 years ago, but also "the greatest transformation that the world has experienced since the war." The governor himself admitted that he considered the "vast changes" that had taken place in such a short time "barely comprehensible."[32]

Indeed, there were those now in the US who were heralding 'The End of History.' This may have sounded plausible from the perspective of the crushing defeat of two totalitarian regimes in a row and the unique victory of the liberal capitalism and democracy that had the US as its supreme leader. But there were those in Europe who feared that some in the US might seize on this unique occasion to espouse a return to a much less interventionist and multilateral stance and one that would inevitably erode transatlantic relations. For countries like the Netherlands that remained convinced, despite serious disagreements with the US in several crises, that American military and diplomatic might was indispensable for European security, this was a worrying prospect.[33]

On 19 April 1990, Dutch-American Friendship Day, Susan Eisenhower, granddaughter of the World War II hero and former American president, in the company of Burgomaster Herman Kaiser, placed a wreath on the grave of one of the 106 unknown soldiers buried at Margraten. A consultant in US relations with what was now known as the Russian Federation, she had been invited over to speak at a conference in Maastricht on the occasion of the 100th anniversary of the birth of her illustrious grandfather to whom the city had also dedicated a temporary exhibition. Susan Eisenhower put most of the emphasis on the importance for the US and other wealthy industrialized nations of providing Eastern Europe and Russia with much-needed economic support. The representative for the Dutch Ministry of Foreign Affairs, however, made sure to use the occasion to build a strong case for the continued relevance of NATO, while issuing a warning that American forces should remain stationed in Europe to ensure peace even at a time when East and West appeared to be moving closer together.[34]

The End of History also begged the question of whether World War II in such a dramatically altered setting would continue to possess any relevance for much longer. In June 1990, an exhibition opened in one of the villages not far from the Margraten cemetery. Its purpose was to commemorate the start of the war half a century ago and to demonstrate the tremendous impact the conflict had had on southern Limburg by focusing on aspects such as the German invasion, the Nazi occupation, the Dutch resistance, and the American liberation. Turnout was very high. Indeed, the exhibition was such a success that soon there was talk in the press of yet another plan to try and create a kind of permanent museum along the Rijksweg and close to the American cemetery.

The endeavor that summer was not, however, without controversy. When, before the opening of the local exhibition, the organizers announced in the press that they intended to ban from it "any weaponry," some in the area were flabbergasted. A man from Heerlen argued that if they decided to go ahead with this, the organizers might just as well prohibit any display of the fascist symbols that had led to the war in the first place. What was wrong, he demanded to know, with showing American rifles or even a Sherman tank, the very weapons that had helped bring to an end the hated occupation? By the end of August, it was becoming obvious also that the financing of any permanent museum was going nowhere as local politicians fell to bickering about the costs, with one alderman complaining in the press that he considered even the financial appropriation for the temporary exhibition "a rather expensive affair."[35]

But again the adopters continued what they had been doing for so long now, regardless of any global upheavals or the antics of local bureaucrats and politicians. As America's Greatest Generation readied itself for retirement, more and more veterans were overcome by a sense of nostalgia for a time when they had been scared to death but young, far away from their families but closer to comrades-in-arms than some later claimed they had ever been to their wives. Many of these comrades lay buried in America's overseas cemeteries where they had remained forever young. By the early 1990s, these hallowed grounds were drawing graying veterans like magnets.

In May 1991, Bill Howland, a veteran from Gloucester, Massachusetts, on the eve of Memorial Day wrote a guest column for his local newspaper. He devoted the long article entirely to "one cemetery a continent away that I have yearned to visit for almost half a century." Bill explained that in November 1944, the very month construction began on the American cemetery at Margraten, he had arrived in the area with the 334th Infantry. He and his two buddies – Charles Rocchio of Rhode Island and Frank Bergen of New Jersey – were given a room in the modest home of August Maassen, his wife, and their two-year-old daughter Annie. Bill jokingly referred to himself and his comrades as 'The Three Musketeers.' Annie and her yellow pigtails always made them laugh when they arrived back at their Dutch home in Nijswiller late every afternoon. Annie's father loved to take the soldiers to the village café. The owner played Bing Crosby records on his Victrola and the regulars would vie with each other to buy the GIs drinks. Although of different religions, on Sunday the three American buddies went to the tiny Catholic church together.

Then suddenly, barely a week after arriving at Nijswiller, they were sent to the front line. Bill remembered bidding farewell to their Dutch hosts and Charlie saying, "I wish we could do more for them." The Three Musketeers became separated on their first day of combat. Charlie was killed almost instantly, running as a messenger. He was among the first to be buried at Margraten, just a few miles west of Nijswiller, and the Maassen family had lovingly adopted his grave not long after.

"So I long to see Nijswiller just one more time," the former high school principal now reminisced, "the apple orchard, the whitewashed house, the café, the road to Germany, the cemetery in Margraten, and of course, the Maassens, their daughter and her family, and where they live. And Charlie, where he lies."[36]

Several months after Bill Howland's public yearning for a return to Limburg, Tony Forcelatti was happily reunited with the daughter of his wartime host family in Heerlen and offered a tribute of appreciation by the town mayor. Like Bill, the New Yorker had never forgotten the many small gestures that had made a world of difference to young men far away from home. Caked with mud from life in the foxholes, Tony had come close to crying when the Beaujean family offered to wash his clothes and bake him some eggs. Upon learning that he was the son of an immigrant family from Naples, they had one day even surprised him by serving him a plate of spaghetti.

The reunion was everything he had hoped for and so much more. "In the United States we are a forgotten group," Tony remarked. "After all, who wants to talk about World War II or the American liberators today. Things certainly are different in Limburg."[37]

6

To make sure that this would stay so, Felix Prevoo, the Margraten adoption committee's 'last Mohican,' a year later launched a determined effort to mobilize Limburgers to step forward and take over as adopters from those who had died or become too old. The response to calls in several regional newspapers was enthusiastic and led to a spike in the number of new registrations.[38]

Many locals had informally taken over from parents or grandparents earlier and were now reminded that it was time to have their names added to the adoption record. One was a woman in her early twenties. Her grandmother, she explained, had always had a special bond with Frank Sonsini, a fighter pilot from Massachusetts, because she "knew how it felt to lose a loved one in a war." Her grandmother's brother, a veteran of the war against the Germans in May 1940, during the occupation had been caught as a member of the resistance and later executed in cold blood.[39]

Yet another woman, this one in her late thirties, was proud to continue a tradition that had been sacred to her father. An inhabitant of Margraten, he had been one of the civilians who had worked at the cemetery as a digger at the end of the war. "He was always very troubled," his daughter remembered, "when he talked about burying so many dead boys." For as long as he lived, her father sought solace in caring for the boys' parents and other relatives from America visiting the cemetery. From the moment organized tours of Gold Star Mothers arrived in the sixties, he had opened his home to them and on each occasion with his wife had moved into one of the children's bedrooms so as to allow the American guests maximum comfort. Until his wife died in 1985, every Sunday morning he could be found wandering the cemetery and at home no one had thought it strange for him to return with American visitors he had run into and offer them some coffee, a bite to eat, or even a place to sleep. When he passed away in the late 1980s, among his papers there were several adoption certificates and many letters from American families he had never mentioned to anyone. In 1991 six members of a branch of the family that lived in Sweden traveled all the way south for a visit to the grave of an Illinois private from the 79th Infantry Division. The relatives made the trip to pay their respects to American soldier Kenneth Peterson, but also to thank the Dutch daughter and her deceased father for having stood by him so devotedly for so long.[40]

Other Limburg families had always regretted having to give up 'their boy' during the massive repatriation of the late 1940s and now, almost half a century later, were pleased at the opportunity to renew their bond with the American cemetery in response to the call in the press. In one such family, Marijke had been 20 when in September 1944 the Germans had forced the inhabitants of Kerkrade to evacuate and escape life in the front line on the Dutch border with the Nazi *Reich*. Her First Aid training had enabled her to help her father, a doctor, to set up a field hospital for the treatment of fellow townspeople who had fallen ill and sustained wounds during long weeks of hiding out in their cellars. In that capacity she had developed many contacts with American military personnel who were never too busy or worn-out to lend a hand. It had been the beginning of a life-long bond with these men, and when Marijke married a Dutchman who had served as an interpreter for American troops during the liberation, that bond became stronger still. After the war, the couple even attended some of the liberators' reunions in Nashville and San Francisco. Although these men had belonged to the 30th Infantry Division, Marijke in 1991, now in her late sixties, was just as happy to adopt the grave of PFC George Berkey, an Oklahoman from the 104th Infantry Division.[41]

Among the new candidates volunteering for adoption, many had been children during the war and events had made a deep impact that kept tugging them back to that time ever more intensely as they grew older. One was a man who had been seven in May 1940 when German invaders passed by his home in Maastricht on their way to Belgium in motorized vehicles, on horseback, and on foot. It had been a hot day, and on his way back from the corner store, the boy had been stopped by a German soldier in a scout car, who had taken a bottle of lemonade from his hands, gulped down half its content, and then handed the rest back for him to drink. In the days and weeks that followed, the endless march to Germany of columns of defeated soldiers had been etched into his mind in even greater detail: the masses of disheveled Belgian prisoners of war, dejected French troops, and men in British uniforms playing sad tunes on mouth organs.

Then, more than four years later, the boy in the same road had watched ragged German troops hurry back home on bicycles without tires, begging bystanders for civilian clothing. On their heels had followed smart soldiers in fast little cars with large radios and sweeping antennas. The now almost 60-year-old man vividly remembered that when Dutch café owners had offered them beer for free, the GIs had been hesitant to accept and had asked locals to take a couple of sips first. At dusk that same day, people in the neighborhood had been loath to see the Americans pack up and leave, and they had only reluctantly let go of the soldiers after they had assured the petrified inhabitants that they would be back the following morning.[42]

Many too were the bittersweet memories that pushed another Limburger, who had been no more than eight at the time of the liberation, to join the long tradition of adoption. The dread caused by German soldiers stamping hobnailed boots; the sinking feeling that set in whenever air-raid sirens started wailing; and the sickening sight of an Allied aircraft caught in the middle of a web of searchlights. But also, on the other end of the spectrum, the sensation of tasting American chocolate or white bread for the very first time, and the outrageous fun, when the first snow fell in the winter of 1944, of riding a sleigh towed by a jeep manned by GIs who behaved like children themselves. Each time he visited Margraten now, all of these memories came rushing back in a jumble as he stood and watched the grave of Corporal Edward Kerr of the Big Red One.[43]

There were many more new adopters his age, and younger even, who experienced similar conflicting emotions during visits to the Margraten boys. The adopter of Lieutenant Nelson Ammerman of New York, for example, a boy of 13 in 1944 who had never forgotten the fear he sensed in American troops billeted in his parents' farm whenever they were about to push off to the front line. The adopter of Sergeant Raymond Russell of Louisiana, a 17-year-old rounded up by the Germans in the last days of the war together with other local men to dig foxholes and trenches for protection against merciless Allied strafing. The adopter of Texan Albert Martin who, although only two years old at the time of the dreadful hunger winter in The Hague, knew by heart the story passed down by his grandmother, which had him pointing up to the sky and Allied emergency drops, jabbering "food, food."[44]

Or the adopter of Private Ernest Lynham, a young child at the time of the Canadian liberation of her family in Amsterdam in 1945 who, now that she lived in Maastricht as a grown-up woman, had decided that the moment was right to adopt a grave with more than one symbolic meaning. On his headstone it said that Ernest was Canadian, but also that he had joined up with the US Army and fought and died with GIs in the 83rd Infantry Division in April 1945, not far from the Soviet allies on the opposite side of the Elbe River.[45]

For a father and son, the decision together to adopt the grave of PFC Warren Grunert from Minnesota after contemplating the call in *De Limburger* in May 1991 was dictated by the horrid memories of the Dutch hunger winter that in the final spasm of the war had cost the lives of an estimated 16,000 civilians. There was again much symbolism in this family tending the grave of a paratrooper. Warren had belonged to the 101st Airborne Division and had participated in Operation Market Garden, the very operation that, had it succeeded, might have caused Germany to collapse before Christmas and, in doing so, would have prevented many Dutch from starving to death.[46]

There were many men and women from families outside of the adoptive community who in 1991 thought it fitting to join the ranks for the first time and begin tending a grave in honor of the World War II experiences of their parents or grandparents. Combat engineer

James O'Laughlin had also been with the 101st Airborne Division in Operation Market Garden in the autumn of 1944. In 1991 his adoption was reactivated by a Dutchman whose father had served in the resistance and had been sent to a German camp as punishment. His father had survived the ordeal but had never been able to talk about it for as long as he lived. At his deathbed, the son had watched his father "go through hell," and he would forever remain convinced that it was because "he tried hard to tell his story at the end." It was a thought he always carried with him to James O'Laughlin, one of countless Allied soldiers whose combined strength had enabled his marked father to return home from Nazi Germany.[47]

Still in response to the media call for new adopters in 1991, a son and his parents in Kerkrade carefully considered how best to go about honoring the grandparents' war experience. It was decided that the young man's parents would ask for the grave of a Christian soldier. This soldier eventually turned out to be Ohioan John Murphy of the 101st Airborne Division, the unit that had fought valiantly and doggedly in the Netherlands among many other places. The son, on the other hand, made a point of putting in a request for the grave of a Jewish soldier. He did so in memory of his paternal grandparents. They had lived in Amsterdam and as market vendors had traded with several Jewish families who had become good friends. The Nazi occupation had quickly done away with the world of business and pleasure. At one stage his grandparents had hidden a small Jewish boy named David, until things had become too dangerous and they had been forced to call on the organized resistance to provide a more secure hiding place. After the war, the adopter's grandfather had made the rounds of various Jewish organizations, only to learn that very few members of the Jewish families he had once known so well had ever been seen again.

The man would have been proud to know that, almost half a century later, his grandson was paying regular visits to the grave of a soldier named Murray Davis, a New York sergeant of the 65th Infantry Division, and that each time he did so, he honored the Jewish tradition of leaving behind a small stone on the marble Star of David to say that he had been there.[48]

7 A Global Village

In the 1990s, while George Bush took over from Ronald Reagan, heralding the arrival of a New World Order, and Bill Clinton trumpeted the power of globalization, the government of the Netherlands remained a firm believer in North Atlantic security cooperation and a staunch ally of the US. Indeed, the Dutch actively contributed to the Gulf War against Iraq in 1991 and joined military operations against Milosevic's regime in the Balkans at the end of the decade.[1]

In that same decade, even the youngest American veterans of World War II were retiring en masse and slowly moving into the twilight of their lives. By the end of the nineties it caused many of what was now dubbed the Greatest Generation to discern the contours of their past more distinctly than ever and to point to World War II as a uniquely defining experience.

Not a few of those with siblings and comrades resting in Margraten thought this an appropriate moment to reach out to the Dutch adopters one last time. In 1996, for example, the 2nd Air Division of the 8th Air Force declared itself "extremely grateful" to be able to bestow a Distinguished Service Award upon the Margraten adoption committee for their "loving care."

The veterans of the 448th Bomb Group did a similar thing that very year. "We wonder," their Certificate of Appreciation said of the fallen, "what a difference their living might have made. Our love for them is unending. For us, the war will never end." And so, the certificate concluded, it was "with great pleasure and pride" that they now honored the Dutch for their own "great love" for these Americans.[2]

Still in 1996, Antonio Cabral wrote a letter to the adoption committee immediately upon his return to North Carolina from Margraten. He had, he explained, visited the grave of his older brother, a dream he had cherished for 51 years since Albert was killed at age 24. Attached to the letter was a photograph of a tall, wiry man strumming the guitar on his porch steps. The careless musician wore white shoes and looked very suave. He had left behind, Albert's younger brother noted, a wife and a two-month-old baby girl he had never had a chance to hold. "If the people of Holland are anything like the few we met," Antonio Cabral said in closing, "then I feel that Al couldn't be in better hands."[3]

Simultaneously, the sons and daughters of those who had fought and died in World War II now began expressing similar feelings. As they watched their own children turn into adults in the 1990s, they became more aware of how very young their fathers had been during the war, and how powerless and desperate the boys' parents and wives must have felt at the thought of them suffering in the front lines overseas.

Alece Egan had lost her father, a lieutenant in a troop carrier group, in March 1945 when she was no more than a baby. It took her almost half a century to have even "the first inkling" that Dutch people had adopted her father's grave and been caring for it all that time. By the late nineties, however, she was an active member of AWON, the American World War II Orphans Network that had been founded at the start of the decade, and determined to thank the adoption committee for the kind gestures the Dutch had displayed during a recent visit to Margraten with her family. "I regret," Mrs. Egan wrote, "that we have been so little aware of all you and the Dutch people have done to continue to honor our fathers. I can assure you that the members of our organization, now middle-aged, appreciate you and will spread the word of what you have done and continue to do."[4]

1

Meanwhile, fears that Dutch interest in the cemetery and its adoption program might dwindle as time marched on, appeared baseless as in the nineties there were clear signs of increased visits and a growing demand to learn how one could become an adopter. In an interview with a local newspaper, Frank Berloth, Margraten cemetery's American superintendent, noted that this trend had begun to swell around 1994, and he surmised that this had everything to do with the many commemorations organized to mark the 50th anniversary of World War II's epic endings.[5]

The problem was, however, that in Margraten the last of the Mohicans now was getting on in years too. Even when he retired in 1986, Felix Prevoo, the adoption committee's sole remaining member, had continued his heroic struggle to prevent the program's administration from falling into disrepair. Indeed, upon leaving his job at the municipality, he had received permission from the mayor to take the heavy antique piece of furniture and the tens of thousands of index cards with him. From his home, Prevoo had led a stubborn but doomed operation trying to update the status and contact details of thousands of adopters. In the past decades adopters had become increasingly mobile and changed addresses several times. By now also, many of the original volunteers had grown too old and frail to be considered active adopters any longer. At the start of the 1990s, the retired town clerk had even appealed to his children to lend him a hand in sorting things out in the scarce time they could afford away from work and families.[6]

Despite Felix's best intentions, the burden proved too much as the decade wore on. More and more of the Margraten boys' siblings and children approached him with requests for information about the adopters. In most cases, however, any reply to such an emotional appeal involved long hours of arduous detective work. Ron Hall from Saint Paul, Minnesota, wanted to know if the grave of his father, an infantry sergeant, had perhaps also been taken care of by Dutch adopters in the program he had learned about during a recent visit to the cemetery. But Felix was distressed to find, after a long and fruitless search, that Sergeant Hall's index card had somehow been misplaced among the thousands of others.

Jack Newman from Terre Haute, Indiana, had also just returned from Margraten. He was so impressed by the experience that he had resolved to write an article for the local press in which the Dutch adoption family of his brother, a private in a tank destroyer battalion, was to be a main feature. Yet the only clues he had were a photo of a woman and her two daughters at his brother's grave in 1946, and a letter and an address dating back to the same year. Felix sent a letter to the old address, but it came back. He wrote a letter to the municipality, but was told that privacy laws prohibited them from releasing the information he was looking for.

When the 30th Infantry Division Association forwarded a list of all 259 men from their outfit buried in Margraten or listed on the cemetery's Wall of the Missing, the Dutchman had to admit defeat. In preparation for a European tour with veterans of World War II, the association's secretary asked Felix to provide the names and addresses of all of the adopters concerned. With pain in his heart, the retiree had to inform the American that it was impossible for him to find so many updated addresses in such a short time frame, and that the best he could do was provide them with a handful so that the veterans might meet at least some adopters.[7]

There were two daunting challenges with keeping the administration updated and protecting the adoption program from sclerosis. The first was that it had proved impossible to stay in touch with all those who had registered as adopters. Over the decades, people had, of course, moved, emigrated, or passed away. Adopters had been asked to inform the committee of changes in their address or family situation but, as might have been expected, many had neglected to do so. In addition, there had never been an adoption newsletter, which, at regular intervals, would have enabled the committee to reach out and keep stock of address changes.

The second and more worrying challenge was that as long as Felix Prevoo remained uncertain as to whether this or that adopter was still active or even alive, he was loath to appoint as a replacement one of the many Dutch who indicated they were eager to get involved. This was mainly so because Felix as an old-timer knew better than anyone else the original adopters to be notoriously protective of 'their' boys.

The extent of the problem was clearly illustrated at the end of the nineties when an initiative was set in motion to find out which Dutch families were still actively caring for the soldiers from Oklahoma. Of the 70 letters that were sent out as a first step, most were returned as 'undeliverable,' and only four actually resulted in a reply. For the Oklahoman graves alone, no more than 120 of a total of 8,300 American graves, it took the better part of two years to establish with sufficient certainty which adopters were still active, and to register new candidates as replacements for those who were no longer.[8]

The only alternative to time-consuming searches like the Oklahoman one was an appeal in the regional press for families to step forward and inform the committee of the adoption status in their midst. Felix was behind such an effort in the newspapers in 1991, and again in 1999. But such appeals, though they caused large numbers of new candidates to come forward, failed to resolve in any systematic and satisfactory manner the issue of which adopters were in effect still active or not. As a result, in the course of the decade, new Dutch candidates for adoption quite often were assigned graves through no more than a lucky coincidence.[9]

Among those who counted themselves fortunate were a mother and daughter in Grevenbicht. Their family had lived in the small Limburg village during the war and had befriended Carl Hodges and Louis Hill. The two were married men from Marshall County, Tennessee. They had been drafted into the 79th Infantry Division in 1944 and had stayed in the Dutch home during preparations for the offensive against neighboring Germany.

Both men regretted having been separated from Harry Sweeney when he was sent to the 6th Armored Division after having gone through basic training with them at Camp Blanding in Florida. Harry too was from Marshall County and in the front lines both men often thought back to their goodbye with the 18-year-old in Lewisburg, the rural county seat, after having been allowed to visit their families for Christmas one last time before being sent overseas.

Forty-five years later, with time on his hands in retirement, Carl Hodges was determined to meet up with Harry again for the first time since their goodbye in the Lewisburg town square. First Carl tried to get in touch again with his Dutch wartime host family, and he was happy to find the family still firmly rooted in the same village. Then he asked his Dutch friends to help him locate Harry's grave.

Harry had never left Europe. In April 1945, Carl's wife, Betty, had sent her husband a copy of the *Marshall Gazette* that said Harry had gone missing in Germany earlier that month. Carl and Louis found the news hard to believe and kept hoping against hope. They were devastated when a copy of the same newspaper, published ten days after the end of the war in Europe, headlined that it was confirmed that Harry had been killed on 3 April 1945.

The news had left a nagging feeling that in 1992 Carl was determined to lay to rest with a visit to Europe. To their surprise, the Dutch family in Grevenbicht learned that all that time Harry had not lain interred in Luxembourg as Carl had thought, but in Margraten, not far from where they lived. Further inquiries established that Harry's original adopter by now was no longer active, and in honor of their friendship with the men from Tennessee, they instantly volunteered to take his place.

Carl's visit to Harry's grave in the company of his Dutch friends made such a deep impression that, when he returned to Tennessee, he immediately sat down to write a letter to the Congresswoman representing his district in Washington, DC, informing her of the wonderful gestures the Dutch had been sustaining at Margraten for half a century.[10]

Another Limburger, too, had sheer luck on his side in ending up as an adopter in the early nineties. For a long time, John Gouverne, a Dutch air force officer and amateur historian, had felt irresistibly drawn to the American cemetery. On one occasion, in a conversation with Felix Prevoo, the subject of American women in the military came up and the officer was intrigued to learn that four of the Margraten boys were indeed not boys but girls.

John Gouverne's surprise was even more complete when he was told that one of those girls, Lieutenant Wilma Vinsant, who had lost her life as a flight nurse, was currently without an adopter. The air force officer did not hesitate for a moment and immediately registered for an adoption certificate with her name.

Wilma had in fact been known all her life as Dolly because of her petite frame and small size. But her physique belied her staunch determination. With her Texan parents, a doctor and nurse in the Rio Grande Valley, as role models, Dolly obtained a degree in nursing in Galveston. Buoyed by the daring feats of Amelia Earhart, she went on to train as a stewardess with Braniff Airways. When war broke out, the frail-looking girl from Texas volunteered for service in the military, completed a rigorous training in air evacuation, and in 1943 was part of the first class to graduate as flight nurses.

Dolly was soon sent to Europe where she was involved in one dangerous flight after another, caring for badly wounded soldiers who were airlifted from the battlefield to hospitals in England and later also Belgium. On one of the English bases she fell in love with Walter Shea, an air force navigator from New York. By the beginning of the war's last year, they were married.

But their dangerous work continued. Walter saw more raids over Europe in a heavy bomber. Dolly now began to accompany casualties

13. Lieutenant and flight nurse Wilma 'Dolly' Vinsant from Texas. One of the four Margraten girls. (Courtesy John Gouverne, Maarheeze, the Netherlands)

on flights deep into Nazi Germany. On 14 April 1945, Dolly failed to return from one such flight as the C-47 Dakota she traveled in crashed near the German town of Eschwege, leaving all six aboard dead.

Neither Dolly nor Walter had any siblings and they had never been given a chance to start a family of their own. With the passing of Walter in 1994, however, Dolly still continued to be remembered in Texas with a hospital in San Benito proudly bearing her name.[11]

If the Dutch officer from Maarheeze unexpectedly found himself playing a part in the remarkable story of flight nurse Dolly Vinsant, the way in which fate caused a Brabant farmer to become a Margraten adopter was even more unusual. As he was plowing a field near Katerbosch on the Mook Plain early in November 1993, farmer Lamers was horrified to stumble across the remains of a corpse. He immediately called the local police.

Upon unearthing jump boots in an area where Allied forces had fought a bitter battle with the Germans during Operation Market Garden, the police in turn contacted the region's Liberation Museum as well as Dutch military authorities. Further examination prompted the Dutch to involve American authorities. Careful testing of the remains followed, first on an American military base in Frankfurt, Germany, and then in the Central Identification Laboratory in Hawaii. Finally, in the summer of 1994, the US Department of the Army concluded that the remains had been positively identified as those of Willis A. Utecht, a glider infantry lieutenant from Marysville, Kansas.

His next of kin decided that they wanted Willis to join the more than 8,000 other boys – and four girls – in Margraten. Under ABMC policy, and in agreement with the host countries concerned, all American military cemeteries are closed to burials except for the remains of the American war dead still found from time to time in battle areas of World Wars I and II. On 16 September 1994, on the eve of the 50th anniversary of Operation Market Garden, Lieutenant Utecht was given a final resting place in Margraten with full military honors. Many American veterans of the 82nd Airborne Division were present. They were joined by a large number of Dutch visitors.

Amongst them was the farmer who had unwittingly caused the 20-year-old paratrooper's name on the Wall of the Missing now to be marked as identified. He was proud to have come all the way from Brabant province to attend the solemn autumn ceremony as the adopter of the American lieutenant's freshly dug grave.[12]

2

The Dutch who were given a chance to become active as adopters in the 1990s brought to the program a renewed sense of purpose and energy. Many of them had been very young during the German occupation or had been born in the postwar era. With memories of World War II and the American liberators vague or secondhand, the desire to learn more about the soldiers whose graves they had adopted now became compelling.

To their frustration, however, the new adopters at the start of the 1990s often discovered that in terms of available research pathways nothing much had changed since the end of the war, with cheaper international telephone calls the only exception. In the standard letter accompanying the adoption certificate, Felix Prevoo made certain to state that for most Margraten boys the home addresses remained unknown. Adopters who turned to the mixed American and Dutch staff at the cemetery were advised that the search for American family members would be a well-nigh impossible task. Privacy concerns even prevented pleas to the US embassy in The Hague from getting any further.[13]

Many remained undeterred by such setbacks, however, and tried various other pathways. A man from Sittard, who had experienced the war as a child, turned to the Department of the Air Force in the US and from the historical officer managed to obtain a copy of the Missing Air Crew Report that told the story of the B-17 on which Sergeant Daniel Lempka had served as a radio navigator. To the Dutchman's surprise, the document revealed that when the bomber had been shot down over Bremen in December 1943, eight of a crew of ten had managed to parachute to safety and had sat out the rest of the war as POWs in a German camp. Still more to his surprise, the report also contained the crew's detailed wartime home addresses. Excited, the adopter sent a letter to all ten addresses with a request for more information. In the letter, he included a picture of Daniel's grave. The disappointment was great, however, when there never came any reply, with the exception of two letters that returned from the US with a grim stamp and the terse message, 'return to sender.' A letter to the city council of Hackensack, New Jersey, the hometown of Daniel's mother, remained unanswered too.[14]

A Limburger who had adopted George Greiner of the 82nd Airborne Division was more fortunate when one of his many letters to the US finally resulted in an address for the veterans association of the 325th Glider Infantry. He managed to have the editor of their magazine, the *Tow Line*, publish an article on George's Dutch adoption with a request for more information about the paratrooper from his former comrades. Many weeks later, a letter arrived in the Netherlands from Jim Trail in California. Jim had befriended George when he was assigned to F Company at Camp Scraptoft in England early in June 1944. Three months later, during Operation Market Garden, George was killed, just minutes after having had a quick chat with Jim while delivering K-rations to his foxhole. "Although I never managed to contact them," Jim told the Dutchman, "I do know he came from a loving, close-knit family in Altoona, Pennsylvania." But it had always bothered Jim that he had failed to get in touch with George's family after the war. Now, with this sudden jolt from the Netherlands, Jim sprang into action and, with the help of George's Dutch adopter, even had a flyer put together with an appeal for more information on George from family and friends. Still, although the flyer was distributed all over Altoona, the belated initiative in this case too failed to elicit any response.[15]

In some instances, however, extraordinary luck went hand in hand with dogged persistence to bring Dutch adopters in touch with American relatives even half a century after the war. A postman from Kerkrade managed to obtain from American authorities a Missing Air Crew Report for Lieutenant Dundon. Since Lewis Dundon was a fighter pilot who, according to the document, hailed from Glen Ridge, a small town in New Jersey, the Dutch postman thought it might not be a bad idea to write a letter addressed directly to the mayor. As it turned out, the mayor not only responded to the adopter's letter, she also helped him get in touch with Lewis's widow as well as with his sister. In the speech the American mayor held on the Memorial Day that followed, she made sure to quote to her townspeople from the Dutch postman's letter at length and with warm appreciation.[16]

In a similar vein, a family in Sint Geertruid considered their quest for more information about their boy from Tennessee important enough to warrant a letter addressed to the governor of the state. The governor's office too was happy to oblige, and in no time their assistance led to contacts with the GI's three brothers and a glowing article on the adoption in the local newspaper of Columbia, Tennessee.[17]

In June 1995, a young English teacher from Nijswiller was even more surprised to learn in a phone call that two of Jim Watson's brothers were currently in Aachen as part of a Victory in Europe tour and that they had contacted the US embassy in The Hague with the message that they desperately wanted to meet the Dutchman.

The teacher had adopted Jim's grave a year earlier, and when a letter to the National Archives in Washington remained without a reply for months, a member of the Margraten staff had alerted the adopter to the fact that veterans of Jim's unit, the 101st Airborne Division, had just recently paid a visit to the cemetery and left behind their home addresses in the cemetery's guest book. The veterans' response to the teacher's appeal had been immediate, and from various bits and pieces the Dutchman had been able to put together at least some picture of Jim's background and army career.

To have Jim's brothers now ask him to be picked up in the nearby German city of Aachen for a visit, however, was something the teacher could never even have dreamt of. Still, within days, the two Americans were walking the cemetery with their brother's adopter and spending time in his home regaling him with stories about what kind of a person the 22-year-old paratrooper from Pennsylvania had been.

In the years following the visit, American relatives provided the Dutch teacher with enough information on the soldier to constitute a small archive. Among these documents was the last sign of life from Jim, a letter to an uncle in which he described his first frontline parachute jump with youthful brashness, calling it "a sensation that cannot be compared to anything else." The paratrooper would be dead a week later.

The adoption brought both families so close together that when Jim's oldest brother, Tom, died several years later, the Dutch teacher was among the first to be informed of the sad news in a phone call from America in the dead of night.[18]

For a family from yet another Limburg town, the catalyst for their close ties with the American relatives of not one, but two Margraten boys, was even more unlikely. Their remarkable journey had begun on the day in September 1994 that paratrooper Willis Utecht from Kansas was buried after a Dutch farmer had discovered his remains on the Mook Plain the year before. The family from Eijsden had attended the ceremony because not long ago they had adopted the grave of a soldier from Willis's 325th Glider Infantry unit. At the end of the ceremony, they had talked about their adoption of Sergeant Howard Ulenburg with a group of 15 veterans who pledged they would do what they could to find out more about him. In the months that followed, Howard's fellow paratroopers were kind enough to forward all kinds of documentation to Eijsden. This included an after-action report that showed that the sergeant from Michigan had been killed on the same day and in the same place as the recently interred lieutenant from Kansas.

The veterans also managed to put the Dutch family in touch with two of Howard's sisters and a sister-in-law, all of them older than 80. The next of kin told the adopting family that Howard had been one of seven children and that he had been killed in the Netherlands shortly after having been rushed to the glider regiment as a replacement. A son of one of Howard's sisters was happy to cultivate relations with the Dutch family to the point where, during his visit to Limburg, he was invited to play his favorite instrument, the clarinet, during a performance by Eijsden's very own brass band.

But that was not the end of the Dutch adopters' wondrous journey with the Margraten boys. In April 1995, during one of the family's visits to Howard, an American walked up to them. The man was curious to know why they were at the sergeant's grave with flowers in their hands. When he learned about the adoption program, the amazed American wondered if it was possible to find out if a Dutch family might have adopted his father too.

After several phone calls back and forth with the help of Felix Prevoo, it emerged that the adopter of Private Bill McLean of the 505th Parachute Infantry had in fact passed away. Bill too had been sent to his regiment, badly mauled in Normandy and the Netherlands, as an urgently needed replacement. He had been wounded in a fight with the Waffen SS at Trois-Ponts in Belgium during the Battle of the Bulge. When he returned to his unit several months later, barely any of the men he had known were still around. Then, during action near the Elbe River towards the very end of the war, Bill volunteered to join a patrol put together to come to the rescue of some American soldiers pinned down by the Germans. He was shot in the head during the attack and it was only after Germany's surrender that his family received the news that Bill had not survived the war.

When the Dutch family from Eijsden learned that, at the time of his death, Bill had been married and a father of three children, none of them older than three, they were horrified. They assured the soldier's visiting youngest son that from now on they would be taking care of Bill's grave too. Not long after, Bill McLean Jr. in his own radio program on New Hampshire's WLNH 98.3 paid tribute to his father in Margraten – and to the Dutch who had promised to watch over him.[19]

It was gratifying for adopters to find that stubborn and meticulous detective work could pay off, especially now that World War II threatened to fade in the memory of those on both sides of the Atlantic. In the era of president and baby-boomer Bill Clinton, adopters were very conscious of the fact that each of the Margraten boys' stories retrieved was one rescued from oblivion in the Netherlands and quite possibly even in the boys' home country.

Like the story, for example, of Private Alex Lewandowski of the 102nd Infantry Division, researched by a young Limburg adopter whose ancestors too were Polish. The adopter's grandfather had ended up in the Netherlands after having been liberated in Germany as a slave laborer of the Nazis. His liberators had been American and, in a decision loaded with symbolism, his Dutch grandson had adopted the grave of a Polish-American soldier in Margraten. His respect for America's sacrifice was given added meaning when he learned that Alex Lewandowski was one of no fewer than three brothers who had been killed in World War II. Alex's brother Walter, a marine, lay buried in faraway Honolulu, Hawaii, while his brother William, an air force lieutenant, rested at the American cemetery in Neuville-en-Condroz in neighboring Belgium.[20]

The story unearthed by a woman in Meerssen too was one she was determined to keep safe for posterity. The woman was ten when she and her family spent five grueling days in a marlstone cave trying to survive the artillery fire that ushered in Limburg's liberation in 1944. She was in her sixties when she learned more about what Lieutenant Hewitt had gone through during the war. It was Ralph Hewitt's nephew, a retired Texan rancher her age, who was happy to send her the story in a big envelope.

Among the documents, there was a letter from one of few of the crew of ten who had survived the downing of their B-17 after a bombing raid against Magdeburg. The letter had been written in August 1945 and was intended for the parents of those who had failed to return. "The hardest thing," the radio operator from Houston confessed, "I have ever done in my life." The Texan had barely survived himself as he claimed that, upon parachuting into Germany, he had been roughed up by German civilians incensed at the destruction Allied bombers were unleashing. But that was not what was haunting him at war's end. It was the sorry fate of Ralph Hewitt and his other comrades. "It is about to kill me," he wrote, "and I could just sit and talk all day about each and every one of them."

Ralph's nephew had added a letter of his own to the envelope and in it he shared some of the more personal details about the Margraten boy. Like the fact that, although his uncle had grown up in a place in Texas with an enchanting name, life for Ralph in Blooming Grove had been full of hardship. His parents had not been able to care for their children and his brothers had ended up being separated to be raised elsewhere. On a much lighter note, the nephew in Texas was also willing to share that three of his grandchildren "have red hair as did Ralph Hewitt."[21]

3

With fading memories and unraveling contacts being an urgent concern in the adoption community, the sudden emergence in the mid-1990s of the wonders of the internet and World Wide Web amounted to a godsend. The Dutch caught on to the new medium with lightning speed. In about a decade, 86 percent of the Dutch population was connected to the internet, a usage density surpassed in few other countries in the world. Thanks to the internet, the adopters by the end of the millennium found themselves part of a rapidly shrinking world that was now dramatically redefining their relationship with the Margraten boys.[22]

Before the age of globally interconnected computer networks, it had taken a man from Sittard many years, and letters to no fewer than 100 US newspapers, to gather at least some basic information about the five soldiers he had adopted in the early 1970s. Even after more than half a century of laborious research and correspondence, to a man in Beek, Sam Slight, a soldier from a tank destroyer battalion adopted in 1946, remained just that: a name without a face or history. Then suddenly, when this adopter logged on to the World Wide Web, he was flabbergasted that, with the help of no more than a keyboard and screen, the new technology revealed to him almost instantaneously not only what Sam Slight had been through with his unit during the war, but also that there were surviving relatives more than willing to reminisce with him about Sam.[23]

The internet by no means guaranteed similar successes for other Dutch citizens watching over American boys in Margraten. Still, the research pathways that had suddenly opened up in the virtual universe appeared to offer limitless possibilities, and this newly galvanized the adoption community. Some at first simply used their computer as an extension of the means of communication they were already familiar with. When international calls became much cheaper in the nineties as a result of privatization and deregulation, adopters had often wished they could just pick up the phone in search of next of kin on the other side of the Atlantic. But without access to American phone directories this had proved largely impossible. Now, however, all that was needed was the American soldier's last name, some connection with a place, and a quick search in whitepages.com. It took the adopter of an infantryman from sparsely populated Montana exactly one phone call to someone who shared the GI's last name to find himself in touch with the brother's widow.[24]

A woman who tried the same approach for a Jewish soldier from New York inevitably found the going much tougher. First she simply went down the directory list with her finger, dialing the number of Weiner after Weiner. When that appeared to lead nowhere, she placed a series of calls to enlist the help of local rabbis in the hope that they would know more about the soldier's relatives. But if such efforts failed to bring this particular adopter any closer to Herman Weiner, others grew increasingly savvy in the virtual world while attempting to learn more about the Margraten boys. Adopters quickly discovered that they had to do no more than turn to the internet's increasingly sophisticated search engines. For some, just keying in the full name and rank of their soldier was enough to make them stumble across a website devoted entirely to their soldier on the initiative of relatives or war buddies. For others, feeding the military unit into the search engine was the start of a process that very quickly gave them access to everything from the titles of books on the soldier's outfit that could be purchased via amazon.com to original after-action reports posted to detail the outfit's battle record.[25]

The more intrepid gradually also found their way to the veterans' forums. These were springing up rapidly as both The Greatest Generation and their children became involved, posting various requests for information. Dutch adopters soon realized that nothing prevented them from participating and launching appeals of their own. English was, of course, the lingua franca in these forums, but for most of the Dutch born after World War II this global language no longer held many secrets. Opportunities to network and gain information in this manner were boundless. A website like armyairforces.com, to cite just one example, was devoted entirely and exclusively to the United States Army Air Forces in World War II. Within a decade of the arrival of the internet, this site alone was hosting close to 300 different forums, neatly organized per bomber and fighter group. In addition to this free service, the site today also offers a number of simple research steps that lead to various links to rich online databases at no extra cost. One of these, for example, contains all of the Missing Air Crew Reports that in preceding decennia adopters had often found so hard, if not impossible, to obtain.

Even as the internet chatter swelled, however, there were still those who preferred to use virtual means solely as a first step to get in touch with real-life people willing to assist them with old-fashioned research. An adopter from North Holland, for example, managed to get in touch with the sister of Ken Staples, a paratrooper from Connecticut, with the help of staff from the Hartford History Center, whose email address he had simply plucked from the center's inviting website.[26]

An adopter from Eijsden reasoned that if anyone should be able to help with his search for information on a B-17 pilot from Illinois, killed in his 14th mission over Germany, it was the history department of the University of Illinois. The Dutchman was right: not only did the professors provide him with lots of documentation, their research also led him to the address of one of the pilot's brothers who was still alive.[27]

In yet another case, an email from Maastricht to the History and Archives Division of the Arizona State Library was all that was needed for the adopter of Theodore Bozarth of the 405th Infantry to be sent the soldier's obituary almost instantly. Something as simple as these few lines from a local newspaper for the Dutchman sufficed to have Theodore restored to a person of flesh and blood among the more than 8,000 names in marble: an Arizonan who had worked in the mines before volunteering for military service and whose life had been abruptly cut short at the age of 25.[28]

In search of such obituaries, many more adopters found their way to the websites of local newspapers in the states engraved on the soldiers' headstones. But reporters, curious and tenacious by nature, proved to be useful for much more than sifting through their newspaper's dusty archives or scanning microfilms. Robert Tappe's adopter, for example, was fortunate enough to make contact with a reporter from the *Pittsburgh Post-Gazette*. She wasted no time getting on the phone with people in the area whose surname was Tappe and before long was passing on to the Netherlands the home and email addresses of no less than the paratrooper's brother and sister.[29]

Backed up by the wonders of the internet, Dutch adopters on more than one occasion demonstrated they could be just as tenacious as any investigative reporter. One woman came close to giving up hope finding out more about the soldier from the 745th Tank Battalion who had been awarded the Silver Star when, on the advice of others in the adoption community, she tried her luck emailing funeral directors in the area. The gamble paid off as one of them remembered that some time ago he had taken care of the service for what he thought had been the soldier's brother. After some emails back and forth, the GI's nephew agreed to have the local funeral director release his name to the adopter in the Netherlands.[30]

There were those who consciously refused to employ the new technology to get in touch with families of the fallen because they judged the matter to be too sensitive for such initiatives and feared that they might be construed as disrespectful. Countless Dutch, however, were increasingly keen to get in touch with relatives of the Margraten boys, and they had myriad reasons for wanting to do so. Elderly adopters seized the opportunity to reconnect with American families whom they had lost contact with long ago. Or they did so to connect with relatives for the first time, hoping to learn more at last about the boys they had been paying visits to for decades. More often than not, they did so by appealing to the younger generation more versed in the virtual arts, thus unwittingly sowing the seeds of interest in Margraten among children and grandchildren, nieces and nephews, and teenage neighbors.

Even those who were not amateur historians determined to reconstruct a soldier's entire life story often found it difficult to let go once they had set out to find what initially was merely basic information. The enduring fascination with a Margraten boy's story sometimes was set in motion by nothing more, for example, than a superficial attempt to locate a picture to put a face to the name or a quick attempt to identify a date of birth so that flowers could be brought on that particular day.

At the same time, many of the new generation of adopters felt compelled to seek contact with American relatives for reasons that were little different from those that had formed the very core of the original adoption scheme at the end of the war. What motivated them to set out on their quest was to make families overseas feel better by expressing their solidarity. If not in terms of comfort and support, as had been the case in the 1940s, then at least to assure that the thousands of young men had not been forgotten more than half a century later, and that awareness of the family's ultimate sacrifice remained alive even now.

Whatever the motivation, and whatever the remaining obstacles, from legal concerns regarding privacy to American relatives occasionally suspicious of the true intent of Dutch inquiries, the results of the quest for the Margraten boys' stories in the internet age proved to be increasingly impressive and sophisticated. Perhaps most remarkable of all were the research results that now began to be delivered to Dutch addresses in fat envelopes by the US Total Army Personnel Command located in Alexandria, Virginia.

The most advanced searches that any of the adopters had ever attempted before the arrival of the internet had involved letters for more information about their soldiers to the National Personnel Records Center in St. Louis, Missouri. These archives contained files on deceased military personnel as well as on surviving veterans, and privacy legislation had made it very difficult for Americans and foreigners alike to obtain information. The Privacy Act of 1974 provided for the release of information only with the written consent and signature of the individual to whom the record pertained. In cases where the soldier concerned was deceased, the Center required the written consent of their next of kin. Confronted with all these restrictions, a mother and son in Limburg who had adopted two infantrymen from Massachusetts compared their inquiries at the Center in St. Louis to "asking for the key to Fort Knox where America is keeping its gold."[31]

Many more adopters had been shocked to learn, however, that the files on their soldiers had quite simply been lost. On 12 July 1973, part of the Center in St. Louis had caught fire. By the time the blaze was brought under control, flames had destroyed the major portion of records of army personnel for the period 1912 through 1959. No copies of the records had been stored elsewhere and so the information was lost forever. Before the advent of the internet, for many an adopter this hugely disappointing news had sufficed to put an abrupt halt to any further investigations into the background of their soldier.

By the late nineties, however, websites and emails were quickly touting the US Total Army Personnel Command in Virginia as a much better place to turn to for information. Adopters were told that here were stored the files on all American army personnel killed during World War II. More importantly, adopters learned that the agency in Virginia was allowed to release World War II casualty information in reply to a simple, written request under the provisions of the Freedom of Information Act. With the detailed address of the agency available on the internet for all to see, it did not take long for the first Dutch letters to find their way to Virginia.

If the adopters were pleasantly surprised by the ease and speed with which the American agency often responded to their requests, they were utterly astonished by the detailed nature of the information that arrived in the form of what was known as an Individual Deceased Personnel File (IDPF). For most GIs who died overseas there simply is no more valuable official record than the IDPF. The file almost always gives information on the soldier's burial, but in many cases also about when and where he was killed, sometimes even backed up by reports of the action in which he died.

Quite a few of the first Dutch adopters to receive such IDPFs were taken aback by the embarrassingly personal nature of the information jumping out at them from dozens upon dozens of photocopied documents. Many forms displayed the detailed addresses not only of parents and wives, but also of grandparents and siblings, information that for decades most adopters had found absolutely impossible to obtain. Other documents just as easily revealed that a soldier's parents had been divorced, for example, or that circumstances had caused them to lose custody of their children. Inventory forms detailed all of the soldiers' personal effects secured by the Quartermaster behind the front lines, casually mentioning such items as letters, combs, slippers, souvenir fountain pens, and highschool rings.

Burial reports even listed the personal effects found on the corpse, and a teacher in Maastricht was horrified to learn that many of the personal items on the paratrooper whose grave she had adopted had been too blood-smeared to return to his mother. For GIs who had gone missing and whose remains had later been discovered in temporary graves in Germany and elsewhere, the procedures of identification before being transported to American cemeteries had been meticulous and had ended up being recorded in much detail. This included, among others, the outline of a body where the official responsible for filling out the forms was bluntly asked to "black out parts of body not received at cemetery."[32]

Many more adopters averted their eyes when in the disinterment directives they stumbled across descriptions of the condition of the remains dug up at the Margraten cemetery in 1948. By the time the son of an American veteran of the 7th Armored Division put up a website in honor of his father and advised others on what steps they could take to reconstruct their dad's wartime story, he knew enough about the nature of IDPFs to caution potential researchers. "When you read these files," he warned, "you are looking at the stark reality of the horror of war and death. The files usually contain mortuary and medical records, and these may be painful for you to read."[33]

4

There was only so much that could be said about mortal remains and silent graves. The same had been true for the Margraten community in the 1940s, when Dutch and American families in their correspondence had gradually moved from discussing the dead to harking back to a prewar past and detailing the progress of their own lives. And it applied even more so to the Dutch adopters who now stood poised to enter a new century far removed from World War II. For many, the information in the IDPFs constituted never more than a starting point. Their search had always been, and continued to be, about finding out what kind of person a soldier had been before war had cut his life short. And the quest to find out more about an American boy's life for many was inevitably driven by a need to find out also who his loved ones had been and, if at all possible, how they had fared since the war had cruelly come between them.

A young woman who took over responsibility for the grave of John Eylens from his IDPF learned that the sergeant's aircraft had crashed near the German town of Piethen and that, before being disinterred and transferred to Margraten, he had lain buried there, his body wrapped in a mattress cover and hands tied with his dog tags. But the American sergeant's story only began to come to life when the adopter, with the help of the website of the 533rd Bomber Squadron, managed to get in touch with some of his comrades. That was especially true when three of these comrades turned out to have belonged to the very crew that had been with John on that fateful day in May 1944 when their Flying Fortress, the *Ole' Swayback*, had been brought down over Germany.

The adopter learned that their mission had been the large Junkers engine plant at Dessau, southwest of Berlin, but that the squadron's B-17s had come under fierce attack from Messerschmidt fighters as soon as they had started their bomb run. The men who had been lucky enough that day to save themselves with their parachutes and become prisoners had never forgotten those who had ended up in Margraten and other American cemeteries.

John Eylens in particular was remembered fondly. He had proved himself to be a bit of a hero when, two months before the deadly crash, he had saved his crew from disaster on returning to base in Britain from a bombardment of factories in Augsburg. While the aircraft was just 25 minutes away from the French coast, a short-circuit had suddenly caused a fire near the top turret. John, the aircraft's engineer and top turret gunner, had thrown off his gloves in the sub-zero cold. With his bare hands, he had battled the blaze, seizing the smoking insulation wires and ripping them out. With the fire under control, the relieved pilot had pulled the bomber back in formation and continued the journey home without further incident.[34]

It was snippets of information like this that for increasing numbers of adopters were turning the rituals of care for American graves into very close and intimate relationships even more than half a century after the war. The young man who adopted the grave of Robert Burgess was very impressed to learn from the sergeant's buddies in a forum on the 102nd Infantry Division's website what the circumstances of his death had been. In mid-April 1945, Bob and his platoon had been ambushed by German tanks in the forests near the town of Gifhorn in Lower Saxony. Bob and another sergeant, Joseph Peluso, had rushed an anti-tank gun to the scene, but their piece had taken a direct hit almost immediately. Bob Burgess was killed on the spot, while Sergeant Peluso had died of his wounds the following day. Sergeant Burgess had been awarded a Silver Star for courage under fire.

But it meant even more to the Dutch adopter to know that, according to a wartime comrade who had grown up with Bob in Mississippi, a highschool yearbook had once described him as "one grand guy." That same veteran also told the Dutchman that he would never forget that on the evening of his birthday overseas, Bob had joined him to quietly celebrate the occasion. Bob Burgess, his proud adopter remarked, may have been a courageous soldier, but he had been above all, "A man with a heart."[35]

It paid to talk with ageing comrades eager to reminisce about the war. But getting in touch with the next of kin sometimes proved difficult even in the age of the internet. When the adopter from Maasbracht was told that Bob Burgess had left behind a wife, but that the couple had not had any children and that she had remarried immediately after the war, something instinctively told the Dutchman "that it was better not to confront the family with the past."

For the fellow Limburger watching over the grave of the sergeant who had gone down with the *Ole' Swayback* in May 1944, a much more tragic find abruptly forced a similar decision. The woman at first counted herself lucky to have tracked down two of the sergeant's half-brothers. They had been small children when John had left for war in Europe, however, and they barely had any memories of him. John's adopter was nevertheless extremely pleased to receive from them two photographs of her soldier. One was of John alone. The other was of John in the company of his wife. The youthful look of both Americans tugged at the Dutch woman's heartstrings. Which made it even more horrifying for her to be told that the girl in the picture had not been able to cope with her husband's loss and had killed herself two months after her country had announced the final victory.

But, by the end of the twentieth century, those who could make a computer talk did not necessarily have to communicate with widows and siblings of the Margraten boys to piece together personal backgrounds. An adopter from Cadier en Keer, a small village down the road from the American cemetery, was keen to know what story lay hidden behind the fact that, according to the information on the marble cross, his soldier had died on 13 September 1945, more than four months after the war in Europe had officially been declared over. What made the story even more puzzling to him was the fact that the soldier had been a member of the 603rd Graves Registration Company, the very unit that in June 1945 had taken over responsibility for the Margraten cemetery.

Like so many others in the late 1990s, the Dutchman began his inquiries with a request for an IDPF. When the file finally arrived from Virginia, the documents in the envelope instantly provided clear answers to all of the adopter's questions. The report of death stated that on that day in September 1945, Michael Bekierski "had taken a vehicle without authority" and had "violated standing orders and thereby stepped out of line of duty." The reckless joy ride had ended in tragedy when the soldier crashed his vehicle in a Belgian town near the Dutch border. Michael, according to the report of burial, had died of a cerebral hemorrhage and was interred with a fractured skull.

But certain elements in the file from Virginia immediately raised a whole set of new questions in the mind of the Dutch adopter. The American soldier had died just five days short of his 32nd birthday in an accident all too typical of the rowdy atmosphere that accompanied demobilization in Europe. But how devastated it must have left his family on Starkweather Avenue in Cleveland, Ohio. Michael had entered military service in February 1943, and it was most likely that his family had not seen much of him since. How heartbroken must have been Michael's father, Casimir, identified in the file as the emergency addressee, and Michael's older sister, Anna, listed as the soldier's beneficiary together with her father.

The list of personal effects found on the body after the accident gave away nothing about Michael and his family: some German marks, a handful of Belgian notes and coins, and a silver "cameo style" ring. But the inventory of the total number of personal effects that Michael had left behind in the European theater of operations did provide some clues. Clues of a fun-loving bachelor who had carried two Zippo lighters, a camera and several rolls of undeveloped film, and one set of dice. Of a Catholic family that had armed their son with a New Testament, a missal, a rosary, and a scapular medal. And of a soldier who had longed to be home and had stashed away three address books, 14 letters, eight envelopes with pictures, and one photograph with frame.

For Michael's adopter, these intimate details prompted a need to find out still more about the American's family. But rather than write a letter to the old address or make phone calls to namesakes all over Cleveland, the Limburger set to navigating the new information highway. From behind his desk in the small Dutch village, he perused the online necrology files of the Cleveland Public Library, and through contacts with American archivists eventually managed to obtain the family's naturalization papers, together with various other documents.

These revealed more to the Dutchman about Michael's origins than perhaps even his relatives could have retrieved from memory. Casimir had been born in the village of Kurniki in Polish Galicia in 1881. He had brown hair and blue eyes, made a girl named Katherine his wife, and by 1905 was the father of two girls, the older of which was Anna. Four years later, Casimir and Katherine with their young daughters traveled to the German port of Bremen, boarded the *Barbarossa*, and embarked in New York to begin a new life in America. A decade later, Casimir had set down firm roots in Cleveland, where he worked as a blacksmith and carpenter to provide for a family to which had been added three boys, of which Michael was the middle one. Michael's ten-year-older sister Anna had the brown hair and blue eyes of her father, and in a photo on one of the naturalization papers she comes across as a soft-natured girl with a sweet smile. She held several jobs in Cleveland, first as a "candy dipper," and then as a cashier. When Casimir became a widower in 1942, however, many of the mother's responsibilities fell upon Anna's shoulders, which is probably why in the War Department's report on Michael's death she was listed as his beneficiary, together with her father. Michael's father had died from "acute cardiac arrest" no more than two years after the war, at age 66.

All in all, the information about the family's odyssey to America and their son's tragic return to Europe in Dutch soil gave Michael's adopter plenty to mull over each time he visited the soldier's grave.[36]

And yet, even in the brave new age of virtual experience, adopters readily admitted that nothing could top personal contacts with living relatives. For Richard Kunne, a young Limburger from the village of Spaubeek, the research into Ralph Willett's background was one of many unexpected twists and turns. Ralph was an air force sergeant from Nebraska who had died on 8 May 1945, the very day that the Allies officially declared victory over Nazi Germany. Richard's research journey commenced when the IDPF revealed that, on that day, a B-26 of the 387th Bomber Group had taken off from airfield Y-44 in Beek for a routine training flight and had inexplicably crashed almost immediately after takeoff. All of the six men on board the Marauder had lost their lives, including 35-year-old Ralph. "The first investigators for the squadron to arrive on the scene," an official American report stated, "found flowers strewn upon the bodies by the Dutch." Beek was only a stone's-throw away from Spaubeek, and the Dutchman was suddenly made to realize that the soldier whose grave had been assigned to him through sheer coincidence now turned out to have been killed in a field not far from his own home.

This startling piece of information convinced Richard to set out on a quest for Ralph's next of kin in the US. The Dutchman consulted the internet to locate the addresses of those in Nebraska who shared Ralph's surname, drafted a letter explaining what he was trying to do, and then carried two dozen envelopes to the post office to be sent to America the old-fashioned way. A modern reply arrived a few weeks later when Don Willett sent an email from Texas at the request of his parents who lived in the small Nebraskan town of Superior. It turned out that Don's father was one of Ralph's cousins.

As the Willett grapevine worked overtime and an article on Richard's adoption appeared in Nebraska's *Hastings Tribune*, the Dutchman soon learned that Ralph's parents and siblings had all died. But he was over the moon when told that the sergeant's widow was still alive. Lois Schuck was in her nineties now. She had no children from Ralph and had remarried after the war. But she had always kept a place in her heart for her first husband and was tremendously relieved to hear that the Dutch had cared for his grave all that time.

Ralph had been employed in Superior's cement plant before the war while Lois worked as a teacher. When Ralph entered military service, they were separated for more than two years. They wrote each other every week of the war and Lois had been heartbroken to receive her husband's last letter from Europe some time after she had already learned he was dead. At the time of repatriation in the late 1940s, Lois on the advice of the pastor had decided that it was better to leave Ralph where he was. Many in his family suffered from ill health and it was feared that the pain and stress of having the coffin shipped home and reburied would be too much for them to bear.

Lois had felt pangs of regret many times since that decision. She had never been able to see his final resting place in Europe. No one in his family had either, with the exception of one of Ralph's cousins who had briefly paid his respects at the grave on his way back home from the war. It was impossible now for Lois to visit Margraten. With her second husband passed away and both her hips fractured in a recent fall, Lois was stuck in a wheelchair in a Nebraskan retirement home.

If Lois was unable to travel to the Netherlands, the young Dutchman decided that he should cross the ocean and pay a visit. He had more than one good reason to do so. During his research he had, through an incredible stroke of luck, discovered that a local collector of World War II items was in the possession of one of Ralph's dog tags. Richard Kunne thought it would be fitting to conclude his search for the soldier's next of kin by handing over the memento with Ralph's name to his ageing widow. He eventually did so during a trip to Nebraska in the company of his father.

A visit to Bostwick, the town in Nebraska where Ralph had grown up, revealed that nothing much remained of the place, except for the cemetery where a weathered plaque near the graves of his family had Ralph's name engraved on it. Few of Ralph's personal papers and documents had survived his widow's move to the retirement home. Richard Kunne was happy to return home knowing that he had done much to rescue Ralph's story for future generations.[37]

5

Richard Kunne used his computer skills to set up an impressive website devoted to Ralph Willett and Donald Bell, the co-pilot of a glider plane adopted by his father. As more and more people learned to surf the future to save the past, there were those also who set out to create research networks among adopters. Their purpose was to provide assistance to those who remained less familiar with computer linguistics and to leverage their expertise. They did so much in the same way the so-called correspondents had done during adoption letter-writing in the 1940s, when English had still been a foreign language.

For a young woman in Hulsberg, the possibilities of the internet had proved a revelation when research into the background of her soldier suddenly took off several years after she had adopted him in 1994. It had taken Nicole Sproncken no more than a couple of emails to the newspaper and public library in Newton Falls, Ohio. In the hometown of Sergeant Charles Ticknor, a paratrooper who had been killed in October 1944, Linda Gordon immediately responded to the Dutch request for help as the mission statement of her library included the preservation of local history.

The assistance provided by Linda and several other townspeople eventually managed to bring the adopter in touch with one of the paratrooper's sisters. But it also led to a unique friendship as emails with Linda turned into phone calls and contacts with the Newton Falls community eventually led to an invitation for a visit. The visit was an unforgettable experience for both sides as Newton Falls' mayor was determined to involve the entire community in commemorating the sergeant's sacrifice and the adopter's compassion.

Before leaving Newton Falls, Nicole had given Linda a small sum of money to be spent on something for the library and to remember the paratrooper by. After some deliberation, Linda had purchased a bench for people to sit on and read in the library's History Room. On the bench was a little plaque that said "In Memory of Charles Ticknor." Nicole so savored the whole experience that several years later she had her hands full conducting internet research for a couple of dozen adopters across the country, and in newspaper articles on her work offered to take on even more.[38]

By the late 1990s, one of the region's main newspapers also had an investigative journalist devote much of her time finding out more about the backgrounds of American soldiers buried in Margraten. Each week, new messages arrived from adopters who had gotten nowhere with their own research. At one point, *De Limburger* announced that people would have to be patient because staff members were unable to handle all of the requests. Meanwhile, the outcomes of investigations that had been successful were being published in a special series called *Without a Trace*. For many in Limburg, the Margraten boys were part of their lives, and it was no surprise therefore that the adoption series had a large number of devoted readers who fervently discussed the twists and turns of each new story.[39]

That was certainly true for the unexpected development in the newspaper's story about William Long from Pennsylvania and the young married couple from Kerkrade. The Bronnebergs had volunteered as adopters when in the late 1990s they learned that no one was actively caring for the infantryman's grave any longer. Research now showed that William had been married when he left for Europe with the 83rd Infantry Division and that he was 29 when he was killed in December 1944. It was revealed also that, immediately after the war, people in Sittard had been caring for William's grave. For several years, this Dutch family had entertained close relations with the soldier's next of kin. William's family had even paid a visit to the adopters' home with the assistance of a translator, and a photo emerged of William's father and sister at his grave dated November 1947. Amy, the soldier's widow, had been sending pictures to the adopters in Sittard too: of herself, of her new husband, and of her baby daughter Carol.

Half a century later, in 1998, the Bronnebergs, William's new adopters, were very happy to learn that the newspaper had managed to re-establish contact with Amy. For Amy, however, the unexpected news from the Netherlands was not without complications. She realized that the time had now arrived for her to come clean with her daughter. For Carol, now in her fifties, the news came as lightning from a clear blue sky. She had never known that William Long had been buried at Margraten cemetery. Worse, she had never even known of William Long's existence. She had been born a month after his death, and her mother had pretended ever since that the man she had married when Carol was still a baby was her biological father.

It was hard for anyone to judge a woman, whose brief marriage had been destroyed by war at the age of 22, for the choices she had made to get her life back to normal as soon as possible. But it was a heavy burden for Carol to know that her mother refused to open up much about William for fear of causing pain to her second husband who was still alive. That is why Carol turned to the young adopters in Kerkrade for support in emails and telephone calls, and why she found herself on a plane to the Netherlands soon after.

The Dutch couple responded by trying to find out all they possibly could about her father. At one point they even traveled to Germany to visit the museum in Vossenack devoted to the battle for the Hürtgen

Forest that had claimed William Long's life. Carol was determined to pay another visit to her father's final resting place as soon as her Dutch friends had all the information. "Then," Mrs. Bronneberg said, "she wants to close a chapter in her life of which she was not even aware that it had been written."[40]

8   The Return of History

At the end of the millennium, it felt as if much of the weight of history had been lifted. After the defeat of fascism, the threat of communism too had been rolled back in what had been an epic struggle of almost half a century. Under the brazen leadership of a US that was now declared a hyperpower, liberal democracy and capitalism were being touted as universal models for the future. Exciting mobility and revolutionary communication technology were giving shape to a global village where people, many anticipated, would be sharing not only increased opportunity, but also Western-style values.

But on Tuesday, 11 September 2001, with the new millennium barely begun, history returned to the US and its allies with a vengeance. That afternoon, life virtually came to a halt in Europe and the Netherlands as word spread of ominous events taking place on the other side of the Atlantic. The Margraten adoption community too watched in astonishment as the World Trade Center, gleaming symbol of American power, came crashing down and dark clouds of dust and smoke gobbled up New York City.

In their Memorial Day speeches at Margraten, successive Limburg governors had been condemning terrorism as early as the late 1970s. But the events of 9/11 could not be compared to anything that had gone before. In the days that followed, shocked and frightened Dutch flocked to the American cemetery. Many of the elderly visitors in particular were shaken as fear of a new war caused the traumatic experiences of World War II to rush back to mind. Prayers were whispered at GI graves. Flowers piled up by the Memorial chapel and by the American flag fluttering half-mast on the far side of the cemetery. People patiently stood in line to write words of support for the American people in the reception room's guest book.

As a sign of respect for the victims of the terrorist attacks, the European Union called on its citizens to halt what they were doing and remain silent for three minutes at noon on Friday, 14 September. Margraten's municipal council issued a media release, in which it pointed to the many ties of friendship with American families that had resulted from World War II, and invited people to come together at the military cemetery that noon. Thousands did, young and old, and the flowers piled up even higher. Above the entrance to the Memorial chapel, large words chiseled in stone read: "In Memory of the Valor and the Sacrifices which Hallow This Soil." At the bottom of the stairs to the chapel, someone had put a letter next to a candle amidst the flowers. "57 years ago you came to help us," the message read. "Now we support the Americans in coming to terms with their grief."[1]

In the wake of 9/11, a new chapter was begun in the long history of insecurity and fear. NATO invoked Article V of the alliance's treaty, which states that an attack against one of the member states will be considered an attack against all. French newspaper *Le Monde* defiantly headlined, 'We Are All Americans.' The Dutch government agreed. It announced that it regarded the attacks on American soil as a declaration of war against the Western world. That meant that the Netherlands too now considered itself to be at war with the terrorists. When, later in the year, a campaign was launched in Afghanistan to destroy their networks and the Taliban that had sheltered them, the Dutch government fully supported the initiative as a legitimate form of self-defense and quickly offered troops for the International Security Assistance Force.[2]

But, as the world braced itself for the long war on terror, a new chapter was begun also in Margraten's long history of friendship and gratitude. In 2002, on a bleak Wednesday evening in November, reminiscent of the Wednesday evening in January 1945 when the Civilian Committee had been created, six people from Margraten and two from neighboring Cadier en Keer met at Margraten town hall. They were from very different walks of life. Fien Opreij, for example, who presided over the meeting, was a successful businesswoman. Jacques Aussems for many years had been a key staff member in Margraten's municipal administration. Jo Purnot was known as the region's indefatigable amateur historian. What brought them and the others together on this autumn evening was their concern for the future of the American cemetery's adoption program that for so long had been a key part of the community's memory and identity.

As they listened to 77-year-old Felix Prevoo's explanation of how outdated the typed and handwritten information on the thousands of index cards by now had become, they realized that if the program was to be saved, immediate action had to be taken. It was therefore decided by those present to form a committee that very evening to be responsible for updating the records, ensuring the continuity of the adoption program, and upgrading local participation in Memorial Day ceremonies.[3]

The new committee differed little from the wartime organization in terms of the drive and efficiency that characterized its operation. Even as the members met for the first time in November, the old information of 60 percent of all index cards on the more than 8,000 soldiers and their adopters had already been stored on one of the municipality's computers. It was Jacques Aussems who had been instrumental in convincing a somewhat reluctant Felix Prevoo that, for reasons of security and continuity, the time had come to have these records returned to their former home. Jacques had been persuasive enough also to have one of the municipal secretaries assigned the painstaking job of deciphering the index cards and rendering them into automated files.[4]

As early as February 2003, the new committee saw itself transformed into a legal entity that would henceforth be formally known as the Foundation Adoption Graves American Cemetery Margraten. By that time too, almost 80 percent of the information on the index cards had been computerized. This meant that the real challenge, the updating of the records, was about to begin. Aware of the tremendous work that this would involve, the Foundation decided to skip all involvement in the organization of Memorial Day activities for May 2003. It also called on more volunteers to lend a hand in establishing a clear picture at last of who could still be said to belong to the group of active adopters. In summer, the good news arrived that Margraten's municipal council had decided to bear a significant part of the costs involved in the massive mailing campaign.

Any help was more than welcome. The names of no fewer than 1,200 adopters appeared on the index cards with addresses that were incomplete or that no longer seemed to make sense. In the frantic days of early adoption, more than 400 American soldiers turned out to have been paired with Dutch names without any mention of an address. To add to the challenges, 60 percent of all addresses were old enough to be lacking the now vital zip code. It took several volunteers a very long time just to determine the exact codes. Then it took many more weeks of hard work to send out more than 5,400 letters to the addresses that had been cleaned up.[5]

In the weeks that followed, some 1,700 of these were returned to sender. It had been anticipated that something like this would happen 60 years after the war. But, as Felix Prevoo had already discovered in the nineties, the real headache was to decide at what point an addressee could realistically be removed from the list of adopters after his or her letter had returned. In most cases, the adopters had simply moved away a long time ago, making it impossible for the postal service to forward the letter. But that meant that the Foundation felt morally obliged to track them down to where they lived now. Even in cases where addressees had been reported to be deceased, the Foundation ideally wanted to ascertain if adoption of the American graves had not been taken over by siblings or descendents often known to be quite protective of 'their' soldiers. To find out, countless hours were spent gathering information through the grapevine, driving out to meet people, and placing phone calls to presumed relatives. Some volunteers were so immersed in their work and so stubborn and meticulous in their searches that they were soon admiringly being dubbed 'the detectives.'[6]

None of the Foundation's members were ready for the tremendous outpouring of support that their letters and phone calls set in motion across Limburg and far beyond. For those who had adopted a grave right after the war, the decision had often been a very personal one that they had not shared even with their children. Indeed, there were sons and daughters now who contacted the Foundation sounding quite emotional, admitting they had never known about this, but insisting they would be most honored to continue a tradition their parents had obviously considered very close to their hearts.

Others approached the Foundation to say they had aspired to be an adopter for years, but had never realized that graves had become available. These people now scrambled to have their names placed on the list. One of them was a middle-aged housewife from Stein who said she had been visiting the cemetery for years with her two daughters. On each occasion, the three of them had walked about with bunches of flowers and, lacking adoption certificates for specific graves, had distributed the flowers across graves lovingly but randomly. Now they were keen, she said, to give their visits a sharper focus and renewed purpose.[7]

As the regional media stepped in to lend a hand with calls for adopters old and new to step forward, and as the Foundation decided to harness the power of the internet too by creating an email address and its own website, the response became overwhelming. "It is almost unimaginable," founding member and local historian Jo Purnot said in a newspaper early in 2004, "to see how much the liberation remains alive not just among the elderly, but among the young too." In that same article, Maria Duizings, who had just retired from her job, but now found herself working long hours as the keeper of adoption records, said she was perplexed by the intensity of emotions that the initiative was generating. "You often find that people want to tell their story," she noted. "And when they do, they talk about 'the boys.' As if they are their own children."[8]

1

If those reaffirming existing commitments to the Margraten boys had moving stories to tell, still more remarkable was what motivated countless Dutch families to register as adopters for the very first time 60 years after World War II had come to an end.

Many of those who had been young during the war were still alive, of course, and they responded to the Foundation's call in large numbers and with memories so vivid they seemed to belong only to yesterday. To them the war was the great watershed of the twentieth century, but also of their own lives. "There was," a married couple of adopters affirmed in the name of those their age, "a time before and a time after."[9]

Wartime itself had left deep marks and ugly scars. For many, adoption of a Margraten boy was an important part of a continuing process of coming to terms with that traumatic past. Although he was 82 when he signed up as an adopter, for the retired leather goods salesman it was his years in the resistance in Eindhoven that overshadowed all else he had ever been involved in. And although some 270 kilometers separated his current home from the Wisconsin lieutenant's grave, it was the memory of those defining years that made him keep his promise to set out on the Margraten pilgrimage not once but several times a year.[10]

The retired sales agent had been a young man of 21 when the Allies liberated the city he lived in. But even those who had been teenagers and very small children during the German occupation had felt much of that traumatic time seep into their soul and bones. As adult adopters they still spoke of those years as "nerve-wracking" and "tense," and many vividly remembered being shaken above all by the sight of beloved parents powerless and eaten away by constant fear. "The fear alone," recalled an adopter who had been no more than seven at the end of the war. "Horrifying."[11]

Many a child had emerged from the war with particularly horrifying events or episodes etched in their minds forever. Quite common among ageing adopters was, for example, the tale of the crashed Allied aircraft in a neighboring field, the mutilated bodies of the crew strewn about. Or still, that of the dead German with bullet holes, staring into the sky from a gutter or ditch. As had happened immediately after the war, even those who had not been liberated by American troops and had been forced to endure the atrocious hunger winter of 1944–45 continued to be drawn to Margraten to express gratitude. A building contractor from the coastal town of Katwijk, who had been five at the end of the war, had been coming back to the American cemetery each year ever since his first visit in 1957. Now at last, with his name on a certificate linked with that of an infantryman from Tennessee, his long-time dream of becoming an adopter had come true.[12]

Ferocious bombardments had also left indelible marks on Dutch families. That much of their suffering could now be categorized as 'collateral damage' brought about by 'friendly fire' did not prevent some from becoming adopters at the American cemetery too. In 1942, Allied air forces had wiped away an adopter's home in Geleen and, with it, all of her family's possessions. "All we had left," recalled the adopter, who was five when the disaster happened, "were the nightclothes on our backs." Still, she just as vividly remembered that when, at the end of the war, four English soldiers were billeted in their temporary shelter, her father had expressed deep gratitude to "these men, who remained liberators. Despite the mistake that was made razing our home to the ground." How then could she refuse to answer the Foundation's call 60 years after the war? In 2004 the woman decided to adopt not one, but two American infantrymen.[13]

For a woman who, as a young child, had survived the Allied bombardment of Venlo late in 1944, the decision appeared to come just as naturally. That Sergeant Harold Hendrickson of Michigan had been part of a crew flying a B-24 in the 466th Bomber Group did not seem to cause her any pangs of conscience. "Because," she clarified, "I find it horrible that he had to die this way. He could have been our son."[14]

Mixed in with the deeply etched pain of war was the continued resonance of the relief and joy of liberation. Asked in 2004 why he had decided to begin caring for an American grave at age 76, a retired school principal who had lived through Operation Market Garden summed it up in one terse sentence. "On 17 September 1944," he said, still awestruck, "I saw the US 82nd Airborne Division land in Groesbeek." Another adopter had been 13 when, the day after the American airborne troops had landed in the Gelderland town, American infantry had arrived in his village in Limburg. He highlighted what to him had been the most remarkable aspect of the American liberation. "Their arrival was not noisy," he pointed out, "as had been the case with the Germans, because these friendly soldiers wore soft-soled shoes, and you barely heard them march by."[15]

This particular experience had stuck in the mind of many Dutch who had been children at the time, because it had instantly set the tone for many good-natured encounters with GIs to follow. A man from Heerlen gladly took over responsibility from two of his sisters for the graves of an infantryman from Georgia and another from New Mexico. He had been six when thousands upon thousands of disheveled Belgian, French, and African colonial troops had trudged by his home on their way to Germany as prisoners in 1940. His mother had filled a tub with water and encouraged the exhausted and thirsty soldiers to fill their canteens, but a German soldier had threatened her with his rifle and barked at her to step back inside. A German officer had intervened and told his mother to continue what she was doing. But the incident had haunted the adopter ever since. In his mind, this frightening moment had become forever contrasted with what for him was the quintessential experience of liberation. When the

14. Shortly after liberation in 1944, children in the Limburg town of Valkenburg have their picture taken near an American piece of artillery. The boys have borrowed helmets from the GIs in the background. The war made an indelible impression on the very young and caused many to become committed adopters later in life. (Courtesy Miets Stevens)

first American Shermans had arrived in his street in Heerlen, he had clambered onto one of the tanks and embraced the soldier standing in the turret. He had taken a coin from his pocket and offered it to the American as a gift. The GI had cried and hugged him and had then yelled something at the soldiers inside the tank. The proud ten-year-old had climbed down from the tank with a pack containing four or five American cigarettes worth more than gold.[16]

For children in particular, the presence among the liberators of African-American soldiers had left an even more indelible mark. "The street was jammed with trucks full of very black people," an adopter from Hoensbroek recalled. "All you saw in the cabins was white teeth and the white of eyes." An adopter who was nine in 1944 fondly remembered the black truck drivers who were regular visitors at her home in Heerlen. "They placed me in their lap and taught me American songs." The outlandish GIs delighted her even more with "huge bars of chocolate" and "tasty white bread that looked gigantic."[17]

Whether in the context of black or white troops, American food remained a central theme seared into the minds of the Dutch. "We sang songs together. Wonderful," the adopter of a New York infantryman reminisced. "There was a lieutenant too, and they brought bread and cheese and chocolate. There were ten children at home. Unforgettable." For a generation whose early lives had been marked by nothing but hardship, the memories of America's blessings remained manifold and powerful. "In a sense," remarked a retired teacher who was only three at the end of the war, "I owe my life to the American doctor who decided to treat me with a new medicine, penicillin, and made the pneumonia go away."[18]

The juxtaposition of Dutch regeneration and American sacrifice had, of course, always been most palpable at the Margraten cemetery. It was therefore not surprising that many of the elderly among the fresh volunteers came to the adoption program haunted by images of the burial ground when it was still no more than a muddy wasteland. Adopters talked of fathers who had been among the civilian diggers and of holding the hands of their mothers during visits to the windswept plateau when the massive cemetery had just opened to the public.

"I witnessed some of the first burials firsthand when I was 15," the adopter of a paratrooper remembered with a mixture of teen excitement and child's horror, "lying on my stomach and peering out from beneath the burlap screens in the autumn of 1944."[19]

An adopter who, as a young woman, had been assigned a freshly dug grave at war's end had always regretted the American family's decision to have the soldier repatriated. Now, as a result of the Foundation's initiative, she was finally offered an opportunity to make up for lost time with the care for another grave. "I am 86 now, and dependent on others for transportation," the woman wrote from Brunssum, "but I will continue to visit as long as possible, at least once a year."[20]

An elderly couple in Heerlen had an even more compelling reason for wanting to do so. The wife's parents had lived in Schinveld and in May 1946 had received from the Civilian Committee an adoption certificate in the mail bearing the name of Maxwell Sullivan of the 44th Bomber Group. During all those years, the Dutch family had acted as loyal caretakers of the lieutenant's grave. But they had to wait until 2005 before receiving a second adoption document with on it the name of the American soldier they had known in person during the liberation. Ernest Byrd had arrived in Europe early in 1945 and been billeted with the Dutch family as an infantryman in the 79th Division. A few days before his move to the nearby front in Germany, Ernest had asked his host family if they could line his military vest with some wool. Mother and daughter had set to work immediately, and Ernest had waved goodbye to them all bundled up against the biting cold. Ernest had returned only a few days later, his frozen corpse piled up with many others on a truck parked near their farm. When the truck had driven off, it had been for the casualties' final trip to Margraten.[21]

2

The overwhelming majority of people who registered in response to the call of the new Adoption Foundation had not lived through any such memorable experience. They had, in fact, no personal recollection of World War II at all, as they had often been born long after their country's freedom had been restored. Still, for countless Dutch families, relations with the Margraten boys had become such an intrinsic part of their identity that terminating adoption was never an option.

An academic from Heerlen, for example, in 2005 took over the graves of no fewer than three infantrymen who had long been in the care of a grandmother, an aunt, and her own mother. When families like hers were asked by the Foundation if they would still be interested in carrying on adoption, the reply was resounding and unequivocal. "I did not hesitate for a moment," a man from Kerkrade said, "because I know how much this had meant to my parents while they were still alive." Most regarded taking over the family's adoption not only as an honor, but also as a duty that was deeply meaningful. She had asked, one woman explained, for the transfer to her name of two American graves that had been in the family since 1946, "in order to continue my mother and aunt's task and care for these graves as if they were family graves."[22]

It bothered Bert Eggen that it was impossible for him to carry on this tradition. He knew how much importance his father too had attached to the ritual for many years. Sergeant Earl Jenkins had been killed in Germany in November 1944. Bert's father had been deeply touched when he received the adoption certificate with the American's name in May 1946. From Simpelveld he had cycled to Margraten each week to carry flowers, pray, and reflect on the war. A picture was taken of Bert as a toddler at Earl's grave. Then, suddenly, in the late 1940s, the cemetery had shut down. When the gates had swung open again, Earl's grave was gone, together with the graves of some 10,000 other Americans. Earl's repatriation had been a big blow to Bert's father. That is why Bert, prodded by the new groundswell of interest in adoption, decided to search for Earl's family in Mississippi. Emails to local newspapers quickly brought him in touch with Earl's daughter, and some time later Bert and his wife were boarding a plane to the US. They returned to Limburg with much treasured pictures of Earl's grave in his hometown in Mississippi. Earl's family had used the occasion to declare their 'adoption' of the Dutch couple and had announced that from now on they were invited to attend the annual Jenkins reunion.[23]

Still others discovered that, for their parents, the pilgrimage to Margraten had been too personal an affair to share with anyone. In May 2004, a middle-aged window dresser received a phone call from the Foundation. She was astonished to learn that, immediately after the war, her mother, who had passed away, had adopted the grave of a soldier called William Kirlin. She had never known anything about this and even a talk with her father and calls to her mother's best friend, sisters, and sisters-in-law revealed nothing about her involvement.

Like many others in her case, however, the window dresser responded with pride and was happy to inform the Foundation that she too would continue the gesture that her mother had clearly thought so important. In September of that year, she put flowers on William's grave the day before the anniversary of his death.

Shortly after, the Dutch woman was left speechless when a woman who said she was William's sister contacted her. She had visited her brother's grave on the day of the anniversary and seen the fresh flowers. With some local help she had found out about the adoption program and managed to find her address. It turned out that Bill Kirlin, a 24-year-old from Shillington, Pennsylvania, who had the broken nose, square jaw, and thick neck of a football player, had been killed as a radio operator on board a B-24 trying to supply paratroopers during Operation Market Garden. All of the ten-member crew had survived the crash landing with the *Baggy Maggy*, but not Bill. He had stood no chance when the top turret had broken off on impact and crushed his strong body. Fate, as the window dresser learned that day, had a way of twisting and turning in mysterious ways – in peace as in war.[24]

The younger generations of Dutch were just as willing to take over adoption from relatives other than their own parents. Respect for their commitment made them carry on the tradition for anyone from aunts to great-uncles. Indeed, in some cases the new adopters were merely namesakes of the old who were more than happy to volunteer when mistakenly contacted by the Foundation as relatives of the adopters they had so far had no luck in tracing.

At the same time, the Foundation's initiative set in motion a process whereby certain adoptions were reactivated after having been dormant a generation long. A software-developer in her forties had long known that her grandfather had adopted a Margraten boy. But he had passed away a long time ago and no one in the family could remember the soldier's name. Then, suddenly, the Foundation's letter found its way to the family, stating the soldier's full details as well as the grave's exact location. The adopter's granddaughter was happy to be reunited with Sergeant George Schiller of the 102nd Infantry Division. She instantly restarted paying visits to the cemetery, this time in the presence of her ten-year-old nephew from a fourth generation.[25]

Still others of the third generation came in the possession of the Foundation's reminder totally unaware of the fact that relatives had become involved in adoption immediately after the war. In Geleen, a couple in their early fifties readily accepted care for two infantrymen whom they learned were mentioned in adoption certificates belonging to two long-deceased great-aunts. With the help of their eldest daughter and the internet, they managed to get in touch with the next of kin of Texan Otis Grant of the 90th Infantry Division. Contacts with the Dutch adopters prompted Otis's family to put together a scrapbook with the soldier's letters and photos, which received pride of place in the church he had attended once upon a time, long ago.[26]

3

Whether they took over graves from relatives or commenced new adoption traditions, motivation for the large majority of the younger volunteers was inextricably linked with family memories of the war. What made many of the postwar generations gravitate to the Margraten boys in the wake of the new initiative were war stories repeated so often within families that they too could now recite them in detail and with the emotion of an eyewitness. Indeed, for many adopters, Margraten more than any other place had played a key role in that oral tradition. As it had morphed from a place of mourning into a site of memory, countless visits to the American cemetery had served as triggers and conduits for just as many stories that had helped keep alive the experience of occupation and liberation.

The hunger that occupation had brought, for example, continued to hold strong resonance even among those who had known only overwhelming plenty all their lives. The new adopter of an airman from New York, a secretary from Margraten, claimed that, even more than 60 years after the war, her father's health problems, as well as those of his two brothers, were attributable to shortages suffered during that time. "Food," she noted, "has therefore always had an extraordinary significance for my father." Many adopters vividly remembered that in their youth they had been forced to empty their plates with the grave threat that "another war would teach them a good lesson."[27]

But new volunteers also brought with them a kaleidoscope of other war experiences they were determined not to forget. The adopter of infantryman Steve Skube, for example, whose mother survived the German bombardment of Rotterdam in May 1940 and whose father was deported to Berlin, escaped, and walked all the way back to the Netherlands evading capture. The adopter of paratrooper Armand Beauchamp, whose father was the skipper of a canal barge and in the summer of 1943 got caught up in the Allied bombing of Hamburg and the terrible firestorm that followed. The adopter of Private Gennaro Esposito, whose parents had to flee the Arnhem front lines in September 1944 when the town's bridge over the Rhine proved to be one too far for the Allies.[28]

The experiences of occupation could be those of victimization as well as resistance. Several Margraten boys came to symbolize harrowing stories that had been acted out by those Dutch who had openly defied the Nazi Germans. Herman Hodge, a sergeant in the 303rd Bomber Group, served to remind the caretaker of his grave of an aunt and uncle who had helped smuggle downed Allied airmen into Belgium and France at the risk of their own lives. The grave of Francis Barrett, a Missourian of the 2nd Infantry Division, was a symbol not just of liberation, but also of the role that the adopter's father had played in the Princess Irene Brigade as the Dutch volunteer unit fought its way across Europe with the Allies all the way from France.[29]

The American graves were especially stark reminders of World War II for those whose next of kin had been sent to the concentration camps, either for what they had done or for what they had been. For a man from Geleen, it had been a sacred duty to take over adoption from his father. The American soldier in question was Lieutenant James Diel, a paratrooper who was killed on 19 September 1944 at the Son bridge in Operation Market Garden and who has been fondly remembered by Major Dick Winters in his memoirs *Beyond Band of Brothers*. But what was even more important for the Dutchman was that which has not been recorded in any bestselling book. His father, he explained, had been among the first Dutch inmates of Buchenwald. He had been there from 8 October 1940 to 15 November 1941. He had been *Häftling* 4425. In a family's memory of such a horrendous time, nothing was ever a mere detail. Regular trips to Margraten were one way of ensuring that nothing of all this would ever be forgotten.[30]

That was true also for a 56-year-old whose father had survived two and a half years in the camps. Arrested as a member of the resistance in 1943, the Germans had first sent the Dutchman to Natzweiler-Struthof, a concentration camp hidden away in the gloomy mountain forests of the Alsace. The Allied invasion of France had prompted the SS to disperse the prisoners to other camps and the adopter's father had eventually ended up in Dachau. His son had never heard him talk much about life in any of the camps. But he knew that he had been wasting away with tuberculosis when liberation at last came in 1945. And he knew that his liberators had been Americans. He did not need to know more to take over from his aunt in 2004 the adoption of PFC Thomas Hastie of the 86th Infantry Division.[31]

4

At the start of the new millennium, Margraten increasingly functioned as a site of memory even for those whose families had suffered in the more distant theaters of World War II. As a consequence of their colonial empire in Asia, the Dutch had been deeply involved also in the war with Japan. One Limburg woman, for example, volunteered for the adoption of two American graves in large part because of her father's past as a sailor. He had fled to England as soon as the Germans invaded the Netherlands in May 1940. There he had joined the crew of the *Jacob van Heemskerck*, a Dutch cruiser that in January 1942 had steamed off to war in the Pacific. Another woman, a young nurse from North Brabant, joined the community of adopters in honor of her grandfather, who had served aboard one of the many Allied ships that suffered defeat in the Battle of the Java Sea in 1942 and who, as a prisoner of the Japanese, had been a slave laborer on the infamous Burma railway.[32]

Dutch soldiers and civilians had suffered terribly at the hand of the Japanese after having been captured during the invasion of the Dutch East Indies. Their children and grandchildren became adopters at Margraten because they were convinced that, had it not been for the American liberators, their relatives might not have survived the war in Asia. For a housewife in her fifties, who adopted a New York lieutenant from the 491st Bomber Group, there was not the least bit of doubt about this. "Because," she explained, "my father was a prisoner of war in Japan and he was liberated by the Americans, and that has meant a great deal to him."[33]

Still, even after 60 years, Margraten remained overwhelmingly a symbol of the role the American liberators had played in the downfall of Nazi Germany. For many Dutch families, there remained now only vague hints of what a particular liberator might possibly have meant for previous generations. A man in Maastricht, for example, was quite surprised by the Foundation's news that his deceased parents had been the adopters of Robert Broding, a Minnesotan who had been part of the 76th General Hospital. He too was happy to continue the tradition and keen to learn more about the reasons behind his father's decision. But the only thing his search revealed was a yellowed picture tucked away among old family photographs in his sister's home. In it were three American soldiers basking in the sun and having fun. One beaming soldier was dressed in a T-shirt and sported a German officer's cap as a trophy; another casually leaned on a civilian's umbrella. This was July 1945, the faded caption on the back of the picture explained, and Robert Broding was the soldier in the middle. He wore a wide grin as well as a black formal top hat. Three months later, and almost half a year after the end of the war in Europe, Robert lay interred at Margraten cemetery. It was a complete mystery to the Dutch family how this had happened and where the intimate photograph might have come from.[34]

For some, however, the deeper meaning of a liberator's adoption could still be sensed very acutely even now. For a woman from Oirsbeek who had been born near the end of the war, there was never any doubt that she would continue the adoption of Sergeant Charles Jefferson from Mississippi. He had been one of the African-American soldiers of the 784th Tank Battalion who had fought on and near the Dutch-German border and befriended her family. Indeed, when in January 1945 bad weather had prevented the woman's aunt and godmother from arriving in time for her christening, the black sergeant had immediately volunteered to take her place in the church service. The arrival of the Foundation's certificate in her name in 2005 only formalized the godchild's role. She had been paying visits to the cemetery with her mother and aunt regularly ever since the sergeant had been killed two months after his kind gesture. There was even a photo of her putting flowers on Charles Jefferson's grave when she was no more than four years old.[35]

There were those also who adopted American liberators in the knowledge that, had fate decided otherwise, their own father or grandfather might just as well have been buried in Margraten. A young woman from Heerlen, for example, took over the adoption of a grave that her grandmother had decided to adopt long ago in honor of the girl's grandfather: an American artillerist who had passed through Limburg as one of the liberators and had evidently made more than a passing impression on one of the girls there.[36]

But Dutch men too had worn the American uniform, and they too had risked their lives up front. Harry van Veen had joined the resistance as a very young man. So impatient was he to welcome the Allied armies in 1944 that, not long after they had landed on the beaches of France, he decided to go and look for them. He gathered some food and his Hohner harmonica and on his ramshackle bicycle spent three weeks making his way through Belgium and into France. Incredibly, he made it all the way to Normandy. In Évreux, Harry ran into troops of the 30th Infantry Division and begged them to let him join up. Reluctant at first, officers of the 119th Infantry Regiment eventually gave in on the express condition that he would serve as a medic and would be given clothing and food but no pay. Eager to prove himself to the battle-hardened Americans, the Dutchman was soon accepting tasks as a stretcher bearer in some of the most dangerous areas at the front. By the time of the Battle of the Bulge, Harry was affectionately known among his GI buddies as 'Crazy Dutchy,' and the Dutchman stuck with his unit until the very end of the war in Germany. Harry van Veen had passed away in 2001. But, in 2004, Harry's son began paying regular visits to two Margraten boys. One of them was a soldier from an infantry regiment similar to the one his father had served in so valiantly.[37]

For an optician from Panningen, that which bound him to the adopted soldier from the 115th Infantry Regiment was even more pointed. On the eve of the war, his father had worked in a radio shop. During the occupation, the Jewish shop-owner and his family were deported to concentration camps from which they would never return. On three occasions, his father attempted an escape to England, but each time he failed. Determined to fight the Nazis, he served in the Dutch underground as a courier and radio operator. In January 1945 he joined the American forces and became a radio operator with the 188th Signal Repair Company in the Ninth Army. He was given a rifle and a helmet that had belonged to a GI named Erwin Bohling.

It had taken a strange twist of fate for his father to find out 20 years after the war that the name inside the helmet was one of the names also on a headstone in Margraten. Erwin Bohling, it turned out, had served as a sergeant in the 29th Infantry Division, and the Silver Star recipient had lost his life on 16 November 1944. The Dutchman who had been given the American's equipment to fight the war in his place had been drawn to the GI's grave in Margraten several times a year. His son was determined to honor the wish of his father to continue this ritual after his death. And on days when his mind wandered off to his father and Erwin Bohling, it often happened also that he paid a quick visit to Panningen's small church to light a candle in memory of both men.[38]

5

What made the new adoption initiative in 2003 such a success too, however, was that by now people from several generations and all walks of life were assigning to the Margraten cemetery a significance transcending both the deeply lived experience of World War II and the singularly personal memories of occupation and liberation passed on within families.

Many of the new volunteers were motivated by a more generic interest in the seismic events of World War II. They merely shared in the strong collective memory of the conflict through everything from devouring entire libraries on the subject to crisscrossing Europe visiting museums, exhibitions, and monuments from D-Day to Dachau. For a 42-year-old health consultant, for example, the motivation for adoption came from having attended commemorations of the battle for Arnhem and the official surrender of German troops in Wageningen on 5 May 1945. But it came just as much, he admitted, from having watched reruns of *Secret Army*, an older BBC television drama series on the activities of the Belgian resistance, with even these episodes "sufficing to make me shed an occasional tear."[39]

Quite a few new adopters indicated they had been completely blown away by the HBO mini-series *Band of Brothers*. The blockbuster television series, produced by Steven Spielberg and Tom Hanks, had told the story of a company of American liberators as they made their way from Utah Beach all the way to Hitler's Eagle's Nest. Released in the US shortly before the tragedy of 9/11, the epic tale of the valor of The Greatest Generation in The Good War for many on both sides of the Atlantic had been a powerful catalyst for wanting to learn more about World War II.

Yet, many more claimed that what had made them decide to become an adopter above all else was a visit to the beaches that the Allied troops had stormed on D-Day. The beaches had become a tourist draw soon after the war. And they had been made even more popular through Cornelius Ryan's bestselling book *The Longest Day* in 1959, the Darryl Zanuck movie version of the same name in 1962, and high-profile commemorations involving American presidents at least once a decade. Dutch tourists too flocked to the area summer after summer. "During a vacation in Normandy," a middle-aged municipal clerk from Bunde explained, "we became so impressed that, upon arriving home, the first thing we did was contact the Foundation that manages adoption."[40]

Still others were drawn to the adoption program as a result of their passion for collecting uniforms and equipment from the war or for battlefield reenactment. Some of these members have since been known to pull up at the cemetery in restored Willys jeeps or to visit graves dressed as American liberators. Such fringe behavior is widely frowned upon within the adoption community, however, and less flamboyant collectors and impersonators have, in their own way, made valuable contributions to preserving the memory of World War II. Members of the living history association Super Sixth, for example, are committed to reenacting daily life in the 50th Infantry Battalion, a unit of the 6th Armored Division. Part of the preparations for re-enactment have involved internet and library research as well as regular correspondence with American veterans regarding the two Margraten boys who belonged to the unit. For one of them, PFC Robert McAlpine, the association eventually managed to put together a file that included, among many other documents, a photo of the smiling Texan in cowboy outfit and another of the same young man wearing a deadly serious uniform.

The latter photo was part of Robert's obituary and told a story that no reenactment could ever convey. Drafted in May 1944, the

22-year-old Texan, who had been working as a ranch hand and car mechanic, had left behind a wife and son. In January 1945, in one of Europe's coldest winters on record, the soldier from Bluff Dale was facing some of Nazi Germany's most formidable troops northeast of Bastogne. In a hamlet called Oubourcy, he was badly wounded trying to save the life of a fellow soldier, an action for which he was awarded the Silver Star. Robert eventually returned to his unit, but on 7 April 1945 there was no one to save his life when he came under fire during yet another vicious battle near the German town of Mühlhausen. For the young family that he left behind in Texas, life eventually resumed its course. Robert's wife remarried, his son took on the stepfather's last name, and when in 1948 a decision had to be made about repatriation, Robert's wife had thought it best to leave things as the war had decided they should be.[41]

Almost 60 years later, many Dutch considered caring for Robert and other American boys at Margraten not just a debt of honor to the liberators and to previous generations of adopters, but a responsibility to history in a much broader sense. No society could afford an era of such massive suffering, significance, and change to be forgotten, and while the Margraten cemetery presented itself as a perfect site of memory, adoption came to be regarded as the ideal ritual of remembrance.

Some considered their responsibility more acute now that the war generation was rapidly fading and even American veterans associations were visiting Margraten less and less. Others were reminded of the importance of what they were doing by the shocking ignorance that people on occasion displayed about World War II. A retired mechanical engineer certainly thought the war sacrifice of Major Tom Skelly worth remembering. On a Sunday in March 1945, the major and his pilot had been attacked by a couple of German Messerschmidts during an observation flight with a Piper Cub for the 252nd Field Artillery Group. The badly damaged aircraft crashed to the ground close to the German town of Rheinberg and American infantrymen rushed the badly wounded men to a hospital. X-rays revealed that the major had such a complicated skull fracture that surgery was deemed useless. The American had gone into a coma that evening and a little later had died in the company of a chaplain and two officers from his unit who had remained at his bedside throughout the ordeal. The Dutchman vowed to keep the adoption and the story of the major from Delaware alive as long as he could. Not least because he vividly remembered his visits to the cemetery with American colleagues in the last years of his active career as well as his astonishment on learning that they knew nothing about Margraten and the more than 8,000 stories similar to that of Major Tom Skelly.[42]

A woman from Maastricht, who in retirement served as a city guide to foreign visitors, had often had similar experiences with Americans. But she remembered as especially disconcerting the day when an elderly American lady had listened intently to her explanation about the nearby World War II cemetery. The talk had suddenly reminded the American woman that her brother had been killed somewhere in Europe, had never been repatriated, and might thus possibly have been laid to rest in the place mentioned. The city guide had hurried to find out more about the lady's brother and had almost instantly discovered that he was buried not at Margraten, but at the nearby cemetery of Henri-Chapelle. Not only had the Dutch guide accompanied the soldier's sister to the cemetery in Belgium, she had also decided afterwards that she should combine her Margraten adoption with care for the grave of this family's long lost son.[43]

Gradually, as the new millennium took shape, not just individuals but local organizations too began embracing the American cemetery, both as a site of memory for the war and as an inextricable part of the region's cultural heritage. In 2005 the Scouts in Landgraaf decided that a new branch should be called Old Hickory in honor of the 30th Infantry Division that had liberated their region in 1944, and they collectively accepted adoption of Charles Hohn, a private from that unit. Still another Limburg Scouts group linked up with Scouts from Henfield in West Sussex. During regular visits from their English counterparts, they never skipped a pilgrimage to Margraten, which always included a tour and short history as well as a ceremony that involved laying flowers at the grave of an unknown American.[44]

Much older than any Scouts organization are Limburg's *schutterijen*. These are ceremonial shooting clubs that have their roots in the voluntary citizen militia that sprung up in defense of towns and cities and in some cases trace their lineage all the way back to the Middle Ages. Given their original function, it was appropriate that they too should be involved in the adoption of Americans who had given their lives for the common defense of the region against Nazi Germany. In July 1945 the *schuttersbond* of southern Limburg had organized a Heroes Day on Margraten cemetery and each local *schutterij* that belonged to the umbrella organization had put a wreath at the grave of a particular soldier. For the *schutterij* from Valkenburg that had been a soldier named Harold Alderman who had, however, been repatriated at the end of the 1940s. Now, in response to the Foundation's appeal, the Valkenburg organization decided that it was time again for its ancient traditions to fuse with this more recent one by adopting the grave of Sergeant Howard May, another soldier from the Old Hickory division, which in 1944 had liberated large swathes of Limburg.[45]

There were new generations also who, in an era of accelerating globalization, came to be involved in the adoption of Margraten boys through various close connections with the US and its inhabitants. A couple from Margraten, for example, decided to care for the grave of Lieutenant Schanke from Minnesota because they had lived in America for several years and, in the wake of 9/11, had witnessed firsthand how young Americans were being sent overseas as soldiers and how devastating this experience proved to be for the families they left behind. Many more Dutch developed an affinity for America and its people during shorter stays in the country as tourists. A significant rise in European travel to the US had begun as early as the 1960s. Since the late 1970s, an impressive 9 percent of all Dutch travel abroad has been to the United States. In 2007 a report from the Pew Global Attitudes Survey found that "individuals who have traveled to the US have more favorable views of the country than those who have not." This was generally true also for the many Dutch who toured the United States. When the Adoption Foundation launched its appeal at the start of the new millennium, several of the volunteers who responded indicated that they did so because of particularly memorable experiences gained during travels in America. Some even insisted on adopting soldiers from such favorite holiday destinations as Florida and California.[46]

A man who registered for the adoption of a Texan lieutenant of the 452nd Bomber Group did so in large part because he was proud to be an employee of the American company Cisco Systems and had come to admire the American "mentality and determination, especially in business." Other Dutch adopters had good reason to feel even closer to the American people because members of their own families had made permanent homes there. For a 59-year-old housewife, the adoption of an infantryman from Connecticut was prompted by "the deep impression the cemetery had made on us," but also by the fact that "a sister had married an American and lived in the US."[47]

For the 67-year-old adopter of Private Melvin Logan from the 75th Infantry Division, America had shaped the course of his life long after World War II. Indeed, in the early 1980s, heart surgery in Houston, Texas, had probably saved his life, while later in the decade his son and only child had attended university in South Carolina and fallen in love with an American girl. Twenty years later, his son was still happily married to the same woman and living a good life in New Jersey, where he was a proud sponsor of a project providing educational support for orphaned children. It was no coincidence therefore that on Melvin Logan's grave marker it said that the private had joined the military from New Jersey.[48]

In recent years, however, quite a few Dutch from Limburg have been able to develop close relations with Americans without so much as leaving their province. As noted earlier, in 1967, AFCENT, short for Allied Forces Central Command, had moved from Fontainebleau to Brunssum in response to an offer from the Dutch government after France had withdrawn from NATO's integrated military structure. The NATO area command underwent significant transformations in the wake of the Cold War and was renamed AFNORTH (Allied Forces North Europe) in 2000 and JFC (Allied Joint Force Command) in 2004. But, despite all this, it has remained firmly entrenched in Brunssum and has close links with the US Army Garrison that was implanted in the neighboring town of Schinnen in 1969. Over a period of almost 40 years, both American communities have developed deep roots in Limburg. Their children receive an excellent education at the International School in Brunssum. The school was created to meet the educational needs of military families serving abroad and officials of the American Department of Defense Education Authority subject it to regular inspections to ensure that it meets educational requirements up to and including twelfth grade. For decades, Dutch civilians have been employed in these American communities as finance managers, legal advisers, electrical engineers, and in various other positions.[49]

The long war on terror has given the NATO command and the American presence in Limburg new significance. Indeed, it is from Brunssum, for example, that support is provided to the International Security Assistance Force in Afghanistan. No wonder then that such close proximity between Dutch and Americans has led to all kinds of relations, some of them very intimate. One Limburg woman, for example, volunteered for adoption of an officer and a private, both infantrymen from the 8th Division, on the day she learned that her American partner would be sent to Iraq with the US Army for a second deployment of 15 months. With her partner's father a veteran of the wars in Korea and Vietnam, the gesture seemed the right thing to do in more than one way, "so that I at least will never forget those who lost their lives in a strange and faraway country for my sake."[50]

For many of the American personnel on the Limburg bases, however, Margraten failed to have any such strong resonance at the dawn of the new millennium. One Limburger, who worked as a bus driver for the Brunssum base, in conversations with Americans was discouraged to learn that even those who had been stationed in the province for two years and longer had often never heard of Margraten, let alone paid a visit to the graves there.[51]

It may have been to counter such amnesia that an ICT specialist in his early forties, who had worked for the US military during much of his career, volunteered to care for the grave of Michael De Febio and then set out to reactivate the memory of this particular Margraten boy with dogged determination. The IDPF was a first start and the file told the Dutchman that the names of the soldier's parents were Gaetano and Angelina, that Mike had three sisters and a brother called Rocco, and that he had married Olga in June 1942, before setting off for the war from his home in Providence, Rhode Island. Mike had served as a sergeant in a reconnaissance unit of the 643rd Tank Destroyer Battalion and earned a Bronze Star by the time he was killed on 12 April 1945, a month short of his 27th birthday.

But a real breakthrough in getting to know Mike better came when one of the Dutchman's many internet searches brought him to the web page of a group of Americans involved in creating a memorial dedicated to all those from Rhode Island who had died in World War II. An email to the committee in no time was relayed to Mike's brother-in-law. The man was thrilled to hear from the adopter as he had visited Mike's grave in Margraten in 1966 during a business trip to nearby Eindhoven and had been very impressed by the Memorial Day ceremony in May. He sent him a photo of Mike with his mother, of Mike posing in uniform with a cocky smile, and of Mike's name on the Rhode Island memorial wall. A little later, veteran Lew Reynolds emailed the adopter to let him know that he had been with Mike when

Germans ambushed their tank destroyer and a Greyhound armored car near the town of Barby as they approached the Elbe River and the Soviet front. In a matter of seconds, a spray of machine-gun fire had mowed down six GIs, one of them Mike who had caught three bullets.

At about the same time that Mike's comrade got in touch, yet another email arrived. Joan, Mike's cousin, just wanted to let the Dutch adopter know that she had been eight when she had last seen Mike and that she remembered him as "the most fun loving boy." "You have," she closed her email, "touched me deeply with your dedication to his memory that I thought was long forgotten by the world."[52]

New volunteers were being drawn to the American cemetery also because its more than eight thousand graves gave them an unmistakable sense, even without specific memories of World War II, of the epic character and continuously resonating impact of this conflict. Strolling between the American names in marble was like walking along a fault line and almost inevitably led to contemplating mass sacrifice and its many consequences. "This way history is kept alive," asserted a 52-year-old who signed up for adoption, "so that it remains clear that, without American support at the time, the Netherlands would now be a different country." A common refrain was that, had it not been for the Americans, "we would now be speaking German." Quite a few took that reasoning to its logical conclusion, noting that, if the Soviet troops had arrived before the Americans, the Dutch today might just as well have been speaking Russian.[53]

"After the liberation too, we Europeans have had much to thank the Americans (allies) for," noted a young adopter who was in the employ of the Dutch Ministry of Foreign Affairs. "Economic prosperity, security, and stability became commonplace in Europe as a result of the American presence." Others expressed a similar conviction but did so more viscerally. "All the choices I can make," a 25-year-old teacher and caretaker of four Margraten boys explained, "and everything I do, and the freedom I enjoy, I owe to the Americans." That seemed true also for a 32-year-old who worked for a retailer in confectionary. He registered for adoption as soon as he learned that he was to become a father. I did so, he clarified, "to thank the Americans who died for us so that the small child that my girlfriend was pregnant with might live in a free world."[54]

"Each time you drive past Margraten you are reminded of what we owe to those boys who are buried there," noted a couple in their fifties who lived in Vaals, a small Dutch town tucked away in the shadow of the German city of Aachen. The couple's gratitude was deep enough for them to want to learn more about the life and death of Charley Rose, whose grave was located in Plot H, Row 15 of the cemetery not far from the road from Aachen to Maastricht. But even before they had so much as taken the first research step, a letter suddenly arrived from a grandson of Charley's brother. In the months after the first contact with Charley's family, the story of the soldier from the 6th Armored Division gradually emerged from more letters and a newspaper clipping from 1946.

A photo showed a young man with such striking Italian looks that he might easily have been mistaken for one of Hollywood's teenage heartthrobs. But the story behind any Margraten boy's photo was, of course, never one with a happy ending. Charley had been raised on a farm in Nevada, Missouri, in a family with very many siblings and at a young age had gone to work for soft-drink company, Double Cola. He entered the army early in September 1944, shortly after he had turned 18, and went through basic training for 17 weeks. Early in 1945, at a time when the Battle of the Bulge was still raging, Charley and other green troops were rushed off to the war in Europe. For some strange reason, once Charley was swallowed up by the Old World's front lines, his family never heard from him again. Even more inexplicably, in February, Charley's mother, Elvina, received her son's watch in the mail, and in March a check for $33.11, the amount of money said to have been in her son's possession. Yet it took the grief-stricken Rose family until 20 April to receive official notification of Charley's death, and when the letter came it insisted rather unconvincingly that the boy had been alive until 8 April.[55]

What motivated adopters like those of Charley Rose was often not mere gratitude for their freedom and prosperity, but a deep conviction also that they owed to the liberators their very existence. For some this appeared quite literally true, even though they were too young to have any personal recollection of the war. Born in 1945, for example, a man from Hoensbroek had been told that his father was very ill by the time of liberation, and that he had managed to pull through in no small part because the Americans had been kind enough to provide him with much extra food. A woman from Noorbeek, also born in 1945, had been raised with the oft-repeated story of how "my mother had been given white bread by the Americans while she was pregnant with me." But similar feelings could motivate even those who had been born long after 1945 and whose families had suffered no obvious special trauma during the war. A man of 40 adopted the graves of three GIs because, he explained, "from my perspective I owe it to the liberators that I exist today and am happily married with three children."[56]

The father of three was reminded quite sharply of how permanent the pain could be that war inflicts on families when he managed to get in touch with the sister of Herbert Berger, one of his own Margraten boys. An emotional Marcia told the Dutchman in an email that Herbie was born and raised in the Bronx and that he had been "a good son" as well as "an exceptionally good student" who was enrolled in college as a premedical student before he joined the army. He also was, she pointed out, "a strong anti-fascist." That was perhaps not surprising for a Jewish soldier, but it did help to explain to his adopter why Herbert was awarded the Bronze Star for courage before being killed as an infantryman with the 75th Division barely two weeks before Nazi Germany finally surrendered. The Bronze Star, however, had never been much comfort to a family that continued to speak of Herbert as Herbie. "As you know," Marcia Berger continued, "Morris and Esther were his parents and both are now deceased for many years. I will say that not a day passed after his death until their death that they did not think of him and miss him. Although it is now 63 years since he was killed that is also true for my brother Robert and me."[57]

6

Ultimately, what made many Dutch respond so overwhelmingly to the renewed call for adoption in 2003 was the inconsolable grief of Marcia Berger and so many others like her. At its most basic level, adoption now boiled down to nothing more than what one volunteer described as "pure decency." Seen from that perspective, the humane gesture transcended nationality and ideology. "It is not just that he is an American," a retired civil servant and adopter of an Illinoisan soldier argued, "but in my eyes a child of 20 years buried in Limburg far away from his country and without relatives." "To be killed," a 35-year-old project manager reflected on the enormity of each individual loss, "in the prime of your life, missing out on all those moments that are now so self-evident for all of us, studying, marrying, building a career, starting a family, growing old."[58]

Such thoughts inevitably came easiest to those who had been close to soldiers in their own family. One adopter of a Margraten boy emphasized that he held the Dutch nationality, but that his father at the time of the war had been a German who had fought against the Allies on both the Eastern Front and the Western Front and had spent several years in Britain as a prisoner of war.[59]

Most of the veterans adopters knew well had, of course, served in the Dutch armed forces. Quite a few adopters had a keen interest in the Margraten cemetery, they acknowledged, because they knew from fathers and brothers what it had been like to fight in the wars that their own country had waged in the East Indies in a desperate and failed bid to regain control over the age-old colony after the defeat of the Japanese in 1945.[60]

Indeed, one new adopter was himself a veteran of the last spasms of those colonial wars as he had been drafted into the Dutch military in 1962 as part of an effort to defend Dutch New Guinea against the claims of the by then independent state of Indonesia. He had been sent there, he recalled, without much training or motivation. He claimed that he had never fired a shot in anger or been in real danger. Nevertheless, he had witnessed the burial of several Dutch soldiers, and this experience so far away from home had left "a deep impression." "How prepared," the 65-year-old wondered as he took on adoption of a West Virginian of the 20th Field Hospital, "had the English and American soldiers been and what fear must they have felt?"[61]

Many Dutch veterans were much younger still. Once its colonial appetite had abated, the Netherlands had changed tack in foreign policy and sent out more than its fair share of troops in multinational efforts to help keep the peace in areas across the globe. Thousands in the second half of the 1990s had been sent to the Balkans as United Nations Blue Helmets. Several of them, often deeply marked by the brutality of the conflict in the former Yugoslavia and the mass murder of Muslim civilians that they had failed to prevent at Srebrenica, linked up with Margraten boys whom they felt they could strongly relate to.[62]

In the new millennium, the war on terror was causing many more Dutch soldiers to be placed in harm's way as thousands poured into Afghanistan and took up position in Uruzgan province with helmets in camouflage colors rather than the blue of the United Nations. Before long, the news of body bags returning to the Netherlands was causing many adopters to reappraise their role with added and urgent meaning. "When now you hear of someone getting killed in Uruzgan," wrote a retiree from Landgraaf who adopted an airman from New Mexico in 2004, "I stop and think about how it must have felt for parents never to have seen their son again, not even after his death."[63]

For one Limburg woman in her forties, the deployment in Afghanistan provided a particularly poignant perspective on adoption in Margraten. She worked for a large pension fund and for many years it had been her business to take care of the affairs of the dependents of Dutch veterans. That included managing the pensions of the generation of East Indies soldiers that was slowly fading away, but also creating new files for the widows and orphans of those who were now being killed in Uruzgan. "For me," the woman observed ruefully, "war is thus not just past, but present too."[64]

In a sense that is what it would always be also to the adopter of Sergeant Ronald Jacobs. In 2005 the Dutchman had registered his name with the Foundation and asked to be assigned responsibility for the grave of an American soldier with a surname similar to his own. The Dutchman was a veteran blue helmet of the UNIFIL mission in Lebanon in 1982, and this background made him particularly keen to find out more about the American sergeant from the 30th Infantry Division.

Internet research proved particularly gratifying as the Dutch veteran soon learned that the sergeant from South Dakota had been employed in a meat packing company in Sioux Falls and that he had been given special leave during his army training when his father had suffered a deadly accident in that same company. Barely four months later, the 20-year-old was on his way to Europe, never to be seen again by his mother, two sisters, and two brothers. Ronald Jacobs received a Bronze Star when on 7 August 1944 he helped stave off a furious German attack against his mortar platoon. Two months later, he was wounded. But he returned to the front and had collected a Silver Star for more courage under fire by the time he was killed in action near Magdeburg in Germany in April 1945.

Referring to his own military service in Lebanon, the Dutchman said self-effacingly: "I have always had the impression that what we accomplished with UNIFIL over there was useful. It cannot compare with what the American boys have meant for us, but it does create a certain bond."[65]

Special bonds were created also between Margraten boys and Dutch who had personal experience of what it meant to have victims of war rest forever in some faraway place. Shortly after receiving an adoption certificate from the Foundation in the summer of 2005, a Limburg woman went to the cemetery where her husband Pièrre had been interred a little earlier. She took some of the flowers from his grave and brought them to Margraten where she placed them on the grave of New Yorker Philip Coloe. She knew that her beloved husband would have appreciated the gesture. The Germans had killed his uncle, and Pièrre had been named after him when he was born five days after the execution. It had taken her husband more than 40 years to learn where his uncle had been buried and to put some flowers on his grave in Hermsdorf on the outskirts of Berlin. It had been Pièrre's dying wish to do for an American soldier what he hoped someone in Germany was doing for his uncle.[66]

There were adopters who had gained firsthand experience of how immensely comforting it was to find that locals in a foreign country were caring for the final resting places of people they did not know. "An uncle of mine was killed in Indonesia," a 39-year-old woman said of her adoption of an infantryman from Vermont, "and there too people take care of his grave."[67]

The adopter of a soldier from South Dakota had vivid memories of a visit with her husband to the Thai war cemetery in Kanchanaburi near the River Kwai, the final resting place for more than 5,000 Commonwealth and close to 2,000 Dutch nationals, most of them casualties of slave labor on the Burma railway. "Although we did not experience the war ourselves," she recounted, "we cried as we walked past the perfectly kept graves with all those Dutch names. Now, the adoption of this American grave feels like returning the favor for what those people in Thailand do for 'our boys.'"[68]

The man from Maastricht who adopted infantryman John McKee from Pennsylvania in 2005 did so with his great-grandfather, George Jamieson, in mind. The adopter was British, but he had married a Dutch woman and now called the Netherlands his home. George Jamieson lay interred in a Commonwealth cemetery in Senlis, 24 miles north of Paris. In October 1915, the married farm worker from the small Scottish town of Forres had joined the regiment of the Seaforth Highlanders. In December 1917, he had been wounded by a gunshot in the left shoulder. The private had recovered from that, only to end up in the Second Battle of the Marne, where a shell explosion in July left him so badly wounded that he succumbed to his injuries a month later. Several years ago, George's great-grandson had finally had the opportunity to visit the Scotsman's grave in the Great War cemetery in France. "We do not manage to go there often," he reflected. "The thought that someone there might put some flowers on his grave from time to time is pleasing, and if I can do the same for a fallen American, I find that pleasing too."[69]

But for those for whom the Margraten boys were first and foremost someone's children rather than an army's soldiers, placing flowers on their graves had a meaning that went far beyond any of the world's countless wars. Several Dutch became adopters because they had lost a child in a car accident or to an illness and had an acute sense of the pain American parents must have felt at not being able to find comfort visiting a grave.

For one couple in their mid-forties, the adoption of Irvin Leech from Pennsylvania was in honor of their parents and their stories of liberation. But it was just as much in memory of the son they had lost several years ago. That was the reason why they had made certain to select the grave of an American soldier who had died on 19 April, the day that their son had been born.[70]

A man who lost his 20-year-old daughter to cancer in 2005 had always been bothered by the memory of how afraid she had been to leave this life without knowing anyone who had gone before her into the great beyond. The Foundation's appeal made him aware of the fact that many of the Margraten boys not far from his home had been her age when they passed away. That is why the grieving father put in a request for adoption and asked if it was possible to take over the grave of a soldier from Georgia, a state he had visited several years earlier and was somewhat familiar with. Now, whenever he paid a visit to the grave of Joseph Culpepper, the Dutchman had his daughter in mind as much as the American soldier.[71]

At the start of the new millennium, the Dutch continued to reach out to the Margraten boys for myriad reasons, many of them still directly related to World War II, others to issues of loss and hope that were of all times.

9 Of Paramount Importance

"We are all Americans," French newspaper *Le Monde* had asserted in the wake of 9/11. And the Dutch and other NATO allies had agreed that the attack against the US should be seen as an attack against them all. Yet the consensus on the War on Terror within NATO began to unravel not long after the offensive against the Taliban in Afghanistan. The issue that set this process in motion was the American pre-emptive and unilateral invasion of Iraq in March 2003 to get at Saddam Hussein's weapons of mass destruction.

Unlike France and Germany, sneered at as 'Old Europe' by Secretary of Defense Donald Rumsfeld for opposing the invasion, a loyal Dutch government gave its backing to the American offensive. But as exhaustive inspections on Iraqi territory gave the lie to the existence of weapons of mass destruction, many in the Netherlands soon felt a sense of betrayal. And, as time passed, many more Dutch turned against the war in Iraq as a result of revelations of shocking American violations of human rights.[1]

1

Even within the Margraten adoption community, the war in Iraq was causing deep divisions. This was nothing new, of course. America's 14 World War II cemeteries overseas, much more so than the eight cemeteries of World War I, had been conceived as instruments of public diplomacy that sought to impress foreign hosts. They were designed with an eye to consolidating the country's international standing, signaling a New World Order in which the US would henceforth be playing a major role. Yet, if these had been the ideological underpinnings of the American fields of honor, nothing had ever prevented the Margraten cemetery from serving as a platform for Americans and Dutch to freely exchange thoughts, and indeed to politely disagree, on the crucial issues of war and peace.[2]

The Vietnam War and Reagan's nuclear arms race in particular had caused spirited disagreements on foreign policy to be aired on the Margraten plateau. Both sides had generally engaged in such exchanges in an atmosphere of respect for free speech, one of the core values for which both allies agreed World War II had ultimately been fought. "The respect for another's beliefs is of paramount importance," former US ambassador to the Netherlands, Philip Young, had remarked in an address in 1965. "The capacity to disagree without jeopardizing a friendship can be of vital significance in the long run."[3]

That is certainly what the Margraten adopters continued to believe wholeheartedly when asked in a survey to convey how they viewed their relation with the US five years into the war with Iraq. On Memorial Day in May 2003, three weeks after President Bush on the aircraft carrier USS *Abraham Lincoln* had triumphantly declared the mission in Iraq to have been accomplished, US ambassador to the Netherlands, Clifford Sobel, in a speech at the Margraten cemetery, had drawn an emotional parallel between the American commitment in the Middle East and the liberation of Europe in World War II. He had, he said, just recently greeted troops of the 101st Airborne Division as they passed through Schiphol airport in Amsterdam for deployment to Iraq. The ambassador told the Dutch audience that the division's first combat casualty in Operation Iraqi Freedom had been Army Specialist Brandon Rowe and that this American soldier reminded him of Sergeant Wingard. Pennsylvanian Jacob Wingard had been killed in a battle to free the Dutch village of Eerde in September 1944, and ambassador Sobel had been happy to visit with the Dutch family that had flown his widow over to see where her husband had died and where he was buried at Margraten. "Brandon Rowe's sacrifice," the American ambassador assured, "like Sergeant Wingard's, was for freedom and the liberation of others." By the time the survey was held in 2008, however, Dutch adopters were less convinced than ever of the American ambassador's interpretation and they were now engaged in much soul-searching.[4]

Sure enough, there were many in the adoption community who staunchly refused to criticize the US even in the midst of the raging controversy. "My father was pro-American," a 52-year-old woman from Eckelrade set the tone. "He regarded them as the liberators of the world. World War II has had a profound impact on me and still does." A man in his forties who cared for the graves of soldiers from Florida and North Dakota resolutely agreed: "A country that sacrifices thousands upon thousands of young people for freedom on the other side of the world cannot but be a good country." The Dutch people owed the Americans "an historical debt," still other adopters emphasized, and therefore the US had to be granted "more credit than other countries." It is, a 68-year-old doctor who had taken over adoption from a great-uncle tried to explain, "an emotional relation that causes one to have an everlasting positive critical view of the USA." For a couple from Maastricht of the doctor's age, that relation was unconditional: "We are grateful for as long as we live: regardless of what happens!" It was no different for an elderly woman from Margraten: "Despite everything, the Americans can do little wrong in my eyes. We remain thankful for the immense sacrifice."[5]

These were the people who continued to have blind faith in the Americans as "the guardians of democracy, peace, and security." They were the people also who managed to see American action, from Vietnam to Iraq, as part of a crusade that had been ongoing almost uninterruptedly since World War II. "It saddens and frightens me," confessed the adopter of an infantryman from Nebraska, "that some cultures which interpret freedom as a weapon of the devil and ban it, share the basic principles of Nazism and Communism." The young man went on to cite the murder by a radical Muslim of controversial Dutch filmmaker Theo van Gogh in the streets of Amsterdam in 2004 and said he was glad that the Americans at least were willing to use massive force to call a halt to such fanatics.[6]

Quite a few adopters who agreed with the intervention in Iraq blamed Dutch media for cultivating an atmosphere of anti-Americanism. One man, the adopter of an Oregonian lieutenant from a medical battalion, blamed both the media and what he called Europe's "pseudo intellectuals." The hardships of World War II had forced his family to become involved in black-market activities during the Nazi occupation and as a result his father, the adopter claimed, on several occasions had been imprisoned. He drew a stark contrast between suffering under German rule and the good life that had befallen one of his aunts when she had married an American soldier and followed

15. Back of the bracelet of S/Sgt Albert Kielblock, killed in October 1944 aboard a B-24 Liberator from the 392nd Bomber Group. From this bomber group alone, the names of 80 men are engraved on Margraten's headstones and walls of the missing. (Courtesy US National Archives and Records Administration and Annette Tison)

him to a town near Chicago. The discussions about Iraq and the attitude of the Europeans towards President Bush, this adopter could only conclude, were "shameful."[7]

A slightly younger man tended to agree, although he worded his discontent less bluntly. For the 56-year-old manager from Beegden, what caused him to withhold judgment on the US was the sacrifice of Margraten boy Amos Doty. On 19 May 1944, Amos had served as an engineer on a B-24 that had taken off from Wendling in England for a bombing mission against targets near Brunswick in Germany. An enemy fighter had pounced on the Liberator near Hessen, causing it to explode in mid-air. German reports stated that debris from the aircraft had been scattered across an area of nearly a mile. None of the ten airmen survived. Indeed, the bodies were so badly burned that only three of them could be positively identified before burial that evening. These were the pilot from California, the navigator from New

York, and engineer Amos Doty from Fort Henry, Tennessee. Among the next of kin registered as those to be informed of casualties by the War Department, the Missing Air Crew Report for the B-24 listed six mothers, two fathers, and two wives. One of the latter was Ruby who had been married to Amos.

Almost every month since the adoption in 2004, the manager from Beegden had driven more than thirty miles to visit the grave of the sergeant from Tennessee. "I believe," the Dutch adopter maintained, "that we have obligations towards America and that it is very important to cooperate as good allies so as to make sure that oppression is eradicated."[8]

The Netherlands and the US, an adopter and lab technician emphasized, were "friendly nations that support and defend each other in good as well as bad times." Many adopters begged to disagree, however. To them, what proved to be of much more importance was, in the words that American former ambassador Philip Young had uttered at the start of the escalation in Vietnam, "the capacity to disagree without jeopardizing that friendship." Renowned historian Hans Blom has remarked that for the Dutch, World War II has long been "firmly embedded in the national psyche as a moral touchstone, as the basis of a clear distinction between moral and immoral, good and bad." In the fiasco that was Iraq, it bothered many adopters that such distinctions appeared to have been erased completely. More importantly, the military intervention in the Middle East once again laid bare what American historian Andrew Bacevich has described as the "radically different conclusions" that the New World and the Old World have drawn from World War II regarding the use of military power. For Americans the 1940s had been "a story of triumph" that had told them that military dominance would allow the US to "perpetuate global primacy and impress its values on the world at large." For Europeans, however, the era had been an unmitigated tragedy and disaster that had caused them to reject war as an acceptable instrument.[9]

By the time of the survey in 2008 there were reasons enough then, even for adopters of American graves, to feel deeply upset and outright angry at what the US had wreaked in the Middle East. "I regard the America of the past," wrote a woman who had been six at the end of World War II, "as different and better." "They were liberators then," one man maintained, "now they are aggressors."

"Given the role Americans currently play in the world," even a man whose father had been liberated from Dachau by GIs could write, "I am not endeared by them." Many adopters thought the military intervention in Iraq senseless and dangerous, and not a few drew parallels with the Vietnam disaster. What appalled them, among others, was the sidelining of the United Nations, the lies that had led to the invasion, and the disregard for human rights from Guantanamo Bay to Abu Ghraib.[10]

For some of those who felt hugely disappointed by America's behavior, the Iraq affair was only part of a much broader problem with the superpower's strategy in the Middle East. "You cannot," lectured a woman whose grandmother had housed American soldiers in Kerkrade in 1944, "bring democracy to Afghanistan and Iraq through the use of arms." Others simply refused to believe that democracy was America's real objective. "Why invade Iraq," one man demanded to know, "and not Zimbabwe?" "It appears to me," said the adopter of an infantryman from Tennessee, "that at present there are other interests at stake than freedom. Power and enrichment are what it is really all about. It is horrible to behold." "At the highest level," a 70-year-old from Scheulder vented his spleen, "economic interests are all that matter and human lives count for nothing." The special relationship with Israel came in for criticism too. "Less support for Israel!" the middle-aged adopter of a Kentuckian urged. "More sympathy for the Palestinians." "I cringe," wrote an elderly man whose family had harbored Jews during World War II, "at the uncritical and unlimited support that America continues to provide to the state of Israel, and the same goes for the slavish attitude of the Dutch government in this matter."[11]

It was one thing to air such political opinions in the private space of one's home or in an anonymous survey. It proved quite another matter, however, for Dutch families to try and convey such heartfelt convictions to American families. A teacher and her parents in Maastricht had been entertaining a lively correspondence with the family of Sergeant Cecil Smith ever since the adoption of his grave in 1946. Letters with his mother and widow had gradually made way for long email exchanges with his daughter in Texas. But when Cecil's daughter asked their overseas friends where they stood on Iraq, the Dutch adopters made the mistake of being a bit too forward in their reply. They told the Texans that they thought what the Americans were doing in Iraq was quite different from what they had done in World War II and that, given that there would not be sufficient support from the Iraqi people, they should not have started this war. After more than 60 years of pleasant visits and warm exchanges, this comment drew no reply whatsoever. "We were given the impression," the Dutch teacher meekly remarked, "that they were of a wholly different mindset regarding this matter."[12]

For the large majority of those watching over the Margraten boys, however, any anger or discomfort that the foreign policies of the Americans might be causing was always more or less assuaged by the memory of their massive involvement in the liberation in the 1940s. "Especially in times when American military action in the world is criticized, often rightly so, it is important," ascertained a man who in 2004 had adopted one grave for himself and one for his two young children, "to continue to highlight the virtues of that same country during World War II."[13]

"I do from time to time," a 42-year-old adopter admitted somewhat reluctantly, "have a negative view of the present-day US. I do not always agree with what they do today." But that had not stopped him from adopting the grave of Leonard Rozwalka in 2007. Internet research had revealed to him the agonizing circumstances that had led to the death of the infantryman from Illinois. Under cover of darkness on Easter Sunday 1945, G Company of the 387th Infantry Regiment had sent a patrol across the Rhine in three boat teams. The men were to probe enemy positions opposite their sector and soon discovered that German strength there was not to be underestimated. So heavy was the German machine-gun fire they drew in response to their landing that before long they were staggering back to the shore. Many were shot as they hurriedly took off their equipment and outer garments and tried to wade and swim to a reef in the river. Leonard Rozwalka was not the only American who failed to return that night. According to the patrol's after-action report, the body of an engineer floated by "with a hole from ear to ear." PFC Schiff "was hit in the jaw by a bullet." Private Gonzalez came to the rescue of PFC Vombey, only to find that "he had been shot all along his right side and through the right side of his head." It was the horrible fate of GIs who had pushed on deep into Germany in 1945, after having liberated parts of his own country, that forced Leonard's adopter to be instinctively cautious in his criticism of America today.[14]

"Even with all the mistakes they make today," a retired English teacher said, "you always have in the back of your mind the tremendous sacrifices they made in 40–45." After all, this adopter had learned that horrible mistakes had been made during World War II too, and that people had somehow reconciled to that in the context of the broader friendship and alliance. In May 2008 the teacher had welcomed Maryanne, the younger sister of Margraten boy Charles Dimmock, to Kerkrade. It was in Kerkrade that her brother Chuck had lost his life when his P-47 Thunderbolt had smashed into a home after having been downed by inexperienced American troops. They had mistaken his aircraft for an enemy aircraft when it returned to the airport of Le Culot in Belgium from a mission in Germany. But Maryanne had come to Kerkrade not just to see where her brother had died. Thanks to the mediation of the former teacher, who was also Chuck's adopter, she was keen to meet up with Bern. Bern's little sister Maria was five when on 7 November 1944 she abruptly abandoned play in the Bockstraat in Kerkrade in response to the shrill wailing of sirens. She rushed home along a narrow path behind their backyard to seek shelter in the sturdy basement. The girl never made it. Debris from Lieutenant Dimmock's disintegrating fighter-bomber cut her down in the middle of her family's backyard. For two families who had lived with the grief of seemingly senseless loss for so long, the meeting in Kerkrade in 2008 brought a profound catharsis. With such painful sacrifice, both Dutch and American, etched into his mind, how was Chuck's adopter to pass easy judgments on wars then and now?[15]

2

Adopters repeated time and again that they would have accepted a duty of care for the graves of the liberators buried at Margraten regardless of their nationality, whether Australian, British, Canadian or Polish. But the fact remained that ever since the reorganization of the resting place in the late 1940s, the graves at Margraten had been exclusively those of American liberators. Many adopters agreed that, despite the commotion caused by the war in Iraq, this continued to give them ample reason to look at the relationship with the US as something quite special.

Some were keenly aware of the deep historical dimension of that relationship. "Countless Dutch are the ancestors of the many new generations of Americans," the adopter of a Jewish soldier from New York pointed out. "The historical relation between the Netherlands and the USA is one of mother and son." Many saw a kind of poetic justice in the fact that a strong New World since its independence had come to the rescue of the old and exhausted mother country on numerous occasions. "Three times they have rescued Western Europe," the adopter of a Californian kept count. "There was World War I, World War II, and Marshall Aid." America's role in half a century of Cold War, from the Berlin airlift to the collapse of the Berlin Wall, continued to have strong resonance in the adoption community. So did the more recent fight against international terrorism, of course, which went hand in hand with an acute awareness that globalization had made people more connected, but at the same time also frighteningly vulnerable. "We will one day," a Limburg mailman and adopter of a Kansas sergeant predicted gravely, "need each other again."[16]

Adopters realized, however, that what often complicated the relationship was the gaping asymmetry in power. "I do," a 56-year-old manager admitted, "sometimes feel ashamed that time and again we let the Americans take the chestnuts from the fire." "When on 6 June 2004 together we visited Omaha Beach in Normandy," a 48-year-old cardiologist and his wife wrote, "we wondered if, when it really mattered, we would be standing on America's beaches." But others reasoned that the Netherlands as a tiny country was doing all it possibly could. Small as the number of Dutch troops in Afghanistan might seem in the overall picture, the Netherlands relative to its size was taking significant risks and casualties in Uruzgan province. This was thought reason enough for their country to be taken seriously. "I consider the relationship between the Netherlands and the US important," the adopter of an infantryman emphasized, "but equality and balance are essential." "We should not," the adopters of a paratrooper clarified, "feel obliged to go along with things we do not agree with."[17]

Many in the adoption community lamented that such balance and respect for the opinion of allies had been gravely lacking in the administration of President George W. Bush. There was some irony therefore in the unexpected announcement from the US embassy in The Hague in March that to mark the 60th anniversary of the end of World War II in Europe on Sunday, 8 May 2005, George W. Bush would be the first American president ever to be paying a visit to the Margraten cemetery. He would do so on his way from the Baltic countries to Moscow. The stopover was to be very brief. But it sufficed to throw much of Limburg in lockdown while Dutch national, regional, and local authorities frantically prepared to have things ready for the most high-profile presence in the rural province since the visit of Pope John Paul II 20 years earlier.

The security implications were soon giving authorities splitting headaches. It was estimated that President Bush would descend on Margraten and its slightly more than 13,000 souls with his own entourage of 800 and another 200 media people in tow from as far away as Japan. Moreover, Queen Beatrix as well as Dutch Prime Minister Jan-Peter Balkenende and American Secretary of State Condoleezza Rice were to accompany the American president at the cemetery. While the regional press raised the specter of the horrible fates that had befallen presidents Lincoln, McKinley, Kennedy, and Reagan, people watched thousands of Dutch and American security forces descend on their neighborhoods and claim control over Margraten and much of southern Limburg. Limburgers watched in awe as sniffer dogs, armored vehicles, Apache helicopters, and snipers wearing black balaclavas took up positions.

Fear of terrorists and demonstrators caused the atmosphere to be tense. As the main roads to the cemetery were reserved for vehicles carrying the VIPs, ordinary visitors were to make their way to the ceremony via secondary roads that could barely handle the traffic. Put in place for the occasion, detection gates at the entrance to the cemetery scanned everyone for suspect metal objects. Security agents thought nothing of confiscating even thermos cans for the duration of the ceremony, leaving people to brave the grey skies and biting wind without the hot coffee they had hoped to be sipping.

As an imposing Air Force One touched down at Maastricht Aachen Airport on Saturday evening, protesters gathered. The organizers of an anti-Bush demonstration in Amsterdam claimed there were some 8,000. Slogans on banners and placards raised all the hot-button issues. The Iraq War, of course, and the violation of human rights at Guantanamo Bay and Abu Ghraib. But everything else too, from Bush's stance on abortion and euthanasia to his refusal to have the US join the International Criminal Court and the fight against global warming.

Things were much quieter in Limburg. There were only a few handfuls of peace activists at the regional airport and in Maastricht. Some of their banners declared Bush a "war criminal" and the US "the dictator of the world." An elderly man sat on a chair and quietly denounced the war in Iraq holding a placard saying, "Not In My Name."

The massive presence of security forces in southern Limburg would have smothered any noisy and potentially disruptive protests in an instant, of course. But that was certainly not the main reason why the atmosphere felt fundamentally different in and around Margraten. Regardless of any policy disagreements they might have had with the current American president, thousands upon thousands of adopters and their families and friends were determined to be present at the cemetery. Indeed, the special relationship between the adoption community and the US had been highlighted as soon as President Bush descended from Air Force One. As the President and First Lady stepped onto the tarmac, two children from local adopting families had been allowed to be the first to greet the honored guests, even before the assembled Dutch politicians and Limburg governor. The children were proud to present the American couple with bouquets of fragrant tulips.[18]

On Sunday morning, 8 May 2005, President Bush addressed the massive crowd at the windswept Margraten cemetery. "In the Voice of America's radio broadcast from London on the first V-E Day," Bush noted, "the announcer asked Europe to 'think of these Americans as your dead, too.' In Dutch hearts, they already were." To the delight of the countless adopters present, the American president went on to praise their "wonderful tradition" and "kindness." "And on behalf of a grateful America," he concluded, "I thank you for treating our men and women as your sons and daughters."

The response was more pensive, however, when President Bush, like his ambassador to the Netherlands before him, insisted on seeing parallels between the Good War and the way America was handling the War on Terror. "As the 21st century unfolds before us," the

16. George W. Bush and Queen Beatrix side by side at the Margraten cemetery during the American president's visit in May 2005. (Courtesy Stichting Margraten Memorial Center)

American leader asserted, "Americans and Europeans are continuing to work together and are bringing freedom and hope to places where it has long been denied: in Afghanistan, in Iraq, in Lebanon, and across the broader Middle East." Despite the Dutch government's broad backing of the American involvement in the Middle East, even Prime Minister Balkenende in his speech at Margraten seemed to be sending subtle signals to the American president. "Freedom is a universal value," the Dutch leader agreed. "Faith in freedom and democracy unites us." But the Dutch leader appeared to be qualifying that statement somewhat when he added: "Freedom has many faces. Freedom is the right to be different." In a country where the Iraq War had become increasingly unpopular, and where gay rights and the right to abortion and euthanasia were part of the social fabric, people understood that the latter could be interpreted on many levels, including the relationship between the Netherlands and the US.[19]

Ultimately, however, for the adopters listening to the speeches as they stood packed between the marble crosses and stars that chill and blustery Sunday morning, the point was not whether and to what extent one agreed or disagreed with the Bush administration. "The US," an adopter of soldiers from Pennsylvania and South Dakota emphasized, "fortunately is much more than Bush." In the 2008 survey, the overwhelming majority of adopters insisted on making clear that, if they had problems with US government policies at all, they had no issue whatsoever with the American people. Strong feelings of sympathy had been cultivated as a result of close relations with ordinary American families that in many cases went back several decades. "The people I have met in the USA," explained an adopter whose family had been taking care of a Margraten boy since 1946, "are the same people I meet here. We can share happiness and sadness with each other." "America seems closer," another family of longtime adopters noted, because "you identify with the next of kin." Adopters admitted to being more attuned to news about the US so as to be more informed and better able to correspond with the Margraten boys' families. Some said they tended to worry whenever they heard that a hurricane or bush fire threatened parts of the US where they knew the boys' families had their homes. "As an adopter," observed a 37-year-old from Heerlen who had signed up recently, "in a sense you feel you belong to the US to a small degree."[20]

The village of Nijswiller was a case in point. Nestled in the gently rolling landscape of southern Limburg, the village counts no more than 750 souls. Proud of its long history, the community had decided to create its own historical society a few months before the American president's visit to the region. Signing up more than 50 members in no time, the society had sufficient manpower to staff a separate work group on World War II tasked with mapping Nijswiller's involvement in the Margraten adoption. Investigators soon discovered that so many of the villagers had been involved with the Margraten boys over the decades that the phenomenon called for the creation of a website on which could be posted all of their stories and accompanying photos. Three years later, the website was documenting the adoption stories of at least twenty families from the small Dutch village. In May 2008 the historical society received a message from a woman in Knoxville, Tennessee:

To the people of Nijswiller:

What a beautiful tribute to our fathers. Knowing that you haven't forgotten and that you care for them as though they were your own family is a burden lifted from my shoulders. Thank you sounds a bit pale in comparison to what I would like to say.

May God Bless You for caring about our fallen fathers. And for me, most especially PFC Andrew James Scalf, who was killed Feb. 27, 1945 in Gerderath, Germany.

"Yes," one of the members of Nijswiller's historical society readily admitted in 2008. "The fact that I am an adopter has changed my view of the US. We have intensive contacts and know now that one cannot generalize when discussing 'the Americans.' And I often find myself defending this point of view because it hurts when someone attacks our friends."[21]

"Friends," an insurance-company employee echoed the adoption community's credo, "do not always have to agree, but they do not let each other down." This adopter as a 41-year-old had signed up to care for the graves of four American infantrymen just a few months before 9/11. None of the political turmoil that had followed in the wake of the terrorist attack had perturbed him even slightly. His focus had remained on the boys whose care, he reasoned, involved not just their graves, but also the memories of who they had been. That is why he had doggedly researched their backgrounds to give faces to their names. What he had learned about some of the soldiers over the years had only increased his respect for the sacrifices that ordinary American families had been forced to make as they became caught up in forces beyond their control.

The Carlsons in Illinois had said goodbye to Sivert in December 1944. Sivert in February recovered from wounds sustained in a landmine explosion in the Hürtgen Forest and a month later was awarded the Bronze Star and promoted to sergeant for rescuing wounded comrades during an intense bombardment after crossing the Roer River. In April 1945, however, Sivert's luck ran out when German soldiers in the Ruhr Pocket tricked his platoon into the open by waving a white flag and then opened fire. It was one of the War Department's standard telegrams that had broken the news to his wife Magdaline. The telegram had also dramatically changed the lives of Sivert's six-year-old daughter and two-year-old son.

The McCollums in Missouri had known that life could be hard long before Clarence was killed in a beet field just outside Prummern in an assault against Mahogany Hill on a Monday morning in November 1944. Clarence's father had given up a successful business in home construction to become an itinerant preacher, leaving his wife to care for ten children on her own for months on end. Clarence himself had left school at age twelve to work in a bakery. He had met his wife at a rollerskate rink in the early 1930s. By the start of the war, they were the proud parents of two daughters and a son. The three children forever remembered how their fun-loving father had often returned from work with donuts for everyone.

The blow had been just as devastating for the Littles in Maryland. Ernie was the eldest of eight children. His father spent his life working in a milk factory while his mother was forced to make regular trips to the sanatorium to be treated for tuberculosis. Ernie had left school at 15 to work in a canning plant. When he married Annie he was not even earning enough money to have wedding pictures made. When their children were born in 1939 and 1940, he found himself employed in a poolroom. Ernie was put in a uniform and rushed overseas on Christmas Day 1944. Within weeks he was thrown into battle in the Hürtgen Forest. Very early in the morning of 30 January 1945,

Ernie's unit went on the attack near Huppenbroich. A snowstorm raged and many of the men said a prayer and kissed the pictures of loved ones before pushing off. When his platoon sought cover in an old mineshaft to escape ferocious German shelling later that day, a direct hit obliterated the shelter, killing Ernie and twenty-one other Americans in the blink of an eye.

In 2004 Sivert's adopter accompanied the soldier's son to the Margraten cemetery. On Memorial Day 2005 he did the same with all of Clarence's children. The Dutchman on numerous occasions also sent small pieces from the turf on the men's graves to their families. In the backyard of Ernie's granddaughter in Elkton, Maryland, one such piece from Margraten, the adopter revealed in 2008, had firmly taken root and "grown quite a bit."[22]

3

Political disagreements over fundamental matters of war and peace kept surfacing at the American military cemetery long after President Bush had returned home. In his Memorial Day speech in May 2007, President Bush's new ambassador to the Netherlands, Roland Arnall, observed: "In an ideal world 'an end to the beginning of all wars' might be conceivable. In an ideal world, the brutality and inhumanity that people suffer would become non-existent." "Unfortunately," he added with some measure of sarcasm, "we have yet to achieve an idyllic existence." With those words the ambassador appeared to have taken a page from neoconservative author Robert Kagan. The American, in a bestselling book, had taken Europeans to task for having shied away from the use of naked power ever since the end of World War II and for insisting that some kind of paradise based on international rules might be possible anytime soon. Limburg's governor, Léon Frissen, however, showed himself unrepentant when, in his speech that same day, he on his part observed: "The past few years have shown that our freedom is fragile and under pressure, and that democratic principles and the rule of law are being flouted." Like the American ambassador, the Dutchman pulled no punches when he added that it was not just "terrorist attacks" that were "indicative" of this, but also "the responses to those attacks."[23]

What was of paramount importance to the adoption community, however, was to ensure that the memory of the Margraten boys in World War II remained untainted by politics past and future. In the 2008 survey, a man in his forties from Landgraaf stated that he was "very critical" of American foreign policy. He then proceeded to explain why, angrily summing up everything from the murder of Lumumba in the Congo to the coup against the regime of Allende in Chile and the right-wing death squadrons in Central America. This same man, however, had been tending to the grave of an American infantryman since 2006. And when asked in the survey if he had ever been criticized for being an adopter at the American military cemetery, he shot back: "I have never had a single negative reaction and cannot imagine that such idiots might exist."[24]

It appeared that the broader Dutch community respected this stance on keeping politics away from the Margraten boys. The overwhelming majority of adopters in response to the same question resolutely stated that no one had ever held their involvement against them in any way. A few adopters even said they resented the very nature of the question. How could, a 70-year-old woman wondered, anyone possibly object to the adoption of American soldiers? "Their blood," she pointed out, "is mixed in with our soil, our grain, our bread."[25]

Indeed, as the memory of World War II inexorably faded into history, the Margraten cemetery was generating increasing interest. The commemorations surrounding the 60th anniversary of the end of World War II formed only the start of a series of official ceremonies involving the Margraten boys and their adopters. In October 2005 the grandsons of Franklin Roosevelt, Winston Churchill, and Joseph Stalin, the leaders who had sat together at Yalta to decide Europe's fate near the end of the war, paid a highly symbolic visit to the Margraten cemetery and participated in a joint wreath-laying ceremony. A year later, the Margraten town council took the initiative, with the support of the province of Limburg, to commemorate the liberation of the region early in September with a Margraten Requiem. In the morning hours of Sunday, 10 September 2006, the Bishop of Roermond celebrated Mass at the cemetery. Later that day on the same spot, the Limburg Symphony Orchestra gave a moving performance of Mozart's *Requiem*. In September 2007, despite threatening weather, the number of visitors serenely listening to Verdi's *Requiem* on Margraten's hallowed grounds had swelled to more than 3,500.[26]

Meanwhile, prompted in part by the mass interest of visitors and media generated by President Bush's visit, the Margraten town council, again with the support of the province of Limburg, had embarked on its most ambitious project yet. In a media release in November 2005, the municipality of Margraten announced that a specialized consultancy agency had determined that it was feasible, given certain conditions, to have what was called a Memorial Park created in the immediate vicinity of the American military cemetery. The first aim of this center was to provide the historical background that Dutch and foreign visitors had repeatedly indicated was sorely missing. It was seen as particularly important to create "new instruments of telling this story in such a manner that it would appeal to younger generations too." There was no escaping the reality that economic motives too were driving this project. The Chamber of Commerce of southern Limburg had co-financed the feasibility study, for example, and the media release in November 2005 made no secret of the fact that the other main objective was "strengthening tourism."[27]

But as the project gathered steam, it remained to be seen how realistic its chances of success might be. After all, Dutch authorities over the decades had several blueprints for projects of this nature drawn up and then shelved again, most often because of lack of funding and serious reservations on the part of the ABMC. The ABMC, which had begun functioning immediately after the Great War, had understandably always been very quick to call a halt to anything that might possibly be construed as commercialization of the cemeteries. But as American historian Ron Robin has shown, another preoccupation of the ABMC from the very beginning had also been "to 'control' and 'censor' battle monuments and cemeteries as 'proper' representations of the United States abroad."[28]

Pleased as they were by the mushrooming ceremonies and initiatives on and around the cemetery, the unpaid volunteers of the newly created Adoption Foundation did what their predecessors had been doing under slightly different names for more than half a century: they battened down and patiently soldiered on. In the wake of President Bush's visit so many additional candidates for adoption from across the country and beyond rushed to contact the Foundation that soon it was decided to create a waiting list. By September 2005 340 candidates were waiting with much impatience and the Foundation therefore agreed that the time had come to give up for adoption the 230 graves mentioned on the so-called B-list. These were the graves for which the adopters on the certificates from immediately after the war had not yet been traced, even after three years of painstaking detective work. Running the risk that at one point in the future these adopters or their descendants might re-emerge, and aware of the emotions surrounding 'their' boys, the Foundation's president thanked the members "for taking this courageous decision."

In March 2006 the Foundation was proud to announce that it was ready to issue adoption certificate number 5,000 and that Limburg governor Léon Frissen had volunteered to have his name written on it as the caretaker of both a known and an unknown American soldier. "Respect and gratitude are my motivation," the governor explained. "But I also find it important that younger generations know what happened and do not take the freedom they have for granted."[29]

In May 2007 an article in *De Limburger* led to yet another wave of requests, with more than six hundred additional candidates getting in touch with a Foundation that had been working in overdrive since its creation in 2002. By the end of 2007, the Foundation was elated to announce that certificates had now been issued to active adopters, old and new, of all of the 8,301 graves in which rest the community's beloved Margraten boys. As the number of names on the waiting list continued to grow, however, this milestone almost immediately marked the beginning of a new challenge. It had been quite an honor for the Margraten adoption community to learn at the start of the new century that the French had copied their system in a program called *Les Fleurs de la Mémoire* for the Normandy American cemeteries at Colleville-sur-Mer and Saint-James. Now the Dutch in turn looked to Normandy for inspiration. Following the French example, early in 2008 they set in motion the adoption of the names of missing American soldiers chiseled in the walls lining the entrance to their cemetery.[30]

Perhaps some of the Foundation's inspiration for the new initiative had resulted also from watching Sharon Estill Taylor at the Wall of the Missing on 27 May 2007. Her father, Lieutenant Shannon Estill, had crashed with his P-38 Lightning in eastern Germany a month before the enemy surrendered. His remains had been recovered only recently and in 2006 Shannon had been laid to rest at the military cemetery of Arlington in Virginia. That Saturday in May, however, visitors including the American ambassador and the Margraten mayor, had witnessed Sharon place a bronze rosette before the name of her father on the Wall of the Missing to signify that he had been found. Of the 1,722 names on the wall it was only the 48th to be accompanied by a rosette more than 60 years after the war had ended. All the other soldiers remained missing and were waiting for adopters to gently run their fingers across their names from time to time.[31]

17. To signal that his remains have been recovered at last, a bronze rosette is placed before Shannon Estill's name on the Wall of the Missing in the presence of the fighter pilot's daughter in 2007. (Courtesy Sharon Estill Taylor)

As the years pushed World War II further and further back, adopters appeared ever more determined to reach across time to salvage the stories of the Margraten boys. The decision to find out more about Sergeant John Barry, for example, put one Dutch woman on a research trail that led to a dark side of the air war she had never even known existed. In an email in 2007, a man called Bob Saumsiegle informed her that he had been part of a B-17 crew together with John Barry. Bob had been the navigator; John had served as the bomber's tail-gunner. "He was a permanent member of the crew," Bob wrote, "and flew all the missions with us." On their 13th mission, however, things had gone horribly wrong. As they released their bombs against targets near the German city of Halberstadt on 30 May 1944, flak hit one of the engines of the *Pistol Packin' Mama*. The crippled Flying Fortress was lagging behind formation when a Messerschmidt fighter appeared to finish off the hapless prey. Smoking and shuddering, the *Pistol Packin' Mama* lumbered through the sky until the order came for the crew to abandon ship. All of the Americans successfully bailed out that Tuesday and most of them eventually ended up prisoners of the Germans. But John Barry and three of his comrades vanished. What the surviving crew had always remained convinced had happened to them was too horrifying for John's adopter to accept without corroborating evidence.

That evidence came soon enough in the form of a big envelope sent from Alexandria, Virginia. The story the IDPF documents told was that, as soon as the war had ended, American medical and graves registration personnel in the German village of Rühen had exhumed human remains, wrapped in burlap cloth, from an isolated grave with a marker bearing the name of John K. Barry. In 1944 already, German records received through the American Legation in Bern, Switzerland, had informed authorities that Sergeant Barry had been killed in action on 30 May and was interred in Rühen. That was the information also that the War Department had eventually passed on to John's mother in New York City. But John's Dutch adopter now learned from the IDPF that as soon as the medical examiners in June 1945 had confirmed that the remains were indeed those of the sergeant, they had also reported they had strong suspicions he had been the victim of a German war crime. Having viewed over 30,000 X-rays of battle casualties, one medical officer stated, he thought it most likely that John Barry had been killed not in a crash, but as the result of small-arms fire.

The medical findings backed up what John's comrades had always suspected. In official testimony after the war, the American airmen had maintained that, while trying to evade capture, enraged German villagers had hunted them down. Indeed, pilot Douglas Van Weelden had reported that his navigator "was nearly killed this way." Sergeant Phillip Olander on his part had forever remained haunted by the fact that his buddy and ball turret-gunner "narrowly escaped hanging by civilians." The pilot, the 303rd Bomb Group Association's historian posted on their website, always believed that John Barry and the other men who failed to return that fatal Tuesday in May 1944 "had been shot and murdered by the Germans."

In unearthing the horrors of war, adopters in the IDPF files also stumbled across the raw pain of American families that even 60 years later never failed to unnerve. John Barry's mother, for example, in May 1945 asked the War Department how to get back some of the 19-year-old's personal belongings, like the football sweater he had taken with him "as a reminder of home." "It's not the value," she apologized, "it's the memory, the only thing we are clinging to."[32]

Another Margraten boy, Sergeant Leonard Henlin had gone down with his Flying Fortress in the disastrous raid against Schweinfurt on 14 October 1943. From Rhode Island his mother in April 1944 sent a letter to the Adjutant General "to find out about my son's effects and whether the tag he had around his neck will be sent to me or whether the Government keeps it."[33]

Mart Etheridge is one of the 1,722 names on Margraten's Wall of the Missing. The Germans had blasted *The Drip*, the lieutenant's B-24, just after its bomb-run over targets near Münster on 5 November 1943. The burning Liberator made it as far as Walcheren, only to disappear behind the Dutch island's dunes and crash into the North Sea. "If we could have stayed up another ten minutes," one of the captured survivors later said, "we would have been home." The grey waters of the North Sea never returned Leonard's body. "These effects," a standard message from the Quartermaster Depot told his wife Margaret a year after the crash, "contained in one carton, are being forwarded to you." It took another six years for the Memorial Division to officially declare that her husband's remains were "not recoverable." "Realizing the extent of your great loss," the letter in 1950 informed the woman in Kentucky, "it is with reluctance that you are sent the information that there is no grave at which to pay homage."[34]

Providing comfort to American families like those of John, Leonard, and Mart is what had motivated the Dutch above all else when at the end of World War II they created Margraten's adoption program. More than 60 years later, unfazed by any political tension, that is what they continued to do. In 2005 Daniel O'Brien, vice-president of the 11th Armored Division Association, was moved to learn from the Foundation in Margraten that the grave of Steve Zoradi had been adopted by someone in Kerkrade. The soldiers both hailed from Nevada and had served together in Company A of the 56th Armored Engineer Battalion. Steve Zoradi had been ambushed and killed when ordered on 7 April 1945 to remove a roadblock on the outskirts of the German town of Schleusingen. Steve had been a "close friend" and his buddy thanked the Foundation's secretary for sharing the address of the adopter. "I greatly appreciate," the ageing veteran said in an email, "the consideration, love, and care that your countrymen are taking to honor our fallen comrades."[35]

That same year, a woman in the tiny town of Mancelona, Michigan, was as surprised as she was moved when a Dutch woman from Berlicum, North Brabant, sent her photos of the grave of her father, infantryman Walter Hood. "I was only two when he died," Walter's daughter thanked the adopter of her father's grave, "and my brother was born two weeks before his death, so I'm not sure the news of my brother's birth got to him before his death." "I'm going to give some of these pictures to him," she added, "he will be so happy."[36]

The 60th anniversary of the end of World War II not only brought an American president to the American cemetery to commemorate the Margraten boys in the company of Dutch adopters. Many of the next of kin also crossed the ocean now, often for the very first time, to visit the boys' graves, knowing that Dutch friends would be there at their side. PFC Philip Seifried had become a casualty of war with the 7th Armored Division in Germany less than a month before the war ended. He had died of his wounds ten days later. In 1946 a Dutch couple and their daughters had adopted his grave. That same year, they managed to get in touch with his family and were soon engaged in an intensive exchange of letters and photos. A photo of Philip was given pride of place on their wall in the living room. Charlotte, Philip's mother, apologized for the fact that she was having one of her daughters write the letters for her. "I was born in the old country," she explained, "and we never got much education there." She asked whether she could have the negatives of the photos taken at Margraten because there were "aunts and friends who would like a picture of his grave too."

Although he was "sort of a quiet boy," his mother told the Dutch family who asked to learn more about Philip, he was "always interested in sports." He had played in a baseball team and had gone to work in a bicycle factory before joining the military. "I have eight children," she went on to describe her family in June 1946. "Five boys and three girls." Then she paused and had her daughter Anna correct this: "I should say seven children because with Philip's death that is all I have left."

In a letter a month later, however, the grieving mother wanted the Dutch to know how much comfort she derived from knowing they were there for Philip. "It is really something," the letter said, "to have a family take over your son's grave and also treat his memory as if he were one of them."

Neither Charlotte nor any of the soldier's siblings ever returned to the old country to visit Philip and his Dutch caretakers. It was 2005 when a grandson of Philip's brother finally made it to the Margraten American cemetery in the company of one of the adopters' daughters.[37]

Also in 2005, on 28 May, a group of some two dozen Americans assembled near Margraten's town hall. They were all members of the American World War II Orphans Network and the next day were to attend the Memorial Day ceremony at the cemetery. But first the sons and daughters of the Margraten boys wanted to express to Margraten and the citizens of the Netherlands their profound gratitude "for 60 years of care and friendship." In an email to the Adoption Foundation paving the way for the ceremony, Gerry Morenski of the orphans network had warned that "the first visit to Margraten can be difficult and emotional." "And after 60 years," she assured, "the tears come even faster then when we were younger." Gerry Morenski could know. She was the daughter of Corporal David Conway who rested in Plot B, Row 2, Grave 31, and she had been at Margraten before. Yet when, on that Saturday in May 2005, the visitors presented as their gift an American red oak to take root in Margraten's soil as a living symbol of enduring friendship, there were only smiles around.[38]

Americans did not have to be related to the Margraten boys to express appreciation for the selfless acts that the Dutch continued to bestow on the fallen so long after World War II. In 2004 a teacher and a nurse from Limburg had volunteered to care for the grave of an infantryman from Michigan and an airman from Kansas. Shortly after, during a vacation in Germany, they ran into a group of American soldiers in a restaurant. They got to talking about World War II and their adoption at Margraten. When, at the end of their meal, the Dutch couple asked for the bill, the German owner told them that the American soldiers had been happy to take care of that when they left.[39]

10   The Audacity of Hope

There is something in Margraten's hushed atmosphere today that seems to suggest to visitors that time has at last softened the suffering of the soldiers and soothed the pain of their families on the other side of the ocean. The sanctuary represents the sublimation of sacrifice and that is precisely what American authorities set out to accomplish when designing this resting place and the 13 other overseas cemeteries of World War II.

In sharp contrast with the shrines of the Great War, historian Ron Robin has shown, Americans in charge of constructing the permanent military cemeteries during the 1950s very consciously abandoned the theme of "lament and mourning," embracing instead the message of "resurrection" and "rejuvenation." Landscape architects, for example, moved away from the Great War reliance on evergreens, demonstrating a clear preference for the extensive use of flowers. This was only part of a more concerted effort to transform the austere into the august, as befitting a world power now ready to accept sacrifice as the inevitable price of leadership. The layout of Great War cemeteries, for example, was that of very simple shapes like squares and rectangles. The blueprints for the cemeteries of World War II, on the other hand, were made up of intricate configurations reflecting "a sophisticated and collective triumph" and exuding unbridled American confidence.[1]

The entrance to the Margraten cemetery today comprises a chapel that allows visitors to contemplate redemption as soon as they arrive. It also boasts a massive sculpture symbolizing regeneration in the form of a young woman surrounded by fluttering birds and a tree stump sprouting leaves. Leon Heuts was nine when in 1944 he saw the gaping graves in the mud and watched trucks stacked with corpses and body parts plow through the slush. "When Leon walks over the cemetery in Margraten today," a local historian notes, "he sees nothing to connect the cemetery as it is today with the things he saw then." "Many visitors," a Dutchman who has worked at the cemetery for 40 years proudly observes, "are impressed by the immaculate lawns: beautifully green and as smooth as billiard cloth."[2]

Yet, at the same time, the abstractions in fresh green and shiny white only serve to accentuate the immense horror of war. There is an inescapable tension between the official attempt to sanctify mass sacrifice and the human need to deconstruct it into the life stories behind the more than 10,000 names on crosses, stars, and walls. Indeed, many find that it is all but impossible to try and unravel the sacrifice while continuing to comprehend it.

That is what the adopters of the Margraten boys struggle with more than any other visitors. "I sit myself down on a cemetery bench for about 15 minutes," says a 34-year-old truck mechanic who became an adopter not long ago, "and silently stare past the many crosses. It gives me goose bumps time and again." "Whenever I see all those graves," writes a 79-year-old woman who has been active as an adopter since 1946, when she was no older than 17, "I cannot help crying."[3]

"Margraten," comments an adopter and civil servant in his fifties, "is a hauntingly beautiful place where I often walk around with tears in my eyes." "I try to absorb," he goes on to explain, "the reality that under each marker lies buried a person who was hoping to return home safely and then to live a long and happy life." "All gone just like that," he reflects. "What pain, what loss, what sadness."[4]

1

If comprehension is rendered impossible, for the adopters of the Margraten boys remembrance remains the next best thing, and so they engage in its rituals with a deep sense of purpose and commitment. Framed adoption certificates with the names of the American soldiers, as well as photographs of the boys posing in uniform or with their families back home, proudly adorn the walls of Dutch living rooms or sit prominently on office desks. It is not unusual for a picture of a Margraten boy to be displayed among those of the adopter's own family members who have passed away. Indeed, in many a household, on special occasions, such as the day on which the soldier died, a candle is lit or some flowers are placed near his portrait.

Many of the older adopters uphold the Catholic tradition of lighting candles in churches for the repose of the soul of the deceased and are happy to include a candle for their American soldier among those for their dearly departed relatives. The small church in Wittem, not far from the cemetery, is the adopters' preferred sanctuary for this ritual, and it can be seen repeated there for soldiers from across America. Another Catholic tradition with a similar purpose, the purchase of Masses dedicated to those who have passed away, also continues to be practiced in the adoption community, and it is not uncommon in churches in Margraten and environs to hear priests invoke in a single breath Dutch names interspersed with somewhat odd-sounding American ones.

A visit to the soldier's grave has, of course, always been, and remains, the most important ritual of all. There are those adopters who drop by the cemetery whenever they feel like it or whenever the occasion presents itself. "I go to the grave," one elderly woman confides, "when I feel happy and also when I am very sad; I take flowers then or a little present." Most adopters, however, make a point of paying a visit on those days each year that hold strong symbolical meaning. Among these are all of the main Christian and Jewish religious days, from Christmas and Easter to All Saints and Yom Kippur. Indeed, the adopter of a soldier from Louisiana voiced a complaint some years ago about the fact that the cemetery cannot be accessed on Christmas Day, one of the rare days of the year that the gates remain closed for visitors. Equally important moments for visits are key dates linked with World War II such as 5 May, the day the Germans put down their arms in the Netherlands; 10 May, the day Nazi Germany invaded the Low Countries and France; and 6 June, the day the Allies landed in Normandy to liberate Europe.[5]

It is quite common also for adopters to visit the Margraten cemetery on the day that the Allies liberated their particular town or village in 1944 or 1945. But the overwhelming majority of adopters prefer to have visits take place on days that are much more personal still. The day on which a soldier was killed certainly ranks among the most important, although adopters who have managed to identify the soldier's date of birth also use that occasion, and there are those even who go and say thanks at the cemetery on their own birthday or that of their children. A family from Valkenburg, on the other hand, has made Mother's Day the preferred occasion for a visit to Margraten "because all those soldiers have a mother who is heartbroken."[6]

Some adopters visit without anyone else in tow so as to be alone with their thoughts. For others it is an occasion to reunite with children and grandchildren or the extended family, or to invite friends from elsewhere in the Netherlands or even from abroad. Although countless adopters continue to gather at the cemetery on Memorial Day at the end of May, as has been the tradition since 1945, many indicate that they prefer to be at Margraten when things are quieter so that they can commemorate their soldier in a more intimate manner. Most take flowers to the graves or place pebbles on the marble Stars of David. Others leave behind a little gift, some candy, or a few words on a card. Some continue to create bouquets the way their parents taught them long ago, using only flowers in red, white, and blue – the colors of both the American and the Dutch flag. Until very recently, a woman in her eighties continued to make a point of paying visits to the cemetery towards the evening, and of placing a single rose on each of the two American graves in her care since the end of the war.[7]

As has been the case for almost seven decades now, the numerous and varied adoption rituals serve to facilitate remembrance of both the European and the American experience of war. A woman from Elsloo was 72 when in 1994 she undertook a trip to Normandy to commemorate the 50th anniversary of the Allied invasion. The experience in France made such an impression that immediately upon her return to Limburg she contacted the adoption committee to sign on as the caretaker for the grave of an unknown soldier at Margraten. "I should have adopted that grave much earlier," she reflects today. "In memory of my father (54) and brother (20) who died in Germany. In concentration camps in Germany. Bergen-Belsen and Oranienburg. Their final resting places unknown."[8]

For adopters of the Margraten boys whose names are known it has often been a sacred duty not only to safeguard the experience of their own families under Nazi occupation, but also to find out as much as possible about those who gave their lives for the liberation. The dogged attempts to rescue from oblivion fragments of personal backgrounds and shards of intimate lives betray an almost reflexive refusal to have total war and mass annihilation wipe out individual identities. The mayor of Margraten was touched when the daughter of Nicholas Bonilla, a paratrooper killed on Dutch soil in September 1944, sent him a book based on the correspondence between her parents during the war. She, the mayor pointed out on Memorial Day in 2007, "and many others like her – children of the 'boys' buried in the cemetery – want nothing more than for the stories of their fathers to be told. It is down to us to make this happen."[9]

Younger adopters in particular continue to oblige, as they have been doing since the internet revolution of the 1990s, by using virtual pathways both to gather information about soldiers and to make their stories known more widely, often with the kind help of American relatives. A man in his late twenties from Purmerend, for example, after having adopted Sergeant Truman Anderson from Arkansas, soon found himself posting personal information not only on 'his' sergeant, but on other Margraten boys too, on a website created for that specific purpose. Even when such research fails to lead to coherent life stories and dense textures, the little that is put out in cyberspace comes across as very powerful and as a victory over the abstraction and uniformity of more than 10,000 names frozen in marble. With help, for example, from his brother Art, who provided the adopter from Purmerend with scans from the American family's private photo album, Robert Morneweck suddenly is no longer just the soldier from Michigan in Plot E, Row 20, Grave 17, killed on 12 April 1945 with the 506th Parachute Infantry Regiment. He now is Bob, who had his picture taken as a child seated on a pony in the summer of 1933; as a young man raising his glass in the company of a pretty blond girlfriend; as a soldier standing next to his brother-in-law Virgil (also in uniform); with his wiry and shy-looking father Weston in 1943; and with his beaming buddy Ray Bascome from Vernal, Utah, in a studio somewhere in France in March 1945.[10]

Such intimate moments in the lives of soldiers inevitably fascinate as they form stark contrasts with the unforgiving brutality of war. And they have given rise to both pilgrimages beyond the cemetery and to rituals meant to be shared only in the privacy of the home. Just recently, for example, a forensic psychiatrist and her husband set out on a long-awaited tour of the United States. They had made sure to map their trip in such a way that there would be plenty of time to see Philadelphia, the city that 23-year-old Lieutenant Thomas Seibel had called his home before being downed with the *Clay Pigeon* just as he and his men were hooking up their parachutes in the C-47 Dakota

18–19. Efforts to safeguard the memory of the Margraten boys continue unabated. Since 1945, four generations of the same family have watched over Albert Gackowksi, a private from Illinois in the 89th Infantry Division. It took his adopters until very recently to get in touch with relatives and obtain family pictures. One photo shows Albert (left) with his brother Leo. Another shows Albert (crouched on the right) with his parents and brothers Leo and Norbert. Albert was the only son not to come home from the war. He rests in Plot A, Row 2, Grave 4. (Courtesy Laura Lange-Gackowski and Inge Burlet)

for the jump into the Arnhem corridor in September 1944. The Dutch couple were hoping that, with some luck, they might also retrace the paratrooper's steps to the church where they knew the American with the sand-colored, curly hair had married a lovely girl called Esther O'Malley before being shipped out to war.[11]

The birth of their daughter has been the reason for an electrical engineer and his wife to adopt the grave of Sergeant John Klippel, another soldier from Pennsylvania. Hoping to instill in the next generation an awareness of the horrors of war and the heavy price to be paid for freedom at times, they have set out to arrange for a simple and solemn breakfast of eggs and coffee in their home on 26 March each year. They have managed to learn very little about John Klippel. Only that he was born in New York, trained as a cook, and was married. But in one of the many after-action reports of the 440th Armored Field Artillery Battalion in Europe, there is one small piece of information that, more than any other, makes their soldier stand out. That is where it mentions in the entry of 26 March 1945: "A breakfast of fresh eggs and black coffee served by Sgt. Klippel, our Mess Sergeant."[12]

2

From the very beginning in 1945, Margraten's adoption has always been about more than caring for graves and remembering the suffering and sacrifice of the boys. Difficult and frustrating as it has been to obtain the soldiers' home addresses from American authorities bent on protecting privacy and preventing abuse, adopting families have never stopped trying. They have considered it a moral duty as Christians and human beings to provide comfort to the devastated families overseas and, even as World War II recedes into the past, continue to regard it as important to let next of kin in America know that the sacrifice of the Margraten boys has not been in vain and will not be forgotten.

Just as it has revolutionized the ways in which the adoption community can put faces to the names of the soldiers, the internet has also since the 1990s dramatically impacted the potential for reaching out to the boys' families overseas. In his 2006 autobiography, Barack Obama, the senator from Illinois and future president of the US, recounts how, during a visit to Google's headquarters in California's Silicon Valley, he stood gazing in amazement at a screen showing the traffic patterns of the entire internet system. Obama recalls it with awe as "a single, constant, thrumming conversation, time and space giving way to a world spun entirely of light." That is certainly what it looks like also to Margraten's adoption community as they venture deeper into the twenty-first century only to find that it is getting easier rather than harder to converse with relatives of the boys who lost their lives as long ago as World War II.[13]

It has to be kept in mind, of course, that today, as in the past, American relatives of the Margraten boys more often than not remain unaware of the fact that there even is such a thing as adoption, let alone a community deeply involved in preserving the memory of the soldiers who rest there. An adopter from Cadier en Keer, for example, was exceptionally lucky when, two days after putting flowers on the grave of his soldier, a call came from the cemetery's visitors' office, telling the Dutchman that an uncle and aunt of the boy were impatient to have a word with him after having been told, to their great amazement, that the flowers they had found on their nephew's grave had come from a local adopter. But a young teacher from Heerlen who takes flowers to four graves several times a year, and each time has letters attached to them addressed to American relatives, has been waiting in vain for a such a call since 2004.[14]

Meanwhile, however, a surprising number of relations with American families that were formed at the end of the war have survived the onslaught of time and, with the help of the internet, continue to thrive. The family that today is caring for Bill Snyder's grave has known the lieutenant in person. Early in 1945, Bill and several other officers of the 79th Infantry Division stayed for quite some time at their farm in Margraten. Bill instantly felt at home in a landscape that resembled that of the Appalachians in Denton, North Carolina, and in a household with a mother who reminded him so much of his own. He gladly helped with the chores and repeatedly played with the baby boy. Jean, another of the farmer's sons, so admired Bill that several times a week he walked seven miles from Maastricht to the farm and then back again to his boarding school in the city just to see the gentle American and talk with him. Bill was killed on 24 March 1945 near Walsum, shortly after crossing the Rhine, just a few days outside Margraten. "Jean," Bill's mother wrote to the Dutch adopting family in January 1946, "I would give anything to be close enough to visit his grave. But so many thousands of miles separate us." "You don't know," she said in the same letter, "how glad we were to get your letter and know of someone in Holland that knew him." Were they absolutely certain, she asked, that it was her dear boy who had come to rest in that grave? How had he been buried? Had they used a casket? "Jean," the mother pleaded, "you must write us often and if you can remember any little thing to tell us about him we will be glad." Jean pledged that that was exactly what he would do. And he and his extended family have kept the promise ever since. Not long ago, when Bill's mother had already passed away, they paid one of many visits to Bill's grave, put flowers on it as usual, and then decided to film the event for the lieutenant's next of kin in America. Assembled around Bill's grave can be seen Jean, his brothers and sisters and their partners, and their children and grandchildren, some of whom in turn are accompanied by partners who hail from as far away as Slovakia and Japan.[15]

Just recently, Ben Allen was overjoyed to learn that Pauline in Kerkrade was expecting a new grandchild. The American asked the proud grandmother to keep him posted and he was quick to send to the Netherlands a book that a pediatrician had recommended as being especially good for very young babies. Ben relished talking with Pauline about the renewal of life almost seven decades after World War II. Pauline was only five when, in the dark winter of 1944–45, Major Robert Arnold and his brother-in-law, Sergeant Bill Allen, were spoiling her rotten. The Americans were part of the 207th Field Artillery Battalion and the 331st Infantry Regiment respectively. Kerkrade, a town a stone's throw from the German border, was their launching pad for the final offensive. In a matter of weeks that offensive voraciously claimed both their lives. Ben Allen was only twelve when he learned of the terrible price his family in Alta, Illinois, had been asked to pay in World War II. News of the death of Robert on 24 February 1945 arrived at the farm just as Elizabeth, Ben's sister and Robert's young wife, had returned to the University of Illinois to complete her degree. "I remember," Ben told Pauline much later, "my father taking the bus to Champaign, where the university was located, to tell Elizabeth and then drive her home in the car." The telegram of Bill's death was delivered to the same farm on a Sunday morning barely two months later. Ben was in the small rural church with neighbors when it arrived. He had always been proud of his older brother. Bill had gone to college and had worked as a teacher at the local high school before joining the army. He had loved books and theater. "I remember," Ben also told Pauline much later, "my father going to the attic to bring down the Nazi uniform and flag that Bill had sent home thinking he would use them in future theatrical performances. He burned all these items in the furnace." Ben's other brother, Lee, returned to Alta safe and sound from war in the Pacific with the Marines. Neither Benton and Lura Allen nor their children Elizabeth, Lee, and Ben ever second-guessed the decision to leave Bill and Robert in peace at Margraten. Nor did they ever regret having both boys watched over by Pauline's parents and what was now announcing itself to be a fourth generation of committed Dutch caretakers.[16]

20. Many American families were made to pay a terrible price in World War II. In April 1944, Ben Allen proudly poses with his big brother Bill on the farm in Illinois. Less than a year later, the final offensive in Nazi Germany had claimed not only the life of Bill but also that of sister Elizabeth's husband. Bill and his brother-in-law both rest in Margraten and are being watched over by a fourth generation of the same Dutch family. (Courtesy Benton Allen and Pauline Roukens-Göttgens, Landgraaf, the Netherlands)

As has been the case over the decades, new bonds between American and Dutch families are being formed in a constant process of adoption renewal, and here too it has by now become hard to imagine a time before the internet. A man in his forties from Sittard recently adopted Robert Erwin, an infantryman from Ohio, and through email exchanges with the staff of the Erie County Library in that same state in a short time managed to locate the children of Robert's younger brother, Jack, who live in Michigan and Montana. Their gratitude for the beautiful gesture with regards to their uncle's faraway grave was such that the family eventually decided it was the Dutchman who should be the keeper of the Margraten boy's memory. Before long, scans were arriving in the email inbox in Sittard of very personal items. A photo of Robert holding his wife Margie in a tender embrace, for example, and pictures of other possessions that had been removed from the soldier's body after he was killed. Scans that followed told an even sadder story. Margie had been pregnant with their first child when Robert left for war in Europe. In a V-mail to Robert dated 26 February 1945 Margie asked if he had received the package with woolen socks and gloves and talked about the final countdown to the happy moment. A telegram sent to Robert's mother ten days later carried the news that "Margie and baby son died today." Robert was killed in Germany a month later. His family never learned the exact circumstances of his death. But the story has always been that he had become utterly careless in the front lines because he no longer valued his own life. Robert's adopter is adamant that the soldier's life story should be preserved at all cost. His resolve was further bolstered when not long ago he received from America a small flat box containing Private Robert Erwin's Purple Heart.[17]

Just recently also, Mary Anne praised the wonders of the internet when her family discovered through some googling that the graves of the two brothers from Duryea, Pennsylvania, had been assigned a new adopter in 2005. Soon after the war, Mr. and Mrs. Dorscheidt in Kerkrade had accepted responsibility for the graves of the brothers resting side by side. In 1949 their own son had been killed in the war in the Dutch East Indies and ten years later their daughter Grada had married an American and moved to Rhode Island. George Evancho's widow Theresa and the Evancho boys' younger sister Helen, Mary Anne's mother, had kept up a steady correspondence with Mr. and Mrs. Dorscheidt for many years. But those contacts now no longer existed. That is why Mary Anne was over the moon to learn that a young man, a carpenter from Belgium who lived not far from the Dutch border, had now taken over from the Dorscheidt family. It was the adoption of Peter Evancho's grave by the Dorscheidts in 1946 that had prompted the American family to ask for the transfer of George's remains from a cemetery in Belgium to that in Margraten. This had been an important factor also in the decision at the end of the 1940s not to have the brothers returned to America. Now, more than 60 years after those heart-wrenching events, Theresa and Helen were being taken care of in the same nursing home in Pennsylvania. Mary Anne regularly paid the elderly women a visit and each time was reminded of the deep wounds that the deaths of Peter and George had caused in the family. The feeling of pain had never really worn off. Through her entire life, Mary Anne's mother had kept a black-and-white photo of her brothers' graves at Margraten by her bedside. It is the photo in which a priest, Grada Dorscheidt's uncle, is blessing Peter and George's final resting places. It gave Mary Anne tremendous satisfaction to be able to show to her mother and aunt the young Belgian adopter's emails as well as photos of marble headstones so shiny and polished and a cemetery so immaculate that it seemed as if time had decided to pass Margraten by. Both elderly women died in about six months after connecting with the new adopter. But these were important months. For Helen and Theresa, for whom it brought some sense of closure. And for Mary Anne, who is glad to have been able to present them with this final gift. "My only regret is," she notes, "that I wish these recent events could have happened ten years ago. However, it is only through the internet that much has been made possible." "I do hope," Peter and George's niece concludes, "the Margraten story is one that would receive more recognition here in the United States. Our soil has not seen the devastation of war as has Europe. All too often, veterans' gravesite markers in small locally operated cemeteries are slowly disappearing – grown over by grass, having no one left among family to remember, to visit, or to safeguard, and diminished funds to maintain. That is why Margraten is so special."[18]

In 2008 the Margraten Adoption Foundation won the prestigious Limburg Award. It did not take the foundation's board long to decide that most of the prize money would be donated to the American War Orphans Network. The board stipulated that the money should

21. Key members of the Adoption Foundation Margraten accept the prestigious Limburg Award in 2008. Most of the prize money would be donated to the American World War II Orphans Network. In the background is a photo projection of Sgt. Walter Pete of the 29th Infantry Division whose name is among more than 1,700 on the Wall of the Missing. (Courtesy Adoption Foundation Margraten and Jo Purnot)

go to those members of the network who had never before had a chance to visit their father's grave and continued to find the cost of travel prohibitive. Never during its existence had the American network, which for years has been organizing such trips to cemeteries across the globe, from Belgium to the Philippines, received this kind of gift. "I'm sure," board member Gerry Morenski commented in their magazine, the *Star*, "all of you share in my excitement at the everlasting generosity of the Dutch to us and to our fathers. Their understanding of the sacrifice of our fathers and the needs of war orphans to visit a father's grave overwhelms me." For the Dutch board members in Margraten, however, the donation had been the most natural of decisions, building as it did on a tradition of almost 70 years of bringing families closer together across the Atlantic divide.[19]

3

It is a deeply rooted tradition too in the adoption community today to regard the Margraten cemetery as a powerful appeal for peace that goes far beyond the particular experience of the Netherlands and Europe in World War II. This sentiment has grown in resonance across decades that witnessed the threat of mutually assured nuclear destruction, the napalm apocalypse of the Vietnam War, and the destructive invasion of Iraq for reasons that to many remain unclear or invalid. "Peace," the adopter of a Californian infantryman remarks, "together with good health, is the most important thing in the world." A recurrent refrain among adopters is that all war is madness and that in armed conflicts there are no winners, only losers. "Each cross," an ICT manager and adopter of a captain of the 29th Infantry Division explains, "also symbolizes killed Germans, murdered Jews, and civilians. The Margraten cemetery in all its beauty is a never-ending scream lamenting the inability of people and leaders to live together peacefully."[20]

Such strong convictions are fueled, of course, by a much older European history darkened by war. "Two world wars suffice," one adopter says tersely. "In my opinion," the caretaker of the grave of an infantryman from Montana notes, "everyone should, at least once in their lifetime, visit the Menin Gate in Ypres and the Margraten cemetery." But the impassioned warnings about the evils of war also build on a proud Dutch legacy that stretches back much further, all the way to Hugo Grotius and his seventeenth-century wish to see a world in which states interact peacefully and within the confines of ethical principles enshrined in law. As late as the end of the nineteenth century, a history of the Netherlands written for a broad audience was proud to conclude with the words: "It is better to be the most virtuous, rather than the most powerful people on earth." Indeed, for over a century the small country had clung to a policy of voluntary neutrality. It had managed to escape even the Great War ravaging the Flemish fields of its unfortunate southern neighbor. Echoes of this age-old, pacifist creed can be found among Dutch adopters deploring the fact that even present-day democratic governments do not recoil from "manipulating" and "brainwashing" citizens into accepting war. In a similar vein, adopters warn that the cost of militarization inevitably undermines "social services" and "healthcare," and hence tends to affect "the weakest in society" more than anyone else.[21]

What adopters find most disheartening, however, is that governments and citizens appear not to be drawing lessons from the horrible mistakes made in the past. "There is still war going on," a middle-aged woman from Margraten agonizes. "Have not enough young lives been ruined already!" For some, such observations are tinged with a sense of despair. "Switch on the television and read the newspaper," writes a man in his sixties whose family has been caring for the grave of an Ohio airman since 1946, "and in many places in the world all you see is misery and cruelties. I think people are becoming immune to it." Never far from the minds of adopters is the sobering realization that war, ethnic cleansing, and genocide returned to their doorstep at a time when no one thought this possible any longer. "Margraten," a firefighter in his fifties urges, "is a message that needs to stay alive in our society. It cannot be made clear enough." Then, in a nod to the Yugoslav wars in the 1990s and the Srebrenica massacre of Muslim men and boys, he adds: "And yet it has happened in Europe again. What a pity."[22]

The tragedy of the Balkans, however, also starkly brings home a painful dilemma. Could the wars and massacres in these bloodlands not have been prevented had Europe decided to intervene with naked power earlier and more forcefully? Is, in other words, war not always pure madness but sometimes unquestionably just and necessary?

Determining the exact conditions that justify war has been the cause of much disagreement among Americans and Dutch at Margraten since as far back as the Vietnam War. And nothing much seemed to have changed when Robert Gates, President Obama's Secretary of Defense, visited Margraten in 2009. Gates was in Europe for a review of the war against the Taliban and al-Qaeda in Afghanistan at a time when tens of thousands of American troops stood poised to join what was being touted as a major "surge." He was also in the Old World, however, to convince allies like the Dutch to stay the course at a time of economic crisis and shrinking defense budgets. Indeed, the Dutch government had already indicated that it was seriously considering pulling its 1,600 troops out of the dangerous Uruzgan province the following year. Misty-eyed after a tour of the American cemetery, Gates emphasized "the continuing high importance of our partners staying with us." But, as many American officials had done before him in the context of other wars, Gates also used the Margraten platform to drive home the powerful and emotional message of an Allied coalition in Afghanistan sharing "a purpose akin to the partnership that liberated Europe six decades ago."[23]

Regardless of whether they agreed with Gates on Afghanistan, there are those in the adoption community who cannot but acknowledge that if the Allied war of 1944–45 has been one of liberation in Europe, other wars may have a similar meaning to people elsewhere. "We do not just owe freedom to the last world war," the adopter of an Hispanic-American from California explains, "but to the various wars that came before it." "Let's be prepared," an adopter, in his thirties, of soldiers from Michigan and Illinois warns, "for when the next well-meaning Chamberlain has the wool pulled over his eyes by the next Hitler so that something can be done in time when things get ugly again." "These days," complains a young man watching over the grave of a sergeant from Maine, "we are afraid of sending soldiers when there is even the slightest chance that some of them might get killed. Often you hear, 'Let people elsewhere take care of themselves.' I think that attitude is wrong."[24]

An adopter who was born in the very year that World War II erupted in Europe would have no problem agreeing with the opinion of his much younger countryman. He regularly says a prayer for the liberator whose grave has been assigned to him and also makes sure to visit Margraten at least six times a year. He is convinced that as a gay man he has even more reason than many others to be deeply involved in the adoption program. "If the Germans had remained in power," he reasons, "Jews, gypsies, and homosexuals would not have had a right to live. So in a very personal sense I owe my life to the courage of these fallen comrades."[25]

The penultimate message that this elderly Dutchman hopes visitors from all over the world will take away from Margraten is that of tolerance. It is a sincere hope he shares with the overwhelming majority of adopters. After all, the message of tolerance contains a convenient solution for those struggling with the dilemma of if and when war can ever be justified. Indeed, if people could learn to live with those who differ in sexual orientation, culture, race, religion, and opinion, then there would never again be a need for war to resolve disagreement. Time and again, adopters in a recent survey have pointed out that what makes the Margraten memorial so powerful in their minds is its haunting ability to make people appreciate the immense value of attributes like solidarity, patience, acceptance, understanding, compromise, dialogue, negotiation, and diplomacy. "It may all take a bit longer," a man in his late sixties acknowledges, "but at least it does not cost any lives."[26]

Understandably, the strong educational value of the Margraten memorial for younger generations in particular has never been lost on those in the adoption community. In 1946 a father and grandfather from Sacramento, California, in a letter to Lucie van den Boorn, the Dutch girl who volunteered to care for the graves of dozens of Margraten boys at the end of the war, praised the young woman and urged: "You are 22 years old and *your* generation *must get together* all over the world and see that no *more* war is made by a few selfish old-style greedy rulers or statesmen, because yours is the generation that will have to fight the war the old men make." But many who are involved in adoption in the early twenty-first century are making sure that the next generation absorb the vital lessons of Margraten at an even younger age. In 1945 a girl of 14 from Brunssum started visiting the grave of infantryman Thomas McKinnie in the company of her mother; more than 60 years later, she is continuing the ritual in the company of grandchildren who are now the same age she was at the end of World War II. Another Dutch woman of retirement age makes a point of whisking her grandchildren to the cemetery whenever they come over to visit from faraway Amsterdam so that she can make them aware of "what war is all about." Many of the primary schools in Limburg have made visits with a similar purpose part of their annual curriculum, teaching very young children in a single breath the story of the Margraten boys and the girl called Anne Frank. These are the same schools that encouraged their pupils to participate in a unique event to commemorate the 60th anniversary of the liberation. Towards dusk on a September day in 2004, a recording at the memorial ground had these children call, sing, murmur, and whisper the names of all of the 10,000 American soldiers etched in marble. At times just one name could be heard followed by an eerie silence. At other times the names of hundreds were uttered in a quick rush. But throughout that evening in Margraten, the effect of children calling out names as warnings never failed to chill the bone.[27]

4

At the start of the new millennium, the swelling chorus for tolerance has had the unlikely effect of transforming Margraten from a vast site of loss and grief into an immense source of hope. In recent years, a number of highly symbolical and deeply meaningful gestures of atonement and reconciliation have done much to strengthen this hope.

One of these gestures has brought full circle the process of healing between former archenemies in World War II. As early as the 1950s, economic imperatives and security concerns with regards to the threat of the Soviet Union had accelerated Western Europe's rapprochement with Western Germany. Indeed, by the early 1970s, few Dutch were making any bones about the fact that German war veterans were using the American military cemetery as a venue to commemorate both their own fallen and those who had once been their adversaries. In a border region like Limburg, where many had intermarried with Germans even before World War II and the start of European unification, this increasingly made sense. As if to drive that point home, at the dawn of both a new century and a new millennium, the newest American superintendent of the Margraten cemetery was a veteran of the Vietnam War who had survived World War II as a German teenager. Frank Schwind's father had died fighting the Russians at Stettin; his mother had succumbed to illness when a doctor in the wartime chaos failed to reach her in time. At the end of the war, an uncle had advised the boy to emigrate to America and Frank had seized the opportunity with both hands. Although the German-born readily admitted that his Vietnam experience had been a nightmare, America had been good to him. Bored by his retirement existence in Florida, he had applied for a job with the ABMC as caretaker of America's World War II cemeteries overseas. In one of fate's strange twists, the new career had carried him from Tunisia to Normandy, and finally to Margraten, no more than a stone's-throw away from the border with his old homeland.[28]

More recently, however, an original initiative from a Dutchman in his late fifties and the overwhelming response from a German community have signaled more clearly than ever before how far former enemies have truly come on the road to reconciliation. The adoption of the grave of Private Michel Ernst unexpectedly led the Dutchman from the Limburg town of Limbricht to Billy Melander in New York. Billy had been one of Michel's close friends in the 29th Infantry Division. On countless long nights spent on tedious guard duty during the war in Europe, Billy had managed to piece together from reluctant fragments the remarkable life story of the fragile-looking and tongue-tied fellow soldier. Born in the Polish capital of Warsaw in 1922, Michel had been raised in a well-to-do Jewish family that manufactured bicycles for export all over Europe. The rise of the Nazis in Germany and anti-Jewish sentiment in Poland had eventually caused his father to make the painful decision to sell the business. Part of the money was used to help his daughters and their husbands start new lives in New York City. The rest of it was spent on resettlement in the Belgian port city of Antwerp, where Michel's father opened a small bicycle repair shop. When the German threat started to be felt there too, Michel's family used their rapidly dwindling funds to finance a move to France and, after that, a dangerous trek across the Pyrenees and all the way to Portugal. In Portugal the Jewish family bribed officials to obtain visas for Canada and, after a rough time at sea, settled in the Toronto area. Not long after, they managed to cross the border with the US illegally so as to become reunited with Michel's sisters in New York City. To make a meager living, the family had no choice but to work long hours in the sweatshops of the city's garment industry. Michel studied during the day and manned the sewing machines at night. Finally, after the US joined the war in response to the Pearl Harbor attack, Michel had enlisted out of hatred for the Nazis and in the hope that his service might be rewarded with American citizenship.

Michel, of course, had never made it back to his newly adopted country. He had been killed in a freak accident in Alsdorf on 17 December 1944 involving a column of the American 2nd Armored Division that was being rushed to Belgium to help stop the German onslaught in the Battle of the Bulge. Although Billy Melander had never stopped mourning the loss of his friend, it was an experience that he and Michel had shared some weeks before this fateful day that still required Billy to have treatment for post-traumatic stress disorder more than 60 years later. In November 1944, Siersdorf, a small mining town not far from Alsdorf, was part of a front line that encompassed Jülich, a city in which barely a wall was left standing by the time the battle ended. In the course of the fighting that month, Billy and his comrades were called upon to help save German civilians who had been buried in a Siersdorf shelter as a result of a direct hit. During the desperate rescue operation, Michel, who spoke German well, played a crucial role as interpreter for American soldiers and elderly German miners who had also rushed to the scene to lend a hand. By the time they reached the civilians, however, it was too late. The scene that followed was one that Billy had been hoping in vain would one day dissolve in his mind: "There were approximately 12 to 14 young children brought out by our rescue team. The German miners carried out the adults (about 7 or 9). All were placed on the rain-soaked street and covered with whatever we could find to shield them from the falling sleet." The victims appeared to be refugees who had fled from the violence on the front lines. No one in Siersdorf managed to identify them and no one ever claimed the bodies.

Moved by the stories of American, German, and Jewish suffering, the Dutch adopter did some quick research and ended up contacting a group of amateur historians who turned out to be part of the evangelical church community of Aldenhoven, the German municipality where these wartime events had taken place. They too were moved by the stories the Dutchman relayed to them and, before long, the German community extended an invitation to the Margraten adopter. The meeting and the contacts that followed were so warm and inspiring that the Dutch adopter eventually offered to have his adoption of Michel Ernst's grave transferred to the German church community. The community responded to this idea with enthusiasm and its pastor soon came up with a plan to ensure the continuity of adoption by assigning responsibility for the care of the grave to the group of young people to be inducted into the church community each year. Since receiving the formal certificate from the Adoption Foundation, people from Aldenhoven, young and old, have been coming together at Michel Ernst's grave in Margraten to whisper the Kaddish and place small stones on the marble Star of David on which his name is engraved.[29]

An equally powerful signal of reconciliation has come from the other side of the Atlantic where, at the end of 2008, Americans elected a young man of African ancestry to be the 44th president of their country. No single event at the start of the new millennium could have implanted more clearly in the minds of people across the globe the belief that nothing humankind dared hope for was preposterous any longer. Commenting on the estimated quarter-million Berliners and other Europeans gathered in Tiergarten Park in the summer of 2008 to see the African-American who was then still no more than a presidential candidate, an American historian and biographer of Martin Luther King stated that "The planet was excited by Barack Hussein Obama as much for what he was as for what he said."[30]

What Obama said was what people so desperately wanted to hear in a world that since 9/11 had not stopped being frightened of terror and the often even more violent ways of responding to it. "We may not look the same," the presidential candidate assured his audience in his famous speech on race in 2008, "and we may not have come from the same place, but we all want to move in the same direction – towards a better future for our children and our grandchildren." When in June 2009 Barack Obama visited Egypt as president of the US and at the University of Cairo in an equally famous speech said that he "had come here to seek a new beginning between the United States and Muslims around the world," a sigh of relief could be heard around the globe. In what was his trademark rhetoric of reconciliation, Obama in Cairo went on to emphasize that America and Islam "share common principles – principles of justice and progress; tolerance and the dignity of all human beings." So powerful and timely were all of these words that the committee in Oslo deemed them more than sufficient to award the black American president the Nobel Peace Prize later that year.[31]

Who Barack Obama was, however, had particular resonance within the Margraten adoption community. That this American president was a Nobel Peace Laureate, of course, formed a source of boundless joy and hope for people who during almost seven decades had been devoted to the memory of more than 10,000 American boys who had perished in war. But that here was a man who had managed to become president of the US despite the color of his skin held an equally special meaning in a community where the memory of the treatment of black American liberators as second-class citizens remained painfully vivid. The moment American troops had arrived in the region in 1944, for example, it had been blatantly obvious that billets with Dutch families were a privilege reserved for white soldiers only and that black troops had to make do with life in segregated tent camps and drab buildings. Black troops of the 960th and 3136th Quartermaster Service Companies were given a similar separate and unequal treatment at the Margraten burial ground, where they carried the mutilated corpses and dug countless graves in soil leaden with rain, while white personnel supervised them and filled out forms. Frans Douven was twenty-one when the liberators arrived in Margraten in 1944. He remembered that most of the black soldiers were relegated to the building that housed the village's fruit auction. And he could never forget that whenever white soldiers dropped by in the nearby hotel, owned and operated by his father, black troops at the hotel bar would suddenly fall eerily silent and meekly slip away.[32]

The flagrant discrimination of African-Americans had continued to cause consternation among adopters of the Margraten boys at a time of Cold War when the US purported to be the leader of the Free World in the fight against what was now Red Fascism. One woman fondly recalled how her parents had accepted adoption of the grave of a white sergeant from the Deep South in 1946 and how the soldier's family sent them long letters and photos of Cecil and his widow and baby daughter. But she also noted that "Cecil's mother was very conservative," and that she distinctly remembered "her father being aghast when reading in one of the woman's letters that she did not care much for negroes and was in favor of apartheid." It was even more shocking for this Dutch family to realize that this was "most probably how she had raised Cecil," the very soldier whose memory as a liberator they held in such high esteem. To anyone in Europe merely skimming the newspaper headlines, the painful black struggle for equal rights had seemed without end. Even when President Johnson in the mid-1960s appeared to have turned the page once and for all with ambitious civil rights legislation, the murder of Martin Luther

22. African-American troops of the 3136th Quartermaster Service Company and Dutch civilians engaged in the backbreaking work of digging graves in Margraten's rich soil in 1945. (Courtesy Stichting Akkers van Margraten and Joseph Layne, Richmond, Virginia)

King, Black Panthers on the march, and riots and fires in America's ghettoes still flaring up in the early 1990s were telling another story.[33]

If African-Americans buried at Margaten had not known equality in life, visitors could be forgiven for thinking that black soldiers were accorded respect at least unequivocally in death. Indeed, the ABMC had made a very conscious effort to project an image of national unity in its overseas cemeteries by allowing white and black soldiers to be buried side by side. It was something that had come to leave quite an impression on visitors very early on. In the spring of 1946, George Taylor, a 26-year-old American from New Jersey who was stationed in Germany, traveled to Margraten to visit the grave of his dear friend Ralph. Ralph Wheeler had been one of seven out of a crew of ten who had been killed when their B-17 was downed over Germany in February 1944. "War," George wrote in a letter to the Dutch adopter of Ralph's grave after his visit, "is a horrible thing, so many helpless people now lie in their graves as a result of it, along with so many young healthy boys regardless of race, color, creed, or nationality."[34]

As an exception to an otherwise strict rule, there was one important distinction that the ABMC did allow to be made between graves in the overseas cemeteries. Those soldiers who had earned the Congressional Medal of Honor, the most prestigious American award for military valor, were accorded the right to have this clearly mentioned on their headstones. After repatriation in the late 1940s, among the more than 8,000 headstones that remained at Margraten, there were only five such very special ones. The names engraved on them, however, were exclusively those of white soldiers. The problem was that during World War II the discrimination against African-American soldiers had been so insidious that these young men had been denied even the recognition of their courage. By all objective standards, Willy James of Kansas City, Missouri, should have been a recipient of the Medal of Honor. On 7 April 1945, the 25-year-old had served as a lead scout for Company G, 413th Regiment, 104th Infantry Division, in an action to secure a bridgehead near Lippoldsberg on the Weser River. As his regiment crossed the river near the German town, the black soldier found himself pinned down by relentless enemy machine-gun fire for about an hour. Despite the imminent danger, however, he never ceased to make careful observations. When he finally managed to make his way back to his platoon, Willy James immediately helped put together a new plan of maneuver and in the attack that followed was instrumental in pointing out key enemy targets. As they pushed forward against continued strong opposition, however, the platoon leader was severely wounded. After all he had already been through that day, Willy James had rushed to the man's aid with complete disregard for his own life, only to be killed by ferocious machine-gun fire himself.[35]

Still, even half a century after the events, there was not the least indication of this extraordinary heroism on Willy James' headstone in the American military cemetery at Margraten. Indeed, the black community for decades had been upset by the fact that not a single African-American had been made a recipient of the Medal of Honor during World War II, even though many thousands of them had served in combat. Finally, after much urging from academic historians, the US military in the Clinton era decided to fund major research on the matter. Specialists combed the government records for a year and concluded that racial bias had precluded many African-Americans from receiving a fair evaluation and that in at least four cases a nomination for the Medal of Honor had in effect been killed as the paperwork moved up the hierarchy. The research findings caused an outcry in the media and eventually led to a ceremony at the White House on 13 January 1997 where President Clinton awarded the Congressional Medal of Honor to seven African-Americans who had fought in World War II. Six of the top military honors were awarded posthumously. Vernon Baker of Idaho was 77 when the president finally handed him the medal that had been rightfully his all that time. The veteran lieutenant from the Italian campaign made certain to salute the recipients who were not there with him in Washington, DC, including Willy James from Missouri.[36]

In an interview after the ceremony, Vernon Baker, reflecting on his experience in a segregated American military, told the *Washington Post*, "I was an angry young man. We were all angry. But we had a job to do, and we did it." In part, he added, he did so because "he knew things would get better. And I'm glad to say that I'm here to see it." Willy James never had a chance to see things get better. But those taking care of the graves of the Missourian and other Margraten boys of all races today are proud to know that the words 'Medal of Honor' have been added to his headstone at last. And they are even more hopeful knowing that, from inside the Margraten visitors' office, the portrait of a black American president, who has so eloquently pleaded for a more perfect union among humankind, is watching over them all.[37]

Postscript

Shortly after President Bush's visit to the American military cemetery in the Netherlands in 2005, representatives of the province of Limburg and the municipality of Margraten created a foundation aimed at erecting an imposing Memorial Center near the burial site by the time of the 70th anniversary of the end of World War II in 2015. It is envisioned that funding for this massive undertaking could come from donations from private individuals and corporations, but especially from the governments of the Netherlands, the US, and the European Union. Indeed, in 2008 a bipartisan delegation from the American Congress paid a visit to Margraten with an eye to becoming better informed about the plans for the Memorial Center.

In a richly illustrated catalogue prepared by the Margraten Memorial Center Foundation, the planned construction was aptly described as a Center of the Permanent Reminder. Similar plans had been drawn up and abandoned again over the past decades, however, mainly because of a lack of funding, but also because the ABMC had shown to be lukewarm about such initiatives in the immediate vicinity of the cemetery for fear that they might compromise the atmosphere of silence and respect surrounding the hallowed site. Still, if question marks continued to hover over the newest and to date most ambitious initiative for a Memorial Center, there was never any doubt at the start of the new millennium that the thousands of Margraten adopters would proudly and gladly persist as a Community of the Permanent Reminder.[1]

The phenomenon of adoption has never been unique to Margraten. Immediately after World War II, for example, many thousands of Belgians volunteered to keep vigil over the graves of American soldiers at Henri-Chapelle and Neuville-en-Condroz. Countless Dutch in the late forties stepped forward to watch over the graves not just of the liberators from the US, but of those from Britain and Canada too. Indeed, by 1946 the NWGC in Amsterdam was using the Margraten adoption program, including its emphasis on correspondence with the families of the fallen, as the model for all of the Allied cemeteries on Dutch soil. What has continued to make the Margraten adoption program unique, however, is the singular fashion in which a highly motivated volunteer organization has managed to rejuvenate itself at crucial moments, thus ensuring that the adoption of American graves remains massive and uninterrupted even at the dawn of a new millennium. Which explains why in 2000 the French decided to copy the Margraten system as the *Fleurs de la Mémoire* program for the famous American cemetery overlooking Omaha beach in Normandy.[2]

Today the Margraten community of the permanent reminder has lost none of the vigor and determination it has been passionately displaying since 1944. Even some of the adopters of the first hour remain astonishingly active and involved. "It has been a true pleasure taking care of the graves and attending Memorial Day all those years," notes an 85-year-old woman from Brunssum. "It was our duty." The only regret this octogenarian holds is that she has never been able to locate her boy's American relatives and send them the pictures of flowers on the grave taken over a span of close to seventy years. For an 86-year-old woman from Meerssen who is the adopter of an infantryman from Georgia, pride in the performance of her duty is tinged with regret of a different kind in the era of the virtual revolution. "I would have loved to obtain more information about the soldier," she confesses. "But I do not own a computer myself, so it is hard to do this. Such a pity, such a pity."[3]

Even for the most strong-willed of adopters of the first hour, however, the moment now unfortunately announces itself when physical impairment makes any further visits to the Margraten boys impossible. For many that moment is very painful and confronting and one they refuse to have pass by without a gesture that is often as emotional as it is symbolical. "I am 92 and no longer able to visit Margraten," a woman is sad to inform the Adoption Foundation in a letter sent from Middelburg, a town more than 100 miles from Margraten. Wrapped in her letter is a rumpled euro bill worth some $70. The money, the retiring adopter explains, is for flowers to be placed on Grave 10 in Row 2 of Plot E, the final resting place of Harold Swan from Nebraska who in April 1945 was killed as a lieutenant of the 102nd Infantry Division.[4]

In a similar letter from Heerlen, a woman who has turned 85 regrets that she is no longer able to visit the grave of Alan Beachler. "I have always done this," she assures, "with reverence and gratitude, especially on his birthday, the day he was killed, and Memorial Day." Together with the letter, the envelope contains all of the information the woman has managed to gather on the American over the years. The liberator was a corporal killed in Germany in March 1945 with the 36th Tank Batalion. But to this Dutch adopter he had always been much more than that. A boy just one year younger than herself who had lived in a small town in Pennsylvania named Lebanon. A boy with a family heartbroken to have only the meager possessions he had on him returned home to 412 Jones Street: one Bible, 16 souvenir coins, six photographs, one religious emblem, one razor, and one harmonica. "On his 84th birthday, Friday, 21 September," the 85-year-old Dutch woman ruefully closes her letter, "I have said a final farewell to him."[5]

If the renewed Adoption Foundation and its automated database ensure that resigning adopters are instantly replaced with new ones on the waiting list, many of the adopters who are getting on in age have nevertheless made certain to arrange for a transfer of adoption in person. Some have closely observed their grandchildren with regards to their interest in the adoption program and the history of World War II and have made a careful assessment as to who will be the most worthy successor ensuring continuity. Indeed, quite a few elderly adopters have left nothing to chance, instructing their family in their final wills about future adoption and specifying the names of those newly invested with that sacred duty.

All this is of great comfort to the ageing veterans of World War II who know they will not be able to continue to embark on the exhausting trip to Margraten much longer. Even at age 89, Leonard Spivey has made it all the way to the graves of Arthur, Walter, and Wilbert. Leonard can be forgiven for thinking he is still only 22 when going over that fatal day in August 1943 when their B-17 was hit by flak over the target in the Netherlands. Three Focke Wulfs finished the bomber off as it attempted to reach the North Sea and the home base in Essex. With the right wing on fire, six of the crew managed to bail out in time over Schiedam. But four comrades remained trapped in the Flying Fortress as it spiraled to earth and broke in two before

23. Gerda Roebroeks-Nelissen shows a photo of her sister Nettie at the grave of Henry Wolf of the 774th Field Artillery Battalion. Gerda was 13 when Henry spent several weeks on their farm before being sent to the Battle of the Bulge. The American asked Gerda's parents to stay in touch with his wife in Ohio. They kept their promise, only to learn at the end of the war that Henry had been killed and buried in nearby Margraten. At the start of a new century, ageing witnesses like Gerda find much comfort in the knowledge that a third and fourth generation are keeping adoption promises made many decades ago. (Courtesy G. Roebroeks-Nelissen, Sint Geertruid, the Netherlands. Photographer José Manuel Alorda, Barcelona, Spain)

crashing into the island of Rozenburg. One of the four, Eugene, was repatriated to Massachusetts in the late 1940s. The other three have remained in Margraten.

Leonard regrets that the grating pain in his back and joints warns him he no longer is 22 and that perhaps there will be no next reunion at Margraten after this. But he does not regret having to leave the boys behind in Europe. He is in the company of a Dutch adopter who is part of a new generation. He has asked him to look after the graves of his friends for the rest of his young life. Leonard Spivey remembers how the Germans captured him and his five comrades after they had parachuted to safety in 1943. Leonard also vividly recalls that, despite the grave danger of Nazi reprisals, the Dutch in Schiedam lined the streets cheering the Allied airmen on as the occupiers whisked them away for interrogation. Leonard has not the slightest doubt that he can count on the Margraten adopters to keep their word.[6]

Notes

Preface

1. Van der Heijden, *Grijs verleden*, 305 and www.abmc.gov/search/wwii.php.
2. The quote is from a report drawn up at the end of the war. HQ AGRC, "Tactical History of Margraten Cemetery," 1, *Unit Histories, compiled 1943–1967, documenting the period 1755–1967*, RG 338, NARA. On the Allied operations in the Netherlands, see Klinkert, "Crossing Borders," 566–74 and Lagrou, *Legacy of Nazi Occupation*, 33, 59–60, 100, and 242.
3. For full details of the American military presence in southern Limburg and some of its impact, see Gouverne, *US Army in Zuid-Limburg, 1944–1945*. Thanks also to John Gouverne for agreeing to an extensive interview on 9 March 2009 further clarifying the background to the special relationship between the population in this region and American soldiers who would remain stationed there until August 1945.

Chapter 1

1. H. Sluysmans was elected president, A. Sluysmans secretary, and H. Brouwers treasurer. Mayor Ronckers was later made honorary president whereas Father Ramaekers received the honorary title of advisor to the Civilian Committee. "Jaarverslag 1945–1946," 23 March 1946, Folder 3, BCM.
2. "Notulen vergadering," 24 January 1945, Folder 3, BCM and Shomon, *Crosses*, 113 and 115. For an excellent collection of Dutch civilian and American military eyewitness accounts of the construction of the cemetery and the impact it had on the area, see the book *From Farmland to Soldiers Cemetery*, edited by Mieke Kirkels and Jo Purnot and published in 2009. The book also contains a brief but valuable survey of the various stages of the cemetery's construction by historian Frans Roebroeks.
3. "Proclamatie," 10 February 1945, PM; "Jaarverslag 1945–1946," 23 March 1946, Folder 3, BCM; "Memorial Day," *GVL*, 30 May 1945; Shomon, *Crosses*, 111–12 and 115–24; and Roebroeks, "Historical Sketch," 13.
4. Shomon, *Crosses*, 116–17 and QAM 1, Roermond, letter 2008.
5. Interview Jef van Laar, 25 July 1994, PJP and Heuschen obituary, *DNL*, 21 February 1961.
6. Shomon, *Crosses*, 117 and 119; "Jaarverslag 1945–1946," 23 March 1946, Folder 3, BCM; and "Schermerhorn spreekt tot Amerika," *De Waarheid*, 5 July 1945.

7. "Herdenking bevrijding Margraten, 8 September 1945," Folder 1.855.2/1392, GAM and "Memorial Hotel for U.S.A. Cemeteries," 26 January 1946, Folder 912, CKL.
8. Mayor Ronckers to Limburg Governor, 12 March 1946, Folder 3, BCM.
9. AGRC to J. van Tuil, Dutch Ministry of War, 20 October 1945, Folder 68, DIB. In many of these cases it concerned men of the more than 4,000 air force personnel shot down in American fighters and bombers in Dutch air space. Klinkert, "Crossing Borders," 573.
10. Ellis S. Middleton letter and circular, 14 August 1945, Folder 1.776.1/940, GAM.
11. Letter from Voorburg, 22 August 1945, Folder 940, GAM and author interview Felix Prevoo, 6 July 2009. Financial statements show that Father Heuschen was receiving compensation for his activities from the committee as early as June 1945. Folder 18, GAM.
12. Bronzwaer, "Maastricht en Luik bezet," 91–4 and 285–92 and author interview Paul Bronzwaer, 16 January 2009.
13. On the GI dance scheme, see letter Emilie van Kessenich to President Harry Truman, 27 September 1945, Folder 293 'Holland,' RG 92, NARA and Willem Michiels van Kessenich, "Probeersel," 13–14, Folder 661, MVK. The quote is from "Ambassadrice van Margraten," *Libelle*, no. 9, 28 June 1946. For the broader context of interactions between GIs and women in Limburg, see Roebroeks, "Strijdbare geesten," 130–7.
14. Bronzwaer, "Maastricht en Luik bezet," 291–2.
15. Mrs. van Kessenich expressed these feelings about the affair early in July 1945. She did so in an entry in what is a combination of journal and scrapbook made up of several leather-bound volumes. (At the time of the research for this book, these volumes were in the possession of Mrs. van Kessenich's children. Just recently, however, they have been handed over to the RHCL in Maastricht.)
16. Mrs. Warren F. Feil to Michiels van Kessenich, 26 August 1945, Folder 657, MVK.
17. "Margraten: Wij zorgen voor hun graven," *GVL*, 14 September 1944 and letter Emilie van Kessenich to President Harry Truman, 27 September 1945, Folder 293 "Holland," RG 92, NARA.
18. Author interviews Felix Prevoo, 6 July 2009; Maria Prevoo-Ramakers, 1 September 2009; and Annie Prevoo-Frijnts, 6 July 2009.
19. Letter Emilie van Kessenich to President Harry Truman, 27 September 1945, Folder 293 "Holland," RG 92, NARA.
20. On the official contacts, see Mrs. van Kessenich's entry in her journal early in November 1945.
21. "Offer by the wife of the Mayor of Maastricht, Holland," War Department, Office of the Chief of Staff, Civil Affairs Division, 30 October 1945 and letter from the Quartermaster General to Emilie van Kessenich, 6 November 1945, Folder 293 "Holland," RG 92, NARA.
22. "Jaarverslag 1945–1946," 23 March 1946, Folder 3, BCM.
23. On 12 February 1946, Mr. Blom of the NWGC sent a letter to Mrs. van Kessenich asking for a meeting and telling her of their intention to use the

Margraten program "as the model for all of the Netherlands." The letter is part of Mrs. van Kessenich's personal papers at the RHCL in Maastricht. See also "Jaarverslag 1945–1946," 23 March 1946, Folder 3, BCM and "Adoptiewerk Margraten" and "Hier is Nederland!" *LD*, 2 and 5 February 1946. For the adoption guidelines as established by the NWGC in 1946, see a copy of "Richtlijnen" in Folder 13, BCM.

24. Author interviews Felix Prevoo, 6 July 2009; Maria Prevoo-Ramakers, 1 September 2009; and Annie Prevoo-Frijnts, 6 July 2009. "Burger-Comité Margraten: U.S. Militaire Begraafplaats, 1945–1955," Folder 26, BCM. Kirkels, *Else Hanöver*, 97.
25. "Jaarverslag 1945–1946," 23 March 1946, Folder 3, BCM.
26. "Jaarverslag 1945–1946," 23 March 1946, Folder 3, BCM.
27. Commander Rijkspolitie District Maastricht to Limburg Governor, 1 June 1946, Folder 902, CKL and "Grateful Dutch Honor U.S. Dead," *New York Times*, 31 May 1946.
28. QAM 2, Vaals, letter 2008 and QAM 3, Spaubeek, letter 2008.
29. QAM 4, Kerkrade, letter 14 May 2008. On the evacuation of Kerkrade in the context of the Siegfried Line campaign, see Paape, *Donkere jaren*, 161 and Gouverne, "US Army in Zuid-Limburg," 46 and 76–7. **Marceau: Plot C, Row 13, Grave 12.**
30. QAM 5, Heerlen, letter 2008.
31. QAM 6, Heerlen, letter 18 May 2008.
32. QAM 7, Geleen, letter 2008. **Stirling: Plot J, Row 16, Grave 12.**
33. QAM 8, Maastricht, letter May 2008. See also, for example, QAM 9, Leiden, email 23 July 2008. For the statistics on the Dutch hunger winter, see Lagrou, *Legacy of Nazi Occupation*, 100–1.
34. QAM 10, Geleen, letter 17 May 2008.
35. The number of Dutch resistance fighters who were killed in action is estimated at 2,800. Van der Heijden, *Grijs verleden*, 280–7 and 305.
36. QAM 11, Nijmegen, letter 7 June 2008.
37. QAM 12, Heerlen, letter 30 April 2008. On forced labor in the Netherlands and Limburg, see van der Heijden, *Grijs verleden*, 302–3 and "50 jaar bevrijding Margraten." On the growing Dutch opposition to forced labor and the promotion of draft evasion as "a patriotic duty," see Lagrou, *Legacy of Nazi Occupation*, 136–40.
38. QAM 13, Maastricht, emails 6 May and 5 June 2008. On the deportation and extermination of Jews in the Netherlands and Limburg, see van der Heijden, *Grijs verleden*, 212, 232–3, and 305; Roebroeks, "Limburg onder de Duitse knoet," 27–32; and Ubachs and Evers, *Tweeduizend jaar Maastricht*, 253. For a comparison with the fate of Jewish populations in the neighboring occupied countries, see Lagrou, *Legacy of Nazi Occupation*, 203, 251–6, and 292–5 and Bronzwaer, "Maastricht en Luik bezet," 181, 191–210, 237, and 248–50.
39. QAM 14, Valkenburg, letter 2008 and QAM 15, Amstenrade, letter 2008.
40. QAM 16, Kerkrade, email 25 April 2008.
41. QAM 17, email 16 June 2009 and QAM 18, Bunde, letter and email 1 June 2009.

42. Thijs Abbenhuis, "De kriebels in mijn buik," *De Natuurgids*, No. 6, 15 September 2007: 206–8.
43. QAM 19, Valkenburg a/d Geul, letter 8 May 2008 and QAM 20, Scheulder, email 25 April 2008.
44. QAM 21, letter 2008 and QAM 22, email 27 August 2008.
45. QAM 23, Landgraaf, email 25 April 2008.
46. QAM 24, emails 17 May 2008 and 10 June 2009.
47. QAM 25, Geleen, letter 2008 and QAM 26, Maastricht, letter 2008.
48. QAM 27, Meerssen, letter, May 2008.
49. QAM 28, Leiden, email 23 July 2008 and QAM 29, Kerkrade, letter 30 April 2008 and email 4 June 2009.
50. QAM 30, Schin op Geul, letter 2008.
51. QAM 31, Eindhoven, email 25 April 2008.
52. QAM 32, Landgraaf, email 18 June 2008.
53. QAM 33, letter 2008.
54. QAM 34, Eygelshoven, letter 2008.
55. QAM 35, Maastricht, letter 2008.
56. Joe and Maria Vaessen, "The Story of Three US Graves in The Netherlands and Belgium," Landgraaf, 1998, Folder "Lopende Correspondentie," SAM. **Diez: Plot E, Row 10, Grave 58 (Henri-Chapelle, Belgium)**.
57. QAM 36, Heerlen, email 1 May 2008; QAM 37, Vaals, email 9 May 2008; QAM 38, Lemiers, letter 2008; QAM 39, Klimmen, letter 2008; and QAM 40, Maastricht, letter 2008.
58. QAM 41, Brunssum, emails 2008 and 19 June 2009. **Le Hoty: Plot L, Row 10, Grave 13**.
59. QAM 42, Margraten, email 2 November 2008 and QAM 43, Maastricht, letter 2008. **Mosbacher: Plot I, Row 11, Grave 19**.

Chapter 2

1. The account of Mrs. van Kessenich's American tour is based on a copy of her detailed travel journal and on a radio interview about her trip for Regionale Omroep Zuid that was broadcast on 12 July 1946. See Folders 659 and 658 respectively, MVK.
2. For Lyndon B. Johnson's instructions, see the Western Union telegram he sent to Edward Connolly in Lockhart on 15 June 1946. The telegram is part of Mrs. van Kessenich's personal papers.
3. The Netherlands Information Bureau (NIB) played a crucial role in planning this successful trip. The Dutch government in exile in London had already established the NIB in the United States as early as 1941, when the Americans had not even entered the war. Through rigorous information management and active cultural diplomacy, the bureau significantly managed to shape the American image of the Netherlands during the war and in the immediate postwar period. See Snyder, "Dutch Cultural Policy," 970–7.

4. *Bridgeport Telegram*, 10 July 1946 and *Atlanta Journal*, 28 June 1946. Transcripts interviews Mrs. van Kessenich for *Headline Edition*, ABC Radio, 17 June 1946 and *We the People*, WABC, 30 June 1946, Folder 658, MVK.
5. Travel journal Mrs. van Kessenich, Folder 659 and letter Mrs. van Kessenich to Katholieke Radio Omroep, 28 July 1946, Folder 658, MVK.
6. The Demopolis and Johnson letters are in Folder 657, MVK.
7. The embassy and Canadian letters are in Folders 658 and 659, MVK.
8. Newspaper clipping in Folder 657, MVK. On the deep-seated social contrasts between Maastricht and rural Limburg as well as city prejudices and village suspicions, see Provinciaal Opbouworgaan Limburg, *Enkele sociologische gegevens over de gemeente Margraten*, 12 and 17 and Ubachs and Evers, *Tweeduizend jaar Maastricht*, 260–1.
9. "Ambassadrice van Margraten," *Libelle*, No. 9, 28 June 1946.
10. Radio interview, Regionale Omroep Zuid, 12 July 1946, Folder 658, MVK.
11. For the Rembrandt comment, see newspaper clipping in Folder 657, MVK.
12. On Heuschen's visit to Liège, see Captain Loudon memorandum for AGRC Versailles, 30 August 1946 and "Uittreksel van brief die J. Heuschen ons bij schrijven dd. 27 juli 1946 deed toekomen," NWGC Amsterdam, Folder 34, DIB.
13. Captain Loudon memorandum for AGRC Versailles, 30 August 1946 and Captain Loudon "Report on trip to Maastricht" for AGRC Versailles, 20 July 1946, Folder 34, DIB. For the Loudon-Heuschen follow-up correspondence, see letters 17 September and 3 and 4 October 1946, also in Folder 34, DIB. On the September resignations, see Folders 1 and 13, BMC.
14. NWGC to Dutch Ministry of War, 29 August 1946, Folder 34, DIB. Transcript NBC broadcast, 26 October 1946, Folder 658, MVK. Emilie van Kessenich to Dutch ambassador, 7 November 1946, Folder 657, MVK and to General Larkin, 6 November 1946, Folder 293 'Holland,' RG 92, NARA.
15. On van Kessenich's contacting the Ministry of Foreign Affairs, see her letter to the Dutch ambassador, 7 November 1946, Folder 657, MVK. On the outcome of the investigation, see Ministry of War to Mrs. van Kessenich, 3 December 1946, Folder 34, DIB. For the Loudon reprimand, see Ministry of War to H. L. F. C. van Vredenburch, Ministry of Foreign Affairs, 4 December 1946. The Dutch embassy's letters to Larkin and Morgan of 2 and 3 December 1946 are in Folder 657, MVK. On the conclusion of the Dutch War Department, see "Nota voor den Minister," 1 August 1947, Folder 34, DIB.
16. On Maastricht's mayor, see Bronzwaer, "Maastricht en Luik bezet," 291–2. On the index cards, see Heuschen to Captain Loudon, 17 September 1946, Folder 34, DIB and financial statements on purchase furniture, Folder 18, BCM.
17. QAM 43, Maastricht, email 26 May 2008.
18. A clipping from the *New York Times* of 28 May 1946 with a photo of such a ceremony has been preserved in Folder 13049, NA/MBZ. See also Elfreda B. Shukter and Barbara S. Scibetta, *War Brides of World War II* (New York: Penguin Books, 1989), 117.

19. Linda Konings, "Flowers for the Fallen," *Pirate Coast Magazine*, May 2007: 30–1.
20. Kirkels and Purnot, *Farmland*, 19 and 99. On the transfer of German dead from Margraten to Ysselsteyn, see Headquarters AGRC, "Report of Operations, 1 October – 31 December 1946," 158–9, *WWII Operations Reports, 1940–48, European Theater*, RG 407, NARA. For dozens of examples of German letters to the Margraten mayor, see Folder 940, GAM.
21. Mrs. Vreedenberg to Margraten mayor, 20 April 1947, Folder 940, GAM.
22. Mr. Emil Müller to Margraten mayor, 22 November 1946, Folder 940, GAM.
23. Mr. Hermann Stockey to Margraten town hall, 6 May 1947 and Mrs. Paula Svoboda to Margraten mayor, 3 October 1947, Folder 940, GAM.
24. "Appendix V: U.S. Military Cemetery, Margraten, Holland," 19 August 1946, Box "WOII," GAM.
25. "Statuten van het Burgercomité Margraten," 5 May 1946, Folder 3, BCM.
26. "Bloemen op Margraten verboden?" *GVL*, 23 May 1946 and "Dutch Forbidden to Honor Graves: U.S. Army Bars Them from Rite at American Cemetery Adopted by Village," *New York Times*, 20 May 1946.
27. "Amerikaansche oorlogsgraven," Minister of War to Minister of Foreign Affairs, 1 October 1946, Folder 34, DIB.
28. HQ AGRC to Commanding Officer, 531st QM Group, 31 October 1945, *Unit Histories, compiled 1943–1967, documenting the period 1755–1967*, RG 338, NARA. Newspaper clipping "Adoptiewerk Margraten: Home addresses?" Folder "Stichting," SAM.
29. Brigadier General H. L. Peckham, HQ AGRC, to J. J. F. Blom, NWGC, 8 August 1947, Folder 15, DIB. For an example of such an unfortunate error, see "Verkeerde naam op graf te Margraten?" newspaper clipping *LD*, October 1946, and Civilian Committee to NWGC, 7 October 1946, Folder 9, BCM.
30. For numerous examples of correspondence on the issue of home addresses, see Folder 44.6 "The Netherlands, 1946–1947," RG 92, NARA.
31. QAM 44, Maastricht, letter 2008.
32. QAM 45, Heerlen, email 14 May 2008. **Smith: Plot A, Row 16, Grave 28.**
33. The Lucie van den Boorn story that follows is based entirely on the private papers that were in her possession until her death in 2011.
34. **Gallion: Plot D, Row 6, Grave 24.**
35. **Lacy: Plot D, Row 11, Grave 23.**
36. **Steele: Plot A, Row 15, Grave 17.**
37. QAM 46, Heerlen, letter 2008 and interview Annie Prevoo-Frijnts, 28 April 2008, AVM.
38. **Cecil and Walter Steiner: Plot J, Row 15, Graves 15 and 16.**
39. The Machen story is based on the private papers that Rita Henssen was kind enough to hand over to Bert Kleijnen in Margraten for safekeeping. **Machen: Plot K, Row 10, Grave 5.**
40. The correspondence between John Adrian Larkin Sr. and Stef Kleijn as well as the Memorial Scholarship booklet are in Folder "Stichting," SAM.

Chapter 3

1. See, for example, "Geallieerde graven worden verzorgd," *Het Parool*, 29 April 1946.
2. "Geallieerd oorlogskerkhof door vacantiegangers ontwijd," *Trouw*, 27 August 1946. Ministry of War to the mayor of Margraten, 30 August 1946; mayor of Margraten to the governor of Limburg, 6 September 1946; mayor of Margraten to the Ministry of War, 6 September 1946; and Ministry of War to the Minister of Internal Affairs, 9 October 1946, Folder 1235, CKL.
3. Robin, *Enclaves of America*, 4.
4. Frey, "Decolonization," 609–14. On page 609 the author notes: "Colonialism and decolonization were the single most divisive issues in bilateral Dutch-American relations in the two decades following World War II. No other colonial power was affected so negatively by American policies to the same degree as the Netherlands."
5. Dutch ambassador in Washington to the Minister of Foreign Affairs, 20 August 1947, Folder 1235, CKL. This démarche was only part of a much broader campaign by the NIB to try and counteract the negative fallout from the East Indies crisis in the United States. See Snyder, "Dutch Cultural Policy," 974–5.
6. Civilian Committee to the governor of Limburg, 3 October 1947, Folder 1235, CKL.
7. Frey, "Decolonization," 613; Ubachs and Evers, *Tweeduizend jaar Maastricht*, 254; and *Riestepot*, 31. For examples of adoption prompted by the war in the East Indies, see QAM 47, Schin op Geul, email 2008; QAM 48, Maria Hoop, letter 2008; and QAM 49, Lemiers, letter 7 July 2008.
8. Author telephone interview with Grada Dorscheidt, 9 September 2009.
9. Letter liaison officer H. A. Loudon to van Tuil, *Afdeeling Gravendienst*, Ministry of War, 8 October 1946, DIB 34. For the agreement, see "Notawisseling tussen de Nederlandse en de Amerikaanse Regering betreffende de Amerikaanse oorlogsgraven in Nederland en in zijn overzeese gebieden; 's-Gravenhage, 11 April 1947," *Tractatenblad van het Koninkrijk der Nederlanden*, no. 31 (1952). Minor amendments were made to the 1947 notes in 1950 and 1951. Copies of these amendments are in Folder 943, GAM.
10. Steere, *Graves Registration Service*, 179 and Sledge, *Soldier Dead*, 139–40. "President Suggests Pilgrimage to Overseas Cemeteries," copy of Department of State wireless, 13 May 1947, Inv. Nr. 13049, MBZ/NA.
11. Dutch ambassador in Washington to Minister of Foreign Affairs, 13 May 1946 and "Draft Proposed Letter to Netherlands Government," enclosed in letter of Minister of Foreign Affairs to Minister of War, 21 June 1946, Inv. Nr. 13049, MBZ/NA.
12. For reports on this in the American press see, for example, "Graves of 19,000 U.S. Soldiers Given Tender Care by Dutch," *Washington Star*, 16 June 1946 and "Flowers, Trees Circle Graves of GI Heroes," *Atlanta Constitution*, 28 June 1946.

13. "'Adoption' of U.S. Soldiers' Graves Often Becomes a Racket in Holland," *Chicago Sun*, 24 August 1947. Memo for the Minister of Foreign Affairs, 4 September 1947, Inv. Nr. 13049, MBZ/NA.
14. The quote is from the standard letter accompanying the Quartermaster General's form "Request for Disposition of Remains," QMG 345 Military.
15. Shomon, *Crosses*, 117.
16. QAM 50, Helmond, email 1 May 2008 and "Dutch Man Who Tends Grave Seeks Info on WWII Paratrooper," *Press & Sun-Bulletin*, 2 March 2008.
17. Both van Kessenich letters are dated 10 July 1947 and are in Folder 1235, CKL.
18. The Anderson letters are dated 25 August and 2 December 1946 and are part of the Lucie van den Boorn papers.
19. Robin, *Enclaves of America*, 110–11. The quotes are from a Dutch translation of the article in the *New York Herald Tribune* published in *De Volkskrant* on 24 March 1947 as "Pelgrimstocht naar Margraten sterkt en troost." It is possible that some of the original wording may have been lost in translation.
20. A copy of the letter is in Warren Miller's IDPF. Thanks to the adopter for enclosing this file in the reply to the author's questionnaire.
21. *Bedford Boys*, 232 and "Na 50 jaar bij graf van broer," *De Telegraaf*, 20 May 1995.
22. The adopters' accounts of the widows' motivations are legion. On widows and blood relatives at loggerheads see, for example, QAM 51, Maastricht, letter 2008.
23. "Imposante Heldenherdenking," *GVL*, 31 May 1948. Telex message no. 5205, sent to the governor of Limburg, contains a list of the representatives for the diplomatic corps and the American embassy, 27 May 1948, Folder 902, CKL.
24. Roebroeks, "Historical Sketch," 13. On John Singer, see "Programma herdenkingsbijeenkomst dd. 10 November 2004," Folder "Perspublicaties," SAM.
25. "Uit Margraten overgeplaatste militaire graven," article by Father Heuschen and published on 17 January 1947. Clipping from an unnamed Dutch newspaper in Folder "Stichting," SAM.
26. Memo Minister of Foreign Affairs to his Secretary-General, 27 March 1947, Inv. Nr. 13040, MBZ/NA. On the fate of the Margraten Soviets, see letter Ministry of War to mayor of Amersfoort, 14 February 1947, DIB 34. See also email Remco Reiding with a brief historical sketch on the fate of the Margraten Soviets, 15 January 2009. Thanks to Jo Purnot and Frans Roebroeks for bringing this email to my attention.
27. Roebroeks, "Historical Sketch," 13. According to notes on the index cards in the Civilian Committee's original card catalogue, now part of the collection of the Adoption Foundation, the Soviet dead were transferred to the cemetery near Amersfoort at the end of May 1948.
28. Roebroeks, "Historical Sketch," 14–15. For the exact dates regarding the start of repatriation and permanent reinterment at Margraten, see a copy of the one-page history "United States Military Cemetery Margraten" in Folder 902, CKL.

29. The statistic on the total number of American casualties in World War II is the one listed by the ABMC, www.abmc.gov/search/wwii.php. On the Antwerp ceremony, see "The Return of John X," *Time*, 13 October 1947, www.time.com/time/magazine/0,9263,7601471013,00.html and also Sledge, *Soldier Dead*, 162–3 and 176.
30. Roebroeks, "Historical Sketch," 14–15.
31. Margraten mayor to Limburg governor, 7 May 1947 and "Kort Verslag van een vergadering inzake het Amerikaans Kerkhof te Margraten, gehouden op Dinsdag 9 Maart 1948 te 10 uur voormiddag in het Gouvernementsgebouw te Maastricht," Folder 1235, CKL.
32. Edward Grider Pegues to Beulah Pegues, 30 August 1949. Many thanks to Patricia Morrow in Houston, Texas, for being so kind to forward a copy of this letter from the family archive.
33. Mrs. Steiner to Lucie van den Boorn, 16 March 1948, PLB.
34. Author interview Lies Köster, 6 July 2009. See also interview Felix Prevoo, 7 March 2008, transcript sections 03:02:57:06 and 03:23:11:22, AVM. On the expected reopening of the cemetery in September 1949, see "Kerkhof Margraten in omlijsting van wuivende graanvelden," *GVL*, 17 September 1949. A copy of the communiqué is in Folder 2 and a copy of the standard reply form in Folder 17 of BCM.
35. For the committee's letter to Liège on 30 July 1948 and the American response on 19 and 31 August 1948, see Folder "Margraten cemetery, Misc. 1946–1948," RG 92, NARA. Civilian Committee to NWGC, 18 October 1949, Folder 2 and NWGC to Civilian Committee, 12 January 1950, Folder 3, BCM.
36. On the ABMC's charter, see www.abmc.gov/commission/index.php. On the Margraten cemetery transfer to the ABMC, see HQ Neuville Cemetery Detachment to Limburg governor Houben, 19 December 1949, Folder 1235, CKL and "Kerkhof Margraten Overgedragen," *GVL*, 29 December 1949. Civilian Committee to NWGC, 4 October 1950, Folder 3 and Colonel A.T.W. Moore of the ABMC's European Office to Dr. W. H. Enklaar, Vice-President of the NWGC, 24 April 1950, Folder 4, BCM.
37. "General Bradley bezocht het oorlogskerkhof te Margraten," *LD*, 1 April 1950.
38. "Duizenden woonden op Amerikaans soldatenkerkhof sobere plechtigheid bij," *LD*, 31 May 1951.
39. On the return rate, see Sledge, *Soldier Dead*, 151.
40. Kirkels and Purnot, *Farmland*, 120–3 and interview Else White-Hanöver, 15 December 2008, transcript sections 10:18:57:07 and 10:58:58:02, AVM.
41. Author telephone interview Grada Dorscheidt, 9 September 2009. QAM 52, Helchteren, including George Evancho's IDPF, August 2009 and email, 17 November 2010. **Peter and George Evancho: Plot N, Row 7, Graves 13 and 14**. Once the permanent reburials overseas had taken place, the US policy was to close the cemeteries to interments except for the remains of American war dead still found from time to time in the former battle areas. Such remains did end up at Margraten long after the war, something that is described later in

this book. Reversely, remains in the permanent overseas cemeteries could no longer be returned to the United States. Research has revealed, however, that for Margraten an exception was made at least once. This was in the case of PFC Joseph F. Hill from Ohio. In 2001 the remains of the paratrooper of the 101st Airborne Division were dug up again and returned to Cincinnati at the request of his daughter Bobbie, who was six at the time her father was killed at Dodewaard in the Netherlands on 22 October 1944. The return took place only after Bobbie was able to demonstrate that a major error had been made with regards to which relative in 1948 had possessed the legal right to make the decision on repatriation. Even then it took Joseph Hill's daughter many decades of legal and political wrangling to have the 1948 decision overturned. See www.awon.org/awhill.html and www.abmc.gov/search/detailwwnew.php.

Chapter 4

1. Harry E. Cook to John M. Butler, 15 October 1951, Folder 477, MVK.
2. The details of Michiels van Kessenich's trip come from his personal travel program, Folder 692, MVK.
3. Harry E. Cook to Reverend Edward Stanton, 16 June 1952, Folder 477, MVK.
4. American Embassy The Hague to Cardinal Spellman, 4 June 1952, Folder 692, MVK; "Groeiende belangstelling voor Maastricht," *GVL*, 2 July 1952; and Michiels van Kessenich to J. B. O'Hara, 7 October 1952, Folder 498, MVK. The National Information Bureau had been renamed the National Information Service in 1951. Snyder, "Dutch Cultural Policy," 975–6.
5. "Dutch Goodwill Envoy Flies Here," *Grand Rapids Press*, 24 June 1952 and "Dutch Mayor Calls for World Friendship," *Baltimore Sun*, 13 June 1952. The note can be found scribbled in red pencil at the top of the first of seven pages torn from a notebook, Folder 692, MVK.
6. Louis Azrael, "Report on Our Dead," *Baltimore American*, 15 June 1952.
7. "Meer begrip voor de achtergrond van het Amerikanisme," *GVL*, 19 September 1952.
8. "Verklaring van het monument op het Koningsplein," Folder 919, CKL.
9. Interview Annie Prevoo-Frijnts, 28 April 2008, AVM.
10. QAM 53, Brunssum, letter 2008. **Zwicky: Plot J, Row 9, Grave 5.**
11. QAM 54, Heerlen, email 2008. **Watson: Plot A, Row 4, Grave 7.**
12. QAM 55, Maastricht, letter 2008 and QAM 56, Maastricht, letter 25 April 2008.
13. Michiels van Kessenich to Ms. Shattuck, 11 February 1953, Folder 504, MVK.
14. Michiels van Kessenich to Mr. and Ms. Hobbs, 17 February 1953, Folder 483, MVK.
15. Singer to Michiels van Kessenich, 26 February 1953, Folder 504, MVK.
16. Ambassador Selden Chapin to Governor Houben, 19 May 1953, Folder 903, CKL and "Nederlands carillon te Washington aangeboden," *De Zuid-Limburger*, 10 May 1954.

17. Stichting tot het Beheeren van Landbouwgronden to Margraten mayor, 26 September 1951, Folder 1.776.1/944, GAM and "Screaming Eagles te Maastricht en Margraten," *LD*, 23 September 1954.
18. The Hobbs letter is quoted in the letter that Michiels van Kessenich sent to his bank and business contacts, 28 July 1954. The Amsterdam bank assessment is quoted in Michiels van Kessenich's letter to Hobbs, 22 September 1954. Both letters are in Folder 694, MVK.
19. Civilian Committee to NWGC, 20 November 1953, Folder 18, BCM.
20. Correspondence between NWGC and Governor Houben, 18 and 24 March 1954, Folder 1235, CKL.
21. Limburg Governor to US ambassador, 28 March 1955, Folder 903, CKL. For more correspondence on the creation of the new committee as well as lists providing membership suggestions, see Folders 903 and 1235, CKL.
22. Koops, "Dutch Emigration," 1005–7.
23. QAM 57, Margraten, letter 2008. **Dziesulski: Plot B, Row 5, Grave 16**.
24. QAM 58, Schin op Geul, letter 2008.
25. QAM 59, email 16 May 2008.
26. QAM 60, Maastricht, emails 25 April 2008 and 26 May 2009.
27. The governor's speech can be found side by side with a report on increased radioactivity in *LD*, 1 June 1954.
28. Text of the governor's speech, Memorial Day, 30 May 1956, Folder 904, CKL.
29. Note on phone call from Margraten mayor to governor's office, 25 May 1956, Folder 904, CKL; *Tractatenblad van het Koninkrijk der Nederlanden*, no. 122 (1956) and Stichting tot het Beheeren van Landbouwgronden to Minister van Oorlog, 12 June 1957, Folder 35, DIB.
30. Limburg governor Houben to H. Freeman Matthews, 25 November 1955, Folder 914, CKL.
31. Letters between Van Kessenich and Notermans, 24 January and 6 February 1957, Folder 4, BCM.
32. For the correspondence on Ms. Ida Barker, see Folder 914, CKL and Folder 6, BCM. **Barker: Plot I, Row 14, Grave 21**.
33. For the correspondence and clipping on Robert Long, see Folder 4, BCM and Folder 500, MVK. **Long: Plot H Row 11 Grave 27**.
34. H. Freeman Matthews to Van Kessenich, 4 June 1955, Folder 4, BCM.
35. Letter 31 May 1958, Folder 5, BCM. **Ralston: Plot L, Row 2, Grave 17**.
36. Letter 12 November 1959, Folder 6, BCM. **Zeigler: Plot D, Row 12, Grave 11**.
37. Letter 17 June 1955, Folder 3, BCM.
38. QAM 61, Heerlen, letter 2008. **Coker: Plot A, Row 16, Grave 32**.
39. QAM 62, Bunde, letter 2008. **Hart: Plot E, Row 2, Grave 2**.
40. US ambassador to Governor Houben, 3 June 1960, Folder 904, CKL.
41. On the 'Globetrotters' and Banneux pilgrims, see Folder 904, CKL and Folders 9 and 21, BCM.
42. Westervelde to mayor, 13 September 1957, Folder 4, BCM.
43. Text of the governor's speech, Memorial Day, 30 May 1959, Folder 904, CKL.

44. Marta Himes, "Netherlands Brussels World's Fair Agent's Tour 1958," 30–1, Folder 660, MVK.
45. For the Klinkisch correspondence between Germany, Margraten, and Ysselsteyn, see Folder 5, BCM.
46. "De Internationale Lamp van de Broederschap," Folder 16, BCM and "Op Margraten wordt lamp der broederlijkheid ontstoken," *DNL*, 8 March 1957.
47. "350.000," *De Margratenpost*, May 1961.
48. Marta Himes, "Netherlands Brussels World's Fair Agent's Tour 1958," 1–4 and 23–7, Folder 660, MVK. On the American travel boom to Europe in the 1950s, see Dierikx, "Beyond the Blue Horizon," 1017–20.
49. Letters between Limburg Committee and Governor Houben, 9 and 21 April 1958, Folder 1, BCM; "Marmeren kruisen op Margraten," *GVL*, 16 April 1953; and General Devers to Governor Houben, 25 April 1960, Folder 914, CKL.
50. Mayor Vrouenraets to Governor Houben, 9 January 1960, Folder 2, BCM and reports on cemetery dedication in *DNL*, 8 July 1960. For the Queen's message, see Shomon, *Crosses*, 197.
51. "Een man kwam terug," *De Margratenpost*, May 1961.
52. J. J. F. Blom to Emilie van Kessenich, 13 January 1958, Folder 5, BCM.
53. "Het kaartsysteem," *De Margratenpost*, May 1961.
54. Report on cemetery dedication in *DNL*, 8 July 1960.
55. QAM 63, Nuth, letter 2008.
56. "Tallozen steken de oceaan over," *GVL*, 20 August 1952 and "Definitieve aanleg van het oorlogskerkhof," *De Tijd*, 9 November 1954.
57. QAM 64, Landgraaf, letter 2008.
58. Letters to Lucie, 13 December 1950 and 30 June and 24 July 1959, PLB.
59. NWGC to Limburg Committee, 1 September 1958, Folder 5 and 23 May 1962, Folder 6, BCM. www.inproudremembrance.com/THE%20MEMORIAL%20 DAY%20I%20WILL%20NEVER%20FORGET.html. **Ross: Plot I, Row 16, Grave 8.**
60. QAM 65, Maasbracht, letter 28 April 2008. **Ratchford: Plot N, Row 2, Grave 10.**
61. Margraten mayor to Limburg governor, 11 September 1959, Folder 9, BCM and "Goldstar Mother strooide Amerikaanse grond," *DNL*, 24 September 1959.
62. Correspondence between J. Kenneth Rippel and Margraten mayor, 13 April and 4 June 1962, Folder 1393, GAM.
63. "Amerikaanse moeders bij graven van hun zonen," *DNL*, 15 September 1962 and Katherine L. Coursey to Margraten mayor, 4 October 1962, Folder 1393, GAM.
64. NWGC to Limburg Committee, June 1962, Folder 14, BCM and Limburg Committee to Sociale Raad Maastricht, 7 April 1962, Folder 6, BCM.
65. Robert Rigby to Michiels van Kessenich, 8 January 1963, Folder 6, BCM.
66. "Margraten komt in juni in 'The Reader's Digest,'" *DNL*, 8 February 1963.
67. Memorial Day reports in *LD*, 31 May 1961 and 1 June 1962.

Chapter 5

1. Governor's Memorial Day speeches 1964 and 1965, Folder 915, CKL.
2. Governor's Memorial Day speech 1964, Folder 915 and American embassy guidelines "Memorial Day Ceremony 1960 Margraten," Folder 904, CKL.
3. Carl L. Davis to Kuijpers, 27 April 1964 and William Baker to Kuijpers, 20 May 1965, Folder 1393, GAM.
4. QAM 66, Heerlen, email 2008.
5. QAM 67, Heerlen, letter and newspaper clipping, 18 May 2008. **Driver: Plot B, Row 4, Grave 24.**
6. The information on Harold Shroka was gathered in the context of a preliminary survey conducted by the Margraten Memorial Center Foundation with a view to creating a digital monument. Thanks to Jo Purnot for bringing this testimony to my attention.
7. *50-jarig priesterjubileum Pastoor Frits Janssen*, 10. Thanks to Bert Kleijnen for bringing this booklet to my attention.
8. QAM 68, Geleen, email 24 April 2008.
9. See, for example, Prevoo's letter to women's magazine *Beatrijs* in October 1964. Folder 6, BCM.
10. "Grote drukte tijdens 21ste Memorial Day," *DNL*, 31 May 1966.
11. "Provo-rel in Maastricht" and "Provo's belegerden kazerne," *LD*, 16 January 1967.
12. "Provo's wilden krans leggen in Margraten," 5 May 1967. Newspaper clipping in Folder 22, BCM.
13. "Massaal jongerenprotest tegen von Kielmansegg," *LD*, 16 May 1967.
14. Memorial Day speech, Folder 915, CKL.
15. Van der Maar, "The Vietnam War," 684–5 and QAM 69, Heerlen, letter 2008.
16. "Al Brodbeck," *DL*, 10 November 1984.
17. "Provo Peace-In Venlo" and "Vredesstoet trok door Maastricht," *DNL*, 17 October and 23 December 1967.
18. "Harde charges van politie in Brunssum en Maastricht," *DNL* and "Gewelddadige vredesmars," *LD*, 16 April 1967. By the late 1960s, there were other indications of what Pieter Lagrou has called the end of a period of Dutch "national consensus" on the meaning of World War II. In Amsterdam, for example, the presence of long-haired Provos in sleeping bags on and around the austere national World War II monument on the Dam square got to the point where it was deemed so scandalous that in August 1970 Dutch marines moved in to oust "its unpatriotic occupants." Lagrou, *Legacy of Nazi Occupation*, 292–5.
19. Van der Maar, "The Vietnam War," 688 and Memorial Day speech, Folder 915, CKL.
20. "Memorial Day 1968 Margraten," *DNL*, 31 May 1968 and "Memorial Day 1968," newspaper clipping, Folder 906, CKL.
21. "Een stille 'stille' optocht" and "Tegen Russisch optreden," *DNL*, 22 and 27 August 1968.

22. "Vredestocht van jongeren," *LD*, 1 October 1968.
23. For the organization of the 1968 Gold Star Mothers visit, see Folder 1393, GAM.
24. QAM 70, Maastricht, emails 7 May 2008 and 26 May 2009.
25. Letters Ministry of Foreign Affairs, 14 March and 23 May 1969, Folder 922, CKL.
26. On the Mass for Eisenhower, see letter Nederland-Amerika Instituut, 13 May 1969, Folder 906, CKL.
27. Limburg governor to Limburg mayors, 21 August 1969, Folder 922, CKL.
28. "Amerikanen bezochten graven van 'hun' dierbaren op Margraten," *DNL*, 31 May 1969.
29. Ambassador Middendorf to Governor van Rooy, 11 August 1969 and governor's 13 September speech, Folder 922, CKL.
30. "Amerikanen bezochten graven van 'hun' dierbaren op Margraten," *DNL*, 31 May 1969.
31. Van der Maar, "The Vietnam War," 688 and "Protesttocht tegen Amerikaanse politiek," *DNL*, 19 May 1970.
32. Correspondence on the agreement and copies of the various drafts are in Folder 913, CKL and Folder 943, GAM.
33. On the visit, see letter mayor Kuijpers to Margraten inhabitants, 26 August 1970 and copies of the various lists, Folder 1393, GAM.
34. QAM 71, letter 2008.
35. For the governor's speeches, see Folder 915, CKL. On Ewell and Middendorf, see newspaper clippings, Folder 907, CKL.
36. Van der Maar, "The Vietnam War," 688 and 690–1 and articles in *DL*, 2 January and 28 December 1972.
37. For examples of the LBJ correspondence, see Folder 657, MVK. Letter to the American Legion, 4 June 1968, Folder 657, MVK.
38. Major General Adams of the ABMC to Baron van Kessenich, 27 July 1970, Folder 474, MVK.
39. Harvard University to Baron van Kessenich, 23 February 1972, Folder 474, MVK. Baron van Kessenich to author Major Thomas Stone, 17 July 1972, Folder 504, MVK.
40. Prevoo to NWGC, 28 January 1972, Folder 11 and list of the financial contributions to Memorial Day of some 30 Limburg municipalities, Folder 12, BCM.
41. "Amerikanen voor het laatst naar Maastricht," newspaper clipping 19 April 1972, Folder 907, CKL.
42. Letter NWGC, December 1972, Folder 13, BCM.
43. *Windhund* Division to Limburg Committee, 15 April 1973, Folder 7, BCM.
44. QAM 72, Amsterdam, letter 2008. **Forein: Plot F, Row 2, Grave 2.**
45. QAM 73, email 28 April 2008. **Riddell: Plot N, Row 21, Grave 5.**
46. Van der Maar, "The Vietnam War," 692–3.
47. Texts of the speeches by Governor van Rooy, General Davison, and Ambassador Gould are in Folders 907 and 915, CKL. During World War II,

Henry Kissinger himself had been stationed at Gulpen in southern Limburg with the 84th Infantry Division. Gouverne, *US Army in Zuid-Limburg*, 155B.
48. QAM 74, Heerlen, email 26 May 2008. **Brown: Plot G, Row 13, Grave 20.**
49. QAM 75, Susteren, letter 18 May 2008. **Bariani: Plot K, Row 20, Grave 19.**
50. Speech Governor van Rooy, Folder 915, CKL and letter NWGC to Limburg mayors, 13 May 1977, Folder 12, BCM.
51. Sereda to Lucie, 1 July 1946 and 30 October 1965, PLB.
52. QAM 76, Heerlen, emails 28 April 2008 and 28 May 2009.
53. Speeches Governor Kremers, Folders 908 and 915, CKL.
54. QAM 77, Beek, letter 2008.
55. QAM 78, Maastricht, email 10 June 2008.
56. QAM 79, Maastricht, email 1 May 2008.

Chapter 6

1. *LD*, 5 August 1980.
2. Righolt, "Second Cold War," 706–15.
3. Governor's speech, Folder 915, CKL and reports in *DL*, 30 October and 17 and 25 November 1981.
4. The text of a revised House Resolution introduced in January 2007 can be found in Folder "Correspondentie," SAM.
5. Governor's speeches, Folder 909, CKL. "Vredesgroepen bundelen hun activiteiten," *DL*, 17 September 1982, and "Limburgs comité dik tevreden," *DL*, 31 October 1983. Righolt, "Second Cold War," 714.
6. Newspaper clipping, 11 November 1983, Folder 9, BCM.
7. Colijn to Margraten mayor, 8 October 1976, Folder 7, BCM. The book was published in 1980, but under another title, *Of Dutch Ways*.
8. For an example, see "After Action Report – 1988 Memorial Day Ceremony," Folder 911, CKL.
9. Margraten mayor to head of the governor's cabinet, L. de Bruijn, 9 September 1983, Folder 911, CKL.
10. "Amerikaanse ambassadeur in bevrijdingsestafette," newspaper clipping, 14 September 1983, Folder 909, CKL.
11. A copy of the tribute of appreciation can be found in Folder 1, BCM.
12. "Adoptie-idee kreeg wereldwijd respons," *DL*, 10 November 1984.
13. QAM 80, Eijsden, letter 2008.
14. "Dutchman seeks out fallen GI's kin," *Milwaukee Sentinel*, 12 December 1985. **Venne: Plot B, Row 17, Grave 18.**
15. "2 miljoen bezoekers," *DL*, 10 November 1984.
16. Righolt, "Second Cold War," 714.
17. QAM 81, Brunssum, letter 30 April 2008.
18. QAM 82, Eijsden, email 28 April 2008.
19. Speech text, Folder 915, CKL.
20. "Vreedzame betoging in Maastricht tegen VS-bommen," *DL*, 18 April 1986.

21. On the security measures, see correspondence and guidelines in Folders 910 and 911, CKL as well as an email to the author from a police officer responsible for the Margraten cemetery at the time, 29 November 2008.
22. QAM 83, Geulle, letter 2008. **Manahan: Plot K, Row 1, Grave 19**.
23. QAM 84, Terschuur, letter 2008. **Kukay: Plot E, Row 13, Grave 10**.
24. Righolt, "Second Cold War," 714.
25. Governor's 1987 Memorial Day speech, Folder 915, CKL.
26. Governor's 1989 Memorial Day speech, Folder 915, CKL.
27. Mayor's 1988 Memorial Day speech, Folder 911, CKL.
28. The full correspondence on this project can be found in Folder 916, CKL.
29. QAM 85, Valkenburg, letter 2008; QAM 86, letter 2008; and QAM 87, Maastricht, letter 2008.
30. QAM 88, Sint Geertruid, letter 21 May 2008.
31. QAM 89, Stramproy, email 27 April 2008.
32. Acting Governor H. W. Riem's Memorial Day speech 1990, Folder 911, CKL.
33. Boxhoorn, "The Reorientation of NATO," 717 and 725–6.
34. "Kleindochter Eisenhower op bezoek in Zuid-Limburg," *DL*, 20 April 1990.
35. See articles on the exposition and museum plans in *LD*, 8 June and 30 August 1990. Peter Pauwels in Heerlen to Bestuur van de Stichting "Voorbereiding Expositie Bezetting-Bevrijding Zuid-Limburg 1940–1945 in Cadier en Keer," 8 June 1990. Box "Archief Adoptie Graven afk. van Van Laar. Herdruk 'Crosses in the Wind,'" PJP.
36. "To See Just One More Time," *Gloucester Daily Times*, 23 May 1991. **Rocchio: Plot E, Row 6, Grave 24**.
37. "Tony Forcelatti even terug in Limburg," *Zondagsnieuws*, 22 September 1991.
38. For the calls in the press, see clippings from newspapers dated 4 and 24 May 1991, Folder 9, BCM.
39. QAM 90, Kerkrade, email 17 May 2008.
40. QAM 91, Margraten, emails 2008 and 27 May 2009.
41. QAM 92, Maastricht, letter 2009.
42. QAM 93, Maastricht, letter 2008.
43. QAM 94, Meerssen, emails 26 April 2008 and 12 June 2009.
44. QAM 95, Kelmis, email 28 April 2008; QAM 96, Heerlen, email 28 April 2008; and QAM 97, Hoensbroek, email 11 May 2008.
45. QAM 98, Maastricht, email 6 June 2008.
46. QAM 99, Sittard, letter 1 May 2008.
47. QAM 100, Linne-Maasgouw, email 9 May 2008.
48. QAM 101, Kerkrade, emails 22 May 2008 and 12 June 2009. **Davis: Plot D, Row 13, Grave 10**.

Chapter 7

1. Hellema, "Politics of Asymmetry," 592–3.
2. For the unit certificates, see Folder 8, BCM.

3. Folder 3, BCM. **Cabral: Plot E, Row 4, Grave 11.**
4. Folder 8, BCM.
5. *LD*, 10 June 1995.
6. *Riestepot*, 70 and interview Felix Prevoo, 7 March 2008, transcript sections 03:23:11:22 and 03:52:43:06, AVM.
7. Folder 8, BCM.
8. Folders 8 and 9, BCM.
9. For the appeals in the press, see Folders 8 and 9, BCM.
10. QAM 102, Grevenbicht, emails 30 April and 18 and 20 May 2008. Thanks also to the son of Carl Hodges who was kind enough to clarify the issue of the letter to Congresswoman Marilyn Lloyd. **Sweeney: Plot B, Row 12, Grave 3.**
11. Gouverne. *US Army in Zuid-Limburg*, 145. Thanks to John Gouverne for providing me with additional documents pertaining to Dolly Vinsant, most notably the "Report of Burial." **Vinsant: Plot B, Row 17, Grave 4.**
12. "Memorial card presented by the 325th Glider Infantry Association in honor of the burial of Lieutenant Utecht at Margraten on 16 September 1994," Folder 8, BCM. **Utecht: Plot N, Row 23, Grave 22.**
13. On the feedback from cemetery staff, see QAM 299, Maastricht, letter 25 April 2008. On US embassy responses see, for example, QAM 300, Roosteren, letter 2008; QAM 103, Baarle-Nassau, letter 28 April 2008; and "Gezocht: Verjaardag van John Jarabek," 11 September 2002, newspaper article attached to QAM 104, letter 2008.
14. QAM 105, email 9 May 2008. **Lempka: Plot M, Row 17, Grave 5.**
15. QAM 106, Schinveld, emails 25 April 2008 and 11 July 2009. **Greiner: Plot G, Row 4, Grave 25.**
16. QAM 107, email 16 May 2008. **Dundon: Plot K, Row 5, Grave 1.**
17. QAM 108, letter 27 April 2008.
18. QAM 109, email 26 September 2008. **Watson: Plot J, Row 10, Grave 22.**
19. QAM 110, email 2008. **Ulenburg: Plot M, Row 2, Grave 5** and **McLean: Plot P, Row 15, Grave 9.**
20. QAM 111, Eijsden, email 4 May 2008. **Lewandowski: Plot L, Row 16, Grave 5.**
21. QAM 112, letter 2008. **Hewitt: Plot D, Row 1, Grave 14.**
22. For internet usage densities with regards to the Netherlands and the rest of the world, see www.internetworldstats.com.
23. QAM 113, letter May 2008 and QAM 114, email 1 May 2008.
24. QAM 115, Cadier en Keer, email 8 May 2008.
25. QAM 116, Kerkrade, email 16 May 2008.
26. QAM 117, Hoofddorp, email May 2008.
27. QAM 118, email 24 April 2008 and www.uiaa.org/illinois/veterans/display_veteran.asp?id=974.
28. QAM 119, email 2008.
29. QAM 120, Venray, email 26 April 2008.
30. QAM 121, Berg en Terblijt, emails 25 April and 5 May 2008.
31. The Fort Knox comment is from "Gezocht: Verjaardag van John Jarabek," 11 September 2002, newspaper article attached to QAM 122, letter 2008.

32. QAM 123, email 2008.
33. The warning on IDPF content is posted on www.wwjohnston.net/dadswar.
34. QAM 124, Stevensweert, email 2008 and www.381st.org/History/WarDiaries/533rdBS. **Eylens: Plot E, Row 15, Grave 26.**
35. QAM 125, email 3 August 2008. **Burgess: Plot E, Row 1, Grave 9.**
36. QAM 126, IDPF and assorted documents on Michael Bekierski sent to the author in 2009. **Bekierski: Plot K, Row 15, Grave 8.**
37. QAM 127, email 24 April 2008 and www.members.home.nl/r.kunne/B26%20mesch%20memorial.htm#vrijdag%203%20oktober. **Willett: Plot L, Row 4, Grave 21.**
38. QAM 128, email 29 April 2008. **Ticknor: Plot M, Row 14, Grave 9.**
39. For the newspaper's call for patience, see copy of the article "Deze graven blijven binnen de familie" enclosed in QAM 129, Maastricht, letter 2008.
40. Based on several newspaper clippings sent to the author by the Bronnebergs in 2008 in addition to their reply to the author's questionnaire. **Long: Plot G, Row 8, Grave 2.**

Chapter 8

1. "Amerika lijkt even een stuk dichterbij" and "Soms moet ik huilen en bidden doe ik ook," *DL*, 15 and 18 September 2001. "Persbericht," Gemeentebestuur Margraten, 13 September 2001, Folder "Perspublicaties," SAM.
2. Hellema, "Politics of Asymmetry," 593.
3. "Beknopt verslag bijeenkomst" and "Presentielijst," 27 November 2002, Folder "Verslagen," SAM. Apart from the four people already mentioned in the text, the new committee's founding members were Mr. R. Croonen, Mr. Eussen, Mr. W. Kamerman, and Mr. M. Royen.
4. "Beknopt verslag bijeenkomst," 27 November 2002, Folder "Verslagen," SAM.
5. Letter Adoption Foundation to Margraten municipal council, March 2003, Folder "Correspondentie," SAM. "Beknopt verslag bijeenkomst Stichting," 24 February and 24 March 2003 and letter Margraten municipal council to Foundation, 17 July 2003, Folder "Verslagen," SAM.
6. "Speuren in adoptantenregister is puur monnikenwerk," *Heuvelland Aktueel*, 14 January 2004.
7. QAM 130, letter 28 April 2008.
8. "Speuren in adoptantenregister is puur monnikenwerk," *Heuvelland Aktueel*, 14 January 2004.
9. QAM 131, Maastricht, email 14 May 2008.
10. QAM 132, letter 2008.
11. QAM 133, Heerlen, letter 2008.
12. QAM 134, letter 2008.
13. QAM 135, Geleen, letter April 2008.
14. QAM 136, letter 2008.

15. QAM 137, Maastricht, letter 2008 and QAM 138, Landgraaf, letter 5 June 2008.
16. QAM 139, Heerlen, letter 26 April 2008.
17. QAM 140, Voerendaal, email 5 May 2008 and QAM 141, Valkenburg, emails 29 April and 12 May 2008.
18. QAM 142, Wylre, letter 2008 and QAM 143, Nuth, email 2 May 2008.
19. QAM 144, Venlo, letter 2008.
20. QAM 145, Brunssum, letter 2008.
21. QAM 146, Heerlen, letter 6 May 2008. **Byrd: Plot D, Row 1, Grave 1**.
22. QAM 147, Heerlen, email 14 May 2008; QAM 148, Kerkrade, email 30 April 2008; and QAM 149, Heerlen, letter 2008.
23. QAM 214, Ubachsberg, emails 15 May and 8 December 2008.
24. QAM 150, email 2008 and www.krijnen.com/archives/000264.shtml. **Kirlin: Plot M, Row 2, Grave 8**.
25. QAM 151, Maastricht, email 26 May 2008.
26. QAM 152, Geleen, email 7 May 2008.
27. QAM 153, Margraten, email 2008 and QAM 154, Voerendaal, email 30 April 2008.
28. QAM 155, Nieuwstadt, email 8 May 2008; QAM 156, Weustenrade, email 2008; and QAM 301, Geleen, letter 2008.
29. QAM 157, Cadier en Keer, email 2 May 2008 and QAM 158, Nuth, letter 2008.
30. QAM 159, Geleen, email 29 April 2008. Winters, *Beyond Band of Brothers*, 117–18.
31. QAM 160, Brunssum, emails 29 April 2008 and 1 July 2009. **Diel: Plot L, Row 15, Grave 8**.
32. QAM 161, Berg en Terblijt, letter 2008 and QAM 162, 's-Hertogenbosch, letter 24 April 2008.
33. QAM 163, Venlo, email 3 May 2008. See also, for example, QAM 164, Papendrecht, email 21 May 2008; QAM 165, letter 2008; and QAM 166, Landgraaf, letter 2008. The total number of Dutch citizens to have been held captive in Japanese camps in the colonies is estimated at 80,000. Lagrou, *Legacy of Nazi Occupation*, 101.
34. QAM 167, Maastricht, letter 14 May 2008.
35. QAM 168, Oirsbeek, emails 20 May 2008 and 10 June 2009. **Jefferson: Plot F, Row 8, Grave 16**.
36. QAM 169, Heerlen, letter 2008.
37. QAM 170, Eijsden, email 27 May 2008 and "Hospik in de vuurlijn," *DL*, 17 September 1994.
38. QAM 171, Panningen, letter 1 May 2008. **Bohling: Plot C, Row 16, Grave 30**.
39. QAM 172, Landgraaf, letter 27 April 2008.
40. QAM 173, Bunde, email 27 April 2008.
41. QAM 174, Susteren, email 25 April 2008. **McAlpine: Plot P, Row 7, Grave 3**.

42. QAM 175, Heerlen, email 24 April 2008. The major's story has been posted on www.fallennotforgotten.nl under "Stories." **Skelly: Plot O, Row 5, Grave 2.**
43. QAM 176, Maastricht, letter 2008.
44. QAM 177, Landgraaf, email 29 May 2008 and QAM 178, Berg en Terblijt, emails 25 April and 5 May 2008.
45. QAM 179, Valkenburg, email 2008.
46. QAM 180, Margraten, email 2008. For examples of tourists, see QAM 181, Eijgelshoven, 28 May 2008 and QAM 182, Urmond, email 2008. On Dutch tourist trends and the impact of travel in the United States, see Dierikx, "Beyond the Blue Horizon," 1020–5 and Martha Bayles, "The Return of Cultural Diplomacy," *Newsweek*, Special Edition/Issues 2009: 66–7.
47. QAM 183, Roermond, emails 30 April and 26 July 2008 and QAM 184, Hoensbroek, letter 2008.
48. QAM 185, Urmond, 18 May 2008.
49. For the American bases and school in Limburg, see www.jfcbs.nato.int/htm/about/history.htm; www.usagschinnen.eur.army.mil/, and www.afnorth-is.com.
50. QAM 186, Voerendaal, email 2008.
51. QAM 187, Nuth, email 8 June 2008.
52. QAM 188, Voerendaal, 24 April 2008 and www.bensavelkoul.nl. **De Febio: Plot E, Row 2, Grave 7.**
53. QAM 189, Voerendaal, email 30 April 2008.
54. QAM 190, Bocholtz, email 2008; QAM 191, Heerlen, email 27 April 2008; and QAM 192, Kerkrade, email 30 May 2008.
55. QAM 193, Vaals, email 19 June 2008, including *Nevada Daily Mail* article, 11 December 1946, and letter from Thomas Rose to adopters, 10 June 2008. **Rose: Plot H, Row 15, Grave 16.**
56. QAM 194, Hoensbroek, email 24 April 2008 and QAM 195, Noorbeek, letter 2008.
57. QAM 196, Nattenhoven, email 28 April 2008 and www.angelfire.com/al4/scheijen/adoptiegravenUSA.html. **Berger: Plot N, Row 16, Grave 8.**
58. QAM 197, Eijsden, email 28 April 2008; QAM 198, Meerssen, email 24 April 2008; and QAM 199, Banholt, email 27 April 2008.
59. QAM 200, Landgraaf, letter 2008.
60. On Dutch East Indies veterans see, for example, QAM 201, Geleen, email 17 May 2008 and QAM 202, Maastricht, letter 27 April 2008.
61. QAM 203, Limbricht, emails 7 May 2008 and 22 June 2009.
62. See, for example, QAM 204, Brunssum, letter 6 May 2008 and QAM 205, Meerssen, letter 2008. Boxhoorn, "The Reorientation of NATO," 724.
63. QAM 206, Landgraaf, email 27 April 2008.
64. QAM 207, Voerendaal, email 4 May 2008.
65. QAM 208, Horst, email 24 April 2008. **Jacobs: Plot F, Row 19, Grave 6.**
66. Letter A. H. C. Smits-Gulikers to Fien Oprej, 17 August 2005, Folder "Lopende Correspondentie," SAM.
67. QAM 209, email 19 May 2008.

68. QAM 210, Hulsberg, email 24 April 2008.
69. QAM 211, Maastricht, emails 2008.
70. QAM 212, Houthem, email 29 April 2008.
71. QAM 213, Stein, email 30 April 2008.

Chapter 9

1. Hellema, "Politics of Asymmetry," 593 and Klep, "Peacekeeping," 729.
2. Robin, *Enclaves of America*, 3–4, 9, 53, 122, and 124.
3. For former ambassador Philip Young's address, see *Halve Maen: Quarterly Magazine of the Dutch Colonial Period in America*, Vol. XL (January 1966): 4.
4. "Netherlands American Cemetery and Memorial, Margraten. Remarks, as delivered, by Ambassador Clifford M. Sobel. Sunday, May 25, 2003." www.thehague.usembassy.gov/052503.
5. QAM 215, Eckelrade, letter 2008; QAM 216, Brunssum, email 1 May 2008; QAM 217, Roermond, email 2008; QAM 218, Heerlen, email 19 May 2008; QAM 219, Heeze, letter 2008; QAM 220, Maastricht, email 14 May 2008; and QAM 221, Margraten, letter 2008.
6. QAM 222, Wessem, email 2008 and QAM 223, Zaandam, email 12 May 2008.
7. QAM 224, Maastricht, email 28 April 2008.
8. QAM 225, Beegden, 7 May 2008. Special thanks also to Annette Tison for the email on this story that she was kind enough to forward on 1 July 2009. **Doty: Plot L, Row 3, Grave 9**.
9. QAM 226, Ohé en Laak, email 1 May 2008; Blom, "Suffering as a Warning," 64; and Bacevich, *New American Militarism*, 225. On the Dutch unease with American militarism after 2003, see also Klep, "Peacekeeping," 728–9 and 733–4.
10. QAM 227, Kerkrade, letter 2008; QAM 228, Cadier en Keer, letter 2008; and QAM 229, Brunssum, email 29 April 2008.
11. QAM 230, Helmond, email 2008; QAM 231, Eijsden, email 30 April 2008; QAM 232, Scheulder, email 25 April 2008; and QAM 233, Roermond, letter 2008. On Zimbabwe and American and Dutch support for Israel, see QAM 234, Nijmegen, letter 7 June 2008.
12. QAM 235, Berg en Terblijt, email 2008.
13. QAM 236, Sint Geertruid, email 2008.
14. QAM 237, Heerlen, email and attached documents, 28 April 2008. **Rozwalka: Plot O, Row 3, Grave 4**.
15. QAM 238, Kerkrade, email 6 May 2008 and Stefan Gillissen, "Verbonden in de dood," *DL*, 30 April 2009. **Dimmock: Plot F, Row 8, Grave 20**.
16. QAM 239, Kerkrade, email 23 May 2008; QAM 240, De Bilt, letter 2008; and QAM 241, Gronsveld, letter 2008.
17. QAM 242, Kunrade, email 5 May 2008; QAM 243, Enschede, email 2008; QAM 244, Landgraaf, email 26 May 2008; and QAM 245, Munstergeleen, email 2008.

18. On President Bush's visit, see *De Limburger*'s special 12-page section in a special edition on 7 and 8 May 2005 titled "President Bush in Limburg."
19. "Speech by President G. W. Bush on 2005, May 8. American Cemetery Margraten" and "Speech by Jan Peter Balkenende, Prime Minister of the Netherlands, commemorating the end of the Second World War, American Military Cemetery in Margraten, 8 May 2005." Copies of both speeches in Folder "Correspondentie," SAM.
20. QAM 246, Hoensbroek, email 23 July 2008; QAM 247, email 28 April 2008; QAM 248, Margraten, email 2 November 2008; and QAM 249, Heerlen, letter 25 April 2008.
21. QAM 250, Nijswiller, email 26 September 2008 and www.heemkundever enigingnijswiller.nl.
22. QAM 251, Deurne, email 25 April 2008 and www.heroesforever.nl. **Carlson: Plot B, Row 9, Grave 12; McCollum: Plot G, Row 8, Grave 25; and Little: Plot F, Row 10, Grave 6.**
23. "Memorial Day Speech by U.S. Ambassador Roland E. Arnall, Netherlands American Cemetery and Memorial, Margraten, May 27, 2007" and "Speech by L. J. P. M. Frissen, the Queen's Commissioner for the Province of Limburg, on the occasion of Memorial Day at the American war cemetery in Margraten on May 27, 2007." Copies of both speeches in Folder "Correspondentie," SAM. Robert Kagan's book is *Of Paradise and Power*, published in 2003.
24. QAM 252, Landgraaf, letter 27 April 2008.
25. QAM 253, Heerlen, letter 28 April 2008.
26. Details on the ceremonies were posted under "Toerisme" and "Amerikaanse begraafplaats" on www.margraten.nl.
27. "'Memorialpark Margraten' moet positie begraafplaats verzekeren en versterken," media release, Margraten, 21 November 2005, Folder "Lopende correspondentie," SAM.
28. Robin, *Enclaves of America*, 39. On the role of President Bush's visit in setting this project in motion, see "Memorialpark Margraten: Onderzoek haalbaarheid oorlogs- en vrijheidsmuseum," (Breda: ZKA Consultants & Planners, November 2005), Folder "Lopende correspondentie," SAM.
29. Secretary of the Adoption Foundation Jacques Aussems to American Ambassador Clifford Sobel, 19 May 2005, Folder "AWON/Bezoek President Bush" and summary report of the Adoption Foundation committee meeting, 8 September 2005, Folder "Verslagen," SAM. On the Limburg governor, see summary report of the Adoption Foundation committee meeting, 9 March 2006, Folder "Verslagen," SAM and QAM 254, Maastricht, email 6 June 2008.
30. Summary report of the Adoption Foundation committee meeting, 22 March 2007 and report drawn up in Cadier en Keer, December 2007, Folder "Verslagen," SAM. On the French adoption system, see www. fleursdelamemoire.free.fr.
31. Details on the ceremony were posted under "Toerisme" and "Amerikaanse begraafplaats" on www.margraten.nl. For more information about Sharon

Estill Taylor's search for her father, see her website www.myphantomfather.com.
32. QAM 255, Uitgeest, including IDPF John K. Barry, and www.303rdbg.com/359vanweelden.html. **Barry: Plot D, Row 6, Grave 10**.
33. QAM 256, Landgraaf, email 7 May 2008 and letter, including IDPF Leonard Henlin, 21 June 2009. **Henlin: Plot B, Row 21, Grave 26**.
34. QAM 257, Baarlo, letter, including IDPF Mart Etheridge, 16 July 2009.
35. Emails Daniel O'Brien to Jacques Aussems of the Adoption Foundation, 30 September and 27 October 2005. With thanks to Jo Purnot for forwarding the emails to me. **Zoradi: Plot M, Row 17, Grave 17**.
36. QAM 258, Berlicum, letter 2008 and copy of letter to her from Nancy Miller in Mancelona, Michigan, 28 February 2005. **Hood: Plot L, Row 21 Grave 22**.
37. QAM 259, Margraten, email 8 May 2008 and letter 28 June 2009, including copies of letters sent to his adopting parents by Philip's mother on 16 June and 21 July 1946. **Seifried: Plot B, Row 7, Grave 24**.
38. Email Gerry Morenski to Fien Opreij of the Adoption Foundation, 6 November 2004. On the event on 28 May 2005, see media release Gemeente Margraten, 23 May 2005. Both documents can be found in Folder "AWON/Bezoek President Bush," SAM.
39. QAM 260, Wittem, letter 7 July 2008.

Chapter 10

1. Robin, *Enclaves of America*, 53 and 126 and "A Foothold in Europe," 66–8. Mayo, *War Memorials*, 101-5.
2. Kirkels and Purnot, *Farmland*, 159 and 163.
3. QAM 261, Kerkrade, email 11 June 2008 and QAM 262, Maastricht, email 1 May 2008.
4. QAM 263, Houthem, email 7 May 2008.
5. Quote is from QAM 264, email 17 May 2008. For the complaint, see QAM 265, Riemst, Belgium, letter 2008.
6. QAM 266, Valkenburg a/d Geul, letter 2008.
7. For the woman in her eighties, see QAM 267, letter 2008.
8. QAM 268, Elsloo, letter 2008.
9. Access to the speech text can be had by clicking on the link "Address by Mayor Van Beers during his words of welcome" at www.margraten.nl/margraten?waxtrapp=fdzDsHkoOloOnHAiFbEhB.
10. QAM 269, email 14 June 2008 and www.ww2online.nl/morneweck.htm. **Morneweck: Plot E, Row 20, Grave 17**.
11. QAM 270, Breugel, email 25 May 2008. **Seibel: Plot H, Row 16, Grave 18**.
12. QAM 271, Voerendaal, email 28 April 2008. **Klippel: Plot M, Row 19, Grave 16**.
13. Barack Obama, *The Audacity of Hope: Thoughts on Reclaiming the American Dream*. (New York: Vintage Books), 141.

14. QAM 272, Cadier en Keer, letter 2008 and QAM 273, Heerlen, email 27 April 2008.
15. QAM 274, Landgraaf, letter 2008, including in attachment a copy of letter from Ms. Snyder to Jean Frints, 26 January 1946. **Snyder: Plot N, Row 19, Grave 3.**
16. Emails from Maurice Göttgens to author, 4 October and 25 November 2009, as well as a copy of the letter written to Ms. Pauline Roukens-Göttgens by Ben Allen shortly after 2005. See also *Dear Folks, Love Bill, 1943–1945*, a collection of Bill's letters home, privately published by his parents shortly after the war. **Arnold: Plot B, Row 14, Grave 15 and Allen: Plot E, Row 2, Grave 1.**
17. QAM 275, Sittard, email 25 April 2008. **Erwin: Plot K, Row 2, Grave 12.**
18. QAM 276, Helchteren, Belgium, email 23 May 2008. See also emails from Mary Anne Fedor to author, 26, 27, and 28 August 2009. **Peter and George Evancho: Plot N, Row 7, Graves 13 and 14.**
19. Gerry Morenski, "Margraten Group Shares Award with AWON," the *Star*, June 2008, 3. See also emails from Gerry Morenski to Jacques Aussems, 28 and 31 March 2008, Folder "Correspondentie," SAM.
20. QAM 277, Reijmerstok, email 28 May 2008 and QAM 278, Limbricht, email 2008.
21. Blom, "Suffering as a Warning," 65–6 and van der Heijden, *Grijs verleden*, 29–31, 88, 91 and 241. For the adopter of the Montanan, see QAM 279, Nijmegen, letter 7 June 2008. For the critique on governments, see QAM 280, Heerlen, letter 2008; QAM 281, Scheulder, email 25 April 2008; and QAM 282, Kerkrade, email 23 May 2008.
22. QAM 283, Margraten, letter 2008; QAM 284, Maastricht, email 2008; and QAM 285, Hulsberg, email 24 April 2008.
23. "Gates Evokes WWII Unity, Resolve in Afghan Fight," *USA Today*, 11 June 2009, www.usatoday.com/news/world/2009-06-10-gates_N.htm.
24. QAM 286, Mierlo, email 27 July 2008; QAM 287, Rosmalen, email 20 May 2008; and QAM 288, Waverveen, letter 2008.
25. QAM 289, Stein, letter 2008.
26. QAM 290, Brunssum, email 2008.
27. Letter from Mr. G. E. Surryhne, 18 September 1946, PLB; QAM 291, Brunssum, letter 2008; QAM 292, Simpelveld, letter 2008. On the Margraten event of September 2004, see www.introinsitu.nl/alle-namen.
28. "Vietnam-veteraan vindt rust in Heuvelland," *DL*, 24 December 2004.
29. QAM 293, Limbricht, email 12 May 2008 and www.spurensuche.aldenhoven.de/soldatengrab.html. **Ernst: Plot I, Row 6, Grave 4.**
30. David Levering Lewis, "Election 2008: How 'Historic' Was It?" *Perspectives on History: The Newsmagazine of the American Historical Association* 47, no. 4 (April 2009): 32–3.
31. www.nytimes.com/2008/03/18/us/politics/18text-obama.html and www.nytimes.com/2009/06/04/us/politics/04obama.text.html.
32. Kirkels and Purnot, *Farmland*, 10, 13, 36–8, and 95.
33. QAM 294, Berg en Terblijt, email 2008.

34. Robin, "A Foothold in Europe," 59–60 and letter written by George Taylor from Karlsruhe, Germany, to Felix Prevoo in Margraten, 8 May 1946 (with thanks to Mr. Prevoo for allowing me to use this letter from his private collection).
35. www.history.army.mil/html/moh/wwII-g-l.html. See the study by Converse et al., *The Exclusion of Black Soldiers from the Medal of Honor in World War II*.
36. www.eurekalert.org/pub_releases/1997-01/UoNC-UPHB-130197.php and www.msnbc.msn.com/id/38251927/ns/us_news-life. **James: Plot P, Row 9, Grave 9.**
37. www.msnbc.msn.com/id/38251927/ns/us_news-life.

Postscript

1. The bid book is "Margraten Memorial Center: A Lasting Memory of the Liberators of World War II in the Heart of Europe." Nuth, s.d. For the Congressional visit, see "Program for Thursday 18 December 2008," drawn up by the Margraten municipality, Folder "Projecten," SAM. As this book goes to press, it appears that the ABMC has indeed given the green light for the construction of a memorial center opposite the cemetery on the other side of the Rijksweg. However, in the difficult economic climate in the wake of the global financial crisis, it remains to be seen where funding for the project can be found.
2. For early references to adoption schemes elsewhere, see "Geallieerde graven worden verzorgd," *Het Parool*, 29 April 1946; "Ambassadrice van Margraten," *Libelle*, no. 9, 28 June 1946; letter J. J. F. Blom, NWGC, to Lieutenant Joseph E. McCluskey, 4 July 1947, Folder 15, DIB; and "Lest We Forget," *Mededelingenblad: Orgaan van het Nederlands Oorlogsgravencomité*, April 1948, Folder 9, BCM. In 2004, AWON member Gerry Morenski noted that Henri-Chapelle in Belgium was another of the few overseas American cemeteries where an adoption organization still existed after all these years. But in 2009, an American official in Henri-Chapelle's visitors' office clarified that Belgian NCOs managed this organization mostly and that the adoption rate currently stood at no more than 40 percent. Email Morenski to Fien Opreij, 10 December 2004, Folder "AWON/Bezoek President Bush," SAM and author interview Henri-Chapelle, 26 July 2009.
3. QAM 295, Brunssum, letter 25 April 2008 and QAM 296, Meerssen, letter May 2008.
4. QAM 297, Middelburg, letter 25 April 2008.
5. Letter Rien Glerum to Adoption Foundation, 21 September 2007, Folder "Stichting," SAM. **Beachler: Plot O, Row 5, Grave 10.**
6. QAM 298, Rozenburg, email 26 June 2010. **Arthur Everett: Plot J, Row 3, Grave 11; Walter Buran: Plot J, Row 3, Grave 19;** and **Wilbert Jones: Plot H, Row 17, Grave 17.**

Bibliography

Primary Sources

I. Questionnaire Adoption Community Margraten

In April 2008 the Adoption Foundation was kind enough to help distribute the author's questionnaire as an insert in the newsletter that annually goes out to all registered members of the Margraten adoption community. The questionnaire asked adopters, among other things, about past and present motivation, the rituals of commemoration, and background information with regards to 'their' American soldier and his relatives overseas.

Close to 1,200 adopters have responded with much enthusiasm since the survey went out in 2008. The replies to the author's questions have come with much additional information enclosed in envelopes or attached to emails. This information consists of various kinds of sources: letters to and from GIs overseas; photos of American soldiers, their families, and homes; Missing Air Crew Reports; War Department telegrams; Individual Deceased Personnel Files; privately published eulogies and memorial booklets; clippings from American and Dutch newspapers; and many more.

All of the adopters' responses (as well as the additional documentation that arrived enclosed or attached) are currently in the possession of the author. They will, in due time, be transferred to the repository that is most appropriate for a collection of this kind. To secure anonymity, adopters are referred to in the notes by a code, the date(s) on which they responded to the author's survey, and their hometowns.

II. Interviews

Author interviews

Lucie Beckers-van den Boorn, Mheer, 22 June 2009.
Paul Bronzwaer, Maastricht, 16 January 2009.
John Gouverne, Maastricht, 10 March 2009.
Lies Köster, Margraten, 6 July 2009.
Jenneke Meyer Viol-Michiels van Kessenich, Lanaken, 21 June 2010.
Felix Prevoo, Margraten, 6 July 2009.

Annie Prevoo-Frijnts, Margraten, 6 July 2009.
Maria Prevoo-Ramakers, Margraten, telephone, 1 September 2009.
Gerarda (Grada) Sumner-Dorscheidt, Cranston, Rhode Island, telephone, 9 September 2009.

'Project Akkers van Margraten' interviews

Felix Prevoo, Margraten, 7 March 2008. Interview by Jo Purnot.
Annie Prevoo-Frijnts, Margraten, 28 April 2008. Interview by Jo Purnot.
Else White-Hanöver, Jacksonville, Florida, 15 December 2008. Interview by Albert Elings and Eugenie Jansen.

These interviews were conducted in the context of the national project 'Erfgoed van de Oorlog' undertaken by the Dutch *Ministerie van Volksgezondheid, Welzijn en Sport*. The complete interviews are being looked after by Data Archiving and Networked Services of the *Koninklijke Nederlandse Akademie van Wetenschappen* and the *Nederlandse Organisatie voor Wetenschappelijk Onderzoek*. Permission to access the interviews has to be granted by the *Regionaal Historisch Centrum Limburg* in Maastricht.

III. Archival Materials

Margraten Municipal Archives

1. Burger-Comité Margraten U.S. Militaire Begraafplaats
Folder 1: Personeel
Folder 2: Begraafplaats
Folder 3: Comité Adoptie
Folder 4: Inlichtingen, 1946–1957
Folder 5: Inlichtingen 1958
Folder 6: Inlichtingen 1959–1964
Folder 7: Inlichtingen 1965–1984
Folder 8: Inlichtingen 1985–2003
Folder 9: Publikaties
Folder 11: Bloemenhulde schoolkinderen
Folder 12: Subsidie Gemeenten ea
Folder 13: Nederlands Oorlogsgravencomité
Folder 14: Klaproosdag
Folder 16: Bond Nederlandse Militaire Oorlogsslachtoffers
Folder 17: Modellenboek
Folder 18: Financiële bescheiden
Folders 20–24: Memorial Day
Folder 26: Burger-Comité Margraten U.S. Militaire Begraafplaats, 1945–1955

2. *Municipal Files*
1.75
Folder 900: Politionele maandrapporten tijdens de bezetting, 1942–44
1.776.1
Folder 940: Militaire Begraafplaats Margraten, 1945–47
Folder 943: Overeenkomsten Amerikaanse oorlogsgraven, 1952–70
Folder 944: Vordering van gronden ten behoeve van het Militaire Kerkhof, 1944–51
1.823
Folder 1254: Landbouwverslagen, 1941–49
1.842.913.9
Folder 1334: Oorlogsschade aan goederen van particulieren, 1940–45
1.851
Folder 1338: Onderwijs tijdens de oorlogsjaren, 1941–43
1.855.2
Folder 1392: Herdenking bevrijding, 1945–52
Folder 1393: Bezoek Amerikaanse *Gold Star Mothers*, 1962–70
1.856.8
Folder 1424: Lijsten van gerepatrieerden wonende in Margraten, 1947–53
1.865.28
Folder 1433: Schade geleden door bezettingstroepen, 1940–48
2.07
Folder 1: Bestuurs- en Beheersbeleid, 1931–44
Folder 2: Geschiedenis van Margraten gedurende de oorlogsjaren, 1940–45
3. *World War II files*
Various files in a separate box labeled "WO II."

Adoption Foundation Graves American Cemetery Margraten

The original index-card catalogue of 1945–46 and the automated and updated database are currently being watched over by Maria Duizings-Croonen in Reijmerstok.

The papers of the Adoption Foundation that was newly created in 2003 are currently in the possession of Jacques Aussems in Cadier en Keer:

Folder: Stichting
Folder: Verslagen
Folder: Correspondentie
Folder: Projecten
Folder: Correspondentie Adoptanten en Nabestaanden
Folder: AWON/Bezoek President Bush
Folder: Lopende correspondentie
Folder: Perspublicaties/Bezoek President Bush

Lucie Beckers-van den Boorn Papers, Mheer

Emilie Michiels van Kessenich Papers, Lanaken, Belgium

Jo Purnot Papers, Cadier en Keer

Box "Archief Adoptie Graven afk. van Van Laar. Herdruk 'Crosses in the Wind.'"
Tape of interview Mr. Joseph Shomon by John Ramaekers, Margraten, 10 September 1994.
Tape of interview Mr. Jef van Laar by Peter Caelen, Margraten, 25 July 1994. (Broadcast by Radio Mergelland on 26 August 1994 and on 2 and 9 September 1994.)

Regionaal Historisch Centrum Limburg, Maastricht

1. Archief van de Commissaris van de Koningin in Limburg, 1944–1990 (2.61)
Folder 898: Toestand in Noord-Limburg, 1945
Folder 901: Oorlogsgraven in provincie Limburg, 1960–1963
Folders 902–911: Memorial Day, 1946–1990
Folder 912: Memorial Hotel, 1946
Folder 913: Verdragen tussen VS en Nederlandse Staat inzake begraafplaats, 1948–1970
Folder 914: Herdenkingsmonument militaire begraafplaats Margraten, 1949–1960
Folder 915: Toespraken gouverneurs Memorial Day, 1954–1989
Folder 916: Memorial Hall, 1988–1989
Folder 919: Oorlogsmonumenten en oorlogsgedenktekens, 1946–1966
Folder 922: Herdenking bevrijding Limburg te Margraten, 13 september 1969
Folder 1235: Comité Limburg Amerikaans Militair Kerkhof Margraten, 1946–1971
2. Archief van de familie Michiels van Kessenich (16.0674)
Folders 474–510: Brieven en minuten van verzonden brieven Willem Michiels van Kessenich en Emilie L. J. M. van Meeuwen, 1919–1991
Folder 657: Emilie L. J. M. van Meeuwen en adoptiewerk Amerikaanse begraafplaats Margraten, 1945–1968
Folder 658: Emilie L. J. M. van Meeuwen en toespraken radio-omroepen in verband met Nederlandsch Oorlogsgraven Comité, 1945
Folder 659: Emilie L. J. M. van Meeuwen en reisverslag USA namens Nederlandsch Oorlogsgraven Comité, 1946
Folder 660: Reisverslagen nabestaanden van in Margraten begraven Amerikaanse soldaten, 1958 en s.d.
Folder 661: Herinnering aan wijze waarop Emilie L. J. M. van Meeuwen betrokken raakte bij adoptiewerk, opgeschreven door Willem Michiels van Kessenich (1981)
Folders 691–695: Reis Willem Michiels van Kessenich naar VS op uitnodiging van 30th US Infantry Division, 1952–1954
Folder 849: Margraten, 1981–1982
3. Archief Parochie Heilige Margarita Margraten (21.244)
"Proclamatie," 10 February 1945
Folder 148: Memorial Day 1947

Stadsbibliotheek Maastricht

Microfilm collection:
Gazet van Limburg
Limburgs Dagblad
De Nieuwe Limburger

Dienst Identificatie en Berging, Ministerie van Defensie, Nationaal Archief, The Hague

Folder 1: Begraafprocedure
Folder 15: Overeenkomsten
Folder 34: Heuschen – van Kessenich
Folder 35: Grondzaken
Folder 68: Herbegraving Amerikanen
Folder 78: Niet-Amerikanen en Duitsers

Ministerie van Buitenlandse Zaken, Nationaal Archief, The Hague

Folder 13040: 1945–1954
Folder 13049: 1945–1954

National Archives and Records Administration, Washington, DC

Record Group 92: Records of the Office of the Quartermaster General
Record Group 338: Records of U.S. Army Operational, Tactical, and Support Organizations (World War II and Thereafter), 1917–1999
Record Group 407: Records of the Adjudant General's Office

IV. Published Materials

Books, articles, and reports
American Battle Monuments Commission. *Netherlands American Cemetery and Memorial*. Washington, DC, 1986.
Margraten, Holland: US Military Cemetery. Heerlen: Limburgs Dagblad, 1946.
Noord-Limburg: Nederland helpt de zwaar geteisterde gebieden. Militair Gezag District Noord-Limburg, 1945.
Provinciaal Opbouworgaan Limburg. *Enkele sociologische gegevens over de gemeente Margraten*. Maastricht, 1956.
Shomon, Joseph J. *Crosses in the Wind: The Unheralded Saga of the Men in the American Graves Registration Service in World War II*. New York: Stratford House, 1947. (Reprint, Geleen: Keulers, 1991.)

Newspapers, magazines, and other periodicals
American:
Atlanta Constitution

Atlanta Journal
Baltimore American
Baltimore Sun
Binghamton Press & Sun-Bulletin
Bridgeport Telegram
Chicago Sun
Gloucester Daily Times
Grand Rapids Press
Los Angeles Times
Milwaukee Sentinel
Nevada Daily Mail
New York Herald Tribune
New York Times
Star: Newsletter of the American WWII Orphans Network
Time
USA Today
Washington Star

Dutch:
Heuvelland Aktueel
Libelle
Margratenpost
Mededelingenblad: Orgaan van het Nederlands Oorlogsgravencomité
Parool
Telegraaf
Tijd
Trouw
Volkskrant
Zondagsnieuws
Zuid-Limburger

Secondary Sources

Books and Articles

50 jaar bevrijding Margraten. Margraten: Oet de Riestepot, 1994.

Algra, Gielt et al. "The Media and the Public Image of Dutch Veterans from World War II to Srebrenica." *Armed Forces and Society* 33, no. 3 (2007): 396–413.

Bacevich, Andrew J. *The New American Militarism: How Americans Are Seduced by War*. New York: Oxford University Press, 2006.

Blom, J. C. H. "Suffering as a Warning: The Netherlands and the Legacy of War." *Revue Canadienne d'Études Néerlandaises* 16, no. 2 (1995): 64–8.

Bodnar, John. *The "Good War" in American Memory*. Baltimore, Maryland: The Johns Hopkins University Press, 2010.

Bodnar, John. *Remaking America: Public Memory, Commemoration, and Patriotism in the Twentieth Century*. Princeton, New Jersey: Princeton University Press, 1992.

Bossenbroek, Martin et al. *Oranje bitter: Nederland bevrijd!* Zwolle: Waanders, 2010.

Boxhoorn, Bram. "American and Dutch Policies toward the Reorientation of NATO after the Cold War." In *Four Centuries of Dutch-American Relations, 1609–2009*. Edited by Hans Krabbendam et al. Albany, New York: State University of New York Press, 2009.

Bronzwaer, Paul. *Maastricht en Luik bezet: Een comparatief onderzoek naar vijf aspecten van de Duitse bezetting van Maastricht en Luik tijdens de Tweede Wereldoorlog*. Vol. 73 of *Maaslandse monografieën*. Hilversum: Uitgeverij Verloren, 2010.

Bronzwaer, Paul, ed. *Zuid-Limburg in de Tweede Wereldoorlog*. Gemeente Margraten, s. d.

Budreau, Lisa M. "The Politics of Remembrance: The Gold Star Mothers' Pilgrimage and America's Fading Memory of the Great War." *Journal of Military History* 72, no. 2 (April 2008): 371–411.

Cammaert, A. P. M. *Het verborgen front: Een geschiedenis van de georganiseerde illegaliteit in de provincie Limburg tijdens de Tweede Wereldoorlog*. Leeuwarden and Mechelen: Eisma, 1994. 2dln.

Capdevila, Luc and Danièle Voldman. *War Dead: Western Societies and the Casualties of War*. Edinburgh: Edinburgh University Press, 2006.

Citino, Robert M. "Military Histories Old and New: A Reintroduction." *American Historical Review* 112, no. 4 (October 2007): 1070–90.

Coleman, Bradley Linn. "Recovering the Korean War Dead, 1950–1958: Graves Registration, Forensic Anthropology, and Wartime Memorialization." *Journal of Military History* 72, no. 1 (January 2008): 179–222.

Converse, Elliott V. et al. *The Exclusion of Black Soldiers from the Medal of Honor in World War II: The Study Commissioned by the United States Army to Investigate Racial Bias in the Awarding of the Nation's Highest Military Decoration*. Jefferson, North Carolina: McFarland, 1997.

Custers, Jos et al. *Sint Geertruid 1939–1945*. Heemkundevereniging Sint Geertruid, 1994.

Damousi, Joy. *The Labour of Loss: Mourning, Memory, and Wartime Bereavement in Australia*. Cambridge: Cambridge University Press, 1999.

De Jong, Lou. *Het Laatste Jaar*. Vol. 10a and 10b of *Het Koninkrijk der Nederlanden in de Tweede Wereldoorlog*. 's-Gravenhage: Staatsuitgeverij, 1980–82.

Dierikx, Marc. "Beyond the Blue Horizon: Tourism and Travel." In *Four Centuries of Dutch-American Relations, 1609–2009*. Edited by Hans Krabbendam et al. Albany, New York: State University of New York Press, 2009.

Endy, Christopher. *Cold War Holidays: American Tourism in France*. Chapel Hill: University of North Carolina Press, 2003.

Etheridge, Brian C. "*The Desert Fox*, Memory Diplomacy, and the German Question in Early Cold War America." *Diplomatic History* 32, no. 2 (April 2008): 208–38.

Frey, Marc. "Decolonization and Dutch-American Relations." In *Four Centuries of Dutch-American Relations, 1609–2009*. Edited by Hans Krabbendam et al. Albany, New York: State University of New York Press, 2009.

Gerritsen, Ger and Henk Langenberg. *Heuvelland bevrijd*. S.l.: Dagblad De Limburger and Limburgs Dagblad, s.d.

Gouverne, J. G. M. J. *US Army in Zuid-Limburg, 1944–1945*. Maarheze: Privately published, 2009.

Hadler, Susan Johnson et al., eds. *Lost in the Victory: Reflections of American War Orphans of World War II*. Denton, Texas: University of North Texas Press, 1998.

Halbwachs, Maurice. *On Collective Memory*. Translation Lewis A. Coser. Chicago and London: University of Chicago Press, 1992.

Hellema, Duco. "The Politics of Asymmetry: The Netherlands and the United States since 1945." In *Four Centuries of Dutch-American Relations, 1609–2009*. Edited by Hans Krabbendam et al. Albany, New York: State University of New York Press, 2009.

Hendriks, Jan and Hans Koenen. *D-Day in Zuid-Limburg: De bevrijding van uur tot uur, van plaats tot plaats*. De Limburger, 1994.

Herring, George C. *From Colony to Superpower: U.S. Foreign Relations since 1776*. New York: Oxford University Press, 2008.

Kagan, Robert. *Of Paradise and Power: America and Europe in the New World Order*. New York: Alfred A. Knopf, 2003.

Kershaw, Alex. *The Bedford Boys: One American Town's Ultimate D-Day Sacrifice*. Cambridge, Massachusetts: Da Capo Press, 2003.

Kirkels, Mieke, ed. *Else Hanöver: Oorlogsjaren in Maastricht*. Den Bosch: Adr. Heinen, 2009.

Kirkels, Mieke and Jo Purnot, eds. *From Farmland to Soldiers Cemetery: Eyewitness Accounts of the Construction of the American Cemetery in Margraten*. Stichting Akkers van Margraten and Heinen, 2009.

Klep, Christ. "Peacekeeping and the War on Terror, 1989–2007." In *Four Centuries of Dutch-American Relations, 1609–2009*. Edited by Hans Krabbendam et al. Albany, New York: State University of New York Press, 2009.

Klep, Christ and Richard van Gils. *Van Korea tot Kosovo: De Nederlandse militaire deelname aan vredesoperaties sinds 1945*. Den Haag: SDU Uitgevers, 1999.

Klinkert, Wim. "Crossing Borders: Americans and the Liberation of the Netherlands." In *Four Centuries of Dutch-American Relations, 1609–2009*. Edited by Hans Krabbendam et al. Albany, New York: State University of New York Press, 2009.

Kolen, Jan, Rutger van Krieken, and Maarten Wijdeveld. "Topografie van de herinnering: De performance van de oorlog in het landschap en de stedelijke ruimte." In *De dynamiek van de herinnering: Nederland en de Tweede Wereldoorlog in een internationale context*. Edited by Frank van Vree and Rob van der Laarse. Amsterdam: Bert Bakker, 2009.

Koops, Enne. "Dutch Emigration to the United States." In *Four Centuries of Dutch-American Relations, 1609–2009*. Edited by Hans Krabbendam et al. Albany, New York: State University of New York Press, 2009.

Lagrou, Pieter. *The Legacy of Nazi Occupation: Patriotic Memory and National Recovery in Western Europe, 1945–1965*. Cambridge: Cambridge University Press, 1999.

Lebow, Richard Ned et al., eds. *The Politics of Memory in Postwar Europe*. Durham, North Carolina: Duke University Press, 2006.

Loeber, H. and G. H. Sprenger, eds. *De Amerikanen en de bevrijding van Nederland*. Amsterdam: Bataafsche Leeuw, 1986.

Lorcin, Patricia M. E. and Daniel Brewer, eds. *France and Its Spaces of War: Experience, Memory, Image*. New York: Palgrave Macmillan, 2009.

MacDonald, Charles B. *The Siegfried Line Campaign*. Washington, DC: Office of the Chief of Military History, Department of the Army, 1963.

Manning, A. F. "Het bevrijde zuiden: Kanttekeningen bij het historisch onderzoek." *Bijdragen en mededelingen betreffende de geschiedenis der Nederlanden* 96, no. 2 (1981): 184–203.

Mayo, James M. *War Memorials as Political Landscape: The American Experience and Beyond*. New York: Praeger, 1988.

McIntyre, Colin. *Monuments of War: How To Read a War Memorial*. London: Robert Hale, 1990.

Mosse, George L. *Fallen Soldiers: Reshaping the Memory of the World Wars*. New York: Oxford University Press, 1991.

Nora, Pierre. *Realms of Memory: Rethinking the French Past*. Vol. I: *Conflicts and Divisions*. Translation Arthur Goldhammer. New York: Columbia University Press, 1996.

Paape, A. H. *Donkere jaren: Episoden uit de geschiedenis van Limburg, 1933–1945*. Assen: Van Gorcum, 1969.

Piehler, G. Kurt. *Remembering War the American Way*. Washington, DC: Smithsonian Books, 2004.

Poole, Robert M. *On Hallowed Ground: The Story of Arlington National Cemetery*. New York: Walker and Company, 2009.

Ribbens, Kees. "De Amerikaanse begraafplaats in Margraten." In *Een open zenuw: Hoe wij ons de Tweede Wereldoorlog herinneren*. Edited by Madelon de Keizer and Marije Plomp. Amsterdam: Bert Bakker, 2010.

Righolt, Hans. "Dutch-American Relations during the Second Cold War." In *Four Centuries of Dutch-American Relations, 1609–2009*. Edited by Hans Krabbendam et al. Albany, New York: State University of New York Press, 2009.

Robin, Ron. *Enclaves of America: The Rhetoric of American Political Architecture Abroad, 1900–1965*. Princeton, New Jersey: Princeton University Press, 1992.

Robin, Ron. "'A Foothold in Europe': The Aesthetics and Politics of American War Cemeteries in Western Europe." *Journal of American Studies* 29, no. 1 (1995): 55–72.

Roebroeks, Frans. "The American Cemetery at Margraten: A Historical Sketch." In Kirkels, Mieke and Jo Purnot, eds. *From Farmland to Soldiers Cemetery: Eyewitness Accounts of the Construction of the American Cemetery in Margraten*. Stichting Akkers van Margraten and Heinen, 2009.

Roebroeks, Frans. "Limburg onder de Duitse knoet." In *De kleine geschiedenis van Limburg in 25 dagen*. Maastricht: Waanders and Regionaal Historisch Centrum Limburg, 2009.

Roebroeks, Frans. "'Strijdbare Geesten' contra GIs: Slag om Maastrichtse meisjes, 1944-1945." *De Maasgouw: Tijdschrift voor Limburgse geschiedenis en oudheidkunde* 125, no.4 (2006): 130-7.

Scates, Bruce. "In Gallipoli's Shadow: Pilgrimage, Memory, Mourning and the Great War." *Australian Historical Studies* 33, no. 119 (April 2002): 1-21.

Scates, Bruce. *Return to Gallipoli: Walking the Battlefields of the Great War*. Cambridge: Cambridge University Press, 2006.

Schoenmaker, Ben and Christ Klep, eds. *De bevrijding van Nederland, 1944-1945*. The Hague: SDU Uitgevers, 1995.

Schulzinger, Robert D. "Memory and Understanding US Foreign Relations." In *Explaining the History of American Foreign Relations*. Edited by Michael J. Hogan and Thomas G. Patterson. New York: Cambridge University Press, 2004.

Sledge, Michael. *Soldier Dead: How We Recover, Identify, Bury, and Honor Our Military Fallen*. New York: Columbia University Press, 2005.

Snyder, David J. "Dutch Cultural Policy in the United States." In *Four Centuries of Dutch-American Relations, 1609-2009*. Edited by Hans Krabbendam et al. Albany, New York: State University of New York Press, 2009.

Steere, Edward. *The Graves Registration Service in World War II*. Washington, DC: Historical Section, Office of the Quartermaster General, 1951.

Tames, Ismee and Jolande Withuis. "'Stilte' na de oorlog?" *Historisch Nieuwsblad* No. 9 (2010): 68-75.

Thelen, David, ed. *Memory and American History*. Bloomington and Indianapolis: Indiana University Press, 1990.

Thuring, G. and J. Heij. *Verdwenen kerkhoven/Vanished Cemeteries Nijmegen Area, Holland: Molenhoek (USA), Nebo (UK), and Sophiaweg (UK)*. Nijmegen: Brakkenstein, 1989.

Tilmans, Karin et al., eds. *Performing the Past: Memory, History, and Identity in Modern Europe*. Amsterdam: Amsterdam University Press, 2010.

Ubachs, Pierre and Ingrid Evers. *Tweeduizend jaar Maastricht: Een stadsgeschiedenis*. Zutphen: Walburg Pers, 2006.

The Unknowns of World War II and Korea. Washington, DC: US Government Printing Office, 1959.

Van der Heijden, Chris. *Grijs verleden: Nederland en de Tweede Wereldoorlog*. Amsterdam and Antwerp: Contact, 2001.

Van der Maar, Rimko. "Dutch-American Relations and the Vietnam War." In *Four Centuries of Dutch-American Relations, 1609-2009*. Edited by Hans Krabbendam et al. Albany, New York: State University of New York Press, 2009.

Van Staden, Alfred. "American-Dutch Political Relations since 1945: What Has Changed and Why?" *Bijdragen en mededelingen betreffende de geschiedenis der Nederlanden* 97, no. 3 (1982): 470-86.

Van Vree, Frank. "De dynamiek van de herinnering: Nederland in een internationale context." In *De dynamiek van de herinnering: Nederland en de Tweede*

> *Wereldoorlog in een internationale context*. Edited by Frank van Vree and Rob van der Laarse. Amsterdam: Bert Bakker, 2009.

Verdery, Katherine. *The Political Lives of Dead Bodies: Reburial and Postsocialist Change*. New York: Columbia University Press, 1999.

Winter, Jay. *Sites of Memory, Sites of Mourning: The Great War in European Cultural History*. Cambridge: Cambridge University Press, 1995.

Winter, Jay and Emmanuel Sivan, eds. *War and Remembrance in the Twentieth Century*. Cambridge: Cambridge University Press, 1999.

Winters, Dick. *Beyond Band of Brothers*. New York: Berkley Caliber, 2008.

Thesis

Bronzwaer, Paul. "Maastricht en Luik bezet: Een comparatief onderzoek naar vijf aspecten van de Duitse bezetting van Maastricht en Luik tijdens de Tweede Wereldoorlog," Leiden University, 2009.

Margraten Boys Index

Allen, Bill (Illinois) Plot E Row 2 Grave 1: 251–2

Arnold, Robert (New Jersey) Plot B Row 14 Grave 15: 251–2

Bariani, John (California) Plot K Row 20 Grave 19: 128–9

Barker, Phillip (Minnesota) Plot I Row 14 Grave 21: 92–3

Barry, John (New York) Plot D Row 6 Grave 10: 237–9

Beachler, Alan (Pennsylvania) Plot O Row 5 Grave 10: 270

Bekierski, Michael (Ohio) Plot K Row 15 Grave 8: 178–80

Berger, Herbert (New York) Plot N Row 16 Grave 8: 212

Bohling, Erwin (Minnesota) Plot C Row 16 Grave 30: 202–3

Brown, Alvin (Texas) Plot G Row 13 Grave 20: 128

Buran, Walter (West Virginia) Plot J Row 3 Grave 19: 270–2

Burgess, Robert (Mississippi) Plot E Row 1 Grave 9: 177–8

Byrd, Ernest (Tennessee) Plot D Row 1 Grave 1: 195

Cabral, Albert (Massachusetts) Plot E Row 4 Grave 11: 157–8

Carlson, Sivert (Illinois) Plot B Row 9 Grave 12: 232, 233

Coker, Henry (Missouri) Plot A Row 16 Grave 32: 96

Davis, Murray (New York) Plot D Row 13 Grave 10: 156

De Febio, Michael (Rhode Island) Plot E Row 2 Grave 7: 209–10

Diel, James (Illinois) Plot L Row 15 Grave 8: 199

Diez, Dan (California) Plot E Row 10 Grave 58 (Henri-Chapelle, Belgium): 29–30

Dimmock, Charles (Pennsylvania) Plot F Row 8 Grave 20: 225

Doty, Amos (Tennessee) Plot L Row 3 Grave 9: 221

Driver, Bill (Kansas) Plot B Row 4 Grave 24: 111

Dundon, Lewis (New Jersey) Plot K Row 5 Grave 1: 166

Dziesulski, Joe (Illinois) Plot B Row 5 Grave 16: 89

Ernst, Michel (New York) Plot I Row 6 Grave 4: 261–3

Erwin, Robert (Ohio) Plot K Row 2 Grave 12: 253

Evancho, George and Peter (Pennsylvania) Plot N Row 7 Graves 13 and 14: 62, 76–8, 253–4

Everett, Arthur (New York) Plot J Row 3 Grave 11: 270–2

Eylens, John (Indiana) Plot E Row 15 Grave 26: 177, 178

Forein, Donald (Illinois) Plot F Row 2 Grave 2: 125–6

Gackowski, Albert (Illinois) Plot A Row 2 Grave 4: 248

Gallion, John (Virginia) Plot D Row 6 Grave 24: 53

Greiner, George (Pennsylvania) Plot G Row 4 Grave 25: 165–6

Hart, Eddie (North Carolina) Plot E Row 2 Grave 2: 96–7
Harte, Frank (Alabama) Plot K Row 2 Grave 21: 36
Henlin, Leonard (Rhode Island) Plot B Row 21 Grave 26: 239
Hewitt, Ralph (Texas) Plot D Row 1 Grave 14: 169–70
Hood, Walter (Michigan) Plot L Row 21 Grave 22: 240

Jacobs, Ronald (South Dakota) Plot F Row 19 Grave 6: 214–15
James, Willy (Missouri) Plot P Row 9 Grave 9: 266–7
Jefferson, Charles (Mississippi) Plot F Row 8 Grave 16: 201–2
Jones, Wilbert (Illinois) Plot H Row 17 Grave 17: 270–2

Kirlin, William (Pennsylvania) Plot M Row 2 Grave 8: 196–7
Klippel, John (Pennsylvania) Plot M Row 19 Grave 16: 248–9
Kukay, Joe (Ohio) Plot E Row 13 Grave 10: 145

Lacy, Ernest (Virginia) Plot D Row 11 Grave 23: 53–4
Land, John (South Carolina) Plot B Row 3 Grave 4: 7–8
Le Hoty, Jerold (Ohio) Plot L Row 10 Grave 13: 31
Lempka, Daniel (New Jersey) Plot M Row 17 Grave 5: 165
Lewandowski, Alex (New Jersey) Plot L Row 16 Grave 5: 169
Little, Ernie (Maryland) Plot F Row 10 Grave 6: 232, 233
Long, Robert (Georgia) Plot H Row 11 Grave 27: 93–4
Long, William (Pennsylvania) Plot G Row 8 Grave 2: 183–5

Machen, Thomas (Virginia) Plot K Row 10 Grave 5: 57–8
Manahan, John (California) Plot K Row 1 Grave 19: 144–5
Marceau, Leo (Massachusetts) Plot C Row 13 Grave 12: 21
McAlpine, Robert (Texas) Plot P Row 7 Grave 3: 204–5
McCollum, Clarence (Missouri) Plot G Row 8 Grave 25: 232, 233
McLean, Bill (Massachusetts) Plot P Row 15 Grave 9: 168–9
Morneweck, Robert (Michigan) Plot E Row 20 Grave 17: 247
Mosbacher, Stephen (Ohio) Plot I Row 11 Grave 19: 31–2

Ralston, Bryce (North Dakota) Plot L Row 2 Grave 17: 94–5
Ratchford, Hugh (North Carolina) Plot N Row 2 Grave 10: 105
Riddell, Johnny (New Jersey) Plot N Row 21 Grave 5: 126
Rocchio, Charles (Rhode Island) Plot E Row 6 Grave 24: 151–2
Rose, Charley (Missouri) Plot H Row 15 Grave 16: 211
Ross, George (Virginia) Plot I Row 16 Grave 8: 105
Rozwalka, Leonard (Illinois) Plot O Row 3 Grave 4: 224–5

Seibel, Thomas (Pennsylvania) Plot H Row 16 Grave 18: 247–8
Seifried, Philip (New York) Plot B Row 7 Grave 24: 240–1
Skelly, Tom (Delaware) Plot O Row 5 Grave 2: 205–6
Smith, Don (Texas) Plot A Row 16 Grave 28: 50
Snyder, Bill (North Carolina) Plot N Row 19 Grave 3: 250–1
Steele, Thomas (New York) Plot A Row 15 Grave 17: 55, 104
Steiner, Cecil and Walter (California) Plot J Row 15 Graves 15 and 16: 56–7, 72–3

Stirling, James (Ohio) Plot J Row 16 Grave 12: 22
Sweeney, Harry (Tennessee) Plot B Row 12 Grave 3: 161–2

Taliaferro, Jack (Oklahoma) Plot G Row 14 Grave 13: xii–xiii
Ticknor, Charles (Ohio) Plot M Row 14 Grave 9: 183

Ulenburg, Howard (Michigan) Plot M Row 2 Grave 5: 167–8
Utecht, Willis (Kansas) Plot N Row 23 Grave 22: 163–4

Venne, Dennis (Wisconsin) Plot B Row 17 Grave 18: 141–2

Vinsant, Wilma (Texas) Plot B Row 17 Grave 4: 162–3

Watson, Hale (New Hampshire) Plot A Row 4 Grave 7: 84
Watson, Jim (Pennsylvania) Plot J Row 10 Grave 22: 166–7
Willett, Ralph (Nebraska) Plot L Row 4 Grave 21: 180–2

Zeigler, Paul (Pennsylvania) Plot D Row 12 Grave 11: 95
Zoradi, Steve (Nevada) Plot M Row 17 Grave 17: 239–40
Zwicky, Alfred (Illinois) Plot J Row 9 Grave 5: 84

General Index

Aachen, Battle of, xiii–xiv, 1, 4
ABC *Headline Edition*, 37
Abu Ghraib, 223, 227–8
Adams, Major General Andrew J., 147–8
Adams, John, 135
Afghanistan
    Dutch troops in Uruzgan province, 214, 226, 258
    Soviet invasion, 134
    war against Taliban, 187, 208–9
African-Americans
    racial discrimination in US society, 35, 264, 266, 266–7
    struggle for civil rights, 98, 264, 266
    World War II troops in the Netherlands, 3, 27, 194, 201–2, 264–5, 266–7
Airborne Divisions
    17th, 103
    82nd, 43, 56, 71, 110, 125–6, 129, 164, 165–6, 167–8, 168–9, 192
    101st, 21, 71, 86, 89, 96, 105–6, 155–6, 166–7, 219
Air Division, 2nd, 157
Air Force, Eight, 157
Allende, Salvador, 234
Allied Forces Central Command (AFCENT), 114–15, 118, 120, 142, 143, 208
Amby, 144–5
American Battle Monuments Commission (ABMC)
    history, 74, 235
    policies, 164, 235, 266

    relations with Dutch in Margraten, 94, 101, 107, 110–11, 124, 147–8, 235, 268
    superintendents at Margraten cemetery: Frank Berloth, 141–2, 158–9; Frank Schwind, 260–1; Johannes Staarup, 100
American Graves Registration Command (AGRC), 10, 41–3, 47–9, 54, 73–4
American Legion, 123–4
American World War II Orphans Network (AWON), 157, 241, 254–6
Amsterdam, 22–3, 135, 156
Anti-Americanism, 220–1
Antwerp, Port of, 70–1
Apollo 11, 120
Arab-Israeli conflict, 115, 127, 131, 223
Arlington National Cemetery, 109, 237
Armed forces
    African colonial, 192
    Belgian, 154, 192
    British, 154
    Dutch, 23, 33–4, 75
    French, 137, 154, 192
Armored Divisions
    2nd, 28, 53, 128, 148
    6th, 161–2, 204–5, 211
    7th, 240–1
    8th, 31–2, 143
    9th, 55
    11th, 239–40
Armored Field Artillery Battalion, 440th, 249
Arnall, Roland, 233

Arnhem, xiii–xiv, 199, 203
Associated Press, 52
Atonement, German, 261–3
Auschwitz, 24–5
Aussems, Jacques, 187–8

B-17 Flying Fortress, 36, 76–8, 138, 144–5, 165, 169–70, 177, 237–9, 266, 270–1
B-24 Liberator, 95, 105, 192, 197, 221, 222, 239
B-26 Marauder, 72
Baker, Major General William, 110–11
Balkans, conflicts of the 1990s, 157, 213, 257
Balkenende, Jan Peter, 227, 230
Band of Brothers, 203–4
Bastogne, 205
Battlefield reenactment, 204–5
Beek, 181
Bergen-Belsen, 246
Berlin airlift, 70, 226
Berlin Wall, 149, 226
Blom, Hans, 222
Bombardment
  of Hamburg, 199
  of Rotterdam, 199
Bomber Groups
  44th, 195
  303rd, 199, 237–9
  305th, 111, 144–5
  306th, 138
  387th, 181
  392nd, 221
  447th, 126
  448th, 157
  452nd, 207
  466th, 192
  491st, 200–1
Bomber Squadrons
  323rd, 84
  533rd, 177
Bradley, General Omar, 74
Bremer III, Paul, 139

Bronze Star, 54, 209, 212, 214–15, 232
Brotherhood of the Lamp, 99–100
Brucker, Wilber M., 101, 103
Brunssum, 114, 117, 208–9
Buchenwald, 199
Bukovsky, Vladimir, 137
Bulge, Battle of the, xv, 1, 28, 96, 122, 132, 211
Burma railway, 200, 215
Bush, George H.W., 157
Bush, George W.
  foreign relations during his administration, 218–25
  visit to Margraten cemetery in 2005, 226–30, 235–6, 268
Butler, John, 79

C-47 Dakota, 163, 247–8
Caen, 119, 139
Cambodia, invasion of, 121
Canadian Broadcasting Corporation, 39
Carter, Jimmy, 131, 134
Catholicism in Limburg province, xiii, 56, 66, 69, 108, 227, 245
CBS *We, the People*, 37–8
Central Identification Laboratory, Hawaii, 164
Chamber of Commerce, Dutch in US, 81
Chapin, Selden, 75
Chicago Sun, 64
Children
  American, mourning loss of fathers: 157, 184–5, 254–6
  Dutch: impact of liberation on, 29, 45, 112, 143, 154–5, 190–4; impact of occupation on, 143, 154–5, 190–2; role in cemetery commemoration, 85–6, 91, 97, 101, 107, 119, 124, 129, 136, 259–60
Clay, General Lucius D., 70
Clinton, Bill, 157, 169, 267
Coal mines, in Limburg, 5

Cold War, end of, 145–6, 149–50
Collateral damage, 22, 92–3, 191–2, 225, 262
Concentration camps, 24–5, 155–6, 199–200, 222–3, 246
Corlett, Major General Charles H., 13
Cruise missiles, 134
Czechoslovakia, 118

Dachau, 200, 222–3
Dance scheme, for GIs in Limburg, 13–14, 17
Davison, General Michael, 127
D-Day, 245
Death squads, in Central America, 234
Decolonization, 61–2, 98
De Limburger, 183–5
Demobilization, 14
Devers, General Jacob, 101
Diplomatic agreements,
  Dutch-American with regards to Margraten cemetery, 62–3, 91–2, 121
Disarmament, 91
Distinguished Flying Cross, 95
Dondero, George, 35
Dossin Barracks, 24
Duizings, Maria, 190
Dutch-American Friendship Day, 135, 149–50
Dutch East Indies
  Dutch attempts at restoring colonial control after World War II, 61–2, 76, 81, 89, 213, 215
  Dutch prisoners of Japanese during World War II, 200–1
  Dutch tensions with US in late 1940s, 61–2
  occupation by Japanese during World War II, 61, 200–1
Dutch New Guinea, 213

Economic Information Service, Dutch in US, 81

Eisenhower, Dwight D., 47, 86, 104, 119, 122
Eisenhower, Susan, 149–50
Emigration, Dutch to US, 76, 88–9, 96–7, 108
Engineer Combat Battalion, 327th, 53–4
Epen, 9–10
European Union, 187
Ewell, General Julian, 123
Eygelshoven, 28–9

Feil, Warren and Mabel Rose, 14–16, 17, 18, 35, 37, 39
Field Artillery Battalion
  207th, 251–2
  774th, 271
Field Artillery Group, 252nd, 205–6
Field Hospital, 20th, 213
First Army, 52
Fleurs de la Mémoire, Les, 237, 269
Flood, in the Netherlands in 1953, 85
Focke Wulf, 270
Forced labor, 24, 25
Frank, Anne, 260
Freedom of Information Act, 175
Friendly fire, 22, 92–3, 191–2
Frissen, Léon, 233, 236

Gates, Robert, 258
Gavin, General James, 43
Geleen, 22, 191–2
Globalization, 157
Gold Star Dads, 106
Gold Star Mothers, 34, 105–7, 110–11, 118–19, 121–2, 124, 153
Gold Star Wives, 43, 47
Goodwill tours, in US with regards to Margraten cemetery, 33–9, 64, 79–82
Google, 249
Gorbachev, Mikhail, 143–4, 145–6
Gould, Kingdon, 127–8, 137

Graves Registration Companies
  603rd, 6, 68–9, 178–80
  611th, 2, 4–5, 6–7, 7–8
Great Depression, xii, 31, 89, 121–2, 141
Grevenbicht, 161–2
Groesbeek, 129
Grotius, Hugo, 256–7
Guantanamo Bay, 223, 227–8
Gulf War of 1991, 157
Gulpen, 28–9

Hamburg, 98
Hanks, Tom, 204
Harvard University, 124
Heerlen, 21–2, 27–8, 28–9, 115–16
Heuschen, Father Johannes, 8–9, 11–12, 16, 18–19, 20, 40–4, 48, 74, 107, 112
Hiroshima, 134
Hobbs, General Leland S., 13, 86–7
Home addresses, of Margraten boys in US, 47–50, 73–4, 94, 148–9, 165, 175, 249
Homosexuals, persecution during Nazi occupation, 258–9
Hornbeck, Stanley, 17, 34
Houben, Frans, 101
Hudson, Henry, 127
Hungary, 91, 93
Hunger Winter, xv, 22–3, 155, 198
Hürtgen Forest, 1, 184–5, 232–3
Hydrogen bomb, 91

Individual Deceased Personnel File (IDPF), 174–6
Infantry Divisions
  1st, 21–2, 111, 125
  2nd, 199
  4th, xii–xiii
  8th, 111, 143, 209
  9th, 27
  29th, 53, 202–3, 261–3
  30th, 7–8, 30–1, 79–80, 82, 85, 86–7, 90, 139, 153–4, 160, 202, 206–7, 214–15
  35th, 122, 128–9
  65th, 156
  75th, 208, 212
  79th, 31, 153, 161–2, 195, 250–1
  83rd, 96, 155, 184–5
  84th, 14–16, 50, 75–6, 104
  86th, 200
  89th, 248
  90th, 198
  97th, 224–5
  99th, 23–4
  102nd, 103, 169, 172, 177–8, 197, 269
  104th, 148, 153–4, 266–7
  106th, 131–2
International Security Assistance Force (ISAF), 187
Internet, impact on adoption community, 170–1, 182–3, 190, 247, 249, 250, 253
Invasion of Iraq in 2003, 218–25
Invasion of May 1940, 23, 26, 127–8, 192, 245

Jacob van Heemskerck, 200
Java Sea, Battle of the, 200
Jews
  American, 212
  Dutch: adoption motivation, 131, 156, 202–3; persecution, xiii, 24–5; rescue, 23–4, 45
  German, 31–2, 56
  Polish, 261–3
Johnson, Lyndon B., 35, 39, 113, 123
Jonkheden, 9

Kagan, Robert, 233
Kaiser, Herman, 146–7, 149–50
Kennedy, John F., 108, 109–10
Kent State University, protests and killings at, 121
Kerkrade, 21, 153, 225, 251–2
Kissinger, Henry, 127, 134
Kiwanis Clubs, 81, 82
KLM Royal Dutch Airlines, 33, 81–2, 100, 106

Korean War, 75, 82, 90–1, 120–1, 209
Köster, Lies, 73–4, 87
Kremers, Johan, 131, 136–7, 143–4, 145–6
Kuijpers, Albert, 106, 110–11
Kwai River, 215

Lebanon, 137, 214–15
Le Monde, 187, 218
Libelle magazine, 40
Libya, 144
Life magazine, 14–15, 18, 37
Longest Day, The, 204
Lumumba, Patrice, 234
Luns, Joseph, 117, 121

Maastricht, 12–13, 62, 81–2, 88–9, 108, 117, 123, 144, 154
Marshall, General George C., 94
Marshall Plan, 61, 81, 118, 210, 226
Matthews, H. Freeman, 88, 94
McAuliffe, Brigadier General Anthony C., 80
McCarthyism, 94
Medal of Honor, 266–7
Memory diplomacy, 61–2, 80–2, 136, 218–19, 243–4
Menin Gate Memorial at Ypres, 256
Messerschmidt, 177, 238
Michiels van Kessenich, Emilie, 13–19, 33–44, 64, 65, 88, 92, 93–4, 100–1, 102, 107, 123, 124
Michiels van Kessenich, Willem, 12–14, 19, 44, 79–82, 85, 86–7, 123–4
Middendorf II, J. William, 120, 121, 123
Military cemeteries of World War II
American: Colleville-sur-Mer, 237; Hamm, 52; Henri-Chapelle, 9–10, 29–30, 52, 54, 69, 70, 206, 268; Molenhoek, 22, 71; Neuville-en-Condroz, 52, 78, 169, 268; Saint-James, 237; Son, 22, 71
Commonwealth: 69; Anzio, 99
Dutch: Kanchanaburi, 215
German: Pomezia, 99; Ysselsteyn, 45–7, 70, 99
Soviet: Leusden, 69–70
Missing Air Crew Report (MACR), 165, 172, 222
Monte Cassino, 99

Napoleon Bonaparte, 146
National Personnel Records Center in St. Louis, Missouri, 174–5
National Tourist Bureau of the Netherlands, 100
Natzweiler-Struthof, 200
NBC *Special Salute to the Netherlands*, 43
Neoconservatism, 233
Netherlands Information Bureau/ Service, 34, 80
Netherlands War Graves Committee (NWGC), 18, 33, 55, 73, 87–8, 91, 93, 95, 102, 105, 107, 112, 124, 125, 268–9
Neutron bomb, 134
New York Times, 47
Nijswiller, 151–2, 231
Ninth Army, xv, 28, 118–19, 124
Nixon, Richard, 119, 120–1, 123, 128, 134
Normandy beaches, 119, 204, 226, 246
North Atlantic Treaty Organization (NATO), 74, 91, 99, 114–15, 117, 134, 137, 150, 157, 187, 208, 218
Nuclear arms race and protests, 91, 98, 108, 130, 134–8, 142–4, 145–6, 219

Obama, Barack
  African-American identity, 263, 264
  Cairo speech, 263
  Nobel Peace Prize, 263–4
Of Power and Paradise, 233

Olympic Games, in Helsinki in 1952, 103
Omaha Beach, 226, 269
Ommen, 24
Operation Grenade, 3
Operation Iraqi Freedom, 219
Operation Market Garden, xiii–xiv, 11, 22, 56, 71, 105–6, 125–6, 129, 163–4, 165–6, 192, 197, 199, 247–8
Operation Plunder, 3
Operation Varsity, 65, 141
Opreij, Fien, 187–8
Oranienburg, 246

P-38 Lightning, 236–7
P-47 Thunderbolt, 11, 95, 225
Pacifism, 91, 115, 116–17, 122–3, 130–1, 150, 256–60
Paris peace negotiations and accords, 118, 123, 126–7
Patton, General George S., 66
Paulen, Adriaan, 28
Peace-In, 116
Penicillin, 194
Philips Electronics, 86
Phillips Exeter Academy, 58
Poland, 91
Poppy sale, 105
Post-traumatic stress disorder (PTSD), 261–2
Prague Spring, 118
Prevoo, Felix, 112–13, 124, 139, 140, 152, 159–61, 165, 168, 187–8, 189
Prince Bernhard, 20, 28, 119
Princess Irene Brigade, 199
Princeton University, 58
Prince William V of Orange, 135
Prisoners of War, American, 165
Privacy Act of 1974, 174
Provos, 114–15, 116–17
Purnot, Jo, 187–8, 190

Quartermaster Service Companies
  960th, 264
  3136th, 264, 265

Queen Beatrix, 136, 227, 229
Queen Elizabeth II, 113
Queen Juliana, 43, 92, 101–2, 113, 120
Queen Wilhelmina, 14, 68

Racketeering, rumors and accusations with regards to adoption, 41–2, 64
Radioactivity, 91
Rapprochement, in Dutch relations with (West) Germany, 98–100, 113, 260
Rationing, 25–6, 194, 198
Reader's Digest, 108
Reagan, Ronald, 135–7, 139, 143–4, 145–6, 219
Red Cross, 46
Remagen bridge, 143
Repatriation, of Margraten boys to US, 2, 60–75, 196, 207
Resistance
  Belgian, 203
  Dutch, 13, 23–4, 28, 131, 132, 152, 155–6, 190–1, 199, 200, 202–3
Rhine River, 3, 96, 141, 224–5
Rice, Condoleezza, 227
Rice, John Stanley, 108
Roer River, 232
Roma, persecution during Nazi occupation, 258–9
Ronckers, J.J.E.H., 2, 6, 8–9, 10–11, 87, 88
Roosevelt, Franklin D., 4
Rotary Clubs, 39, 81, 107
Rozenburg, 271
Rumsfeld, Donald, 218
Rusk, Dean, 117
Russell, Richard, 35
Ryan, Cornelius, 204

Sakharov, Andrei, 137
Schermerhorn, Wim, 9
Schiedam, 270–1
Schinveld, 208

Schutterijen, 206–7
Schweinfurt, 144–5, 239
Scouts, 206
Secret Army, 203
Senecal, Lieutenant Colonel Leo, 17
September 11 attacks in 2001, 186–7
Shad, John, 146–7
Shomon, Joseph, 2, 3–4, 5, 6–7, 64–5, 102
Siegfried Line, xiv, xv, 1, 113
Signal Repair Company, 188th, 202–3
Silver Star, 31–2, 59, 177–8, 214–15
Simpson, General William H., 4–5, 13, 118–19, 124
Smuggling, of downed Allied airmen, 23–4, 25, 34, 199
Sobel, Clifford, 219
Son bridge, 199
South Africa, 98
Soviets
    meetings with Americans at Elbe River in 1945, 53–4, 155, 210
    tensions with Dutch during Cold War, 69, 118, 134, 210
Spaatz, General Carl A., 101
Sparks, Chauncey, 35
Spellman, Cardinal Francis, 80
Spielberg, Steven, 204
Srebrenica, 213, 257
SS-20 missiles, 134
Stoottroepen, 28
Suez Canal Crisis, 93

Tank Battalion
    14th, 118
    36th, 24, 141–2, 270
    745th, 173
    784th, 201–2
Tank Destroyer Battalion, 643rd, 209–10
Terrorism, 131, 135, 137, 144, 186–7
Tet Offensive, 117
The Hague, 137
Third World, 114, 146

Tourism
    American travel to the Netherlands and Margraten, 103–6, 116
    impact of Dutch travel to US on Margraten adoption, 103, 207
    Margraten cemetery as a tourist attraction, 81–2, 100–1, 235
Troop Carrier Group, 437th, 66
Truman, Harry S., 16–17, 47, 63, 80–1
Tyler, William, 117–18

United Nations, 43, 75, 127, 223
US Total Army Personnel Command in Alexandria, Virginia, 174
Utrecht, 123

Valkenburg, 134, 193
Van den Boorn, Lucie, 51–7, 65–6, 72–3, 104, 129–30, 259
Van Gogh, Theo, 220
Van Laar, Joseph, 7–8
Van Mulken, 102–3, 112
Van Roey, Cardinal Jozef, 70
Van Roijen, Herman, 17, 80–1
Van Rooy, Charles, 109–10, 113–14, 118, 122–3, 126–7, 129
Van Veen, Harry, 202
Venlo, 192
Venray, 113
Veterans of Foreign Wars (VFW), 95
Vietnam War, 113–24, 126–7, 129–31, 134, 135, 137, 142, 209, 219, 223, 258, 260–1
Vijlen, 28
Voice of America, 228
Volksbund Deutsche Kriegsgräberfürsorge, 46
Vrouenraets, Hub, 88, 101

Wageningen, 203
Walls of the Missing, at Margraten cemetery, xiii, xv, 142, 164, 236–7
War brides, 45, 253
War on Terror, 218–34
War veterans
    American, 151–2, 157–8, 167–8

Dutch, 213–15
German, 125, 137, 260
Italian, 99
War widows, 15–16, 18, 37, 90, 99, 104, 178, 181–2
Watergate affair, 129
Weert, 118
Weser River, 266
West Side Story, 114
Whittington, William, 35
Women, role in adoption, 82–4
World's Fair, in Brussels in 1958, 98, 100

World War I
    American cemeteries in Europe, 74, 164
    American troops in Europe, 84–5
    Commonwealth cemetery of Senlis, 216
    repatriation of American war dead, 63

Yalta Conference, 234
Young, Philip, 97, 219, 222

Zanuck, Darryl, 204